BEST ALTWEEKLY WRITING 2009 & 2010

BEST ALTWEEKLY
WRITING
2009 & 2010

Edited by the

Association of Alternative Newsweeklies

Introduction by

Mike Sager

Northwestern University Press
Evanston, Illinois

Northwestern University Press
www.nupress.northwestern.edu

Printed in the United States of America

10   9   8   7   6   5   4   3   2   1

ISBN 978-0-8101-2737-1

CONTENTS

SPECIAL TOPIC—ELECTION COVERAGE

Interviews with the award-winning authors explaining "How I Got That Story" follow their articles throughout the book.

PREFACE

Julia Goldberg
AAN Editorial Chair and
Editor of the *Santa Fe Reporter*

With more than 130 member papers, the Association of Alternative Newsweeklies (AltWeeklies.com) is a diverse trade association that represents alternative journalism from big cities and small towns across North America. In turn, the journalism that is recognized each year in AAN's contest reflects the bad-ass news, opinion, criticism, and innovation that characterizes our still-thriving altweekly world.

In 2010, the AAN awards turned 15, and the rewarding but hard work of putting together this book took place. The success of the contest and this anthology are due in large part to the efforts of several people.

Jason Zaragoza, who serves as AAN's editor for AltWeeklies .com, also has the unenviable job of overseeing the AAN contest, which typically attracts more than 1,100 entries each year. For this book, Jason also was tasked with preparing the texts of the winning entries. Jason has overseen all of these duties—most of which were tedious, frankly—with humor and precision. This book would not exist without him.

AAN's Editorial Committee plays an integral role in the contest by reviewing on an annual basis participation, categories, and contest rules for the two dozen categories spread among two circulation divisions. For 2009 and 2010, committee members also interviewed contest winners for the "How I Got That Story" Q&As in this anthology. Editors Jimmy Boegle (*Tucson Weekly*), Patricia Calhoun (*Westword*), Scott

Dickensheets (*Las Vegas Weekly*), Steve Jones (*San Francisco Bay Guardian*), Anne Schindler (*Folio Weekly*) and Hank Sims (*North Coast Journal*) contributed many uncompensated hours to this project, and deserve massive thanks (and extra drink tickets at the next AAN convention).

Former AAN Executive Director Richard Karpel was the instigator of AAN's collaboration with Northwestern University Press for this book, and deserves our thanks (but not a free copy).

Behind the scenes, dozens of journalists and educators serve as AAN's judges each year. Judging an AAN contest is not a small commitment—our writers still produce 10,000-word stories, after all. We thank the judges for their time and commitment.

Many AAN judges are altweekly alum, as is author and *Esquire* contributing writer Mike Sager, who graciously contributed his time to introduce this collection.

Finally, Jenny Gavacs and her colleagues at Northwestern University Press provided AAN with detailed attention and commitment to this project.

The winners highlighted in *Best AltWeekly Writing 2009 & 2010* are just a selection of two years' worth of contest winners. Want more? You're in luck. No matter where you live, chances are you've got a great (and free) AAN paper in your community. Keep supporting it.

INTRODUCTION

Mike Sager

In honor of this volume of award-winning altweekly stories, and in celebration of writing this opening—like all the altweekly writing I've ever done it will be performed gratis— I have gifted myself with a visit to my personal archives. This collection of books, magazines, and loose-leaf scrapbooks is housed in a series of 900-pound, fireproof file cabinets that various unlucky Teamsters have transported to and from the domiciles I've inhabited.

Some years ago, while doing a story on a deadly California wildfire, I watched a crew of firefighters engage a similar file cabinet—rated among the best—with the heavy-duty tool called the Jaws of Life. The brave, ash-covered firemen worked as men in teams do: they each took shifts while the others smoked and observed.

At last the steel- and concrete-reinforced box was breached.

All the paper inside had turned to char.

Luckily the same has not happened to me . . . yet. I dig down until I find the black loose-leaf binder I'm looking for, a big honker with four-inch rings and label-maker dates on the spine. When I set out to become a writer, this binder became the symbol of the life's work I sought. I wanted to be a person who could make words appear on a blank page (or later a blank screen), who could make something from nothing, who could exist on his talent and drive and personal wiles. A person whose life was his own, whose voice was his own.

Partway into the binder, working back to front, I find my first story for Atlanta's *Creative Loafing*. I am proud to say that the Loaf was one of the first altweeklies in the country, and that it is still in existence. And I am proud to say that without *Creative Loafing* I wouldn't be who I am today.

You see, deep into my senior year of college, determined to become a writer, I was headed for law school.

Yep. I know it sounds stupid. But then I got this internship at the Loaf. I drove my car to this cool, rundown house in a cool, rundown neighborhood; the offbeat people working inside seemed just my type. Upstairs, under the eves, was the most wonderfully odd one of them all; his name was Steve Jones. I am proud to say he was my first professional editor. I remember to this day how he used to pick up his telephone and announce himself: "Steve Jones." Though his voice was somewhat reedy, he answered that phone like a man who knew the world. I still answer the phone that way when I'm on the clock.

Steve gave me my first assignment soon after I began, and I went off to do my first interview. The article ran on April 15, 1978, under an appropriately plucky altweekly headline: "Get Yourself Off . . . The Ground." Weighing in at 500 words or so, bylined with my lawyer name—Michael A. Sager—the article detailed a course in advanced transcendental meditation that was being offered the upcoming week.

Thus began my amazing three months at the Loaf. I did a roundup of neighborhood pubs. (My first expense account!) I wrote a first-person action piece about a day at a go-cart track with some frat bros. The Sci-Fi convention, mopeds, edible plants, river rafting on the Chattahoochee. They even let me shoot a few covers; back then I did photography, too. To say my internship at *Creative Loafing* was epiphanous would not be an exaggeration.

I had found my calling.

As it turned out, the year I had the internship at *Creative Loafing*, 1978, was the founding year of the Association of Alternative Newsweeklies, the force behind this book. The AAN began with 30 newspapers, including the *San Francisco Bay Guardian*, the *Chicago Reader* . . . and *Creative Loafing*.

Today there are 130 member publications. There are a lot of doom mongers who dismiss the future of publications, and surely the members of the AAN have faced some lean times of late. But I dare anyone to envision a future without *content.* The need to tell and read stories, the need for fun and graceful and committed writing, the need to have something to *read,* the need to be kept up to date . . . these things will never go away. Our paradigm might shift but there will always be a place for the sensibility and content that altweeklies bring.

And what content there is: altweeklies have always made it their mission to tell great stories in different ways, and to go the distance to be watchdogs for the public good. The award-winning pieces from 2009 and 2010 collected in this book reflect this diversity of purpose and reporting: Randall Roberts's account of following the band Ozomatli on a surreal, State Department-sponsored trip through Burma; John Dickerson's multi-part investigation of Phoenix, Arizona's lax regulation of doctors; Pulitzer Prize–winner Jonathan Gold's ode to food and wine; and Christina Waters's in-depth look at trickster winemaker Randall Grahm. From a hair-raising public service report on one community's heroin problem to the bittersweet story of a gay football player, the work being produced by American altweeklies today reminds all of us how great journalism is supposed to feel. And it makes us hopeful that the news well will not be forsaken by the suits. We are all of us nothing without our content.

Frequently I hear from young writers. They want to do and see and report. They want to exist on their talent and drive and personal wiles. They want to be people whose lives are their own, whose voices are their own.

To those still in school I say: get thee an internship at your local altweekly. From there begins all good things.

To those young writers hungry for clips and experience I say: get thee an assignment from your local altweekly. (Offer to write the first one for free, or on spec. You might just surprise them, as I apparently did so many years ago.)

And believe it or not, the universe willing, 30 or more years will pass, and you will have your own dusty archives.

Maybe by then they'll have something better than those damned, expensive, *useless* fireproof cabinets.

BEST ALTWEEKLY WRITING 2009 & 2010

ARTS CRITICISM

🏅 🏅 🏅

CIRCULATION 50,000 AND OVER

"Why Hard Times Won't Mean Good Times at the Movies Again"
"Robert Frank's Real America"

by Jim Hoberman, *Village Voice*

"Hoberman's erudition and fluid writing remain an inspiration."—Jeet Heer, York University

🏅 🏅 🏅

CIRCULATION UNDER 50,000

"Madhouse"
"Once Upon a Time Forever"

by Jim Ridley, *Nashville Scene*

"Very good film criticism from a writer who's equally at home making sense of the classics and expressing exasperation with the contemporary."—Dan Kois, Washington Post / Vulture

Why Hard Times Won't Mean Good Times at the Movies Again

Jim Hoberman

FEBRUARY 4, 2009

"We have seen that our product is, at worst, recession-resistant." So DreamWorks Animation CEO Jeffrey Katzenberg assured a conclave of Hollywood studio execs and Wall Street investors, hosted by Goldman Sachs last September amid the din of falling stock prices.

The movie industry had already endured a year-long credit crunch. Two days later, Universal backed away from Dream-Works' $130 million 3-D animation *Tintin* (and within a week, Goldman Sachs ceased to be an investment bank), but, as Katzenberg explained, time was on their side. "More optimistically and historically," he recalled, the motion-picture product "has actually been recession-proof." Optimistic? You bet: back in 1930, Hollywood had considered itself "depression-proof," too.

For the American people, the first five years of the Great Depression—1930 through 1934—were the worst of times and the *really* worst of times. For the American movie industry, the period would also bring the worst of economic times. In another way, though, it was the best. The early '30s were the days of "Breadlines & Champagne," as Film Forum has dubbed its month-long, all-35mm celebration of the pre-Code, the Socially Conscious, and the Screwball—three manifestations of the richest period in Hollywood history.

Crisis may be stimulus to popular art—the Nixon years were great for movies as well—and the Great Depression created chaos for all. Busily rewiring their theaters for newly developed "talking pictures" and importing verbally adroit talent from the Broadway stage to make them, the Hollywood studios initially ignored the stock market crash. The crash, however, did not ignore them. The novelty of sound soon faded. By the end of 1931, the record motion-picture audience of the previous year was down by a third and falling. So were ticket prices. Production costs, however, had doubled.

Warner Bros., the studio that led the initially profitable shift to talking pictures, was now hemorrhaging money. Universal terminated hundreds of employees and would soon join RKO in receivership—followed by Fox and, in what was then America's second largest bankruptcy to date, Paramount. As movie houses darkened, exhibitors played exploitation angles, promoting double features, dish giveaways, and weekly lotteries called "bank nights"—which, as part of its retro, Film Forum plans to revive. By the time Franklin Roosevelt took office in March 1933, theaters were empty, production slates slashed, cash flow dried up. The industry was near collapse. But the product was better than ever.

Sound brought a new hyper-verbal cinema, racy and insolent. The talkies also changed the nature of stardom. (The great voices of the early '30s are recycled to this day: Cagney, Hepburn, Peter Lorre, Groucho Marx, W. C. Fields, and Mae West.) Hard times pushed desperate producers toward sensationalism. The studios ignored their own Production Code. Crime paid, so did sin. Street-smart criminals traded brazen double entendres with fast-talking chorines. Gangsters ruled the 1931–32 season; bad girls followed, as *Variety* estimated 80 percent of the pictures released in the 1932–33 season had a "sex slant." The trend peaked with West, whose first feature, *She Done Him Wrong,* was the biggest hit of 1933, returning 10 times its production costs in North America alone and precipitating a national crusade to clean up the movies. Fittingly, "Breadlines & Champagne" opens with West's follow-up, *I'm No Angel*—selling tickets at the Depression price of 35 cents.

The movies of the early '30s were at once more naturalistic and more theatrical than silent movies—and, thanks to tight budgets and the exigencies of the double feature, far snappier. In addition to trafficking in sex and violence, talkies assimilated the vaudeville aesthetic of ethnic stereotype and crazy comedy, creating a rowdy new American idiom in which every other line seemed to include an appreciative "Swell!" or questioning "On the level?" Extravagant fantasies alternated with cynical realism. The period brought forth a remarkable number of enduring celluloid archetypes: Paul Muni's Scarface and Jean Harlow's Platinum Blonde, the Universal horrors

Dracula and Frankenstein, Tarzan and King Kong, Betty Boop and even Mickey Mouse. The chaos (and lack of supervision) allowed filmmakers like Ernst Lubitsch, Josef von Sternberg, and Busby Berkeley to do their best work—unlike today, when every project is necessarily pre-sold and vetted.

"Breadlines & Champagne" doesn't showcase the full range of early-'30s Hollywood, but it is particularly rich in "preachment yarns"—movies that trafficked in lurid topicality while expressing a measure of passionately confused social protest. Banks go kerflooey in Frank Capra's *American Madness,* teenage hobos ride the rails in William Wellman's *Wild Boys of the Road,* and the unemployed turn to collective farming in King Vidor's *Our Daily Bread.* The countryside was in turmoil, yet Hollywood was never more urban. The movies at Film Forum are mainly set in big cities—nearly half in New York, four among the homeless inhabitants of Manhattan's Hoovervilles. Not since the days of the nickelodeon had audiences been so encouraged to identify with the destitute and the desperate. Class warfare was rife. Capitalism was equated with crime. Predatory businessmen debauched their innocent employees—although with the New Deal's new order, sexual relations between capital and labor became a subject for comedy.

As the 1932 election neared, with nearly half the nation's labor force out of work or marginally employed, the call resounded for "strong" leadership. Hollywood shifted from the outrageously cynical to the hysterically crypto-fascist—*Washington Merry-Go-Round* (the government is run by lobbyists and crooked pols) gave way to *Gabriel Over the White House* (new president divinely inspired to declare martial law) and *This Day and Age* (teenage vigilantes wage a war against crime), both of which opened near the beginning of Roosevelt's term. In early 1933, Warner Bros., the studio most identified with FDR, declared its own "New Deal in Entertainment": In *42nd Street,* Warner Baxter's tyrannical stage director demonstrates that one might defeat the Depression by making a Broadway show. The utopia of full employment had never been more vividly dramatized than by Busby Berkeley's screen-filling dance formations.

The following year's *Stand Up and Cheer!* had Baxter tapped by FDR himself to head the new Federal Department of Amusement, a cross between Hollywood and the WPA. The new agency's first megaproduction, "I'm Laughing," featured everyone in America—welders and seamstresses, cops and chorus girls, blacksmiths, hillbillies, and the white actress who performs in burnt cork under the name "Aunt Jemima"—united against self-pity. "I'm laughing, and I have nothing to laugh about," is the new anthem. "But if I can laugh and sing and shout—brother, so can you!"After a dozen more numbers, including one introducing five-year-old Shirley Temple (embodiment of optimism and, soon, Hollywood's biggest star), *Stand Up and Cheer!* ends by proclaiming the end of the Depression. The movie's visceral metaphors of social organization have cured the malaise.

Can Hollywood do it again?

The U.S. suffered through three and a half years of economic misery before the New Deal arrived; the Obama administration arrives after only three and a half months. Since October, Hollywood studios have been terminating franchises and buying out employees. The audience has remained constant, although revenues have declined. Warner Bros. saw a nine percent fall in its third-quarter earnings—despite the colossal success of *The Dark Knight*. Stock prices are down, but much scarier, from the industry's point of view, has been the drop in DVD sales. (Especially scary since a movie's theatrical release is largely a means of promoting DVD sales.)

This is only the beginning. Fox has announced a sequel to Oliver Stone's *Wall Street* (yawn), but nothing like Depression-era topical showmanship has begun to kick in. The independent *Wendy and Lucy,* with Michelle Williams as a jobless vagrant, now seems prescient, and recent releases ranging from *WALL-E* and *Milk* to *The Wrestler* and *Gran Torino* have certainly profited from the current mood of anxious Obam-optimism. The rags-to-riches romance *Slumdog Millionaire* is the prime beneficiary, although the 13 Oscar nominations accorded $150 million bummer *Benjamin Button* suggest the industry's touching vote of confidence in itself. And therein lies the rub. Hooked on tent poles and blockbusters, dreaming of dinosaurs, the movie industry has long since ceased to be nimble enough to adapt to crisis.

A reorganized and self-regulated Hollywood bounced back in 1935, but times were different then. Movies were America's universal culture. Now, they're not even close. Like then, the technology is changing—but in a far different way. Movies are expendable. Folks will give up $12 tickets, cancel Netflix, and cut cable to save their high-speed Internet connection. With the president's fireside chats posted online, the new Hoovervilles will certainly have broadband. Is there a downsized future for Katzenberg's product? As one bankrupt mogul said to another, "*YouTube?!*"

Maybe free online movies are strictly for the indies. But if times get worse and the studios want to get real, they'll have to find the audience where it lives: Hulu for Hollywood. ●◆

Robert Frank's Real America

Jim Hoberman

SEPTEMBER 29, 2009

America changed between the summers of 1955 and '56—and so did its sense of itself. During those 12 months, we got "Hound Dog" and "Howl," *Invasion of the Body Snatchers* and *The Searchers,* Marilyn Monroe and Arthur Miller, Martin Luther King and the Montgomery bus boycott. Disneyland opened. HUAC's interrogations were upstaged by *The $64,000 Question.* James Dean died and was resurrected, eternally young, in *Rebel Without a Cause.*

The Alexis de Tocqueville of this new New World was Robert Frank. From June 1955 into the following summer, the 31-year-old Swiss-born photographer crossed and recrossed the continent in a used Ford. Frank's project, the subject of the Metropolitan Museum's current exhibit, was, so he wrote to his parents, to document "how Americans live, have fun, eat, drive cars, work, etc." Did that "etc." include the magic word, "dream"? For once Frank published these photographs as a book, provocatively called *The Americans,* it was evident that he had also documented a landscape as much psychic as physical.

Frank's initial road trip took him from New York through the smokestack cities of western Pennsylvania and Ohio to Detroit; his second, from New York to antediluvian Savannah. Supported by a Guggenheim, Frank again headed south in late '55, driving a circuitous route down through the Old Confederacy to New Orleans, then Texas, taking Route 66 to Las Vegas, and on to Los Angeles. Frank and his young family spent the winter in California, returning to New York by way of Reno, Salt Lake, Butte, the Great Plains, and Chicago— which the photographer revisited for the Democratic Convention in mid-August.

Over the course of his travels, Frank exposed nearly 800 rolls of film. He took snapshots at rodeos, picnics, funerals, and political rallies; his subjects included Detroit assembly line workers, Hoboken politicians, New York City drag queens, the midday crowd on New Orleans' Canal Street, and countless automobiles. Working ahead of the curve, he completed his trip before the U.S. Congress authorized a 40,000-mile interstate highway system (and before *Time* gushed that such highways were "really *the* American art").

Intimating the loneliness inherent in American notions of freedom, Frank's photographs reveled in empty two-lane blacktops, seedy bus depots, solitary lunch counters, and all-night diners inhabited by a restless tribe of waitresses, truckers, and midnight cowboys. *The Americans* suggested an alternate America of dissident subcultures—the black Brandos on their motorcycles, the Native American hitchhikers photographed driving the photographer's Ford, the New York teenagers clustered around yet another outsize jukebox. Frank also acknowledged that freedom might be just another word, paying particular attention to black America—separate and unequal. That might be why, as a shabby, unshaven, camera-toting foreigner driving through the Deep South with New York plates and a "smart-alecky attitude," Frank struck at least one local sheriff as a Communist agent—and was arrested in an Arkansas town on the Mississippi border.

There's a sense in which that cop was right: Frank was an alien spy. His photographs were collected first in France in 1958, illustrating *Les américains,* a book of short, critical texts by Simone de Beauvoir, Henry Miller, Richard Wright, and de Tocqueville, among others. In early 1960, Grove Press published an American edition. There was no text—rather, Frank's 83 photographs were the text, as well as the subtext, with Jack Kerouac providing a suitably ecstatic introduction. A few notices were positive. Gilbert Millstein, the *New York Times* reviewer whose 1957 rave put *On the Road* on the cultural map, thought Frank had talent. But mainly, Americans took *The Americans* personally. The book was characterized as "sick," "warped," "joyless," "dishonest," "sad," "neurotic," "marred by spite, bitterness, and narrow prejudice." Coming from a foreigner, the title was an insult. Why not "Some Americans"? (Noting the "irritable" nature of American patriotism, de Tocqueville had observed that if one appeared to criticize America, an American typically responded as if he himself were under attack.)

Worse, perhaps, Frank depicted God's country as a wasteland. For centuries, America's "natural paradise" had been a source of transcendent value—"Is not the landscape, every glimpse of which hath a grandeur, a face of Him?" Emerson asked. *The Americans* turned that paradise inside out. What had been exalted was ignored, and that which, overly familiar, had been ignored—roadside America's nowhere-but-everywhere stretch of billboards, drive-ins, and gas stations later called the Strip—was now made strange. In 1955, Walt Disney created one sort of theme park; Robert Frank found another.

We all live in Frank's America now. Following the initial shock of recognition, *The Americans* would become one the most influential American artworks of the twentieth century. The Met is selling the new Aperture book, *Photography After Frank.* And *An American Journey,* the hour-long documentary at Film Forum this week, treats Frank's *The Americans* as holy writ. Looking for traces, French filmmaker Philippe Séclier revisits Frank's locations—the hotel room overlooking downtown Butte, the apartment in Hoboken, the North Carolina barbershop where the photographer cast his shadow on the screen door. Hoping to recover the sacred relic of the barber's chair, Séclier discovered the shop is long gone. Still, some of Frank's subjects are alive—typically with no idea that they'd been photographed, let alone immortalized.

The Met's catalog—a 500-page, seven-and-a-half-pound door-stopper—surrounds *The Americans* with massive exegesis, including maps, chronologies, 81 pages of contact sheets, and a guide to Frank's variant croppings. The book testifies to the labor involved in the photographer's snapshot, as does the Met's wall of work prints. Frank exposed 27,000 images, printed 1,000, and used 83—a shooting ratio of 330:1. The work prints are not so much alternate takes as an alternate *Americans.*

Although *The Americans* is a book, the exhibition clarifies Frank's structure. His sense of montage is more apparent; it's easier to see his visual puns and cross-references when sequenced on the wall. Frank arranged his photographs in four roughly differentiated movements, each announced in the book by the image of an American flag. The first introduces his cast, as well as the artist's knack for expressionist parody: The Jersey pol with his pursed lips, the exultant Kefauver campaign worker making like Il Duce, the conspiratorial fat cats in the club car to Washington, the frozen-faced starlet, the simpering queens, the portly soldier and his hard-faced companion out for a stroll. All are almost Weimar caricatures.

America is divided, powerful figures alternating with a skeptical, unsmiling population. These stark oppositions continue into the book's second movement, as Frank focuses on the landscape, discovering unlikely monuments and vistas (a New York City newsstand, a mailbox bisecting the Nebraska plains, a man genuflecting before a jukebox, the view from a mining town hotel window). In some cases—as with the benches of elderly Floridians—people are the landscape. The opening shot of a translucent flag presages a series of mutations: A segregated New Orleans trolley becomes a roll of exposed film; a shrouded car dissolves into a shrouded corpse and then an empty highway.

Heralded by the images of Washington and Lincoln presiding over a Detroit bar, the third chapter is the most complex. Here, images of images are mixed with signs of salvation. Some of the photographs are weirdly pastoral, even transcendent: the gas stations of the cross; a Miami elevator that, the operator's weary expression notwithstanding, might be the lift to paradise; an empty café with Oral Roberts preaching on the TV against the blast of sunlight that obliterates an adjacent window; cars worshipping an illuminated movie screen; the fierce lyricism of a black evangelist raising his staff down by the river.

The Americans' final section seems the most overtly political. Here, the flag blares from a shiny tuba and an outsize neon arrow directs a tiny, hastening pedestrian down a dark street: As was asked in the '30s, "Little Man, What Now?" Halfway through, images of mass-produced images and signs of alienated collectivity segue to brutally tender portraits of loners, then couples, some of whom make eye contact with the camera, and finally families, often shown with their cars— as is the photographer's family in the last image, bringing it all back home.

As Frank's sign-rich images demand to be read, particularly in context, so his year-long trip has its literary analogues. Taken as lived experience, *The Americans* is an anti-*Walden,* a whaling voyage, a sojourn on the Mississippi. Shortly before Frank embarked, the *Paris Review* published a chunk of *On the Road;* around the time the photographer left California, Allen Ginsberg gave the first public reading of "Howl."

Like the beat writers, Frank presented a chaotic countryside at once concrete and allegorical, vital and haunted. His photographs of a Los Angeles street evangelist brandishing a copy of *Awake!,* the "Christ Died for Our Sins" card taped to an old Chevy, or the statue of St. Francis blessing skid row could easily have inspired a Ginsberg poem, a Kerouac riff, or a Dylan line. In his enthusiastic introduction to Frank's book, Kerouac hailed, "The humor, the sadness, the EVERYTHING-ness and American-ness of these pictures!" In that, however, the writer was expressing his own affirmative sensibility. Taken as narrative, *The Americans* suggests a dark pilgrim's progress through a hardscrabble land where beauty sprouts like weeds in a vacant lot—a place subjugated by images and ruled by machines, hypermodern yet underdeveloped, banal but apocalyptic.

With their iconic use of flags, billboards, and TV sets, Frank's photographs presaged Pop Art; in their dramatic personae, they anticipated the iconography and attitudes of films that would not be made for another dozen years. Frank's road trip was recapitulated in American movies from Ron Rice's underground *Senseless* and Ken Kesey's unfinished Merry Pranksters epic through the echt'60s youth films *Easy Rider* and *Two-Lane Blacktop* to the more eccentric travelogues of *Stranger Than Paradise*, *Thelma and Louise,* and *Fear and Loathing in Las Vegas,* not to mention Sacha Baron Cohen's *Borat.*

Photographing himself in America, Frank dramatized a particular sort of American heroism. Soon after he arrived in New York—March 1947, the same Cold War season in which *On the Road's* narrative begins—he wrote to his parents, saying, "I feel as if I'm in a film." (Driving cross-country some 40 years later, French philosopher Jean Baudrillard would make the same observation.) After *The Americans,* Frank's artistic production shifted toward motion pictures—in some, he was the overt subject.

Perhaps the total involvement of *The Americans* exhausted Frank's interest in photography. He was already working with Kerouac and painter Alfred Leslie on his first movie, *Pull My Daisy,* when *The Americans* was published—and has expressed no small ambivalence toward the youthful enterprise that has remained his defining achievement. Both exhibit and catalog end with a section called "Destroying *The Americans.*" As curator Sarah Greenough notes, Frank's relationship to his famous creation is "inextricably linked with his innate suspicion of success, his abhorrence of repetition," and "a restless desire" (that some might call quintessentially American) "to push his art in new ways."

Although not many of them travelogues, Frank's subsequent movies often share *The Americans'* sense of being a stranger in a strange land. A number of these are screening this fall at the Met, including the never-released, 1972 Rolling Stones documentary *Cocksucker Blues,* in which, for one shining moment, Mick Jagger finds himself in an actual Southern juke joint (and thus inside *The Americans*), and the 1987 feature *Candy Mountain,* an end-of-the-road film co-directed with novelist Rudy Wurlitzer that, with its northern journey from Lower Manhattan to deepest Nova Scotia, is essentially a disappearing act that mirrors Frank's own.

A few years later, Frank made a masterful, if little-seen, video piece, *C'est vrait!,* composed of a single hour-long shot taken mainly from a beat-up van that repeatedly circles through the artist's Noho neighborhood. More than *Candy Mountain,* this declaration of truth parodies even as it expunges the memory of the artist's long-ago trip from sea to shining sea. ◀▸

"HOW I GOT THAT STORY"

Jim Hoberman got through high school reading the Village Voice *and has written for it for more than 30 years. He teaches film history at the Cooper Union and is the author of 10 books, most recently* An Army of Phantoms: American Movies and the Making of the Cold War. *The following interview was conducted by email with Santa Fe Reporter Editor and AAN Editorial Chair Julia Goldberg.*

These pieces of journalism struck me as going far beyond criticism into the realm of being stunningly instructive. Do you undertake massive research to provide such historical and cultural contexts for your articles, or do you tailor your subjects to those for which you already are well-versed?
Calling these pieces "instructive" is a great compliment. To my mind, the great function of journalism is to inform the reader—that is, to tell people things they don't necessarily know, or enrich their understanding of facts they may already have. There's always some amount of research involved in any article, and there should be—I like to learn things too! However, I do have some long-established interests and areas of knowledge and consequently welcome the opportunity to draw on that. Each of these articles made use of material that I had either taught or written, albeit in a new and different context.

Sometimes arts critics fall into a trap of writing more for people who already are interested in or knowledgeable about a given subject, rather than for a wider

audience. Who do you see as the audience for your pieces, and how do you approach the task of reaching them?

This is a tough question to answer. I take the reader's interest in a particular subject as a given, although I certainly understand the significance of a headline and lead in prompting that interest. The reader's knowledge is, of course, highly variable. I try to be lucid but I don't want to write "down" to people (nor do I believe readers want that). I also take it for granted that there are readers who may know as much as I do about a subject, or even more—it's a challenge then to both make something clear and to come up with a new perspective or say something fresh.

With the volume of arts events to consider each week in your market, what process do you apply to decide which ones you will write about?

I like to cover that which excites my curiosity or seems interesting or would be fun to write about—it's one of the great things about the job.

Has the online environment changed how you approach your work?

It's certainly made research more convenient—and also feedback more available. I've done some blogging and appreciate its spontaneity. But that's also a problem— it's hard to take unedited writing entirely seriously. I recognize that the future belongs to online journalism but I long ago fell for print and, for better or worse, love it still.

What advice would you give aspiring arts critics?

Practice reading as well as writing, recognize the gift of a talented editor, cultivate your enthusiasms, interrogate your prejudices, and never forget your job to inform the reader.

Madhouse

Jim Ridley

JULY 29, 2009

House (Hausu)

Sid and Marty Krofft, meet Salvador Dali. There are movies for which advance word in the newspaper seems like insufficient notice. In the case of this thoroughly insane feature—a 1977 Japanese horror film now making erratic stops across the country, like a spaceship crashing in your backyard—it's hard to imagine what method could conceivably herald its contents:

a three-story gong, maybe, or an army of acid-crazed Brownies shrieking through the streets.

For now, this'll have to do: Run. Wake your neighbor. Slap your children. Eye your cat with suspicion. Every once in a blue-screen moon, a movie will remind even the most jaded of cult-film aficionados that, no, in fact, they have *not* seen everything. Here, director Nobuhiko Obayashi dispatches six schoolgirls to spend their summer vacation with classmate Oshare (Kimiko Ikegami) at her ailing aunt's remote estate. A friend described the movie's first half as an experimental film made by an 11-year-old girl, and that fits: Avant-garde devices such as screens within screens may be underscored with pancake-syrupy pop, or framed with the kind of gauzy borders a kid might sketch around a doodled unicorn.

And the second half? Why spoil some of the only surprises to rattle movie screens all summer? I don't think this is giving away too much: There's an evil housecat, and it convinces a piano to eat one of the girls. All I will add is that Obayashi's body of work extends from experimental shorts to apocalyptic teenage sci-fi (1987's *The Drifting Classroom*) to those notorious 1970s Charles Bronson "Mandom" perfume ads—and in *House*, he manages to compress them all into one brain-boiling spew of psychotropic, psychedelic, sense-deranging WTF imagery. It's scary not in any conventional sense, but because a viewer feels so utterly without bearings—as if whatever glue holds the universe together had suddenly turned to Jell-O.

Brought to you by (of all people) the canonical custodians at Janus Films, *House* is the reason midnight movies were invented: so you will have other people to confirm that, yes, you really did just watch a deadly assault by animated lampshade. (Shows midnight July 31–Aug. 1 at The Belcourt)

Humpday

True situation comedy may be the hardest kind to pull off, because it's the least reliant on obvious cues like punch lines or pratfalls. But when done properly—as in writer-director Lynn Shelton's sharply observed indie hit—it can keep you laughing even when nothing overtly funny seems to be happening.

Mark Duplass and Joshua Leonard play old friends who've grown apart as Duplass has settled into married life and Leonard has clung to his *On the Road* self-image. Reunited and nagged by worries that they've lost their old edge, the buddies notch up their rivalry until they've committed to a colossally misguided show of daring—starring together in an amateur gay porn film.

What could have been a predictable gross-out farce instead takes one unexpected turn after another, as the characters respond believably to their unbelievable predicament—and that includes everything after the brosephs enter the hotel room they've rented for their moment of truth.

Duplass, last seen in the NaFF selection *True Adolescents*, and *The Blair Witch Project*'s Leonard have spry comic chemistry. But the performer who steals her every scene is Alycia Delmore as Duplass's wife, who descends the rungs of cold fury with hilarious tight-lipped concealment. Never have the phrases "You're right" and "I shouldn't get mad" sounded more like preludes to Armageddon. (Opens Friday at The Belcourt) ➥

Once Upon a Time Forever

Jim Ridley

AUGUST 27, 2009

"Once upon a time in Nazi-occupied France," reads the chapter heading that opens Quentin Tarantino's *Inglourious Basterds*—a commando mission in counter-mythmaking where a movie theater, a projector, a handy editing deck and a great big heap of flammable film stock (not to mention the climaxes of *Carrie* and *The Wizard of Oz* and the theme song from *Cat People*) team up to wipe out the Third Reich's high command. It's a movie about the power of movies to change history, in that celluloid parallel universe where memory and imagination stand off with the record.

How fitting that Tarantino's chapter heading tips its visor hat to the movies of Sergio Leone, an alternate history of

America conjured up from gunsmoke and mirrors. The first time I saw *Once Upon a Time in the West,* screening this weekend as the finale to the Belcourt's Sergio Leone Month and its summer-long series of Westerns, I was a kid watching the WNGE "Award Movie" on Sunday afternoon, on the floor of my grandmother's living room. For lots of reasons, it was the worst possible way to watch one of the most visually striking movies ever made. But I can still see this image, burned into my mind's eye: a gaunt bald gunslinger standing impassively, staring into the camera, as a drip from the ceiling fills the wide brim of his hat with a thup! thup! thup!

Over the years, I've found something more to appreciate every time I've seen *Once Upon a Time in the West.* But every time, it leaves me feeling like an awestruck 10-year-old. It has something to do with the scale of Leone's gloriously excessive 1968 Western. Every dusty street is a football field's width. Every grizzled face, shot in screen-filling close-up, looms like a head on Mount Rushmore. Every gunfight is a duel of the gods. A viewer becomes an HO-scale brakeman walking through a regular-sized trainyard. In this, the most elaborate and exhilarating of his grandiose pistol operas, Leone took the Western he envisioned as a child—an Old West of quick-triggered warriors, enormous open spaces and superheroic deeds—and transferred it to the screen with its mythic distortions intact.

Apart from the scale (and the title), there's nothing child-like about *Once Upon a Time in the West.* An inextricable mix of cynicism, violence and delicate lyricism—as voluptuous and perverse as you'd expect from a story dreamed up by Bernardo Bertolucci (*The Conformist*) and Dario Argento (*Suspiria*)—the movie was a critical and commercial failure when released here in 1969, as the genre's audience was either riding into the twilight with the Duke or grooving on the revisionist bloodbath of The Wild Bunch. It was not the time to be romanticizing manifest destiny, even if Leone's quasi-Marxist take equates business with bloodshed.

Over the years, though, a funny thing has happened. Leone's outsized rethink of the Western, an exaggerated pastiche of the John Ford films and gunfighter mythology he absorbed as a boy overseas, has gradually edged aside the John Wayne and Roy Rogers models in the popular imagination. You can see it when you close your eyes: the figures at opposite ends of a dust-blown street, the close-ups of "two beeg eyes" glaring edgily, the duster coats whirling like a bullfighter's cape. Thanks to Leone's invaluable collaborator, composer Ennio Morricone, you can hear it, too: the matadorial trumpets, the celestial female vocals, the trebly electric guitar that stabs and slashes.

Morricone's score clarifies a convoluted plot that concerns four main characters: a shadowy avenger (Charles Bronson); a prostitute, Jill (Claudia Cardinale), on her way to a blood-soaked wedding day; a scruffy outlaw named Cheyenne (Jason Robards); and a pale-eyed angel of death known only as Frank. He is played by Henry Fonda, who demolishes his decades of good-guy rectitude at the moment of his terrifying entrance. This is Tom Joad's evil doppelganger—a guy who's present wherever there's a fight so hungry people can eat, all right, but always working for those with a whip hand on the drawstrings of plenty.

Morricone composed the music before the movie even started shooting, and it is as much screenplay as score. Each character has a theme—Jill's motif is a soaring solo wail, Cheyenne's a pokey, halting clip-clop—and the composer interweaves them, stating the connections between characters without a word of dialogue. No one needs to state that Frank and his pursuer are bound; Morricone's menacing theme uses an ever-present harmonica to link them. Bronson's harmonica is literally an instrument of vengeance. It's the totem he wears around his neck, for a reason he means to explain to Frank at the point of death.

Oh, there's so much more. There's the tremendous opening sequence, in which Western icons Woody Strode and Jack Elam converge on a railway depot to the John Cage-like accompaniment of various squeaks and clatters. There's the hangdog decency of Robards's Cheyenne, the outlaw doomed by the suits moving West. And above all, there's the almost inhuman perfection of Leone's widescreen images, with their rhythmic alternation of flyspeck long shots and bulbous close-ups. Each frame has a painterly precision and clarity, as if the director had somehow eliminated anything standing between the screen and the image he had in his head. *Once Upon a Time in the West* is the kind of movie whose total intoxication with moviemaking can lead to a lifetime's love. ➙

"HOW I GOT THAT STORY"

When he isn't a writhing victim of a madman's lust, Jim Ridley is a howling hellcat humping a hot steel hog on a roaring rampage of revenge. He lives in Nashville, where he edits the Nashville Scene. *The following interview was conducted via email by Santa Fe Reporter Editor and AAN Editorial Chair Julia Goldberg.*

Your film reviews are extremely visceral and loaded with recalled detail. How do you accomplish this? Do you take prodigious notes when you're watching movies? Watch them repeatedly? Have a mind like a steel trap?

More like a plastic colander. I think it depends on the movie, really. It's hard to forget something like *House*. On the other hand, I saw *Predators* a few nights ago and I can't even remember how some of the characters got killed. As for notes, I used to pride myself on not taking notes, in part because notetaking can distract you from movie-watching. But I rely on them more these days, especially when I'm working on long-form pieces.

How much do you consider the movie marketplace when deciding what to review? Do you feel pressure to review big box office hits, or do you stick to what you think will be interesting to you?

Big box-office hits are interesting to me. Love it or hate it, tell me there was a more interesting movie to write about this year than *Inception*. I would cover those movies naturally, so I never really feel any pressure. To me, reviewers should feel emboldened, not disheartened, by the brush-off they're getting from studios. You didn't get an advance screening of *Predators*? Fine: write about something like *Winter's Bone* or *I Am Love* that deserves the space and the attention. Readers will thank you for it. The reduced number of advance screenings has liberated reviewers from the tyranny of opening weekends; they just don't know it yet. Besides, the megaplex in my mind has room for *Jeanne Dielman* as well as *Booty Call*. My imaginary reader is the other guy who's figured out how to make those screenings work as a double feature.

Has the online environment changed how you approach your work?

No, not really. I've accepted that I'll always be a slowpoke. The same is as true of thought and reflection as it is of a traffic violation: speed kills. But I'm really excited by the way a lot of younger critics are using the audiovisual capabilities of YouTube et al. to create new hybrid forms of criticism, going straight to the film text.

In "Once Upon a Time in the West," you write about watching the film for the first time as a child. Are movies just in your DNA?
I grew up loving movies. My mother, who just passed away, encouraged me to see all kinds of things: one of her greatest gifts to me was the night she dropped me off at a college screening of Truffaut's *Shoot the Piano Player* when I was a teenager. It blew my mind that a single movie could be both elevated and goofy, lyrical and slangy, serene and violent. If it didn't put movies in my DNA, it certainly rearranged the wiring of my cerebral cortex.

What advice would you give aspiring arts critics?
There is no shame in panhandling.

ARTS FEATURE

✿ ✿ ✿

CIRCULATION 50,000 AND OVER

"On the Road to Burma"

by Randall Roberts, *L.A. Weekly*

"A strong combination of vivid scene-setting—visual, aural, political—and consideration of big questions related to the role and meaning of state department tours."—Alisa Solomon, Columbia University

✿ ✿ ✿

CIRCULATION UNDER 50,000

"Art on Trial"

by Edwin Slipek Jr., *Style Weekly*

"This is really top notch. The reporting (so much of it) all feels so seamless. It's really gorgeously done, a perfect length, so well-handled throughout, and opinionated without being jeering."—Choire Sicha, The Awl

On the Road to Burma

Randall Roberts

JUNE 25, 2009

Four days into a five-day tour of Rangoon, Burma, we thought we'd had our fill of weirdness. But after Ozomatli are led through Kawechan School for the Blind's darkened hallways and up a flight of stairs, the sound of a flailing guitar solo and the thump of a bass drum punch through the corridor. Around a corner, standing on a stage, four conservatively dressed men wearing sunglasses and matching pink-and-blue polo-type shirts are banging out a rock song. They look like a '60s surf band, the Ventures or something—square and stiff.

Ozomatli, a band born in Los Angeles in 1996, are scheduled to perform a few songs for students, orphans, and disabled kids as part of an outreach program arranged by the U.S. Department of State. They didn't count on any competition, and they watch from the side as a band called Blind Reality, facing 100 people of varying degrees of disability, creates a chaotic, freakazoid sound that only four sightless rock dudes living in the pocket of one of the world's most beaten-down countries could possibly make.

New-genre alert: Burmese blind-metal.

Ulises Bella's jaw drops. Wil-Dog Abers gasps, and Raúl Pacheco, a thoughtful former Tom Hayden political intern with "Chicano" tattooed on the back of his hand, witnesses, eyes agape, as the guitarist does a double-fingered fret run that would make Eddie Van Halen shift uncomfortably in his seat. The members of Ozomatli have a catalog of mind-blowing images stored from the two years they've been working as musical diplomats for the U.S. Department of State, but this one surely ranks: an expert Blind Reality guitarist whose main influences, he will tell the band, are fretboard gymnasts Yngwie Malmsteen and Steve Vai.

As if Blind Reality couldn't take it any further, after a mean cover of a Bon Jovi song, a lady guest vocalist, also wearing sunglasses, is led slowly to the microphone stand. She touches it with her hand and, the room silent, moves into Creedence

Clearwater Revival's "Have You Ever Seen the Rain?" She sings the words in Burmese: "Someone told me long ago/ There's a calm before the storm/I know, it's been coming for some time/When it's over, so they say/It'll rain a sunny day/I know, shining down like water."

"Getting up there and seeing these four blind dudes just killing it? I never witnessed anything like that in my life," says Ozo percussionist and MC Justin "El Niño" Porée a few days later.

Ozo sets up, still buzzing from that lightning-bolt moment. Even in a little corner of the world with way bigger concerns than one-upmanship, pride enters the equation when an opening band smokes it. Soon the seven in Ozomatli—guitar, bass, percussion, drums, keyboard, saxophone, trumpet—are playing hard, their rhythms running through the room. A row of children with Down syndrome bounce and fidget; blind kids in middle rows direct their ears at the music and absorb it. Nurses in the back smile.

It's after the first couple of songs that a man sandwiched in the second or third row starts making a commotion. It's not clear whether he's having problems or is somehow disturbed. He's contorted with what looks to be cerebral palsy, and is struggling to stand. Ozomatli watch from the stage, swinging to their poppy hit "After Party." Grasping his neighbors' shoulders, the guy pushes his way toward the aisle, arms taut, legs and torso cockeyed, and moves to the empty space in front of the stage. Bella bursts forth with a tenor-sax solo.

Then, as if plugged into a socket, the man starts whaling his arms with the rhythm, a look of joyful determination on his face, bouncing at his knees, punching as he fights to remain balanced while tabla player Jiro Yamaguchi, Porée, and longtime Ozomatli drummer Mario Calire offer a cumbia rhythm. You know the iconic image of the man facing down tanks in Tiananmen Square? Imagine the opposite: An observer standing before an invisible force, willfully getting plowed over.

After the gig, the handshakes, and the photos, Ozomatli load back in the van and wave goodbye, a little bit different in the head from before.

✻

When you drive along the boulevards of Rangoon in a white late-model Chevy van, you might as well be rolling in a polka dot Rolls Royce. Monks in saffron robes rubberneck and nudge their companions. At stoplights, as we idle next to old pickup trucks retrofitted to be people-movers, riders in the back and on the bumpers crane their necks to look with kind but curious eyes. In a country in which even a junky compact car costs $25,000 and anything new will run you at least $100,000 after licensing fees and kickbacks, a fresh U.S. government–issue Chevy is something to behold.

The van moves in dense traffic through roundabouts and curving lefts and rights, past Inya Lake, where, three days earlier, an American named John Yettaw had been arrested on its southern shore after swimming to Suu Kyi's compound. A few kilometers later, the Schwedagon Pagoda, constructed a few millennia ago to house eight strands of the Buddha's hair, appears like a hallucination. Shimmering in the morning sun with a new coat of gold leaf, the bell-shaped pagoda looks like it was on loan from another—better—planet.

The first stop of an early-May, three-country U.S.–sponsored tour that ultimately takes Ozomatli to Vietnam and Thailand, Burma will jar even the most jaded travelers. One of our guides warns us that the country is at least 20 years behind the rest of civilization; soon thereafter we drive past a billboard excitedly advertising the arrival of a new Yellow Pages. The name of the country's most beloved leader, Aung San Suu Kyi, is forbidden from being spoken aloud; rather, she is known simply as "The Lady." The exchange rate of American currency is based as much on the cleanliness of the bill as on what numbers are on it. Hand the hotel receptionist a crinkled or torn $100, and you may as well have just handed her a leaf.

In addition to the moment-to-moment oddities, it has been a strange few days for the band—and the country. On the same day that Yettaw is pulled from the lake and Ozomatli arrive in Burma, two American journalists traveling in Mandalay, to the north, are detained by Burmese immigration authorities. The week of Ozomatli's tour of Burma is also the first anniversary of Cyclone Nargis. The storm, thought to be the most deadly natural disaster in the country's recorded history, killed an estimated 100,000 people.

And if that weren't enough weight, the house-arrest sentence of Suu Kyi, the leader of the National League for Democracy, who has been confined to her compound on Inya Lake for 13 of the past 19 years, is up for renewal in a few weeks. The Lady won the Nobel Peace Prize in 1991. She's a living symbol of the prodemocracy movement in Burma but is imprisoned under the orders of the military junta that controls the country. She is allowed no visitors, save for her doctor, and her home is guarded 24 hours a day. This is one reason that many nations refuse to recognize the legitimacy of the junta, or the new name it has chosen for the country—Myanmar.

Richard Mei, chief public-affairs officer in Burma for the U.S. Department of State, doesn't know whether any of these factors—the swimmer, the journalists' detention, the anniversary—are connected, or whether Ozomatli's visit has anything to do with any of it. But news and rumors of the curious happenings have wormed their way into the heads of the American visitors, their State Department guides, and the two Burmese translators assigned to serve as Ozomatli's attachés.

Mei, a tall Asian-American born in Queens, has a simple catchall explanation for anything that occurs in his oft-baffling station: "This is Burma. Strange things can happen."Ozomatli have already traveled the world a few times over, and Burma is just the latest hot spot. Since 2007, the Grammy winners, born of protest rallies in East L.A. in 1996 as a 10-piece salsa/cumbia/hip-hop/rock amalgam, have been playing cultural-outreach gigs at the behest—and with the support—of the U.S. government. On past travels, they've been escorted in a bulletproof SUV through a Palestinian refugee camp in Jordan and asked by a little boy, who confused the band with U.S. soldiers: "How come you let your friends kill my little brother?" They've played songs to kids rescued from an Indian orphanage that was a front for a child-prostitution ring. Guitarist Pacheco was nearly electrocuted onstage in Madagascar.

These tours occurred during the Bush administration, at a time when the last thing a left-leaning Chicano/Jewish/Black/

Whatever band from the hood wanted was to be known as enablers for an embattled Republican government.

But if there's one thing the band has learned on these State Department–organized tours, it's that the closer you are to situations, the more murky the so-called "politics" become. When Ozomatli were first approached to participate in these outreaches, some of the most forceful U.S.-government advocates for Asian cultural and democratic efforts were former first lady Laura Bush and then–Under Secretary for Public Affairs Karen Hughes.

The fact that longtime Bush cheerleader Hughes once danced to your band in D.C. isn't something you want the Ozoheadz in Boulder to catch wind of. When the band hit the ground on their first missions, though, they were greeted by America's midlevel public-affairs officers, outreach organizers, and charity workers, and realized that left, right, and center mingle more than they imagined.

Jack Healey was president of Amnesty International for 12 years, founded the Washington, D.C.–based Human Rights Action Center, which works with the U.S. Campaign for Burma, an advocacy group. In April 2008 Healey met with the National Security Agency at the White House. What he saw surprised him: "The Bush people—and I hate the sons of bitches—but on this topic, they were as good as you could be."

Wil-Dog Abers first hooked up with his eventual Burma entourage at Ozomatli's debut outreach program there, at the tiny Gitameit Music Center in the Moe Kaung Yankin township, a labyrinthine, *Slumdog*-type neighborhood in Rangoon. The building is surrounded by a tangle of dirt pathways and makeshift avenues lined on both sides by one- and two-story homes that look like rural fruit stands.

The posse thing was bound to happen. Ozomatli's bassist and co-founder, Wil-Dog, as he's known to everyone (his mom goes by Mom-Dog), is a big personality and loves playing to kids. Wil-Dog perhaps knows more about Mexican music than any other Jew on the West Coast, but his first love was punk rock. He got a taste of a future when, as an 11-year-old with a Mohawk, he was taken by his Communist-activist parents to see the Clash at the Hollywood Palladium. "That was it," he says. "I knew that night I would be doing this." He treasures the notion that he could be a Joe Strummer to some Burmese kid.

Wil-Dog spots his Rangoon posse, a half-dozen five-year-old students, in a second-floor recital room that feels like a jungle tree house. Five girls and a boy, they're poised before music stands, with baby violins on their shoulders. The lessons here cost $15 a month, which seems a pittance until you learn that the average annual income throughout the country is less than $300, and probably far less in this neighborhood. They stare at the sheet music, and with great concentration they scratch out an oblong melody. When it's done, the band applauds, and Wil-Dog is officially smitten.

Afterward, Ozomatli and the students walk down to an adjoining performance space about the size of an Appalachian church. It isn't Glastonbury, Coachella, or Kathmandu, but when the band, standing on a small stage, begin their "Ya Viene El Sol," a melodic, Latin-tinged pop song with rolling rhythms and the joyous and eruptive voice of lead Ozo vocalist Asdru Sierra, the eyes in the audience emit a warm glow, and the little boys and girls immediately become enrapt, as though they're watching a favorite movie. Soon, Wil-Dog is in front of them, playing bass and doing funny dances along with the song, bouncing and clapping like a clown and making the six giggle.

After the show, the kids and their teacher, an elegant Burmese woman carrying a sun umbrella, take the band on a tour of the neighborhood, and the reality of the children's situation reveals itself. Seldom do the residents of this village see Westerners, let alone Latinos, and as we walk dirt paths lined with open sewers, skinny dogs tromp alongside and people peek out of their doorways and look at the Americans blankly.

We learn later that what we did during the hourlong stroll—videotape and photograph the state of the Burma ghettos—was dangerous. Unaware, we pointed and shot, waved as we walked the paths, an eerie silence giving the feel of some sort of postmeltdown dystopia. Ozo's sound guy, Mack, remembers the silence, but even more, he was struck by the mysterious theraminlike music emanating from somewhere within many of the homes and food stands, like the soundtrack of some horror movie.

Music is perfectly legal in Burma, as long as any song you write or perform is first approved by the Scrutiny Board—the state censors. But video cameras are a dangerous technology here, one used as a weapon by the junta's minions to document dissident activities; shoved in the faces of protesters in a malicious attempt at quelling dissent; smuggled out of the country by democratic activists to document protests—and aimed at American bands walking through alleyway markets by men straddling mopeds.

"That was the most surreal moment, walking through that neighborhood," recalls sax player Bella, talking about our guides' concern that operatives were watching us. "It almost seemed unbelievable, to a degree. Like, 'Bullshit, there's people keeping track of us through this neighborhood? Yeah, right.' But then, that's not our reality."

The regime has a right to be paranoid, as do its people, because their reality is different. Our two translators, a man and a woman, were careful about what they said. In the restaurant on our first night, our male guide was very nervous. Ozomatli manager Amy Blackman recalls saying something and the guide replying quietly, "People are watching and listening." In the hotel, he'd hardly say anything. At an outdoor market restaurant, and especially in our vans, however, both were much more talkative.

During one window of opportunity, the male guide told the band that when Cyclone Nargis hit last year, none of the Burmese people knew of its impending arrival, even though satellite images predicted its path. Nargis was all the more destructive because of the suddenness of its arrival. Along Burma's 1,200-mile coastline, few saw it coming. It hit, then passed, and time stopped.

Over the following days and weeks, the State Peace and Development Council, the name of the 11-general junta that governs the country, refused all offers of foreign aid. In the Count Basie Room at the American Center in Rangoon, there are of the disaster children's drawings that will hurt your heart: of big stick figures stranded in palm trees and littler figures drowning in scribbled water below. In a country where one in three children is chronically malnourished, the cyclone was a hit matched only by the blowback realization that its rulers care more about perceived threats from abroad than helping their people.

Eight months before the natural disaster, the SPDC was on the butt end of a political disaster. In September 2007 the Buddhist clergy marched through Rangoon in an unprecedented show of civil disobedience to protest the government's gasoline price hikes. Over the next two weeks the monks created a sea of saffron robes along the roads surrounding the Schwedagon Pagoda. The monks were soon joined by citizens, who marched to Aung San Suu Kyi's residence.

Then came the obligatory shielded-soldier crackdown, troops locked in rows marching at unarmed monks. In the ensuing violence, captured by renegade video journalists and uploaded to networks across the globe, security forces breached a line they had never before crossed: they beat monks. In the weeks to follow, SPDC officers arrested a few thousand more, many of whom remain locked up.

Human Rights Action Center's Healey says that the cyclone and the military actions reveal the potential for change. "Any respect that was left for the military, among the young soldiers in particular, and among the young in general, is gone. That they didn't take care of the people drowning? Huge loss of respect. When they hurt the monks, chased them to the border, tortured them, that's a big break. So there's a tipping point possible that isn't seen outside. The people are ready to go."

Guitarist Raúl Pacheco knows a little bit about organizing The People. Before joining Ozomatli, he spent nearly five years in Sacramento, working for politicians. In the early 1990s he landed a job in Willie Brown's state assembly office, and interned with former state senator and Democratic activist Tom Hayden. The word "Chicano," written in neat cursive on Pacheco's left hand, makes him look like a gangbanger. But he's the polar opposite, warm and soft-spoken. He toured Burma while reading Gabriel García Márquez's autobiography and letters Aung San Suu Kyi wrote in the mid-1990s.

While Suu Kyi was crafting those letters from a home prison, Pacheco was getting resettled in L.A., intent on writing about Chicano politics. He started volunteering at the L.A.-based People's Union for Democratic Rights, organizing an afterschool program for kids, and decided to play music again. So he called up Ozomatli's then-drummer and asked about a gig. "He said, 'Come to the Peace and Justice Center. We're gonna start making music.'"

Asdru Sierra, who was a kid in South-Central when they sent the National Guard in, was there. Sierra started singing when he was young, then moved on to trumpet and keyboards—music was always around. His grandfather had been signed to RCA-Victor in Mexico, his father and uncles were professional musicians. Sierra followed the music to CalArts. Ozomatli's mission fit right in with his aesthetic: "It was raw and undefined, but it had so much passion, and it was fun. We could bring any instrument, any idea and any style of music and no one would judge you."

Ulises Bella grew up a trench-coated punk rocker in the blue-collar East L.A. township of Bell and fell in with the ska crowd in his teens. He played saxophone with Yeska, whose stated goal was "to be the Latin Skatalites." Yeska was getting great gigs in the mid-'90s, and Ozo was Bella's second band. The two outfits would gig together at the Viper Room, and as Ozo's star rose, Bella quit Yeska to commit full-time.

Wil-Dog had followed Joe Strummer's lead, moving from punk to hip-hop, and became the persistent center of the band, one whose dubby and funky bass-playing is the perfect reflection of his demeanor, open and honest, filled with enthusiasm for the adventure of it all. He invited percussionist Porée to jam with Ozo, but he was skeptical. "The thing that caught me, though, was when he said, 'I got turntables and tablas,'" Porée says. On practice day, he walked in to see Yamaguchi and DJ Cut Chemist, one of the city's preeminent turntablists, practicing. "I was, like, this is insanity, but this is dope. How can I not be a part of this?"

From early protest gigs, Ozo sold out residencies at the Viper Room and Opium Den with lines stretching down the Sunset Strip. The band signed to a label called Almo Sounds, the post-A&M project of Herb Alpert and Jerry Moss, and released their anthemic, self-titled debut, which established them as one of the go-to bands of the so-called "Latin rock" scene. They've won two Grammys and a Latin Grammy. The awards have fed more opportunity, especially in a changing media landscape trying to adapt to the much-belated realization that the Spanish-speaking markets were not only demographically ignored but also that television shows need funky Latino music to support certain scenes.

Blackman says when the band is feeling jaded, they call their demographic niche "Spanish-language music for gringos," a truth that they've all had to grudgingly accept. The band itself has appeared in an episode of *Sex and the City* and performed on last season's *Dancing With the Stars.* "NBC loves their stuff," Blackman says. They've done *CSI, Ugly Betty, Shark, Las Vegas.* HBO used "Saturday Night" for their fall promos; the Los Angeles Lakers use their song "City of Angels" a lot. Last week they performed "Afterparty" on *The Today Show,* and Al Roker did his funkiest dance.

"They've become their own paradigm," Blackman says. "Supervisors will say, 'I need some upbeat, Latinesque, party-sounding Ozo-like music in this scene.' It's like they are their own genre, in a way."

It was this so-called paradigm that attracted the State Department's Bureau of Public Affairs, via a broadcast on one of America's most popular gringo news outlets, National Public Radio. A department official had heard an interview with the band, and was looking for an act to perform in different parts of the world where the bureau believed it might send a message.

Blackman did a little research on the history of the government's cultural-diplomacy efforts, and what she learned helped her to make a case to the band. Beginning in the 1950s, President Dwight D. Eisenhower started what was to become a landmark series of globetrotting musical programs sponsored by the Department of State. Among those who traveled on the 20-year program were Dizzy Gillespie, Duke Ellington, Count Basie, and Louis Armstrong.

"The State Department still kind of looks back and admires what they did in the '50s and '60s with Gillespie and Louis Armstrong, and Dave Brubeck and all these people," says Tim Receveur of the Bureau of International Information Programs at the State Department. "It was really effective with sending jazz musicians over, but we're trying to evolve, see what people are listening to now, younger kids, hip-hop/rap and rock."

Blackman took the idea to the band in early 2007, and was ready to argue her point: "Our mantra in general has been to say yes to most opportunities. Just say yes. And this was just one of those things. It was like, 'Okay, this sounds cool and kooky and weird—and let's try it!'"

It was a polarizing pitch.

"I was, like, 'Fuck this shit,'" Porée says. "I was totally against it." When the band started, he says, he wasn't that politically active. But he learned and absorbed, and became part of an L.A. musical movement that was based on protest and consciousness. So his reflex response at the time was, "Basically, they're just using us, and we're like puppets. The U.S. government's image around the world is shit, and they're just using us to soften the blow."

Pacheco, though wary, paid close attention to his moral compass, one that gets tested a lot in a business where the best-paying gigs often come from the cigarette companies. "We had contradictions within ourselves even without going to the State Department. We've played music for booze companies. People say we sold out—but we sold out when we signed a record deal. Do you know what it means to start caring about money coming in every month?"

Plus, he adds, "We were the only band they could ask. We're mixing up way more stuff. We're rocking, using beats that are Middle Eastern, playing reggae music over cumbia beats and all this type of fusion."

Ultimately, it came down to a vote. Over the years, the band has supported as many as 15 full-time touring musicians. A core of six remain from the initial lineup, along with drummer Calire, and though it hasn't been all roses, and the band has nearly disintegrated a few times for reasons either financial, chemical, or personal, they banged out a deal among the half-dozen members that splits all publishing rights evenly, which creates a democracy among them. It's a bitch being in the studio with six equal voices—apparently they nearly break up every time they step near a mixing board. (In fact, the band is in the beginning stages of recording a new full-length for the New York–based Mercer Street label, an offshoot of the high-flying Downtown Records imprint.) The democracy makes for a lively discussion when something like songwriting structure, sequencing or "representing the Bush administration" gets thrown in the mix.

They decided to give it a try. Pretty quickly, the band realized that the black-and-white of political right and wrong goes gray once you meet your perceived antagonists face to face.

Blackman remembers the first time she met Karen Hughes, in 2008 at the Latin Museum in Washington, D.C. By then, the band had toured India, Nepal, and the Middle East, and the longtime George Bush confidante had been getting positive feedback regarding Ozomatli's trips. But she had never seen the band, and she wanted to meet them.

Hughes and her staff showed up at 7:30 p.m.—"on the dot, of course," Blackman says with a laugh. Hughes, whose steely demeanor and forceful opinions Blackman and the band had watched on TV as she defended Bush's positions, admittedly had preconceptions. "She was actually very pleasant to talk to," Blackman recalls. "She isn't smarmy, which is so weird. She is kind. She asked me a ton of questions about the band and where they came from, who they were and what makes them tick and what parts of the trip struck them the most."

"She was really into Ozomatli," confirms Receveur at the State Department. "It was really pretty cool." He adds that as a rule, the State Department doesn't insist on any restrictions regarding what Ozomatli can say onstage, "and this was the Bush administration. Ozomatli did interviews where they were talking about how they were antiwar, that they didn't like the Bush administration, but that they were there to represent America."

Despite the many public-policy disasters of the Bush administration, even some of its most vocal critics acknowledge that, in specific countries, the administration provided a much-needed injection of both attention and funding for public-diplomacy programs.

"Laura Bush—as good as you could be. She knew the issue, she could talk about it," says Human Rights Action Center's Healey on the government's Burma policy.

Hughes's replacement as undersecretary of Public Diplomacy is Judith McHale. Before being nominated by the Obama administration to fill the position, she was president and CEO of Discovery Channel. At her Senate confirmation hearing last month, McHale discussed her goals in the job, at least one of which alarmed advocates for Ozomatli-style outreach programs. "New technology, used effectively and creatively, can be a game-changer," she told the committee, citing communications advances that offer opportunities to engage people more efficiently.

Whether this sort of diplomacy would work in Burma is debatable. Most citizens don't have access to computers. For those who do, however, only one social network, Facebook, is allowed, and it's closely monitored. Despite Big Brother, the network is incredibly popular in Burma, and Ozomatli have a lot of new friends in the country. The downside is, every single status update, photo, or video posting runs through servers controlled by the Scrutiny Board.

Hence, ground-level outreach like Ozomatli's is a vital tool.

The American Club is an oddly juxtaposed chunk of tennis courts, swimming pools, softball fields and a clubhouse built on property owned by the U.S. government, and tonight Ozomatli will perform. By Burmese law, any public gathering of more than five people is illegal, so any large event requires permission from the authorities. Because tonight's concert is being held on the grounds, though, it wasn't necessary for the State Department to ask permission. Still, the office informed the Burmese foreign ministry of its plans via a diplomatic note, so it wouldn't be surprised.

The day before, Richard Mei and Burmese Regional Security Officer Bill Mellott had convened the band for a briefing. He told them that they have to be particularly careful about how they act and what they say. If they mention Aung San Suu Kyi's name, he explained, not only will they jeopardize themselves and risk being deported but they could also endanger anyone who attends the concert. He advised them not to mention "The Lady" at all.

Mei had explained as much on the morning the band arrived in the country. He gathered the 11-member entourage in a hotel meeting room, and spoke very specifically about the proper way to move around Rangoon: quietly and anonymously, except when you're onstage. After they had left the country, he encouraged them to say whatever they wanted, and to tell what they saw. But here, delivery of an incendiary message wouldn't help. "They hear the music, but I'm not sure if they're going to get too much of the message. But that's what we're interested in, and we want you to do your normal thing." His voice lifted a little bit as he stretched to explain his next point: "It's just that because of this country, and the way that you have to operate in this country, you have to be sensitive of certain things. And that means not being overt about the political situation."

Twenty-four hours before the concert was scheduled, representatives of the local township gave a note to the guards at the American Club that said the State Department had not informed the township of the event. The department responded on Friday morning by sending a copy of the earlier diplomatic note, which seemed to satisfy them.

By this point, news had started to spread about Yettaw, the American who was captured in the lake on the morning the band arrived in Burma. On the evening of May 4, he sank into Inya Lake with homemade fins, toting with him a strange collection of items that he wanted to get to Suu Kyi. Uninvited and seemingly unconcerned that his visit would violate the terms of The Lady's house arrest and jeopardize her possible release, Yettaw swam to the shore of her home and, carrying what state news reports say included a video camera, two black Muslim robes, veils, sunglasses and several books, including the Book of Mormon, he entered her compound and met with her. She urged him to leave immediately, but he said he was too tired. He left two days later, and was arrested on May 6 on the opposite shore.

Suu Kyi, her two caretakers, and her doctor were all arrested and charged soon thereafter. Suu Kyi remains at Insein Prison, where she was taken after the incident, and with the recent removal of the security surrounding her house, which included drop-down gates, barbed-wire fences and full-time guards, it appears that the government has no intention of releasing her back into house arrest. (Yettaw has since been dubbed "The American Fool" by the *Bangkok Post.*)

By 5:30 p.m., a few hundred people have gathered, many of them Western expats desperate for something, anything to do. The locals start trickling in, and the second of two opening acts performs—a local rapper named J-Me, who, while forbidden to rap about politics, focuses on the universally understood language of, in his words, "bitches, money, and weed."

Wil-Dog's six-student entourage from the music school arrives. Wide-eyed and wearing their best clothes, they look a little frightened, especially the little boy, who hasn't smiled once. This is the first time they've ever been out of their neighborhood.

They take a spot standing in the front row, their heads peeking just above the stage. J-Me the rapper prowls around, at one point nearly stepping on the children's fingers. The crowds keep coming, and the concrete space, about the size of two tennis courts, is soon filled.

Ozomatli step onstage right at 6 p.m., and pretty quickly it's clear that the Scrutiny Board hasn't screened the lyrics to "Saturday Night," as Porée rhymes the lyrics: "People to places the message basic/from raised fist to sit-ins resist to change shit/ Peep this scenario/to the future, bro/2020 and some number of years ago/people rose up, governments froze up/worldwide block party, everybody shows up."

If only it were that simple. Sing a song with words of hope, the crowd hears them and decides that tomorrow night the revolution will begin.

Nobody's naive enough to believe in that, not least Ozomatli. But that doesn't stop the band. During the encore, Wil-Dog runs over to his little posse and motions them up. They look confused. He smiles, takes one of them by the hands, lifts her up onto the stage and outfits her with maracas. Soon all six are up, and they're jumping and playing in rhythm. The boy, nervous down below, has a confused smile on his face. He looks around, takes a shaker, and starts jumping enthusiastically while staring at the crowd before him.

As the final song winds down, Ozomatli do their signature move. Each of the band members grabs a portable instrument, and as the crowd continues to dance, the band descends from the stage into the citizenry and starts a dance train. The trumpet and the saxophone blare through the night as the rest of the band bangs on tablas, maracas and tambourines and the crowd bounces and claps along, laughing and dancing behind the best Latin/cumbia/salsa/hip-hop drum corps ever to grace a Burmese stage. ➼

"HOW I GOT THAT STORY"

Randall Roberts is the pop music editor at the Los Angeles Times. *Prior to that, he was the music editor at* L.A. Weekly. *He grew up in Edwardsville, Illinois, and attended the University of Missouri, Columbia. The following interview was conducted via email by Santa Fe Reporter Editor and AAN Editorial Chair Julia Goldberg.*

So, does every arts writer at *L.A. Weekly* get to go to Burma with Ozomatli? How did this story come to be?
The first time I met Ozomatli's manager, Amy Blackman, she told me in passing about the arrangement the band had with the State Department as cultural ambassadors, and I was surprised to learn that no one had ever documented this as fully as I thought it deserved. The next time we ran into each other was at a party a few months later, and she excitedly informed me that the band had just confirmed a tour of Burma, Vietnam, and Thailand, and said, in no uncertain terms, "You have to come." After doing more research and communicating with the U.S. State Department, I pitched the story to my editor at *L.A. Weekly*, Laurie Ochoa, who echoed Amy's sentiment by saying "You have to go." Despite some opposition from the higher-ups, Laurie steadfastly pushed forward as a result of our belief that this was a story that should to be told.

Within the first day of our being in Burma, an American was arrested for swimming in Lake Inya, and the story of him illegally visiting Aung San Suu Kyi gradually unfolded. All that obviously couldn't have been planned. But as it was occurring and I was learning from the U.S. consulate in Burma what was going on, I knew that the story had become something much bigger. Then it was just a matter of documenting it accurately. The surreal nature of the circumstances made it rather easy to write, honestly. All I had to do was document what had happened, and the strangeness spoke for itself.

The story, of course, ends up being just as focused on human rights and politics as music, but you lead with the music. Did you know right away the Burmese blind metal scene would be your lead?
When I'm working on a story, I always pay attention to the parts of it that I can't wait to tell friends about—the stories within the story that are so exciting to me that I absolutely have to share them as soon as possible. In this instance, I was telling everyone I knew about this band and this moment, and most were pretty fascinated by it.

As well, the experience in that little auditorium was incredibly emotional for me. It was a really intense afternoon, so of course I felt that this could be powerful on the page. Finally, when the woman sang "Have You Ever Seen the Rain?,"' well, it just made sense thematically to open with the story: It's a song that on the surface isn't political at all, but given the plight of the Burmese people—dealing with a catastrophic cyclone and a government that seemingly cares nothing for its citizenry— the message of hope amidst the darkness felt like the perfect curtain-raiser.

Sometimes music writers fall into a habit of only wanting to write about certain genres or bands. How do you view your role as a music writer; what guides your decisions about what to cover and what not to cover?
If you only write about certain genres or bands, you're only writing for the people that like those genres/bands. The rest of the readership couldn't care less, and they'll flip the page the moment they realize this wasn't written with them in mind. I very much follow my curiosity, and feel like I've learned to trust that nagging part of my brain that won't keep quiet when a good story idea presents itself.

I'm drawn to musicians who are pushing at the edges of whatever genre they're working within. I have no interest in writing about the bands whose influences are obvious; I'm more interested in the iconoclasts, loudmouths, and freaks. They're much more fun to talk to—and more entertaining to write about. It helps to have a narrative, too. Basic band profiles, are, for the most part, boring to read and boring to write.

How has the online environment changed your approach to your work?
It's made me work harder to find stories that haven't been told yet. With so much information online and everybody chasing the latest trend and hottest band, the value of good relationships with a vast network of sources is essential. On a more basic level, I'm putting the compelling stuff higher and higher in the story because people are very impatient when they're reading online. And I've started including kittens in most of my stories.

What advice would you give aspiring music writers?

Learn how to report non-music stories. Music writers these days are a dime a dozen, and rare is the voice that rises above the chatter. But writers who know music and also know reporting skills have a much better chance of making an impact by finding a compelling story and documenting it. These stories aren't the ones that the publicists email you. They're the ones that you find by meeting people who work behind the publicist. Once you have a story with a narrative arc, you can attach to it the stuff about how awesome the lead singer's voice is or how amazing the new record is.

Also, it's hard to find good stories by surfing the internet. You have to be out on the town asking questions and paying attention. The Ozomatli story came about because I was out at lunch with a source, and the band's manager happened to be at the same restaurant. That never would have happened over email.

And you have to know music history and expand your knowledge base as widely as possible. Readers can spot a fraud a mile away. People who read music stories are by definition very passionate about music. If you don't have a broad context in which to place your ideas, they'll roll their eyes and turn the page.

Art on Trial

Edwin Slipek Jr.

JULY 21, 2009

You may know this: Richmond and Manchester once were separate entities.

You may not know this: when the two cities merged in 1910 Manchester residents, just south of the river from Shockoe Slip, didn't altogether trust their neighbors to the north. So they placed some caveats in the agreement. Richmond was to build a modern, toll-free bridge across the James River at Mayo Island. Taxes collected from Manchester would be deposited in South Side banks. And the courthouse at 920 Hull St. would continue to hear local cases in perpetuity.

The merger's 100th anniversary next year will see the completion of a remodeled and expanded Manchester Courthouse and some kind of public ceremony. But don't expect to find public sculpture on the site funded by Richmond's popular and successful One Percent for the Arts program.

Apparently, Manchester's three judges think about as much of aesthetic tastes from north of the river as their predecessors trusted Richmond's capacity for honest tax collecting and delivering justice. It's not in their job description, but last month General District Court Judges D. Eugene Cheek, Phillip L. Hairston, and Gregory L. Rupe squelched plans for a proposed 30-foot ebullient and glitzy sculpture by Philadelphia artist Ray King, whose work is collected internationally.

The Public Art Commission had voted unanimously to install the piece in a landscaped plaza at the southeast corner of Hull and Ninth streets. To be placed just steps from the courthouse's new front, a classical portico, it was envisioned as a reflective and illuminated beacon—visible from up and down Hull Street and Commerce Road as well as the James River bridges—to signal a new day for a hardscrabble neighborhood.

The court was unimpressed.

"It was not appropriate," says David M. Hicks, clerk of the Manchester court. "Maybe in Las Vegas or in front of a big shopping center, but the judges were adamant: they weren't going to have that sculpture in front of the courthouse."

"I was stunned," says Richmond artist and freelance curator Vaughn Garland, who's completing the first year of a three-year appointment as chair of the city's Public Art Commission. "We were excited because it was not just a major site-specific piece for Manchester but also a work for all of Richmond. It was designed to glow. We saw it as symbolizing healing and that the courthouse is a place for the community to gather."

King's "The Stainless Sphere" design consisted of one spherical structure of stainless steel and laminated glass within a larger 13-foot-diameter sphere, set on a cast-concrete base. It would be a decidedly contemporary addition to an impressive collection of public sculpture in the self-proclaimed City of Monuments, where memorials to Confederate pride and military valor share communal space—in a sometimes uneasy face-off—with tributes to civil rights and race relations.

But the recent brouhaha raises interesting issues. Who are the arbiters of taste here for public art? And should three judges determine where a specific, public-funded piece of art is—or in this situation, isn't—placed?

Richmond has been distinguished by and known for out-door sculpture since 1858, when the equestrian statue of George Washington by artist Thomas Crawford was shipped from Germany and installed in Capitol Square.

By the turn of the last century, it was Confederate-themed works that marked intersections, parks and cemeteries.

But times and power bases change, and because history belongs to those living, one of the city's first monuments of the twenty-first century marks the 200th anniversary of the end of international slave trafficking: the Slavery Reconciliation Statue near Shockoe Bottom. Another salutes Virginia's civil-rights leaders: the Virginia Civil Rights Memorial at Capitol square.

Also, since the late twentieth century, contemporary art-works—not necessarily historical or commemorative—have been placed in public places with increasing frequency. The patrons are usually corporations and developers who situ-ate generic and abstract artworks—"plop art"—near major approaches to their buildings as a way to humanize otherwise deadening and minimalist architectural settings. Two examples of the genre in the financial district are sculptor Robert Eng-man's silver-and-blue "Quadrature" at the SunTrust building and Lloyd Lillie's depiction of muscular male nudes hoisting sails in "Wind's Up" at the James Center.

There are also temporary public-art installations. The Arts Council of Richmond used to sponsor temporary exhibits in such venues as the Richmond International Airport, empty downtown store windows and arts festivals as well as the ubiq-uitous Go Fish project. But in 1996, under the Arts Council's leadership and then-City Manager Robert Bobb's advocacy, art in public places was institutionalized with a One Percent for the Arts program. It allocates 1 percent of the cost of city-sponsored construction projects to commission artwork specif-ically for that site. (School buildings are excluded.)

Among the most recognized public art from this program are "Skyrider," a multimedia piece suspended from the Inter-state 95 bridge in Shockoe Bottom, across the street from Main Street Station, and "Thin Blue Line" by Michael Stutz, a metal-mesh depiction of a police officer's head that glares from the police headquarters buildings at East Grace and Jefferson streets.

"It's become an icon, it's a meeting place," says Sally Bowring of "Thin Blue Line." Bowring is a Richmond artist and member of the City Public Art Commission who spearheaded the initial public art projects back in 1996. She says the wall sculpture at police headquarters exemplifies public art at its best. "It helps identify the building and has become a part of the personality of the neighborhood," she says.

It's also outdoors. Although a number of successful and handsome public artworks have been placed inside city buildings, Bowring thinks the greater the exposure to the citizenry the better. "I wanted art to be out in public and not in the boardrooms," she says. "I insisted that stuff started coming outside."

In determining how to spend $120,000 on a public-art commission at the Manchester courthouse site, there was nothing unusual in how the 12-person Public Art Commission approached its task (the City Planning Commission appoints each member to a three-year, renewable term).

The art commission's site-selection committee consisted of two members, including Garland and Sarah Shields Driggs, who's written books about the city's historic neighborhoods. Other committee members were Lu Guy Lanier, landscape architect of the courthouse plaza; community representative Laura Bryant; courthouse architectural designer Claes Tholand; Catherine Easterling from the city's department of community development; and David M. Hicks, representing the Manchester court.

For Garland the assignment marked an exciting chance to build on public art projects he'd previously undertaken in Manchester. He certainly knew the territory as well as anyone after serving as instigator and co-curator of the Richmond Outdoor Sculpture Exhibition, which was held in Manchester in 2005 and 2006. For each exhibit he had pinpointed potential spaces and then persuaded property owners to allow their parking spaces, vacant lots, or even drainage ditches to become temporary venues for site-specific art. Where others saw urban neglect and decay, Garland and participating artists saw aesthetic and transformative potential. The two consecutive sculpture exhibitions attracted hundreds of visitors and illuminated the rusted neighborhood in imaginative and surprising ways.

Also, Manchester in recent years has increasingly emerged as an arts Mecca, with converted industrial spaces finding new life as galleries, studios, and living spaces.

For the courthouse public-art project, once the committee had selected a site adjacent to the courthouse, there was the usual call for entries. About 50 artists responded from across the country. From these submissions the selection committee picked four proposals for further consideration.

Then the full committee convened for a meeting at the Banquet Place, an event space near the courthouse. Among those present was Hicks, Manchester clerk of court. But apparently the three judges he represented were already miffed that they hadn't been included in earlier deliberations.

"They didn't include the powers that be," Hicks says. "This was the first meeting that I had been to and they had already picked the finalists."

But Hicks reported back to the courthouse that Ray King's proposal was the first choice among the finalists: "The artists had presented their little things [project proposals] in packets and I took them back to the judges."

The three judges took one look and reacted the same way, he says: "'Not in front of our courthouse.'"

When the Planning Commission, which must pass on the art commission's recommendations, heard of the judges' displeasure, it asked the Public Art Commission to meet personally with the tribunal.

On the afternoon of June 1 four commission members, two city staff members, and artist Ray King, who'd traveled from Philadelphia, met with the judges in a trailer near the courthouse construction site.

According to the Public Art Commission's meeting notes, King led off by introducing his work and then offered metaphors as to how the piece symbolized balance.

Judge Cheek apparently shot back that justice wasn't as simplistic as balance and suggested that justice was about the dignity of the law. The courthouse design, he pointed out, was austere and therefore allowed the public to respect the law. Cheek then asked King how he intended to tie the challenges that the neighborhood faced to the artwork.

King responded that the sculpture would be "a bright spot in the neighborhood, a beacon of hope."

Judge Cheek responded that "festive and futuristic" didn't complement the brick and frame courthouse and reportedly called the piece "offensive" from a historic point of view.

This is when Commissioner Sarah Shields Driggs, an architectural historian, joined the discussion. She reminded the judges that the piece was meant to engage people and that it symbolized a neighborhood that was overcoming its challenges.

Judge Rupe retorted: "The average user of the courthouse won't understand how this piece ties to the neighborhood."

Hicks says the judges were concerned the piece would be vandalized. "I like contemporary art," he says. "But what they were proposing was not appropriate for the space. It would have been destroyed in no time. That would have been $120,000 down the tube."

The judges told the commissioners they wanted something that would maintain the dignity of the courthouse. "This space is like Colonial Williamsburg," one of them explained. "We need something the common man can understand."

This was apparently too much for artist King: "I see the piece as contemporary. We aren't in a colonial day."

Judge Rupe shot back: "Why can't we just get a knockoff version of the brass scale of justice? We would prefer that this piece be somewhere else in the city. I'm not big on modern, I don't buy into it. Looks like Epcot to me."

After 90 minutes of back and forth and things sliding south fast, the public art commissioners asked the judges why they hadn't given input earlier in the process.

They replied that the Public Art Commission hadn't invited them to participate until the final round.

"People who aren't in the legal loop might not realize that judges aren't accustomed to being told what to do," Hicks says, some weeks after the meeting.

The Public Art Commission says that the courthouse did not respond to its communiqués.

This isn't the only recent example of judges applying the brakes on a major public-art project locally. At the new federal courthouse downtown, which opened in the fall, the U.S. General Services Administration proposed a specific piece of contemporary sculpture for the atrium. It was a realistic depiction of a large, all-seeing eye. The judges shot it down. According to a source familiar with the project, the response from the GSA public art officials in Washington to the judges' response was: "'Oh, those conservative Richmond judges.' But I thought the judges were sophisticated and had valid criticism. And in no way did the artist's metaphor fit the 'justice is blind' context of the setting."

Richmond isn't unique in its experience with judges rejecting contemporary art. It happens in the most sophisticated art capitals. John Ravenal, the Sydney and Frances Lewis Family Curator of Modern and Contemporary Art at the Virginia Museum of Fine Arts, cites a 1981 conflict in New York City. "Tilted Arc," a sculpture by Richard Serra, who Ravenal calls "internationally known and one of the most important living artists," was installed in lower Manhattan at Federal Plaza. A federal judge was among those vehemently opposed to the work. "There was quite an outcry between those people who used the parklike space and those who thought they knew what would work there," Ravenal says. "But the piece was eventually removed because of community opposition."

Area curators agree that it's essential to include constituents in the design process from the earliest stages.

Ashley Kistler, director of the Anderson Gallery at Virginia Commonwealth University, spearheaded one of the city's most ambitious and critically acclaimed public art projects in 2004 when she was curator at the Visual Arts Center of Richmond. "In Peace and Harmony: Carver Portraits," was a presentation of dozens of huge photo murals of Carver neighborhood residents and pupils by internationally known artist Wendy Ewald that were attached to neighborhood buildings and displayed for 18 months.

"There were many preliminary discussions with various constituents—community associations, businesses, residents, and folks at Carver Elementary School," Kistler says. "They had a say before anything else was done. Those conversations took place with the artist and helped shape the final project."

She says the exhibition was meaningful because it engaged the Carver community on one level while also engaging the broader community. "This is an essential element," Kistler says. "It was extremely successful on an aesthetic level as well as encompassing a broad public— without dumbing down."

Balancing community acceptance while offering challenging art should be the goal of public art, the museum's Ravenal says. "It's a thorny issue, I'm sort of ambivalent about public art," he says. "It makes sense that the recipient—the audience—is pleased and that it speaks to them and addresses their needs. However, if that's the guiding principle you feed the status quo. I want art to encourage people to stretch.

"That's why you bring in the experts who understand quality and content," he continues, endorsing public art commissions. "Also, they're familiar with the resources that are available."

"You have to lay the groundwork," Ravenal says. "It has to be win-win. . . . But it's important that the final project be forward-looking and can stand the test of time. If it's forgettable, come the next revolution it will be melted down for the bronze."

Despite the judges' objections, the Public Art Commission agreed unanimously on Friday, June 5, to proceed with commissioning the Ray King piece for the Manchester Courthouse. It was ready to take its recommendation to the Planning Commission for final approval.

By midday, however, an undated letter had been received by the Department of Community Development and Planning from the Manchester court clerk, Hicks.

If the recent meeting between the commissioners and judges had produced no meeting of the minds, now the gloves were off. Stating that he was writing on behalf of the three Manchester judges, Hicks reiterated their objections in writing:

"Would you put a 12-foot chrome filigree ball atop a 12-foot pedestal, looking like it came from Epcot at Disney World, in front of the Virginia State Capital [sic]? Would you put that sculpture on Monument Avenue between the Lee and Jackson Monuments? . . . No. Why would you put it in front of the Manchester Courthouse, which was originally erected in 1874, is a historic site, and for which there have been great efforts to preserve its architectural continuity during the previous five expansions? It makes about as much sense as the French placing the gargantuan glass pyramid in front of the Louvre.

"While the self-styled art experts, may think it is appropriate, they seem to have taken leave of their historical preservationist senses on this matter. One is left to wonder what they may have come up with had they been asked to erect a large piece of artwork in front of Monticello."

He concluded by saying the judges "strongly opposed" the proposed sculpture.

The Public Art Commission decided not to place the sculpture at the courthouse.

Incredulous and angry, some art commissioners wanted to soldier on.

"There were people thought that there should be a big fight," commissioner Bowring says. "As soon as I realized the judges weren't there, I realized there was no use. There was no opportunity for dialogue; there were missed opportunities. . . .

"A battle is only good if all parties are engaged," she says. "What benefit would there be if it was put up in someone's face?"

What next for the "Stainless Sphere"?

"The timing of all this is important because next year marks the centennial of the merger of Manchester and Richmond," says William Thomas, vice president of the Manchester Civic Association, which was not included in the discussions. "We like that the new courthouse faces the river—the river is the front door of Manchester. And we are for anything that adds decorum to our neighborhood."

Still committed to the King sculpture, the Public Art Commission has regrouped and is seeking a new location for the work.

"I like the idea of placing it somewhere in Manchester," Bowring says, a twinkle in her eye. "It would be really nice if it could be seen from the courthouse." ❧

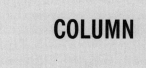
COLUMN

🎗 🎗 🎗

CIRCULATION 50,000 AND OVER

"Globe High School Censors Its Student Newspaper"
"Sarah Fenske's in Dogged Pursuit"

by Sarah Fenske, *Phoenix New Times*

"These columns are the best in class—she reported the hell out of each piece, even the personal one, and the results are fair but strongly argued, presented in an easy, persuasive style. The newsier passages are clear and move nicely, and then every once in a while, there's a writerly sentence that's more than pretty—it's moving or even paralyzing in its power: 'You never meet anyone who regrets having kids, only people who regret not having them.' Probably someone has written those words before, but it works beautifully here. Great stuff." —Marc Fisher, Washington Post

🎗 🎗 🎗

CIRCULATION UNDER 50,000

"History Lesson"
"Sugar Land"

by Anne Schindler, *Folio Weekly*

"Good passion here, especially in the history piece, where institutional knowledge and strong reporting remind us why there's such a thing as a professional journalist. The arguments throughout are strong and couched in an easy, conversational style."—Marc Fisher, Washington Post

Globe High School Censors Its Student Newspaper

Sarah Fenske

FEBRUARY 7, 2008

Every morning, students at Globe High School are forced to watch TV. Sounds weird, I know, but it's not unusual. An estimated 6 million kids—one-third of all American teens—start their day with a 12-minute news program broadcast by a company called Channel One.

The deal is a bit tawdry: Channel One donates TVs to school districts and, in return, the districts promise to force their students to watch the insipid broadcast—and, of course, commercial after commercial. Buy Skittles. Drink Coke.

Lately, Channel One has also been broadcasting ads for the TRUTH, the 10-year-old but still oh-so-edgy ad campaign warning teens about Big Tobacco's skullduggery. The latest TRUTH ads are called "Whudafxup," and the word appears prominently in most of the spots.

Controversial, right? With that f-bomb tucked into the slang, you'd think the puritans would be raising hell. But at Globe High School, the controversy came only because a student dared to—gasp!—write about the campaign in the school newspaper.

After the December 7 issue of the Globe High School *Papoose* was printed, but before the student journalists could begin distribution, the principal announced that he was confiscating all 700 copies and destroying them. Future issues of the paper, the principal warned, would be subject to strict review.

The paper's co-editors, seniors Nathan O'Neal and Shelby McLoughlin, say that they were given two reasons for the school's censorship.

One was an editorial written by O'Neal, who described a "sullen and gloomy atmosphere" in the hallways and a lack of motivation among both students and teachers.

The nerve of that kid!

The other problem, O'Neal and McLoughlin say, was a headline: "Whudafxup with that?" Staff writer Taylor Rainwater had written an essay criticizing the TRUTH campaign—and dared to put the ad's title in the story's headline. That was inappropriate, the students were told.

So, it's appropriate for Globe students to be subjected to propaganda featuring the word "Whudafxup," but if a student dares to repeat the word while critiquing the propaganda in question, 700 newspapers need to be destroyed?

And high school administrators wonder why students are so sullen these days. Pretty hard to smile when your education is being managed by idiots.

High school students don't enjoy all the rights that adults do. They can't drink and can't vote. Most of them can't even buy a pack of those demon cigarettes.

But they do have the freedom of speech. The First Amendment applies even to high school newspapers—and when I consulted a lawyer who specializes in the issue, I was surprised to learn just how many rights high school journalists have.

Frank LoMonte is the executive director of the Student Press Law Center in Arlington, Virginia. He says that high schools have greater latitude to censor publications than, say, colleges, "but that is not unlimited."

"Even in a situation where a school sets itself up as the absolute arbiter of what goes into a student newspaper, they can't just censor willy-nilly," LoMonte tells me.

For 25 years, U.S. Supreme Court precedent has held that schools censoring student publications must have a "valid educational purpose," LoMonte says. If the students have done a terrible job and the paper is littered with grammatical errors, for example, the school can intervene. Or if, say, the students wanted to publish a graphic sexual description, the school could argue that it needs to protect its students and remove the offensive story.

But destroying the entire print run because a student used a word frequently shown on classroom TVs? That's a hard sell. For that matter, so is banning an editorial just because it has a negative take on the school.

If administrators allow a student newspaper to write positive editorials about school functions, LoMonte says, it needs to allow negative ones, too.

"If a student wrote an editorial saying that school spirit is at an all-time high, I have a feeling that editorial would be published," he says. "From the facts as you describe them, the school engaged in the most noxious form of censorship."

Suffice it to say, Sherrill Stephens, the principal at Globe High School, doesn't quite see things this way.

Globe is a small town, with just about 8,000 residents, and it seems even smaller by virtue of its isolation. Tucked into the Pinal Mountains, at the edge of the Tonto National Forest, it feels a world away from the bustling Valley—never mind that it takes only an hour and a half to drive there.

Principal Stephens agreed to take my call, after an admirably short period on hold. But when he got on the phone, and I again explained my purpose, Stephens's befuddlement was clear.

Why, he asked, would anyone in Phoenix care about the *Papoose*?

"It's really not much of a story," Stephens drawled, good-old-boy style. Then he refused to tell me why he ordered the issue's destruction. "If you saw it, you'd know why," he said.

I told him I had seen it. And I simply couldn't fathom what the problem was.

"The superintendent and I decided it was not appropriate," he said, again refusing to give particulars. "There were inappropriate things. We are in a small town. That is why. And we're doing a lot of good things here."

Maybe that's true. Maybe the football team notched some wins and the cheerleaders are pretty. But Globe High School is certainly not teaching its students much about good journalism—much less critical thinking.

The *Papoose* used to come out five or six times a year. I looked at a few years of back issues, and I was impressed. It's an attractive tabloid, with design good enough for a small college newspaper. It wins awards—including, last year, second place in "overall excellence" from the Arizona Newspaper Association's high school division. The two co-editors are serious enough about their work that both attended journalism workshops during last year's summer break.

This year, though, the *Papoose* has struggled. The longtime adviser retired, and last semester, the paper was stuck with a new teacher just arrived from the Philippines, a guy who made it clear he had little interest in newspapers. It didn't help that the school district auctioned off the newspaper's Macs and replaced them with a new computer system incapable of printing the newspaper's layouts, co-editors O'Neal and McLoughlin tell me.

It wasn't until December that the students managed to complete their first issue. Just getting it to the presses was something of a triumph.

It's a shame that the rest of the school never got to see it. What's even worse: O'Neal and McLoughlin tell me their next attempt at an issue didn't even get that far.

After the December 7 issue was junked, they say, they were told that the next issue would have to be vetted by no fewer than four teachers and administrators—and one school office worker. Not surprisingly, the late December issue didn't even get through half that roster before someone objected to an editorial about the Plan B "morning after" pill.

That issue has yet to be printed. (Principal Stephens denied knowing anything about its existence, much less the controversy over the Plan B editorial.) McLoughlin and O'Neal say it's no longer timely; they've given up on getting it out.

And here's the kicker. Now, the students say, the school is suggesting that its journalism class ought to help the district to publish a newsletter instead of putting out a real newspaper.

"They tried to assign us to do articles about the school and articles that could go out to the parents," McLoughlin says, rolling her eyes.

"They wanted a public relations tool," O'Neal says.

LoMonte, of the Student Press Law Center, says the students could have a decent lawsuit over the censored issues—and that there are plenty of lawyers around the country who take cases like this pro bono. God bless America, eh?

But neither editor wants to pursue it. They're getting ready to graduate, and they can't wait to get out of Globe to study journalism at Arizona State or, in O'Neal's case, perhaps, the University of Southern California.

McLoughlin says, "I want to see justice done, but . . ."

"But we only have four months left," O'Neal finishes.

I don't blame them for moving on. Still, it's unsettling that the students at Globe High School got to see plenty of commercials this year but, so far, haven't seen a single issue of their supposedly student-run newspaper.

"We are constantly being preached 'professionalism' and responsibility, but how can we be expected to perform to these standards if the boundaries are constantly being altered?"

That's the last line of Nathan O'Neal's editorial from December 7, the editorial Globe High School wasn't allowed to read. Principal Stephens may not agree, but I think it's a really good question—and it's safe to say the students aren't going to find the answer on Channel One. ☞

Sarah Fenske's in Dogged Pursuit

Sarah Fenske

MAY 8, 2008

By the time my mother was my age, she'd already had three children. Me, I've yet to figure out how to keep a plant alive. This has been freaking me out a bit lately, and not in a my-biological-clock-is-ticking kind of way. (It isn't.) It's more like it suddenly occurred to me that I'm 31 years old and, if anything, more footloose than I was at 21. I've got no mortgage, no kids, no pets—only a forlorn cactus positioned on my apartment's balcony so it can collect its annual two inches of rain, no watering can necessary.

I am living a completely selfish life, which, now that I realize it, scares me a little. At least in my twenties I had a pair of fish!

So I decided to get a dog.

I'm not really a dog person: never been around them, never really wanted to be around them. But cats can't come with you to the park, they don't like parties, and they certainly don't want to fly to San Francisco for an impromptu weekend getaway. I'm not sure my dog will want to do all this, either, but I'm hopeful.

I'm also petrified.

At first, when the idea was abstract, it was fun. I spent hours making lists of dog names. Henry? Trotsky? Buckley!

But when the breeder was selected, and the puppy picked, I started to worry. There's good reason I don't have pets or plants or babies in my life. I like staying out late and drinking too much. I don't have a primary-care physician and I don't take my vitamins. I don't want to take care of myself, much less anyone else.

So what, I thought, if I come home too late one night, and the dog's peed all over my apartment?

What if he gets sick? What if I accidentally starve him to death?

What if, asks a small voice inside my head, he doesn't like me?

And now I'm thinking frantically about how I need a puppy gate and a puppy crate and puppy food and I need to find a vet and—how do people do this? And how do they afford it?

Maybe it's only because ads for Mother's Day are everywhere this week, but I thought of my mom.

She was 26 when she got pregnant with my older sister. Not all that young, of course, but younger than I am today. And here I'm freaking out about a dog.

How could my mom possibly have known what she was doing?

How does any mother?

There are five of us Fenske kids, and I used to think how alien we must have seemed to my mother.

My mother comes from a family of Indiana farmers, one that's tilled the same fertile soil since 1830 without ever questioning their calling. I don't want to say they're simple people, but calling them complicated would be not only inaccurate, but an insult to their good humor, their heartiness, their all-around niceness. My mother was the only girl among three brothers and was the apple of her daddy's eye. An Indiana princess.

No one has ever accused me or my siblings of being royalty. As kids, we were all elbows and Coke-bottle glasses; I'm not really sure my mother knew what to do with fourth-graders who read Thomas Hardy and played "French Revolution" in the backyard. We were young royals on the lam from marauding peasants. (I know, I know.) My sisters and I always felt that we were letting Mom down because we weren't pretty and we weren't popular. But what could we do about it? We were clueless.

My mom says that none of this ever occurred to her. She doesn't overthink things the way I do, I guess.

I called her last week to talk about my dog fears. Of course, I didn't frame it that way; I could hardly admit to my mother that I was petrified about something so silly. So we talked about kids—specifically, her decision to give up any semblance of a glamorous life and have the five of us.

She said that, at the time, she never really stopped to think about the choices she was making. That's how it was then. You got married, you bought a house, and then you had kids. You didn't agonize over children the way my girlfriends do because, in part, your choices were fewer. You could not, for the most part, decide to have a baby if you weren't in a committed relationship. Nor could you wait until you were 45 and try something tricky with hormones. Or just pick Daddy out at a sperm bank.

So after my mom and dad got married, they bought a house. They decided to have a baby soon after that mostly because, my mom says, she didn't like her job.

"I was pretty restless," she says.

When I was 25 and restless, I got divorced and moved cross-country. That was not how things worked in 1975. And so my sister Amy was born, and then me, and then my three younger siblings. (Amy and I used to fantasize about how much happier we'd be if they'd stopped at two.)

My mother's life changed completely. By the time she went back to work, Bill Clinton was president. By the time she and my dad shuttled my youngest sister off to college, 30 years had passed.

Now, you'd think someone who stumbled into motherhood might regret spending that much time on it. Okay, maybe you wouldn't think that—I think that, because I love my job and love having enough disposable income to shop (occasionally!) at Stuart Weitzman.

But not my mom. She was genuinely good at being a mom, and as weird as it seems to me now, I think it was quite fulfilling for her. She blossomed.

In fact, she misses little kids so much that she and my dad typically spend half their weekends driving to visit my sister in Milwaukee. That's 16 hours in the car, round trip. And I might point out they haven't been to Phoenix in three years.

Milwaukee is where their grandchild is.

They love this little guy so much that my mom actually cites him as one reason they're glad they had kids. I'm thinking, what, we're this bridge generation to your perfect little baby boy? Thanks a lot, Mom!

You never meet anyone who regrets having kids, only people who regret *not* having them. Even parents who have the most awful kids seem to think they're great.

That can't just be about the kids. I think it may say more about the process of parenting.

When my mom tried to explain to me how wonderful motherhood is, she spoke only briefly about how cute we were and how much fun it was to watch us running around. In retrospect, I think she loved having us partly because she sees now how much parenthood changed her. That it moved her, forcibly, from her own selfishness into something challenging—and wondrous.

"If Dad and I hadn't had all you kids, we would have worked all those years," she says. "So we would have had a lot more money. Why? To pay for the nursing home?"

Nothing like a chat with Mom to make me question my own life choices. So I crack a joke. "Hey, at least I'll have a dog to grow old with."

"Sarah, getting a dog is a *lark*," my mother says. "It's not going to be anything close to a child! You're not going to have to get up in the middle of the night with your dog. You're not going to have to quit your job, or shift to something less demanding, in order to raise him! You're not going to have to change diapers."

Yes . . . *Exactly*.

A dog may sound like a small step to a woman who raised five kids without complaining. But for this frazzled career girl, it's giant-leap time.

Happy Mother's Day, Mom. I'm off to PetSmart. ⊷

"HOW I GOT THAT STORY"

Sarah Fenske, 33, has been a staff writer at Phoenix New Times *for almost six years and the paper's columnist for three. A native of Cleveland, Ohio, she got her start busting politicians at the (Lorain)* Morning Journal. *She's a two-time winner of the Clarion Award for column writing and has also received top honors from the National Association of Black Journalists, the Maggies, and the Arizona Press Club. She lives in Phoenix. In November 2009 Fenske participated in AAN's live chat series. The following is an edited version of that interview, which was conducted by* Santa Fe Reporter *writer Zane Fischer, a 2008 winner of AAN's column-writing award.*

OK, softballs first: What does it mean to win the AAN column award? Acknowledgement of hard work or just another day at the office?
It's kind of cool . . . most of these awards things are so apples-to-oranges. Here you're competing against the people who do what you do . . . so their kudos are really nice.

Your column is very newsy and your reporting is excellent and detailed. To what extent do you rely on public information and archives versus live sources?
I rarely, if ever, get any ideas from public information or other publications. That said, once I start looking into something, that's the first place I head. I try to put in at least two public information requests per week and on top of that, I love how much public records and archives are now online. I rarely, if ever, write about a person (much less an agency) without doing a thorough background check.

There's a lot of range, but usually a good balance between your hard reporting and your own somewhat lively and intimate editorial voice. Is it a natural combination or a balance you strive for?
It was hard at first. I'd been a news reporter for seven years when they gave me the column, and working as a hard news reporter, especially at a daily, they tend to beat your voice out of you. . . . It was hard, initially, to be honest about what I really felt about things and to let my guard down a bit and have fun with it.

What's your relationship with your editor like? How much does it inform the planning and execution of your column?
I'm edited by Amy Silverman, the managing editor here. She's awesome. I can't say enough about how great it is to work with her . . . she was an awesome reporter before

she chose to focus more on editing (she's still a great writer/reporter—just doesn't get to do it as much) and we have a great give-and-take. . . . I've learned to trust her judgment, though. If she thinks something will be boring, and I fight her and win, I have regretted it every single time! So we talk through a lot of ideas on the front end and, after that, it's usually a pretty easy edit.

Every once in a while you break things up with more personal storytelling, like your tales about your dog, Buckley. Does that mean it's a slow news week or Amy canned your idea or does it mean you need a break from hard-nosing it?
Really, it's mostly that I get bored. This is a curse for any columnist, I think, but once I've written about a topic, I really want to do something else, ASAP! So Amy has encouraged me to mix things up a bit. I try to write about something personal two or three times a year and the biggest challenge, really, is finding a week when there's no breaking news we want to jump in on—that and setting yourself up for the inevitable crap from the online readers.

You've had people comment and write letters this past year that are full of personal attacks and allegations about you. How do you handle people who respond to your work that way?
Well, if they ever used their real names, I would respond plenty, let me tell you! This stuff is always, always anonymous, and it's always Web-based. So I just ignore it. I used to get upset, when I was young and sweet. Now I'm just kind of a bitch and I'm really happy I've pissed 'em off to the point that they have to make it personal.

One of the things I most enjoyed about plowing through a wheelbarrow full of your columns is that I feel that I have this distinct picture of Phoenix. Do you ever feel like your muckraking is also creating a kind of civic portraiture?
Portraiture is a very, very flattering idea and you're very kind. I think, though, that it's more like if you're out there talking to people, and working sources, a portrait of the city emerges on its own . . . of course my Phoenix is not my editor's Phoenix and it's not my coworker's Phoenix. But since I write about what most interests me, hopefully there's kind of a coherent picture that emerges, maybe!

You're not shy about ribbing the daily. Do you feel like you have a vague adversarial relationship related to market share or a responsibility to point out shoddy reporting or a genuine battle against a force that repeatedly appears to suppress truth and distort facts?
Not market share! Just that they're so, so awful . . . I hate to say this—I have friends there—but often it's downright insulting how much they kowtow to whoever's in power. And the laziness in reporting—my god. I can open a paper any day of the week

and already know nine-tenths of what's in there before I read it . . . it's either press releases or old news. Just terrible.

You sometimes get stuck, as we all do, with referring to 'your sources.' How do typically handle sources that don't want to be named or go on record?
I hate anonymous quotes, but I love anonymous sources, so that is a balance. If I can prove something through the public record or whatever, I don't feel like I need a sound bite in quotation marks . . . but if someone wants to cast stones, there better be a bunch of them, or they better be doing it on the record.

Was losing the reliance on sound bites part of becoming a columnist or did you write news like that as well?
I tried to do it when I was writing news, but it was harder and I often failed, really. I love now that I can explore something, get to the bottom, and report back to my readers. Back pre-column, you'd have to find something a bit more concrete, some document you could cite or someone on the record. I would hate to have to go back to that just because it was difficult. A column really makes this stuff easy!

Advice for the aspiring columnist?
I guess you have to learn to trust your own judgment. It's important to report things as hard as you can, but when you realize a spade is a spade, you've got to learn to call it that.

History Lesson

Anne Schindler

MARCH 11, 2008

Last week, residents of the massive 2,200-home Palencia development in St. Johns County converged on a County Commission meeting to ask for help. At issue was a proposed recycling facility located less than a mile from the entrance to the subdivision—proximity that homeowners felt would cheapen property values and impinge on their quality of life. As one resident put it in an email to commissioners, "My guess is it's . . . not conducive to residential living." Another expressed concern that the operation would imperil the "welfare and safety" of residents.

The furor over the recycling facility seems reasonable if one looks at Palencia as it is today—a growing, family-friendly community of high-end homes and condominiums, centered around a walkable town center design and dotted with wetlands and forested areas.

But to look at Palencia in this way would be naïve, even hypocritical. In the first place, the proposed recycling facility, located across U.S. 1 from the development, is hardly an industrial anomaly. The strip is already home to a county landfill, two cement plants, three cell phone towers, one steel-reinforced double-sided billboard and a set of railroad tracks. Long before Palencia's developers turned the first shovelful of dirt, the industrial presence on U.S. 1 was a fact of life.

To be fair, residents may not know about some of that activity. Tree buffers protect some industrial areas from view, and unless homeowners researched local land-use designations before buying, they might not know what surrounding parcels could become.

There are, in fact, a lot of things that Palencia residents may not know. They may not know that their development prompted the most heated, protracted legal battle of any development to date in St. Johns County. They may not know that their homes are built on wetlands destroyed in the name of increased developer profits. They may not know that numerous historically significant Native American sites, including ancient burial grounds, were destroyed, so that their upper middle class homes could be built. They may not realize that it was this development's appalling encroachment on creeks and marshes (referenced in the original development's name, "Marshall Creek, DRI") that prompted the county to hire a consultant to develop new wetland buffer guidelines.

They may not know that the developers of their new homes forced out longtime residents along Shannon Road, north of the development's main entrance, buying up property and pressuring families to leave. They may not know that these same developers retaliated against the one family that refused to sell, blocking access to their house, cutting off their power and locating a public bathroom steps from their front door to punish them for their intractability.

Of course, this is Florida, land of the transplant, the clueless newcomer, the ahistorical interloper. Many if not most of us live and trod upon lands that once held a different, arguably higher purpose. But this particular project, just six years old, may be vulnerable to a unique form of collective amnesia. In order to build this sprawling planned community—one that developers unironically promised would offer a "sense of place"—they had to cover over its history, its ecology, and any evidence of its earlier human inhabitants.

The extent to which developers bought into their new reality is perhaps best encapsulated by a comment made by Palencia Project Manager Walt O'Shea to the *St. Augustine Record* in late 2001. Dismissing concerns that lawn fertilizers and golf course pesticides would harm the delicate waters of the Guana Tolomato Matanzas Research Reserve, which Palencia abuts, O'Shea explained, "Any water [runoff] coming off this project will be of better quality than the water coming off today." Now that's revisionist history with panache.

There's nothing wrong with the residents of Palencia rallying their neighbors to activism in the name of a better quality of life. But they ought to know there were many battles fought over the property they now seek to defend. Their homes, their lawns, the very existence of their community is proof of the failure of similar efforts in the past.

It's a history lesson that every resident of Florida could stand to learn. ••

Sugar Land

Anne Schindler

NOVEMBER 4, 2008

The world is a lonelier place than it was this time last week. The robo calls have stopped, mass emails no longer clog the inbox, direct mailers are now outnumbered by holiday catalogues. The election is over. And while you may be depressed or elated by the outcome, there's little choice now but to move on.

Of course, that's not as easy as pulling the signs out of your lawn or scraping the bumper sticker from your rear window. Like the Halloween candy consumed last weekend, the residue of the past year will remain with us for some time—our own political avoirdupois.

Shedding that burden will take effort, but it's worth it. Americans have created many great things in this 232-year-old democracy, but we have not yet developed a language to discuss our politics. Whether yours draw from right-wing radio or left-leaning chat rooms, the angry argot is the same. Every statement is a salvo, every retort wrapped in withering prose. There are plenty of smart, thinking people who voted for John McCain. There are plenty of Barack Obama fans who aren't Stalinist pinkos. But you wouldn't know it from the death stares and middle fingers that surfaced on suburban roads, or the rampant theft and vandalism of political signs on private property.

It's nice that citizens care who runs their government, but it would be nicer if they cared about their neighbors. Or, more generally, if they cared about everyone's right to speak freely, endorse openly and campaign actively. We love democracy until it runs up against our entrenched beliefs. Then it's good-bye marketplace of ideas, hello secret police.

Such attitudes have clearly been exacerbated by the Religious Right, which has attempted to conflate politics and morality through issues like abortion and gay marriage. The left isn't without blame, however, having turned the issue of global warming into a battle between those who care about the fate of the Earth and irrational despoilers gunning for the End of Days.

Viewed through the prism of partisanship, the opposing sides couldn't be more different. But the confluence of two recent calendar dates—Election Day and Halloween—points up just how absurd such perceptions are. The first, steeped in divisive politics, involves converging at a central community building and peacefully filling out paperwork. The other, born of a desire for candy, involves dressing as zombies and ax murderers, and threatening neighbors for handouts. Martians would be hard-pressed to understand why one causes our blood pressure to rise, and the other only our blood sugar.

I should probably point out here that, as of this writing, Election Day has not yet dawned, much less ended, and there is no certainty how the vote will roll out. But it isn't too soon to begin focusing on the things that unite us as a community, as a nation, as a species. Almost to a person, we want our children to grow up cared for and well educated. We want to have good jobs and safe homes, clean air and drinkable water. We want to enjoy our brief time on this planet with a minimum of suffering and a maximum of joy.

With that much in common, policy differences seem positively niggling. So beat your swords back into ploughshares, replace the sign divots on your front lawn, and remember that whatever's ahead, it has to be better than the past eight years.

As for that that lingering partisanship? Try feeding it something sweet. •➔

"HOW I GOT THAT STORY"

Anne Schindler began her tenure at Folio Weekly *in 1995 as a staff writer, after moving to Florida on a whim the year before. She took over as editor in 2003. Before that, she writes: "I was a journo grad from University of Wisconsin, Madison, where I overcame my aversion to patchouli (sort of) and learned how important it is to examine one's own cervix (Women's Studies 760, Perspectives on Gender). Which I never did, so I was punished by cervical cancer (ahaha—seriously, but it's OK now). Moved to Minneapolis, worked in a bar, met David Carr, interned and wrote for him there at the (now defunct) Twin Cities Reader." Schindler is a member of AAN's editorial committee and in November 2009 she participated in AAN's live chat series. The following is an edited version of that interview, which was conducted by* Santa Fe Reporter *Editor and AAN Editorial Chair Julia Goldberg.*

Does Editor's Note have specific beats or do you mix it up week to week?
I've worked at *Folio* since 1995, so I've developed some areas of interest that I tend to revisit—local politics, the environment, development issues. But there is no beat. The column's topics are just driven by whatever's in the news that interests me.

How did you initially envision the column?
Well, I inherited it, with very little prep time, when my predecessor Bob Snell left in 2003. So initially it was very much by the seat of my pants. At first, I envisioned it as a heavily-reported piece, one that would be less about issuing proclamations or recommendations, which I was less comfortable with than straight-up news reporting.

And sometimes, it still is like that. A few weeks ago, I used the space to break a story about the local transportation authority, and how they've been lying for years about the number of bus stops they have. But more often than not, it's an effort to provide context, and what institutional memory I can offer, to something that's already in the news.

With your longevity at the paper, is it hard to keep it fresh when you're dealing with ongoing issues in your community?
Yes, keeping it fresh is a challenge, and I don't always succeed. Areas of interest tend to devolve into repeat beats pretty easily. My art director says if I write one more column about water issues, he's going to quit.

Of course, you're a columnist and the editor. What's the relationship of your column to the rest of the paper? Do you riff off reporting from your news staff or do you tackle stories and issues no one else is covering?
I occasionally write about something we've covered, maybe once every six or eight weeks. I should do it more. It's a good way to give stories a little more shelf life and, for those people who just don't read cover-length stories, it's sometimes they only way they'll be exposed to the issue. Of course, sometimes it just feels like piggybacking— a little too easy.

So the question every editor who doesn't write a column wants answered: how do you get this column written? I consider it a good day when I actually manage to listen to my voice mails.
I've stopped listening to voice mails, in fact . . . which might help. I often don't begin until Friday noon, and it's due that day by three or four (or five if I'm pissing off everyone in the art department). On a good week, I've been thinking on the issue for some time, calling sources and reading up on it. On a bad week, I'm flying by the seat of my pants. But, to be honest, some of my favorite columns are ones that have less to do with reported material—or even current material—and more with trying to contextualize information.

Like the election day/Halloween connection in "Sugarland."
Right.

Now, in "History Lesson" you pretty much call out the residents of a development for hypocrisy in their protest of a proposed recycling plant nearby. What kind of reaction did you get to that?
Um, none, as a matter of fact—not from the residents. A few people who remember the efforts to stop their development from ever happening were glad to see the piece. . . . But even though I focus on the residents of the development in that piece, they are

really just a symbol of the transient Florida interloper. There are 1,000 people moving to this state a day (or there were, before the bubble burst) and we get 80 million visitors a year, and virtually everyone here is from somewhere else. But almost nobody knows what this state looked like before the suburbs arrived, you know?

The residents of Palencia were an attractive target, because their home so recently emerged from the swamp, but what I hoped to drive home in that piece is that every Florida resident would do well to consider that their presence here displaced something or someone else's way of life.

I have a columnist who calls out residents on that sort of double-standard. And then I take some of their angry calls. Do you ever feel the need to self-censor in your column because you're also the editor? As in, you hold a strong opinion but you also need to be seen by potential sources as accessibleand balanced on issues, etc?
I'm not sure everyone views me as balanced on the issues, though I do try to be accessible. We've been pretty straightforward that our pieces have a viewpoint. That's off-putting to some, but even those who disagree with our editorial content tend to support the aggressiveness of the reporting style.

The columns I read don't employ the first-person voice as many columns and blogs do. How do you view the difference between writing a column as the editor of the paper versus writing an editorial on behalf of the paper?
I don't use first person much, because I'm not comfortable with it. My reporting background makes me skeptical of that all-knowing "our opinion" stuff. . . . But the column appears on page three, before even the table of contents, so it does serve as a placeholder for an editorial opinion, even if I'm just writing from my perspective.

Your voice in the columns is a great combo of scathing and polite (in person you're just the latter, even when drinking tequila), but I did want to know if you're a total word nerd . . . because otherwise I'll feel stupid that I had to look up 'avoirdupois.'
I come from a family of word nerds. My mom's a science writer, and my dad is fond of reminding everyone of the Latin root of this or that. So I come by it honestly. As for scathingly polite, I think that probably is my natural voice. I honed it during my years as a waitress in Minneapolis.

Can you offer some advice for the aspiring columnist?
Really, I'd offer the same advice I offer any of my writers, which is read as much good stuff as you can and write about things that interest you. Those two things, I think, are the best ingredients for good writing.

FEATURE STORY

CIRCULATION 50,000 AND OVER

"The Good Soldier"

by Joel Warner, *Westword*

"Outstanding blend of strong reporting and fast-paced narrative writing. Unforgettable descriptions from Iraq. A moving look at a soldier fighting an important battle. Wonderful piece."—Stephanie Simon, Wall Street Journal

CIRCULATION UNDER 50,000

"Private Trauma"

by Patrick Michels, *Texas Observer*

"Damn near perfect. Excellent structure and layered details and clean unpretentious writing and deep reporting."—Amy Argetsinger, Washington Post

The Good Soldier

Joel Warner

Do you like green eggs and ham?

I do not like them, Sam-I-am. I do not like green eggs and ham!

It was September 28, 2003, Andrew Pogany's second day in Iraq, and he was steering a Land Rover through the night toward Samarra with another Special Forces soldier on board and an M4 rifle in his lap. This stretch of road, which ran through the especially nasty enclave of insurgent strongholds called the Sunni Triangle, was known for ambushes of Army convoys just like his. "This is Indian country down here," a Green Beret had told him earlier in the day. "You'll be lucky to make it out alive." Pogany should have been completely focused on the road, scanning the surroundings for signs of trouble, but he was a little distracted.

Would you like them in a house?

Would you like them with a mouse?

A 32-year-old staff sergeant stationed at Fort Carson, Pogany had been assigned to fill a vacancy in a highly trained, twelve-man Special Forces A Team just two weeks before they shipped out to fight in the still-young war. And now he was learning something about one of them. Sitting next to Pogany, gripping his own rifle, medic Ken Lehman had decided it was the perfect time to recite lines from Dr. Seuss. Over and over again.

Would you eat them in a box?

Would you eat them with a fox?

It seemed to be the only way Lehman could calm himself, but it was rattling Pogany. On and on it went—in a car, in a tree, on a train, in the rain. Pogany told him to shut up, asked him, begged him, and finally managed to plug him up with a cigarette.

What an introduction to war, Pogany thought to himself later that night after the convoy had made it safely to Samarra and he tried to fall asleep in a mortar-scarred barracks, gunfire echoing through the city. He didn't have much time to reflect. Soon, explosions sounded in the distance, and truck engines roared nearby. Outside, Pogany found chaos: Soldiers were screaming and running through the compound as smoke billowed around them. A strange, metallic odor filled the air. It was the smell of blood.

There had been an ambush; several Iraqis had been captured and brought back to the compound. All that was left of one of them was in a body bag—a body bag being unzipped as Pogany turned to look. Six seconds. That's how long the bag was open, but that was all it took. It was enough to see exactly how the heavy artillery round had ripped straight through the man's torso. Enough to make out all the blood and shredded flesh. Enough to know it was difficult to call what was left a body.

Pogany turned away and went back to his room. He had the fortitude to stomach this, he told himself. He'd trained for war for years, and before that he'd been a volunteer firefighter. He'd received stellar military reviews and had been recommended for immediate promotion. Most important, he was Special Forces. But the body bag had set something off inside his head, something that didn't make sense. Everything started moving in slow motion. Then came nausea, trembling, and terror. He tried to sleep again, had horrible dreams, and woke up to discover his room exploding around him. A mortar must have exploded, he thought, as he watched the ceiling cave in.

It was all in his head. Pogany realized later that he'd been hallucinating.

The next day, he told his team sergeant he needed help, that he was having a nervous breakdown. An Army psychiatrist agreed. "Solider reported signs of symptoms consistent with those of a normal combat-stress reaction," he wrote in his report. But Pogany's commanding officers wouldn't hear of it—he had to start acting like a soldier. It wasn't as simple as finding some guts and going back to work, Pogany replied; there had to be something physically wrong with him. "So, well, if you can't help me here," Pogany said, "I guess you are going to have to send me home."

They did so on October 7, and a week later, Pogany received his coming-home present: The U.S. Department of Defense charged him with cowardice. It was a military crime that hadn't been used to convict a soldier since 1968—and it was punishable by death. With a hook like that, national media was all over the story. Jessica Lynch, America's hero, was just then front-page news. Now Pogany was America's coward.

"I am not trying to screw the Army," the staff sergeant tells Pogany. They're sitting in a chow hall at Fort Carson, the massive Army installation south of Colorado Springs, early one bright morning several weeks ago. "But I am looking out for myself," he says. "I've been here for 12 years, and to get treated like this? Hell, no."

The Army has told the 31-year-old staff sergeant that he's no longer fit for duty because he has sleep apnea, a medical condition involving breathing problems during sleep. An Army medical evaluation recently concluded that his problems aren't related to combat, so he'll be sent home with a single severance check. No retirement pay, no access to life or health insurance. Before he knows or understands it, he'll be out of the Army, and his problems will be a matter for others to deal with. The great military machine will move on, recruiting new soldiers to replace him, able-bodied men and women who aren't *broken.*

But the staff sergeant knows something's different inside of him, something beyond sleep problems. It's been that way ever since a mortar exploded next to him in Iraq. He walked away without any physical wounds, any outward signs of damage—but something was wrong. "When I got back from Iraq the last time, I was irritable, and lately it's been worse. It's rough when I can't sleep, and I get home and get in an argument with my wife. . . " His voice trails off.

Pogany, now 36, listens quietly, his eyes trained steadily on the soldier—the only part of Pogany that doesn't seem to be in constant, agitated motion. His legs bounce absentmindedly; his hands, sheathed in his black leather jacket, pull thoughtfully on the brown goatee adorning his boyish face when they aren't flipping through the documents the staff sergeant has brought with him. On one document, he notices something.

"According to this, you have a mild traumatic brain injury," he says. Traumatic brain injuries (TBIs), caused by sudden head trauma such as a mortar attack and marked by lingering psychological and physical symptoms like sleep apnea, have become a common memento of the war. In fact, Fort Carson has reported in a study that nearly 18 percent of its soldiers returning from war had suffered a traumatic brain injury. And that's not the only baggage they were coming home with: since 2003, the base has also diagnosed 2,189 cases of post-traumatic stress disorder. "What are they doing for that?" he asks the staff sergeant.

"Nothing."

Pogany's heard enough. A TBI is serious enough to warrant medical retirement and benefits. "That diagnosis was not included in your [medical evaluation]. The question is why." Pogany wants to see all of the staff sergeant's medical records. They're going to appeal his medical evaluation, he says, and the soldier doesn't need to worry about legal fees. Pogany's going to get him a pro bono lawyer.

Four years after being charged with, and later acquitted of, cowardice, after riding his own tumultuous wave through the Army, Pogany is a Denver-based soldiers' advocate helping veterans who are living through much the same experiences he had.

Over the past few years, he's worked for several veterans organizations, and in January he was hired as a special investigator for the Washington, D.C.-based National Veterans Legal Services Program (NVLSP) to seek out stories like this, soldiers who are coming back from the wars in Iraq and Afghanistan and finding the Army has deemed them expendable. Retired from the Army, he's a one-man civilian commando unit, working to untangle the bureaucracy behind the Defense Department's medical, military justice, and veterans' benefits systems—and if that doesn't do the trick, he can always call his powerful contacts in the press corps or on Capitol Hill to help him.

There's lots to keep him busy. The Army, which begins its sixth year of war in Iraq this week, has been hammered on multiple fronts for its poor treatment of injured soldiers, especially those suffering from mental and psychological injuries. Fort Carson, with 17,500 military personnel assigned to it, has become a flashpoint in the extended controversy, with soldiers there claiming they've been punished or kicked out of the Army without proper benefits because they have TBIs or mental-health problems like post-traumatic stress disorder (PTSD). The allegations have led to front-page headlines, investigations by U.S. senators and military officials, and promised improvement by Fort Carson brass.

Pogany has been in the center of it all, working to help the soldiers, telling reporters and Congress about the problems, and pushing for changes that are now starting to happen. And he certainly has the attention of Fort Carson's new commander.

"I have talked to Andrew on several occasions," says Major General Mark Graham, who took charge of Fort Carson last September. "I think Andrew has much the same goal as we do, which is to help soldiers and their families. Andrew has raised some concerns to us, and I appreciate him doing that.

"I think we are showing that multiple deployments is tough on soldiers and their families," Graham adds. "But I think the good part of this is that we have a system in place where we talk to soldiers and tell them we are always open. We tell them it is a sign of strength, not weakness, to come forward and say they need some help. We are changing the culture. It takes time, but I think we are making some progress in that area."

Pogany agrees that Fort Carson and the Army are making progress—but there are still soldiers who need help, like the staff sergeant sitting across from him. "They made it look like I was trying to get out of going to Iraq again," he tells Pogany with a snort. "I have been to Iraq twice. I'm not scared to go." Still, he adds, bad stuff did happen over there—stuff he can't shake.

"You need to be completely re-evaluated for a traumatic brain injury," Pogany tells him. In fact, does he have time to go to Fort Carson's traumatic brain injury clinic right now? No need to worry about making an appointment; people at Fort Carson are used to Pogany's unannounced visits.

The staff sergeant will make time. "The Army uses you and uses you," he says, "and then throws you out."

Pogany knows exactly how that feels.

✿

Pogany says he doesn't like talking about his past, his voice betraying no hint of an accent, no hint of growing up in Germany as Georg-Andreas, the son of an expat Hungarian insurgent who fought against the Soviets in his country's failed 1956 revolution. It took months for Pogany's girlfriend, Jen Collins, to learn about his time in the military, about how, after he emigrated to the United States as a college student and studied criminal justice at the University of South Florida, he joined the Army and was trained as an interrogator. And it's been years since he's signed off his e-mails with the Special Forces' motto, "De oppresso liber"—liberator of the oppressed—which he started doing, even though not a Green Beret himself, after he was assigned to the 10th Special Forces Group at Fort Carson in 2001. Instead, Pogany prefers to quote from the *Bodhisattva* or *The Art of War*, or tell a wry joke adorned with a few choice selections of his still-vibrant barracks vocabulary.

But driving through Fort Carson after dropping off the staff sergeant at the clinic, it's hard to escape his past. The brick office buildings, the "GI Jolt" coffee shop in the base strip mall, the fenced-off trucks and cargo containers waiting to be shipped to the desert thousands of miles away—everything comprised by "greatest home town in America," as the guards at the entrance gates are required to call it—bring back memories. Last week at the Army hospital, for example, Pogany ran into Lehman, the *Green Eggs and Ham* guy, whom he hadn't seen in years. Lehman said he was messed up, that he had PTSD and a TBI, and that he was in trouble with the law.

Pogany knew what Lehman felt like, lost and alone in the middle of Fort Carson. This was where Pogany returned after being charged with cowardice and ordered to complete one menial on-base task after another. It was where he struggled through the diminishing but still debilitating symptoms of his mysterious condition—blurry vision, balance problems, stomach ailments—and tried to make sense of the cowardice charge.

"I never bought into what they were saying," he says. "The question was, 'What happened?' This was not me. I didn't understand what had happened."

To try and figure it out, Pogany called a soldiers' advocate he'd heard of: Steve Robinson, a Gulf War veteran and head of the Washington, D.C., veterans' advocacy group National Gulf War Resource Center (NGWRC), who agreed to help.

"I believe the military realized it was in a different fight in Iraq. It was no longer limited tank battles; it was going to be up-close urban combat, and that was going to create fear in the soldiers, and fear is like a cancer in a war," Robinson says now. "This guy Andrew had an emotional reaction to this broken and destroyed body, and they decided they were not going to put up with it. They said, 'Let's kill this cancer right now.' It had a chilling effect throughout the entire military."

Pogany and Robinson dug in, trying to find out what, exactly, was wrong with Pogany, looking for a smoking gun— and they believed they found it in Lariam, a commonly used anti-malarial drug he'd been prescribed by the military for Iraq that was known to cause serious psychiatric side effects in some people. Military officials told Robinson they weren't prescribing Lariam in Iraq, but Pogany still had the blister pack of Lariam they'd given him; he'd taken three pills, the third on the day of his breakdown.

Soon other soldiers who'd served in Iraq were contacting Robinson—and the media—saying they, too, had been given Lariam and were experiencing troubling side effects. With that news, Pogany began boning up on his pharmacology. He learned about a medical study showing that 29 percent of 500 travelers and tourists who took the drug had experienced neuropsychiatric side effects. He talked to reporters who linked the drug to instances of suicide. He read about Canadian troops who'd beaten a boy to death in Somalia in 1993 and about three Special Forces soldiers at Fort Bragg, North Carolina, who'd killed their wives and then themselves in 2002. They'd all taken Lariam. Soon reporters stopped calling Andrew Pogany, coward, and began calling Andrew Pogany, Lariam expert.

The Defense Department began to feel the pressure. It dropped the cowardice charge, instead accusing Pogany of dereliction of duty, for which he could spend six months in prison and receive a dishonorable discharge. But they'd underestimated him.

"They picked the wrong person to call a coward," says Collins, his girlfriend. "He turned it around and came at them with a vengeance."

As his protracted legal battle wore on, Pogany heard disturbing news that increased his suspicions about Lariam. On March 14, 2004, a 36-year-old Fort Carson soldier who'd just returned from Iraq threatened his wife with a revolver in their Monument home and then, when the police arrived, shot and killed himself. The solder, it turned out, was William Howell, who had been part of Pogany's twelve-man team in Iraq.

In May of that year, Pogany's supervisors agreed to send him to a specialized Navy medical lab in San Diego for proper diagnosis. There, in a doctor's written notes, he received his vindication: "Drug toxicity antimalarials. . . . Likely Lariam toxicity."

Later, after he'd similarly diagnosed several other soldiers and his findings had reached the press, the doctor changed his tune; he was no longer certain if Lariam was the culprit. But the damage had been done. The Army dropped all charges against Pogany and, on April 14, 2005, he was medically retired because of permanent brain-stem damage due to Lariam toxicity. "Then I was unceremoniously walked to the door and told to take off," Pogany remembers. "I was told to never set foot on the 10th Special Forces Group compound again."

Peace is every step.

The words are written in elegant cursive on a strip of paper pasted inside the windshield of Pogany's Volkswagen, above the dreamcatcher dangling from the rearview mirror and the tangle of wires covering his center console that powers his cell phone—which, as he makes his way across Fort Carson, is ringing constantly, filling the car with a Monty Python ditty: *Always look on the bright side of life . . .* An NPR reporter wants to meet with him in Colorado Springs. Pogany, juggling the phone and the steering wheel, schedules it into his electronic calendar.

Always look on the bright side of life. . . It's the screenwriter who's pitching a movie about Pogany. He's thinking Colin Farrell could star in it, or maybe Matt Damon.

Always look on the bright side of life . . . A soldier found one of the business cards Pogany distributes around the base; he's hoping Pogany can help him. "Send me an email with everything that happened, including your deployment dates. Do you have any of your medical records? Do you have copies of your mental-health care records?" he says before hanging up. "That will be a new case"—one of the handful he may get today.

This is Pogany's mobile workplace, one he drives to and from Fort Carson several times a week, on workdays that usually begin at 6 A.M. It's an extension of a home office in the basement of his brick bungalow in central Denver that features a heavily armed G.I. Joe doll, faded prayer flags on the wall, bookshelves stocked with veterans' benefits guides and mental-disorders manuals, and boxes and boxes of soldiers' case files. He pulls his VW office over at a barracks building and flashes the ID card hanging around his neck to the guard in the front lobby. He is there to meet with Nicholas.

"Fucking wild," Nicholas, 21, says of the 20 or so roadside bomb explosions he was exposed to in Iraq. "You hear it, but it's more like your ears start immediately ringing. It feels like a very strong, hot wind that knocks you back when they go off." He only realized their lasting toll once he got back from the war and ran a guy off the road in an inexplicable fit of rage. Later, he recounts with a wry laugh, he flipped out during a training exercise and put a gun to a passerby's head. "I just kind of lost it for a while."

Things weren't so funny when Nicholas's mother first called Pogany several months ago, the night her son was taken to the Evans Army Community Hospital for having suicidal thoughts. Nicholas had just been told he was being redeployed in four days—even though he'd been diagnosed with post-traumatic stress disorder, a fractured femur, and a traumatic brain injury and labeled temporarily unfit for deployment.

Because of privacy considerations, the Army can't respond publicly to allegations such as Nicholas's, says Fort Carson Public Affairs Officer Dee McNutt in an email. "Each case needs to be looked into separately, and the Army cannot release or discuss information regarding specific cases without a soldier's expressed written consent." But "soldiers are human and will tell their side of the story as they see it," she adds.

As for claims that Fort Carson has been deploying injured soldiers to Iraq, she says, "Medical personnel are responsible for making recommendations to commanders on what resources or level of care a soldier requires to be considered fully capable for deployment. Commanders know the assets available to them in theater and what accommodations can be made for the limitations of each individual soldier. Many times soldiers require care that is readily available in theater."

Pogany helped Nicholas's mother, Dawna Lynn, track down documents proving that his ailments and no-deployment status had been ignored. He encouraged her to contact a congressional subcommittee on military affairs, Fort Carson's inspector general, and the installation's commanding general. Soon her son's story was one of the examples reporters were using to demonstrate that the Army was improperly shipping out injured soldiers in order to fill diminished ranks. "There was no way I could have sorted through the military bureaucracy if I didn't have somebody tell me how to do it," she says. "If I hadn't been aggressive and had the right person tell me what to do, my son would have been sent back to Iraq without the proper medical care."

Instead, Nicholas's deployment was called off, and he's expecting to be medically retired. For him, that moment can't come too soon. "I hate this job," he says. "I needed some help, some support. They didn't want to give it to me. They didn't care."

Pogany was angry like Nicholas once, especially during the months leading up to his medical retirement. Angry at the Army for being his whole world and then turning on him and making him a national pariah. Angry that his injury didn't make any sense—whoever heard of a soldier laid low by a stupid pill? Angry that, despite all he'd been through, he still ended up better off than some of his teammates, like Howell or his team sergeant, Kelly Hornbeck, who was killed by a roadside bomb in Iraq.

"Sometimes I feel like I was the luckiest guy in this whole war," he says. "I went over for what, 15 days, and came home with two arms, two legs." And he was angry that he was entering civilian life with no job and no idea what he wanted to do with his life. "I was in the toilet," he says now.

He took time off, traveled to Europe. He met Claude AnShin Thomas, a Vietnam veteran turned Buddhist monk who told him, "Once a soldier, always a soldier. It's what we do with the experience that makes a difference in our lives." And then, finally, he got it. "I had to come to grips with the fact that I was shattered. That I was broken. And that being broken wasn't such a bad thing," he says. "And, in a nutshell, I had a choice. I could either get busy living, or I could get busy dying."

He soon found something to live for, something perfectly suited to his background. While he was still in the Army, soldiers had started coming up to him, asking for help. They knew no one else to turn to other than the guy who'd taken on the system and won. A month after leaving the Army, Pogany started working with Robinson at the NGWRC, helping him build on veterans-advocacy tools first developed by Vietnam veterans, shifting the programs to focus on a new generation of soldiers.

"I felt that now that Andrew had successfully survived his battle, he could become a powerful advocate. Intellectually, he was very well put together. He had the intelligence-gathering skills and paperwork skills and organizational skills to be very effective," says Robinson. "The people who are most passionate about these issues are the ones who've dealt personally with them."

The two men, first at the NGWRC, then at Veterans for America, discovered that they had their work cut out for them. While soldiers were no longer returning with apparent Lariam side effects—the drug is still commonly prescribed to people traveling to regions where malaria is resistant to some other anti-malarials, but the Army has stopped using it—they were coming home with other problems, like PTSD and TBIs.

More than 1.6 million soldiers have been deployed to Iraq and Afghanistan, and they've been finding that these battlefields are very different than those of their predecessors. In Vietnam, one soldier was killed for every two and a half wounded. Now the survival rate is one killed for every sixteen wounded. The Veterans Administration is expecting to treat an estimated 333,000 Iraq and Afghanistan war veterans in 2009 alone, and many of these injuries will be mental, brought on by constant, omnipresent danger dotted with brain-rattling roadside bombs.

"Combat in Iraq is 360-365," says Paul Sullivan, executive director of the nonprofit Veterans for Common Sense. "That means our service members are completely surrounded, all day, every day, for a year."

The undersecretary for health at the Veterans Health Administration recently noted that of the 300,000 veterans of the wars treated at VA hospitals, more than half were diagnosed with a mental health condition, 68,000 of which were PTSD. In addition, 30 percent of veterans treated at Walter Reed Army Medical Center have been diagnosed with a traumatic brain injury. These are injuries that aren't as gruesomely simple to treat as a lost arm or leg—and much easier for the Army to overlook or ignore.

Pogany put his Army interrogator training to good use tracking down and helping soldiers with these injuries. He began digging into Army regulations—military justice volumes, medical manuals—and hanging around Fort Carson, finding those who needed help as well as those who could help them.

He worked within the system, making sure to distance himself from antiwar groups. "It's not an issue about the war, and it never has been for me," he says. "When that question is brought into the picture, it becomes very political. And when it becomes very political, you tend to not open as many doors."

While Robinson helped document abuses at the Walter Reed Army Medical Center in Washington, D.C., leading to front-page headlines and several prominent military leaders stepping down, Pogany trained his sights on his former Army post.

"Andrew has proven to be a tireless and dedicated advocate for troops suffering from invisible injuries such as PTSD," says

Republican Senator Kit Bond of Missouri, whose office has used Pogany as a resource. "He knows the challenges these warfighters face in getting the care they need because he has lived the experience."

Pogany, the "Puppet Master," as his girlfriend jokingly calls him, was soon traveling to other states, poking around their military installations. In upstate New York, he discovered soldiers at Fort Drum were waiting six to eight weeks to get a mental health appointment. In California, Pogany and Robinson reported to the press that at Camp Pendleton, Marines with post-traumatic stress disorder were being given little treatment or respect. And at Alaska's Fort Richardson, Pogany found only three social workers, two substance-abuse counselors and zero psychiatrists for almost 4,000 soldiers.

"Everywhere, I found the same problems: People left and right falling through the cracks," he says. "There was this huge disconnect between what happens in the trenches and what the Pentagon and Army put out."

Until he was hired full time by Veterans for America, Pogany worked for little or no pay, cramming his investigations into nights and weekends when he wasn't working a security job at Buckley Air Force Base. His new position with the NVLSP program is similar to his past work, with one major advantage: He can connect his cases with one of the NVLSP's network of 1,000 plus pro bono lawyers, many from major law firms. The Army has long had its phalanx of legal mavens; now Pogany has one, too.

Not everyone appreciates his crusade. "Chain of command doesn't like that I am talking to you," Nicholas says to Pogany as they wrap up their meeting. "They said you are out to bash the Army." Pogany gets this a lot. For a while, there were posters plastered around Fort Carson with his face on them, warning people to call military police if they spotted him. In 2005, Colorado Springs mayor Lionel Rivera withdrew his promised support of Operation Just One, a program Pogany created to connect soldiers with off-base therapists, reportedly because he was skeptical of Pogany's motivations.

"We aren't the bad guys. This is not about ending someone's career," says Pogany. "While they are calling me names,

I am going to be presenting facts. We are going to keep moving the pieces across the chessboard, and one day it's going to be checkmate."

It's a beautiful day," Teresa Mischke tells Pogany as he pulls into her driveway, greeting him like an old war buddy. They've been through a lot together.

Her husband Darren's story is so long, so convoluted, it's sometimes hard for her to know where to begin. There was his first deployment to Iraq in 2003, before he met Teresa, when his soft-skin Humvee was rammed by an Iraqi truck. There was no blood, no obvious damage, so he went right back to work. Sure, when he got home and met Teresa, there were some headaches, but nothing to be concerned about. Then, during his second deployment in 2005, a mortar hit his vehicle, blowing a hole in the turret right by his head. At the time, Darren considered himself lucky to be alive. But back in Colorado Springs in December 2006, right around the time the two got married, he stopped acting like himself. He'd get real quiet, lash out at unexpected moments and forget the most basic things. Training simulators became impossibly mystifying, his hands and mind rebelling against him, and bright flashes plagued his vision.

Then there was the night he brought his battle demons home and shoved Teresa. She called 911—not to have him locked up, but to get help. Still, he was arrested and pleaded guilty in exchange for counseling. When his superiors heard that he was on probation and could no longer carry a weapon, they had grounds for an administrative discharge.

But Darren was getting worse. He started having seizure-like attacks, and for a while, doctors had him on 20 different medications. The military thought he was making it all up, says Teresa, to avoid going back to Iraq.

Teresa's tale didn't surprise Pogany when she first called him last spring. He'd heard lots of stories of soldiers too sick or injured to serve who'd found themselves removed from the Army without what they believed was proper treatment and support. Like Darren, some were discharged because of legal or discipline problems and were never fully medically evaluated for underlying mental-health problems. Others who did undergo a Medical Evaluation Board process claimed the assessments ignored serious injuries like PTSD and TBIs and instead focused on minor ailments or diagnosed them with general pre-existing conditions like "personality disorders" that made them unfit for duty but not eligible for pensions or for health and life insurance.

Army spokeswoman McNutt counters these claims, saying Evans Army Community Hospital at Fort Carson "has an outstanding Medical Evaluation Board section which takes pride in dispositioning soldiers in a comprehensive and timely manner. All soldiers undergoing the Medical Evaluation Board process receive a thorough examination to ensure that all medical and behavioral health issues are documented. During the process, if additional medical issues are identified, they may be added to the record. In addition, soldiers are counseled and afforded multiple opportunities to appeal decisions made during the Medical Evaluation Board, the Physical Evaluation Board, and the physical disability rating process. Anytime we become aware of something that may have been missed or inadvertently overlooked, we ensure the error is corrected."

So Pogany connected Darren and Teresa with the right medical experts, who agreed he had signs of head injury as well as dementia—and a brain scan this past October found multiple lesions on his brain. And now, finally, Teresa tells Pogany they seem to be getting somewhere. Darren was just sent to a Veterans Affairs medical center in California for evaluation and treatment. And the chief psychiatrist at the Evans Army hospital noted that "disinhibited behavior is quite common amongst individuals with brain injuries of this kind, and may have contributed to his episodes of behavioral dyscontrol in the past 6–8 months." Teresa's hoping it's enough to convince the district attorney to throw out his domestic-violence conviction and to get the Army to switch his administrative discharge process to a medical retirement with benefits.

Darren's potential medical retirement is the latest of several promising developments at Fort Carson. The installation and others like it have implemented "warrior transition units," where soldiers with physical or psychological injuries are allowed downtime for care and rehabilitation.

"In response to an identified need that soldiers and leaders required further awareness and education on mental health, Fort Carson developed a training program to help leaders and soldiers better understand how to identify behavioral health problems and provide assistance to their battle buddies," says McNutt.

The Behavioral Health Department at Evans has also stepped up its mental-health care efforts, she says, developing programs to readily identify and treat these problems. "With very few exceptions, soldiers can walk into the clinic without an appointment," she says. "By implementing these changes, it will reduce the time it takes to get an appointment and time spent waiting in the clinic to see a provider."

And—most surprising—Pogany, whose mug was once on Wanted posters across the base, now has the ear of Fort Carson's commander.

The phone calls are endless. *Always look on the bright side of life* . . . Soldiers, mothers, wives, looking for someone, anyone, who will listen, understand, maybe even help. *Always look on the bright side of life* . . . They come at night, on weekends, even during vacations. *Always look on the bright side of life* . . . They're calls Pogany has a hard time ignoring. One of the latest is from Denver resident Joel Hunt, a former Army specialist who was medically retired in October for chronic foot pain, a disability his Fort Carson superiors concluded didn't warrant a medical pension or health insurance. But Pogany has met with Hunt and knows that this veteran, who had a hard time filling out his own forms, has more problems than just a bad foot.

Collins, Pogany's girlfriend, worries about the constant phone calls. Maybe it's genetic, she thinks, a rebellious gene passed down from his insurgent father: "Asking him not to do this is like asking him not to breathe." Sometimes she wonders if it's something else, if he's fighting the same battle over and over again that started with his cowardice charge. "I think he struggles to keep balance in his life," she says. "What's his quote? 'If you want peace, fight for justice.' I think that's what drew him to the military, and that's why he does what he does now. I don't know anyone who is so persistent and committed."

Pogany's friends and colleagues say he's come a long way since he left the Army, since he was stuck in the toilet. He's found his calling, they say, and it's helped him get busy living. But even Pogany admits he's still broken, shattered—a fact he lives with every day. "It's a process," he says. "I'm definitely not all the way there. You have to understand, healing is ongoing. It's not something you do once and it's done."

Every time he drives through Monument on the way to Fort Carson, for example, he sees the face of his teammate Bill Howell, who put a gun to his own head and pulled the trigger. He used to dream about Howell, him and Kelly Hornbeck, his team sergeant who was killed in Iraq. "The Bill Howell dream was always the same. He and I meet up and talk. And he just says, 'Everything is going to be fine. Everything is gong to be okay. You will be okay.'" His dreams of Hornbeck, who called him a coward and refused him help in Iraq, aren't so encouraging. In one, Pogany runs into an old girlfriend at an airport. "She said, 'Hey, I want you to meet my new husband,'" Pogany remembers. "Then the guy turned around and it's Kelly, and half his head is blown off."

Now there's another casualty from his Special Forces team. Pogany just got the call: Lehman, the medic who'd passed out the Lariam pills, the *Green Eggs and Ham* guy, had checked himself into an on-base hotel last week, numbed his arm with Lidocaine, and then sliced himself up and bled to death—the day after Pogany had seen him. "What are the odds of me running into him the day before he takes his own life?" Pogany wonders, shaking his head. "I wish I could have . . ."

He trails off, thinking of their brief conversation. Lehman had talked about Iraq; how, in hindsight, Lariam had messed up everyone on the team. "Manic Mondays," they'd call the days they took the pills. Laughing, he even brought up the *Green Eggs and Ham* thing. But Lehman, looking disheveled, also mentioned his problems now, his PTSD and TBI, and said he was hoping Pogany could help him. Pogany gave him his card, and then that was it. "He took his green beret out of his pocket, put it on and walked out the door," Pogany remembers. "That was the last time I saw him."

The next time he sees him may be in his dreams. ⚬⟶

"HOW I GOT THAT STORY"

Westword *staff writer Joel Warner's writing career at the paper began in November 2005 with his first-ever food story (a profile of a McDonald's restaurant owner who'd set out to take over the world), one that landed him a nomination for a James Beard award. Prior to Westword, Warner worked at a variety of Colorado alternative newspapers, including the* Boulder Weekly *and the* Rocky Mountain Bullhorn *in Fort Collins, and also did a stint at the* Boston Globe. *Currently he's embroiled in covering Colorado's booming medical marijuana scene, but if anyone has any good story tips that could help him get off that never-ending beat, please do let him know. In October 2009 Warner was interviewed about his award-winning story on veteran Andrew Pogany by* Westword *Editor and AAN Editorial Committee member Patricia Calhoun as part of AAN's live chat series. The following is an edited version of that interview.*

Joel, I think it might be useful for you to talk a little about your background—since you've worked at a couple of alts, and the story started at the *Boulder Weekly*.
Sure thing. I've been working on and off for altweeklies since 2002.

And you first encountered Andrew Pogany when?
When I was working at the Boulder Weekly in 2005. I was actually inspired to look into military issues after attending the AAN West conference that year.

AAN at work! So you did it for the weekly, and then when did you decide to get back into it for *Westword*?
I maintained contact with Pogany after the story. While he had left the Army, he became a soldiers' advocate. He became a source not just for me, but for other reporters around the country: NPR, CNN, etc.

We've got a case in Colorado right now with one of those fake veterans who seem to pop up periodically. How did you know he was the real deal?
When I first met Pogany, he was already national news. He'd been labeled a coward in the media, sort of a counterpoint to "America's hero," Jessica Lynch.

It's interesting that his own war against the bureaucracy has been going on as long as the action in Iraq. Was that part of your reinitiating contact?

I had always maintained contact with him for story ideas. It wasn't until I started looking at the totality of the problems at Fort Carson that I realized *he* was a great story idea. Instead of finding one or two soldiers with PTSD or traumatic brain injuries and telling their stories, I contacted Pogany and told him I wanted to shadow him for a few weeks. I went with him when he visited soldiers and I tried to be as unobtrusive as possible. Later, as we were leaving, I would ask if I could spend some time with the soldiers at a later date. Many were willing to let me do so. They were eager to get their story out.

The combination of stories is so compelling. What kind of access did you have to military officials? Was it tough getting stories confirmed?

Fort Carson actually gave me a good amount of access. That's one of the techniques I've always used. I'm probably too nice to people. I came out right from the start and told the Fort Carson PR rep what I was doing.

Has Fort Carson become more accommodating as the war has gone on—and the returning vets continue to face such huge problems?

I think Fort Carson has become more willing to deal with the press. They've realized they don't have much choice. Also, Fort Carson and the Army seem to have finally accepted Pogany's role.

Is that true of military bases in general now? Or has Pogany really played a key role in changing things?

Finally, since we have more time to work on stories, PR reps at Fort Carson and elsewhere seem to appreciate the extra time we can give them to work with us. Pogany has become a well-recognized character in military circles. They know he's amassed some firepower—both with politicians and national media.

For all the attention Pogany has gotten, what surprised you most when you got to spend more time with him? It seems a very lonely, exhausting quest.

The most striking thing I took away was that Pogany, while much more healthy than he was when I first met him, still struggles with what he's gone through every day. It fuels him—but it's not an easy life.

Did other stories come out of this one?

Several other stories of soldiers in trouble came up. The challenge with those additional stories is a real tough one. There are so many horrible stories like that. How do you find the "right one" to write about? Sort of the same issue with all the people being detained because of their immigration status. I'd been trying to find a way around that before I hit on using Pogany as the central narrative.

Here's one: Army press releases. Since everything about the Army is so unique, even their boring old press releases can be useful. Example: I found one a few years ago that mentioned a fake Iraqi town that had been built on Fort Carson to help train soldiers in cultural sensitivity. Since it wasn't that controversial, I was allowed to visit it and got several stories out of it—about the soldiers training there, the props expert that built it, and, most interestingly, some of the Iraqi-Americans hired to play insurgents.

Yeah, instead of Army issues, lately I've been writing about Colorado's medical marijuana explosion. It's a fascinating, complicated issue, but I think I'm ready to focus on some other issues. It's good to find a balance, though—of fun, attention-grabbing stories like pot, and harder stuff like Pogany. Keeps us altweekly folks on our toes.

Private Trauma

Patrick Michels

MARCH 20, 2008

Preston Wheeler woke up disoriented in a ditch along U.S. Highway 71 in western Arkansas.

Gradually, it came back to him: the 18-wheeler passing on the two-lane road, the sharp pop, the cloud of dust from a blown rear tire. The flashback came as he veered right to avoid the blowout's debris.

As his car left the asphalt, a scene replayed: Preston was back on a dead-end road in Ad Duluiyah, north of Baghdad, trapped behind a flipped tractor-trailer. Four gunmen coaxed a fellow driver out of the truck ahead of his in the convoy. He heard the shots as the men executed the driver in the street. Their white pants flapped in the wind, the road behind them streaked with blood. Preston regained consciousness alone in his Chevy Cavalier.

His psychiatrist had warned him against returning to his job as a driver on the open road. So instead, he drove semitrailers in circles around a Tyson Foods Inc. lot, hauling live chickens to the slaughterhouse—100,000 a day.

It wasn't supposed to be like this. He, of all people, should have known.

The U.S. employs more civilian contractors than soldiers in Iraq. Preston's former employer, Houston-based KBR Inc., formerly a subsidiary of Halliburton Co., is the largest company operating there. During five years of war, the Army and some contractors have improved the ways they detect and treat post-traumatic stress disorder. KBR has not, according to its wounded employees. KBR's screening procedure is left to on-site counselors who identify employees who've faced trauma, rather than a routine screening for all workers when they return home. Workers often have to recognize their own symptoms and request, or sometimes fight for, treatment through the company's insurance carrier. "When employees/former employees contact KBR, the company assists them in making a claim," says Heather Browne, a KBR spokesperson.

Many civilian contract employees come from East Texas and neighboring states like Arkansas, the result of recruiting in dead-end towns. A job in Iraq that triples your current pay doesn't look so bad when you're in debt even after a long, hard year of trucking at home.

Preston had a simple dream: He wanted to build his own house in the woods near his hometown of Wickes, Arkansas. Given the local economy, it was more fantasy than plan. Sometimes you have to leave your hometown for a job; he knew that. Tired of chasing oil, cement, and trucking jobs, he hoped a year or two in Iraq would be his shortcut to a new home, a clear credit record, and enough money to support his son.

"'Round here, you either got something or you don't," Preston says, driving through Wickes. "Most people are content as they can be with the way their life is."

With the local logging industry running on machines instead of manpower, the Tyson plant is the only major employer left.

It was a cold day last January, and Preston, who'd just turned 40, wore a green Carhartt jacket and a camouflage hat. He sat behind the wheel of his girlfriend Kellie's truck while she and her kids, Sierra and Allan (all but Kellie call him Bubba), rode in the back. Preston is of medium height and average build—a few dozen pounds lighter, he says, since he quit drinking a few months earlier.

He drove past the Wickes housing project, a long row of structures tucked behind a thin stand of pines, where he lived when he was young. Older cars shared the front yard with lawn mower parts and mud-covered toys. "I guarantee you, if my dad knew I went to Iraq, he would flip plumb out," Preston says.

The year before Preston was born, his dad came back from Vietnam missing both his legs. Wayne Wheeler was with the Marines in 1966 when he stepped on a land mine in Da Nang. When he returned, he was sullen, often drunk, and prone to fits of rage at home. Over a few years, Preston's mother, Yvonne, realized she had a painful decision to make—tougher still with four children and no job of her own. "Daddy was real abusive," Preston says. "I don't really remember them breaking up. I just remember we moved."

Yvonne remarried and moved to Texarkana. Preston spent high school getting into fights and skipping class. He flunked out of his junior year twice, then dropped out, got his GED, and went to work at the chicken plant. Later he left for oil field work in Bakersfield, concrete work in Oklahoma City, and a string of trucking jobs. He married and divorced twice. His son, Blaine, from his first marriage, lives with him today and is a senior at Wickes High. After every job and each woman, Preston always came home.

By 2005, he was deep in debt from house expenses and medical bills, and didn't see a way clear. If there were two kinds of folks in Wickes, the ones with something and those without, he could see which group he was headed for.

Preston knew of people from town who had driven trucks in Iraq. "They came back no problem, so I decided maybe I'd go over there and I wouldn't have a problem," he says. "It wasn't desperation. I just knew that was a lifetime opportunity to go make that kind of money. I wanted a home so bad, I was willing to pay that price."

In 2005, when his second wife admitted to cheating on him, he asked her to move out, making his choice to leave simple. Summing up his state of mind at the time, he remembers thinking, "I got nobody else. It's just me, and I'm gonna do this or get killed."

As it happened, fate found a third way.

Five hundred million served," signs should read at KBR's dining halls. The scale of KBR's accomplishments, enumerated in a company press release, is awesome: 272 million pounds of mail and 3.5 billion gallons of fuel delivered, over 3.7 million miles of road traveled, 32 million clothing bundles laundered worldwide—just since December 2001.

The private sector that accompanies the U.S. military in Iraq is an elaborate patchwork of contracts and subcontracts, but with the Army's all-purpose support work in its pocket, KBR is the two-ton gorilla. Through May 2007, according to the *Washington Post,* KBR received $19.7 billion under a contract known as LOGCAP III. Pentagon boosters promised the contract would lead to a more responsive approach to the war. Private employees would be cheaper to train and easier to get rid of when the job was done.

Whistleblowers and the media have called out KBR for waste and overbilling, such as recording more meals than were actually served, or favoring new equipment orders over repairs. Yet in April 2007, KBR was one of three companies awarded the Army's next LOGCAP contract. Depending on how much mail and laundry the military generates, KBR could gross as much as $50 billion from the work over the next decade.

Like other new hires, Preston knew there was big money in KBR when he reported to orientation at Greenspoint Mall in Houston. All he wanted was a piece.

Dimly lit and often eerily vacant, Greenspoint isn't an ideal place to spend one's last weeks before going off to war. The mall can't shake its old nickname—"Gunspoint"—it took on after a spate of violent crimes in the mid-1990s. A few days after Thanksgiving 2007, as the holiday shopping season began, Greenspoint was evacuated after a murder-suicide at the Body Luxuries lingerie store. A mall Santa Claus led one wave of fleeing shoppers to the parking lot.

Nearly every worker KBR sends to Iraq passes through orientation in Greenspoint, in a large unmarked space that used to be a Montgomery Ward store. Trainers show recruits how to put on chemical suits, warn them to drink plenty of water, and remind them how much money they'll be making. The other end of the mall has Army, Navy, and Air Force recruiting stations, so lunchtime at the food court can look like a Green Zone mess hall—except that in Iraq, the KBR recruits serve the food.

Preston says he didn't mind the surroundings or the two weeks of waiting without pay. His mind was occupied with dreams of how the money would change his life back home. He signed on to drive a truck for around $8,000 a month—"More money than I'd ever seen in a month's time," he says.

At the end of the second week, his name finally came up on the flight list, and a bus took him 30 minutes down the road to Bush Intercontinental Airport. When he left Houston in April 2005 it was his first ride in an airplane.

After security contractors, truck drivers probably have the most dangerous private jobs in Iraq. Running from base to base in long convoys, they make easy targets for improvised explosive devices, snipers, even rock-throwers. But with pay starting near $100,000 annually, a trucker can earn twice what his military escort makes. On base, where most private contractors work, the danger is much more limited, and the pay can be even better.

As Preston learned, though, the cash comes at a price. Soldiers carry guns; truck drivers don't, although Preston kept a knife in his cab. While troops generally get a warm welcome home, a trucker coming back is as likely to be called a war profiteer as a patriot. Contractors often return without anybody nearby who can relate to their experience, and without a Veterans Affairs office they can turn to for help. Private insurance carriers take on that role.

Preston lived in Camp Anaconda, a sprawling, makeshift town of tens of thousands where KBR bases its Iraq operations, about 65 miles north of Baghdad, at Balad. He drove a refrigerated truck—a "reefer"—on convoy runs every couple of days, and between runs, he killed time in his one-room hooch. Fine desert dust collected on his clothes. He sat around watching pirated DVDs bought from Filipino laundry workers, and called home to talk to his mom, Yvonne, and his son, Blaine, who was staying with her.

Preston asked his mom to take $600 out of his bank account and send him a digital camera. At first he thought the silver Sony CyberShot was too small, but he was happy with his pictures of exotic arches, run-down buildings, and Iraqi children waving from the roadside. On a laptop he bought in Dubai, he made a slide show set to the Toby Keith song "How Do You Like Me Now?" and dedicated it to his ex-wife.

"How do you like me now, / Now that I'm on my way? / Do you still think I'm crazy / Standin' here today?"

Preston had $20,000 saved by the end of August, when he came home for R and R. He visited his family in Texarkana and took them all out to dinner. Preston took Blaine and a friend on a weekend trip to Dallas, and spent $8,000 on a new four-wheeler. "I just got a taste of the money," he says. He relished the easy lifestyle that came with the extra cash and was unconcerned as his savings dwindled. "It don't take long. $20,000 is nothing," he says. There was plenty more waiting in Iraq.

When he returned to Anaconda, he found he'd been transferred from reefer trucks to flatbeds—news that hit him hard in the gut. Reefer assignments had given him a day on base between runs, but flatbed drivers left the wire almost daily. The odds had just doubled against him.

On the morning of September 20, 2005, a week and a half after his return, Preston joined a few drivers for a briefing with their Virginia National Guard escorts. They were headed to Forward Operating Base McKenzie, 45 minutes away. The drivers were told they'd be back in time for lunch. Preston's white Mercedes-Benz was the No. 5 truck, near the front. Yvonne had asked him to try out the video mode on his camera, so as he left Anaconda he pressed the record button and aimed the camera at the road.

As Preston barrels down the highway, the video catches a dusty road, with green brush and occasional palms. The video doesn't reveal it, but a military navigator had accidentally directed the convoy down the wrong road.

The pavement narrows, and low buildings creep close to the road as the convoy passes through Ad Duluiyah, a town about halfway to Camp McKenzie. Preston pulls closer to the Humvee ahead of him as they roll down the middle of the street past markets, homes, and Iraqis paused at the roadside to watch.

"KBR just took two rocks, right side," calls a voice on the radio. Preston turns his camera to the left and trains it on an Iraqi boy. The child bends down to grab a rock, takes a few running steps, and hurls it against Preston's truck. More drivers report rocks, then broken windows and windshields. "It's raining rocks," one driver says. Preston's driver's side window shatters.

The road dead-ends at the banks of the Tigris River, and the trucks regroup. Realizing they've taken a wrong turn, the convoy commander decides to turn around and push on to McKenzie. "We just missed our turn. We gotta go through that hellhole again," Preston tells the camera. "This is gonna be one good video right here, boy."

The camera continues to run. The streets of Ad Duluiyah reappear, this time without the people who had lined them minutes earlier. Other drivers would later recall passing an old man who made an ominous chopping motion with his hands. A distant cracking noise and a small bullet hole in Preston's windshield signal the onset of real trouble. "Goddamn!" he screams. The bullet has passed just above Preston's head. The camera pans down for a moment.

The lead truck's driver, Christopher Lem, is killed by a gunshot to the neck. His truck overturns, blocking half the road. Preston's truck shakes as a rocket-propelled grenade hits where the trailer is hitched. The cab pitches forward off its back wheels as warning buzzers let out an urgent whine. Voices on the radio tell him to push through, but Preston repeatedly radios back that truck five is stuck, and he needs help.

"You're damn right I'm scared," he tells the camera, hiding in the sleeper space behind the passenger seat. The city street is eerily empty, its silence occasionally broken by staccato gunfire. "I'm going home when this shit's done."

Far ahead, too small to distinguish on camera but clear enough for Preston to see, four men stop at the immobilized No. 3 truck and coax out the driver, Sascha Grenner-Case. Moments later they execute him in the street. They move on to truck four and fire up into its cab, at driver Kevin Dagit. "Oh Jesus, they just killed him," Preston shouts.

Up to that point, he's kept the camera recording without knowing quite why. After Dagit's killing, he puts the camera down and turns it off.

Two bullets pierced his truck after that, tearing through his right arm and settling under his shoulder. He had enough time to tear off a sleeve and tie up the wound as the four gunmen walked slowly toward him. "The truck wouldn't move, so I was just stuck there. It wasn't a matter of do or die, 'cause there was nothing I could do. My only option was to die," he says. Fighting an urge to get out and run, he took out a long black knife and gripped it tight, waiting to defend himself. "All I knew was, the first feller that stuck his head up in my door, I was stickin' him," he says.

"I was just going into a panic, 'cause I knew my number was coming up. I was on the radio with somebody, I don't know who. I saw them walking to my truck, and I told him to tell my son I loved him. They kept telling me, don't say that, you're gonna be alright. And I told him, I'm not gonna make it out of this one."

The men walked slowly, laughing with each other, he recalls, until they heard the Army helicopters arrive. The sound sent his would-be attackers running, and in that instant Preston was handed back his life.

Preston's mother Yvonne always assumed someone from KBR would call if Preston were hurt, but the first she heard of the attack was from her son. "He said, 'Momma I've been shot,' and I just went all to pieces. There was no way I could get to him," she says. "And he said, 'Momma, but I'm alive.'"

After a week in the Army hospital in Ramstein, Germany, Preston flew home to Texarkana, where Yvonne, her husband Odis, Blaine, and other family members awaited. The hospital in Texas suggested sending him to a nursing home to recover, but Yvonne decided he would stay with her in Hooks, Texas, just west of Texarkana.

The hospital couldn't send a nurse every day, so Yvonne learned how to take care of Preston all over again. Doctors put an IV port in his chest, and his mother injected him with antibiotics every six hours. Preston had to keep the wound dry, so he depended on her for sponge baths. She'd remove the bandages, clean the wound, and cover it again. Preston says it was big enough "to fit a Skoal can." "I would set the alarm, get it all ready, and get him through the night," Yvonne says. "But when he started having those flashbacks, it was bad."

Preston says, "I didn't realize the effect it had on me till after I got home. I'd wake up dreaming about it, and be up at four or five o'clock in the morning, setting on the porch and crying by myself. Didn't want to wake up my mom or [step] dad, so I'd just sit out there and cry. I had a lot of mornings like that, man."

For six months, Preston lived with Yvonne, trying to raise his right arm and waiting for the wound to heal. He left the house only to smoke cigarettes in the driveway and watch traffic pass. He didn't get many visitors, but he didn't want them anyway. A musical wall clock became the soundtrack to his days, playing recorded chime versions of "Hey Jude" and "Here Comes the Sun" while he ticked away the time. Day after day began with Preston crying on the porch. "Mostly it was from the dreams. The reality of what happened went on forever. It seemed like it was never gonna end," he says. A psychiatrist in Texarkana diagnosed Preston with PTSD.

For a while he considered returning to Iraq, but his therapist convinced him that was a bad idea. The psychiatrist told him he shouldn't drive big trucks anymore. Preston understood why: Loud noises tend to trigger the most intense flashbacks. "That's my biggest fear driving a truck, that I'll blow a tire on the highway and end up taking out an innocent family," he says.

Preston had loved trucking since he was a boy, loved the freedom he felt racing down open road. Now that he couldn't haul on the highway, he found the job at the chicken plant near Wickes, making the same four right turns 20 times every shift.

To date, about 1.5 million people visiting YouTube have witnessed the intense, emotional moments Preston was sure would be his last. The digital recording of the attack has become one of the most extraordinary pieces of Preston's story, making a traumatic, near-death experience an oddly public event. Often war memories cloud over with time until just a few details remain, but what Preston saw and felt that day is inextricably tied to footage he can replay whenever he likes. He says he's watched the video—"studied it"—hundreds of times.

Preston had emailed the video to other drivers in the convoy, or their families, but says it went public after another driver's wife sent the movie to Canadian television. The video made the mainstream media rounds within a year after the attack. Preston did a remote interview with CNN's Anderson Cooper, and the ABC Evening News flew him to New York. After his appearance on ABC News, he earned a second trip around the news cycle for his accusation that the Virginia National Guard escort had abandoned his convoy. (In his video, the Humvee ahead of him drives past the wreckage as Preston calls for help. While the rest of the escort fought off the attack behind him, the lead gun trucks had pushed forward to regroup for a counterattack.)

Five hundred YouTube users have added comments to Preston's video. Most write about the war, America, or Iraq in general, often in the raw, crass style typical of online comment threads. A few are aimed at Preston: some are sympathetic, but others criticize what he says in the video, his unarmed presence in a war zone, his decision to go to Iraq in the first place. Preston has fired back at some of the comments.

Preston became a cult sensation in Australia after a TV station accidentally played a few of his terrified words on a loop, over and over, for five minutes, during a prime-time documentary about a train wreck. "I tell you what man, you Google

'Jesus Christ, help us all Lord,' and my name comes right up," he says.

If his new job didn't give him that old thrill of asphalt rushing under his feet, at least it took his mind off his memories. It also helped that his old friend Kellie worked in the office; he spent his entire shift driving circles around her. A few months after she divorced her husband—an old friend of Preston's—the two started dating, and when Preston moved into a rented house in Wickes, Kellie and her two kids moved in with him.

The memories remained, though, and something felt unsettled. It was more than Kellie and her kids, or Blaine, could distract him from. Preston began following the news from Iraq, looking for people who had been through what he had. "I got TV 'cause I was bored, but next thing you know, 'Everybody Loves Raymond' wasn't so important to me—it was CNN," he says.

While Preston was broadcast, published, and streamed online around the globe, in person he grew more and more shut in. He watched CNN compulsively. "He confined himself to the house, and there was no outside world," Kellie says.

"I didn't know what I could get out and do," Preston says. "My getting out and doing something was going to get a 30-pack of beer, and I'd come home to drink it."

Worse than the memories of what he had seen was the urgent sense of being penned in on that street. It came back to him driving, when he got stuck behind a slow driver; it came back in a crowded room. That need to take control, to fight his way out if necessary, grew more intense. "It would be my pleasure to oblige the next feller that wanted to try me out," he says. "Win or lose, I wouldn't care. I just got so much built up inside of me, you know? I've always been good at driving a truck, and hurting somebody. Those two things."

While he avoided leaving his home, he became resentful when Kellie spent time away. After one argument in October 2007, Preston ordered Kellie to leave the house.

Coincidentally, a week later some truck drivers from his old convoy had a meeting in Porter, Texas, a suburb north of Houston. Preston drove down to see them.

American Contractors in Iraq is one of the only national support networks for injured contractors. It's made up of a loose affiliation of contractors and their families. The group's website, americancontractorsiniraq.com, was founded by Jana Crowdet, a contractor's wife, who posts information about filing insurance claims and coping with PTSD.

Art Faust, the truck driver who organized the conference, had been five trucks behind Preston in the convoy. The No. 2 truck driver, Terry Steward, who spent weeks recovering beside Preston after the attack, was there, too; Preston stayed with Steward and his wife in their RV. Other drivers welcomed him warmly. Some told Preston his video helped them recover after their own attacks.

A Houston therapist named Sandra Dickson spoke to the group, describing the signs of PTSD. Being quick to fight, developing relationship trouble, and sitting in front of the news for hours on end were all typical signs, she said. Though Preston had already been diagnosed, he was surprised when her description nailed him so well. He thought that the shut-in he'd become wasn't really him, that maybe he'd never find what he was looking for on the news. Preston raised his hand when Dickson asked for questions.

"Is it my fault that I'm an asshole?" he asked. "It's not your fault, but it is your responsibility," she said.

Preston drove home and took down his satellite dish.

He reminded himself not to let the memories take over, the way his father did. "I understand him now, to an extent, because of the post-traumatic stress. But it took me a long time to forgive my dad," Preston says. "I went out there to his grave and told him. He let it consume him. It's something I don't intend to let happen to me."

Kellie came back, and the two remained together until mid-March, when she left again after Preston and her 10-year-old son, Bubba, got into a shouting match. The boy's exuberance, and loud balloon popping in the living room, had long tested Preston's will, but the two clearly shared a bond. Preston said Bubba, a constant shadow in a matching camouflage jacket, helped him focus on the future and keep his memories from taking over.

Ironically, Preston may yet end up with the money he wanted from Iraq—possibly much more—precisely because of the attack. The claim he filed under the Defense Base Act, a World War II-era law providing generous worker's compensation for civilians supporting the U.S. military overseas, may settle soon, and he could end up with a lump sum that would more than pay for a new house in Wickes.

His lawyer, Gary Pitts, who represents many contractors in similar claims, says Preston is lucky, legally speaking. Some of Pitts's clients are fighting drawn-out claims with American International Group Inc., the insurance carrier for KBR, over soft-tissue and back injuries that are tougher to document than two bullets in the right arm. In disputed PTSD claims, Pitts says, the case often comes down to opposing opinions from the contractor's therapist and AIG's in-house expert. "It's a shootout every time," Pitts says. Preston's case is unique because if AIG asks him to document his trauma, all he has to do is push "play."

Preston keeps a sketch of the floor plan for the house he says he'll build someday, settlement or not. His son Blaine has signed to join the Navy after graduation, and may go off to war himself. "If I can build my home, then I'm satisfied I've reached the goal I set out to reach in my life," Preston says. No matter how well the money works out, he wishes he hadn't gone to Iraq. "I can live with the physical part, the injuries," he says. "But I would give it all back to not have the memories." ❖

"HOW I GOT THAT STORY"

Patrick Michels is a staff writer at the Dallas Observer, which he joined as web editor in 2008. A San Francisco native, he studied magazine journalism at Northwestern University and photojournalism at the University of Texas at Austin, with two years above the Arctic Circle in Kotzebue, Alaska, in between. His long-term work includes continued coverage of civilian contractors and competitive eating. In October 2009 Patrick Michels, along with his former Texas Observer editor Jake Bernstein, participated in AAN's live chat series; the following is an edited version of that interview, which was conducted by North Coast Journal editor and AAN Editorial Committee member Hank Sims.

So where did this story begin, for you? Did you discover Wheeler's story from news coverage, and realize that it also spoke to conditions of returning civilian contractors? Or were you already looking for a way into that larger story when you came across him?

Patrick Michels: Yeah, at first I was looking for a way into the story of injured contractors. I was starting work on a master's project at UT-Austin in photojournalism, looking for a subject to follow around with a camera.

But this guy, on your turf, had become something of a media sensation, I take it.

Patrick Michels: It's true, but I hadn't heard of him until I met him at a gathering of injured contractors. He sort of blew in off the highway from Arkansas at this meeting in Houston, and everyone seemed to know who he was.

When did you focus down on him, and why?

Patrick Michels: A few other truckers from his convoy were at this meeting in Houston, and he was the one they were all glad to see. I approached Jake at the *Texas Observer* about a story on the subject, and we got to talking about which of the contractors I'd met would fit the bill best. Preston's story jumped out for a couple of reasons—the first one was that he had a physical injury—he'd been shot. That didn't leave much gray area because he'd been videotaping the attack and there was plenty of footage to draw from.

And it was his sort of renown in that room, rather than in the world at large, that made you decide on him?

Patrick Michels: To an extent, but at that time, I was trying to meet as many of these guys as possible for a photo series. Only after the fact, looking at whose story would sustain that narrative best, did we settle on Preston's story in particular.

Jake Bernstein: I think we realized that Preston as 'the Internet sensation' cut both ways. It also allowed us to tell a story about a guy that people thought they knew rather than who they really knew. The video itself also became a great narrative device.

You have to cover a lot of ground in this story. You want as much of Wheeler's personal narrative in there—both his gripping war tale and his compelling life pre- and post-Iraq. But his story is also emblematic, so you want to broaden the focus. Was it difficult to balance the two? Space is obviously finite.

Patrick Michels: Jake is probably still having nightmares about this, but the original draft was a bit longer than the piece that finally ran. There were so many interesting nuggets to the story, cutting it down was a challenge. From the beginning, though, it was his life at home—what drove him over there, and what happened after he came back—that interested me

Jake Bernstein: Yes, his first draft was a novella. What I loved about what Patrick brought to us was the amazing detail: stuff like the first time he ever rode on an airplane was when KBR flew him to Iraq. It was a very compelling package.

There's a sort of family chain in there: his father, him, his son, all going to war. It was subtle, but it was present in the story. Did you make a conscious decision to keep that in the subtext?
Patrick Michels: That really was one of the things that drew me most to his character—the idea that he's a new kind of soldier dealing with the same thing his father went through. The detail of his son was almost an afterthought, something his son mentioned in the driveway as I was getting into my car. Just a quick note, his son was planning to join the Navy before, but since has enlisted in the Army and he'll be driving a Bradley in Iraq soon.

It may be a small thing, but I noted how you refer to him by his first name throughout. Is that house style at the *Observer*, or did you make a conscious decision to personalize him in that way?
Jake Bernstein: It was a conscious decision. We usually used last names but it was a story about this guy's inner-life as much as his outer one. We wanted it to be as immediate and intimate as possible.

Patrick Michels: I felt like using his first name was most natural in such a personal story.

Is the fact that Preston's incident was documented part of why you chose him—because we talk about this issue a lot, trying to vet stories from Iraq.
Patrick Michels: It certainly made that aspect simpler—more than that, though, I was thankful to have that detail to draw on when I was writing. I was also lucky enough to have three different drivers from that convoy to talk to and gather anecdotes from.

What kind of time did you spend with Preston?
Patrick Michels: After that initial weekend in Houston, when I spent a couple days with him and other drivers, I made a trip up to his home in rural Arkansas for a long weekend visit. I stayed at his house, and shadowed him for four days straight.

Do you have any idea how he's doing now, if he has stuck to his resolve?
Patrick Michels: Sure, I just spoke with him today and his PTSD has actually been worse since the story came out. He's still receiving his checks from AIG, but he had to quit his job and is back living with his mother in Texarkana.

Was he open to the idea of a profile from the beginning? It's always difficult to get people to talk about their hardships, and I would have supposed it would be doubly so in the case of this kind of severe trauma.

Patrick Michels: It's true, many of the guys I've met who've been through this kind of thing are more guarded, understandably. But Preston was always very open, right from the start.

What advice would you have for other journalists who want to try to tackle this big subject? Any pitfalls, resources, warnings, thoughts?

Jake Bernstein: Resources are a huge issue. We were able to piggyback on other work that Patrick was doing, so it made it more manageable.

Did the story change policy in any way, as far as you know? Was it well received by the injured contractors?

Patrick Michels: It was well received by the other contractors I've heard from, and I keep in touch with them as their legal issues move along. In terms of policy changes, there's just now some attention coming from Congress—I think *ProPublica*'s more recent work, for instance, has made a bigger impact on policy changes underway—and that's encouraging.

FOOD WRITING

CIRCULATION 50,000 AND OVER

"Breaking Free"

by Jonathan Gold, *L.A. Weekly*

"The weave of humor and erudition is irresistible. It's hard to come up with better prose-stylists writing about food today."—Brett Anderson, New Orleans Times-Picayune

CIRCULATION UNDER 50,000

"The Jester's Quest"

by Christina Waters, *Santa Cruz Weekly*

"Deeply researched, crisply written, richly informative."—Mollie Katzen, *author of* The Moosewood Cookbook

Breaking Free

Jonathan Gold

The magic of wine is this: Even at a restaurant you don't particularly care for, say a Venice wine bar populated with trust-fund dudes and winking navel rings, rubbery scallops and cured-meat platters that wouldn't be out of place at the Olive Garden, even after six duff courses, it is possible to chase a simple plate of gnocchi with a glass of South African Syrah, and the combination of food and wine is so stunningly right that the floor drops away and the ceiling turns to clouds, and you are left with an animal sense of well-being that lasts all afternoon. Wine people know all about these moments—that's why the wines capable of providing them can cost several hundred dollars a bottle. But they, along with many chefs, know wine's dirty little secret: You don't have to spend a fortune. If the wine is good enough, transcendence is only a lamb chop away.

The best wine program in Los Angeles at the moment may be at Bastide, which is a tiny, staggeringly chic restaurant tucked away in the Melrose Place decorator district, on a block where almost every shop bears notices from *Elle Decor* or *Vogue*. You know what you've heard about the writers' strike driving all of Hollywood back to takeout Chinese food and microwaved burritos? Somebody here didn't get the memo, because reservations are as hard to snag as Lakers floor seats, and Bastide—run at the whim of Joe Pytka, a television-commercial auteur who has directed talents as diverse as John Lennon and Bugs Bunny—is just lousy with Hollywood guys, who wear the kinds of thrown-together designer outfits that H&M knocks off at about 5 percent of the price. Pytka displays a lot of art here, but the most stunning visual in the restaurant may be the array of bottles in the dining room holding the chef's table, including some vintages that were on the vine when Abigail Adams was living in the White House.

Not long before Pytka lured Walter Manzke to become the third chef of the restaurant, he managed to hire Pieter

Verheyde as his sommelier, a young Belgian who had become well-known in the wine world for his work as wine director for Alain Ducasse's restaurants in Paris and New York, a spry cat with the impish, otherworldly presence of a medieval alchemist and a mind for wines that may rival that of Garry Kasparov's for chess. Bastide's 1,400-strong wine list, once famous for its depth and obstinate Frenchness, suddenly ranged all over the wine-growing world.

At Ducasse in New York, Verheyde's list was classic, but idiosyncratic and expensive, with a strong specialty in wines that were otherwise unavailable, and he discovered a gift for persuading customers to drink wines outside their comfort zone. At Bastide, he's like a teenager with a powerful new motorcycle—he knows he should be responsible, but he can't stop popping wheelies. The first weeks the restaurant was open, the cellar wasn't quite ready, and Verheyde's by-the-glass wine pairings were included in the price of dinner—stunned customers found themselves drinking things like Transylvanian Kiralyleanyka, a six-dollar wine whose bright acidity happened to make a piece of seared sea bass pop in a way that no grand cru Chablis ever could. At the moment, more than 90 percent of Bastide's customers sign on for the wine pairings he designed to go along with the tasting menus, at the not-insignificant price of $60, $90, or $190 per person.

I'm not usually much for wine pairings. With tasting menus, I like to order a bottle or two of food-friendly Alsatian pinot blanc or Piemontese dolcetto and let the dishes sort of lean into the wine: There are only so many flavors one's mind can process over the course of a meal. The surprising thing about Verheyde's pairings is not just that they are appropriate and delicious—anybody could do that. It's that the mind-blowing wines are not only the tastes of $500-a-bottle Echezeaux with the roasted duck or the sweet SGN pinot gris from Zind Humbrecht with the perfectly ripened Epoisses. They include the salty, slightly oxidized Coenobium made by the sisters at a Trappist monastery in north Lazio, the rose champagne from Sacy, Syrah from California's Central Coast, and twinned vintages of Gruner Veltliner from Donabaum's Danube-adjacent vineyards, all of which you could find for $30 a bottle or so if you knew where to look (most of us assuredly don't), and all of which not only complement Manzke's cooking but combine into a new thing, a third taste, the kind of harmony that you look for every time you pop a cork. Let the snobs and the proper East Coasters have their Lynch Bages, their Opus and their oaky Chardonnays. Verheyde's list tastes like freedom.

Every important restaurant city has a wine culture of its own. After that first meal at Bastide—after sublime experiences at Cut, where the sommelier Dana Farner looks like an indie-rock goddess and insinuates the sublimity of her $152 Blaufrankisch with grilled Japanese beef loin; after surgical-strike wine pairings at the now-defunct Bin 8945; after a flight of biodynamic Loire wines at Lou; after Chablis and oysters at Sgt. Recruiter; after a glass of Scholium Vermentino at 750ml; after the 14th time a Los Angeles sommelier brought out cold sake instead of wine with the marinated hamachi sashimi; after an oldish Loire white at Hatfield's . . . after hundreds of L.A. restaurant meals—it is clear that there is a vivid wine scene in Los Angeles at the moment. It is not always clear what it happens to be.

In the United States, at least, the wine culture of a city often has more to do with the efforts of a few obsessed people than it does with factors that you'd think would be more important, such as climate, the ethnicity of its population, and the physical proximity of vineyards. My favorite Bay Area restaurants, which should be awash in the big, glossy wines from nearby Napa and Sonoma, tend instead to specialize in handmade wines from the Rhone and the south of France, probably because of the influence of Chez Panisse and local wine importers like Kermit Lynch and North Berkeley Wine. The best Portland lists, while featuring a comprehensive roster of Northwest wines, are often deep in the sorts of boutique Northern Italian wines that rarely make it out of Piedmont. It is easier to find rare Burgundy in Manhattan than it is to find wines from nearby Long Island.

Greater Los Angeles may be the single biggest wine market in the United States, and it is situated just a couple of hours from the important winegrowing areas of Santa Ynez, Ojai, Temecula, and the Guadalupe Valley, but it rarely seems connected to those regions, and the shape of its taste is often hard to discern.

(It says something, I think, that some of my best wine experiences last year were at Ludobar and Laurent Quenioux's Bistro K, two excellent, now-defunct restaurants that happened to have a BYOB policy. There is something subversive about bringing your own '91 grand cru Alsatian Riesling and ancient bottles of Clape Cornas to dinner—it lets you think that you are getting away with something, and you are drinking really, really well.)

Fifteen-odd years ago, the boundaries of local taste were more clear. Manfred Krankl, now a revered winemaker but then the general manager at the restaurant Campanile, was obsessed with both Italian wines and tiny-production California wines. He, along with Valentino's Piero Selvaggio, educated Angelenos on the necessity of paying serious money for then-unpronounceable super-Tuscans, whites from the Alto Adige and and ink-dark Montepulciano d'Abruzzo. (For years, I don't think there was a cult California or Italian wine that hadn't at one time been poured by the glass at Campanile's bar, which was also early on Austrian wines.) Philip Reich and other sommeliers at Michael's shaped the idea of what a great California-dominated list might look like. Joachim Splichal put serious French wine back into play, although Hollywood has always nurtured a large corps of Francophile collectors. The most important chef in Los Angeles, then as now, was probably Wolfgang Puck, and his head sommelier Michael Bonaccorsi helped to form the idea of the eclectic modern list.

You remember pictures of the old wine guys, old-fashioned sommeliers, the stout, florid, usually foreign men wearing tuxedos two sizes too small, worn Florsheims, and bunch-of-grapes pins stabbed into their grosgrain lapels? They wore heavy pewter tastevins around their necks, possibly awarded at a grand ceremony in France, and they muttered a lot about vintages. You saw them in the movies—Hungarian actor S.Z. "Cuddles" Sakall made a career out of playing them. Charles Laughton corrected their pronunciation of "Montrachet."

Then one day we woke up, and the wine dude was the coolest guy in the room—profiled in magazines, rocking Comme des Garcons suits, riding motorcycles to tastings, cramming for certification exams with his cool friends. Sommeliers like Caitlin Stansbury, formerly of the Lodge, wore sexy pantsuits and brought serious wine to restaurants where the Aerosmith on the house iPod rarely dipped below stadium volume. Mark Mendoza at Sona matches wine to David Myers's precise cooking with the painstaking care of a project architect. David Rosoff at Mozza, who in a previous gig at Opaline was one of the few sommeliers to actually persuade the chef to cook to the contours of his wine, juggles the under-$50 Italian wines in the pizzeria and the pricier wines in the adjacent osteria and actually comes up with a coherent wine philosophy, even if that philosophy sometimes seems like Obscure + Italian = Good. Where else are you going to find the Slovenian Edi Simcic Merlot blend from Goriska Brda? Where else would you want to?

We started seeing curated wine shops, not full-service general emporia like Wally's, Red Carpet, or the Wine House, but groovy joints like Silverlake Wine, the Champagne-intensive Wine Expo in Santa Monica, and Mission Wine in South Pasadena, reflecting not just an inventory but a worldview, often with a subspecialty in esoteric but well-priced and satisfying bottles, in Ribolla Gialla and Teroldego and Cold Heaven Viognier. And after too many run-ins with the wrong Chilean Carmeneres, we've come to rely on the curators too.

(You have undoubtedly experienced the stages of wine disillusionment yourself: you fall in love with a California wine; you realize the French wine that the California wine is modeled on is cheaper than its clone; the French wine rockets to three figures; and then you sneak back to the first wine only to discover that you can no longer afford to drink that one, or even its New Zealand equivalent. It's a complicated process. It is why you are probably drinking more wines from Argentina and South Africa than you used to.)

If chefs can sometimes seem like studio engineers, technique-obsessed artists laboring for hours to create a single, dazzling effect, wine guys are like DJs, digging stuff out of the crates and rocking the party. Chefs have to spend long hours buried in carcasses to the elbow. Wine guys spend their mornings spitting and swallowing. Chefs spend their working vacations grilling quail for charity benefits in North Carolina. Wine guys fly to Paris and Verona. Chefs stagger home at two in the morning with blood on their clothing and bits of flour in their hair. Wine guys may also stagger home at two in the morning with blood on their clothing, but it is not generally part of the job description.

Sommeliers in Los Angeles operate under certain disadvantages. Angelenos don't drink as much as New Yorkers or Londoners—that second bottle of wine is incompatible with speeding home on the 405—and we're much more likely to drink our Petrus, should we be in the mood for it, at home. When we feel like a Santa Barbara Chardonnay, it's harder to talk us into ordering a bottle of Merseault. But we are people who live in neighborhoods with Tudor castles, Spanish haciendas, and modernist slabs all on the same block, and we're pretty much up for anything. Radikon Vitovska? Sure. The world is our vineyard.

RESTAURANTS FOR WINE LOVERS

A.O.C. The cheese-and-charcuterie-intensive inspiration for basically all of the new generation of wine bars, Suzanne Goin's A.O.C. is the kind of place you drop into for a glass of Cassis and maybe a bit of octopus, then a glass of Sancerre and a few grilled sardines, then a glass of Friulian Tocai and a plate of sliced prosciutto, then a glass of Corbieres and the tiniest plate of skewered grilled lamb with mint. Unless you were in the mood for the bacon-wrapped dates with Parmesan on the bar menu, which would go so nicely with one of those big southern Italian reds, or a ripe Crozier blue with a late-bottled port, or whatever creature comes with a bit of Goin's romesco sauce, or quite possibly the 12-hour pork belly. You could drink and eat like this all night if you remembered to make a reservation—and if A.O.C. didn't unreasonably stop serving at 11. *8022 W. Third St., L.A.*

BASTIDE To the small, food-obsessed population of Angelenos who know the difference between a sliver of Jabugo ham and a chunk of mere *jamon serrano,* Bastide is the Montrachet-slinging equivalent of Willy Wonka's chocolate factory, with *Space Jam* auteur Joe Pytka, its mad proprietor, taking the place of the estimable Mr. Wonka. After months on hiatus, Pytka reopened the doors with Walter Manzke, an ex-Patina chef, taking over the range, and Pieter Verheyde, the former sommelier at Ducasse in New York and Paris, assuming control of the wine list (see more in main essay). The menu is prix-fixe, $100 for seven courses; another $100 or $190, depending on how far you want to go, lets you experience Verheyde's eccentric wine pairing, which is one of the best shows in town. As in the last incarnation of Bastide, the food wobbles on the edge between familiarity and utter weirdness, things like deconstructed lobster tacos, abalone noodle soup, oyster shooters with wasabi ice and cylinders of roasted Beijing duck. Many, many cheeses. Dessert. A fifth or sixth glass of wine, probably a vintage port. And then out on the street. *8475 Melrose Place, West Hollywood.*

BLUE VELVET Wrapped around a glowing swimming pool that turns every vantage into a David Hockney painting, Blue Velvet is a hyperdesigned lounge fitted into the ground floor of a former Holiday Inn, with the cool blues of Staples Center and the financial-district skyscrapers just beyond. Some of the herbs and vegetables are harvested from an organic rooftop garden overlooking the Harbor Freeway. The well-priced wine list includes hard-to-find things like Failla Chardonnay and Denis Alaray's delicious Cairanne. From a spot by the window, downtown is as glamorous as the view from a penthouse in a Fred Astaire picture. It is doubtful, though, that Astaire ever dined on deep-fried yogurt balls with pureed greens and raisins, or on a vaguely Malaysian squid salad with kumquats, or on a Thai-flavored roast duck accompanied by its tempura-fried liver, or on smoked tofu with black lentils and cherry tomatoes. Kris Morningstar, who did stints at Patina, A.O.C., and the late Meson G, is the chef at Blue Velvet, and his engaged if inconsistent version of the eclectic world cuisine thing ranges over more of the globe than Angelina Jolie. I especially like the squab crepinette, which involves rare slices of the breast arranged over a sort of pillowlike sausage stuffed with pureed corn bread, pureed mushrooms and bits of the bird's own liver cooked into what tastes a little like Thanksgiving dinner on a small plate. *750 S. Garland Ave., L.A.*

BOTTLE ROCK The tables at Bottle Rock are the size of phonograph records, and the wobbly metal stools seem perpetually on the verge of collapse. The location, tucked behind a parking structure, is obscure, even if it is just a step or two from Culver City's new restaurant row. But Bottle Rock, which doubles as a wine shop, is among the most appealing of the wine bars that have opened on the Westside—because of the housemade pates, because of the tomato bread and the pressed sandwiches, because of the cheese board, but mostly because of the wine, which tends to be obscure, well chosen, and reasonably priced. The proprietors will open any bottle in the shop, from a simple California white to an aged Barolo, if you commit to two glasses of the stuff, and the chalkboard list of available wines can change 20 times a night. The little grilled chorizos are delicious. And there is always something good to drink for $5 a glass. After a screening at Sony or a show at one of the local theaters, Bottle Rock is the perfect place to kick it. *3847 Main St., Culver City.*

CAMPANILE Campanile has had one of the country's most influential Italian wine lists since the waning days of the 1980s, although sommelier Jay Perrin moved it solidly into the tannic territory of the French. Still, the restaurant is probably best-known for the prowess of Mark Peel, the LeBron James of the grill, who showcases more shades of fire and heat than any chef on Earth: rosemary-charred lamb, cedar-plank salmon, grilled prime rib with bitter greens. Grilled-fish soup is a sort of deconstructed bouillabaisse, a dish involving four or five sea creatures, each with a different cooking time and a different capacity for heat—a feat of kitchen virtuosity with the same degree of difficulty as a reverse 360 dunk. You'll be wanting a chilled bottle of Cassis with that. *624 S. La Brea Ave., Los Angeles.*

COBRAS & MATADORS Steven Arroyo is the Bill Graham of tapas in Los Angeles, the impresario who made the concept of Spanish drinks 'n' snacks as popular as sushi platters after dozens of others had tried and failed. And his dark, buzzy tapas parlors are teeming dens of olive oil and garlic, octopus and cured pig, grilled meats and pungent concoctions of seafood and paprika and beans rushed to the table still crackling in unglazed crocks. The Los Feliz restaurant has a nicely curated list of Spanish and South American wines; at the Hollywood restaurant, you buy your wines from the shop conveniently located next door. When you bring your prize back to the table, don't be surprised if the counter guy is standing right there, corkscrew in hand. *7615 W. Beverly Blvd., L.A.*

COMME CA David Myers's new brasserie has the look of a dining room restored to use after 70 years of disuse: black and white, lined with mirrors, dotted with actual French speakers. The oysters are briny, crisp and alive. The housemade terrines and pates are first-rate. There are snails in garlic butter and frisee salads with bacon and poached eggs, choucroute garni on Wednesdays and braised pork belly on Saturdays as well as great onion soup. At lunch, they have the best cheeseburgers in Los Angeles. The wine list includes French village wines that are uncannily appropriate with the food; the house carafe is a decent Cotes du Rhone. And there's that great, happy roar of music and people with a little too much wine in them, and the sense that somebody, somewhere in the restaurant is having the most memorable evening of her life. *8479 Melrose Ave., West Hollywood.*

CUT If Spago is at heart Wolfgang Puck's restaurant, its menu plumped out with his easygoing air, his enriched stocks and his Austrian favorites, Cut, despite obvious signs of the master's touch, is actually the love child of Puck's capo, Spago chef Lee Hefter, whose obsessions lie as much in technique as they do in produce, and whose menus of warm veal-tongue salads, succulent maple-glazed pork bellies, potato "tarte tatin" and flan-stuffed marrow bones tend to be more modern but less user-friendly than the dishes Puck turns out on his own. If you have $120 to spend on a steak, you might want to consider visiting Cut—and splitting the Kobe strip four or five ways, because unless you happen to play in the NFL, there is no way you can digest even a small example of the plutonium-dense meat by yourself. Ask sommelier Dana Farner to pour you something you've never seen before. Look out for the gnarliest Malbec of your life. Cut, designed to the teeth by Getty Center architect Richard Meier, is to the other steak houses in town what Spago was to the pizza parlors back in 1981. *9500 Wilshire Blvd., Beverly Wilshire Hotel, Beverly Hills.*

ENOTECA DRAGO In New York City, Italian wine bars multiply like mosquitoes. In Beverly Hills, we have Enoteca Drago, an outpost of Celestino Drago's pasta-driven empire, where you can chase a plate of prosciutto, a mess of baby octopods, or occasionally the elusive *lardo* — cured pig fat in the style of northwestern Tuscany, melted onto a slab of fried bread—with a glass of crisp Verdicchio from the Marches. Some of the wines are served in flights—sets of small pours arranged by grape or by region. Enoteca Drago does function as a full restaurant, although it is occasionally hard to remember this when you're floating in the middle of a Brunello reverie, but you will also find great pasta with pesto and one of the few proper versions of spaghetti carbonara in town. *410 N. Canon Drive, Beverly Hills.*

FORD'S FILLING STATION Ford's, whose chef-owner is Benjamin Ford, formerly of the restaurant Chadwick, is a bar that happens to have ambitious, organic food as opposed to a restaurant that happens to have a bar attached, a gastropub where you can enjoy pretty decent cooking while being bounced around like a pachinko ball. If you manage to power your way to a barstool or to an actual table, you will find most of the usual Los Angeles gastropub classics. If you like the fried Ipswich clams at Jar, you will probably like Ford's rudely indelicate version. There is a hamburger tricked out with blue cheese and an onion compote, the requisite butter-lettuce salad with bacon, and a decent selection of cheeses and meats, some of them procured from Armandino Batali in Seattle, to help down the White Dog Grenache. And there's butterscotch pudding for dessert. *9531 Culver Blvd., Culver City.*

FRAICHE Again we are in Culver City, where new, vaguely Mediterranean-influenced restaurants multiply like roly-poly bugs after a rain. And again we are in the presence of stripped brick, an open kitchen, an ambitious wine list rich in Rhône reds and Loire whites, and women who wear interesting eyeglasses and eat blood sausage instead of tofu. But the project from chef Jason Travi and Thierry Perez, a bluff Frenchman of classic maitre d' temperament who could probably sneer at your wine choice in any of nine different languages, is clearly a restaurant of love and obsession, from the meticulous *plateaux de mer* that rival the majestic displays of shellfish at Parisian brasseries to Travi's house-cured guanciale, from the careful juiciness of the Kurobuta pork chop with violet mustard to the subtle sweetness of the rabbit tortelli with brown butter, to the sweet delicacy of the smoked eel in a salad with arugula and mint. Fraiche is a tough reservation, but there is a separate bar area where you can drink "sangria" concocted from Grey Goose and farmers-market strawberries soaked in Grand Marnier, inhale giant portions of mussels and fries, and gingerly sip a Fernet-Branca when the bacchanalia becomes too much. *9411 Culver Blvd., Culver City.*

GRACE If Los Angeles restaurants are like rock bands, Neal Fraser is the glamorous indie-rock hero, a chef with a wobbly, idiosyncratic style that couldn't be further from the finish-fetish crowd pleasers, a detailed, strongly flavored New American cuisine, heavy on French technique and inspired by farmers-market produce and big slabs of animal. From pork belly to boar tenderloin, Fraser is clearly aspiring to greatness here—this is tremendously ambitious food. The wine list is strong on small California producers and big global reds. There's a program that introduces the occasional cellar-aged wine at a reasonable price. And there are freshly fried jelly doughnuts for dessert. What more could you want? *7360 Beverly Blvd., L.A.*

HUNGRY CAT To aficionados of the ruddy beasts, Crab Day at the newly expanded Hungry Cat is an annual event up there with Christmas and the Fourth of July, a chance to take a mallet to as many spicy boiled crustaceans as their wee stomachs can hold. Somebody call the mayor: It is an occasion worthy of a city holiday. But even on the other 364 days, the Hungry Cat is a civic treasure, a place to drop into for a dozen oysters or a bowl of shrimp, a crab cake or a bowl of chowder, a greyhound or a glass of Picpoul. The wine list is tiny and delicious. The primary object of desire here is the lobster roll, an abstracted rendition of the New England beach-shack standard transformed into a split, crisp, rectangular object about the size of a Twinkie. In Maine, the $20-plus it costs would buy you a lobster the size of a small pony. But we are in Hollywood, where the next acceptable lobster roll may be 2,800 miles away. *1535 N. Vine St., Hollywood.*

IL MORO In Bologna, one tends to eat very well—on prosciutto, Parmesan cheese and mortadella, on creamy emulsions and butter-basted chickens, on long-cooked ragus that incorporate the entire barnyard into a few tablespoonsful of sauce. It is not for nothing the city is often called Bologna the Fat. Il Moro, which recently transformed itself from a better-than-average office-building restaurant to a center of Bolognese cuisine, may be the only place in Los Angeles where you can taste the cooking of the region: the tiny, meat-stuffed cappelletti floating in a deep-yellow capon broth; the baked lasagna enriched with a wheelbarrowful of bechamel; the house-made pasta, alive under the teeth, buried under an ultradense sauce fashioned from tomatoes and minced pigeon. Prosciutto and salami are served in the traditional Modenese way, with *gnocco*—oblong, unsweetened beignets that would be equally appreciated by New Orleanians and Homer Simpson. What do you drink? Fizzy Lambrusco, of course. Tucked into the corner of the Westside where you might least expect a restaurant, busier at lunch than at dinner, it backs up onto a rather romantic patio, has an attached bar with occasional live music—and is usually pretty easy to slip into without a reservation even on a Saturday night. A useful restaurant. *11400 W. Olympic Blvd., W.L.A.*

JAR Any place in town can serve you a grilled T-bone, but Suzanne Tracht's snazzy steak house is strictly postmodernsville, chefly riffs on the strip steak and the porterhouse, the hash brown and the French fry that may or may not incorporate every last pea tendril and star-anise infusion in the Asian-fusion playbook, if that happens to be your desire. Some people we know have never even tried the steak here— the braised pork belly, the glorious pot roast and the duck fried rice are just too compelling. And there's a wonderful, mostly Italian wine list to contemplate. But the steak, seared at 1,100 degrees, is about as good as it gets. The decor is straight off the set of a Cary Grant movie. And there's banana cream pie for dessert. *8225 Beverly Blvd., L.A.*

JOE'S Everybody loves an underdog, and at Joe's, which has been an institution since it was the size of a rent-controlled studio beach apartment, half of Venice has a crush on Joe Miller's uncomplicated cuisine and small but intelligent wine list. You may not have a transcendent experience at Joe's, and you'll spend more than you think you should for a supper of Little Gem lettuce and salmon, but there is this to be said for the restaurant: The kitchen never, ever screws up the fish. *1023 Abbot Kinney Blvd., Venice.*

LITERATI II Literati is just as happy to serve you a really good pork chop as an exquisite organic salad, a stiff drink as a bottle of Viognier, and it seems as if some of the customers have practically set up their offices here beneath the framed pencils and the old photographs of Santa Monica, borrowing novels from the dining-room bookcase to read over lunch—like Literati Cafe next door, from which it spawned, Literati II is popular with screenwriters and others eager for a second home. Chef Chris Kidder and pastry chef Kimberly Sklar are both veterans of Campanile in the very best way, in love with woodsmoke and seasonal farmers'-market produce, generous portions and plenty of herbs; tapping old Mediterranean traditions and making them their own—don't miss the pasta with arugula pesto or the hot churros with bitter chocolate. *12081 Wilshire Blvd., W.L.A.*

LOU If pigs had their way, pig candy would be made out of chocolate—better yet, out of chocolate that made its way into their troughs. But for better or worse, pig candy is the vernacular name for a snack made out of smoky, thick-cut bacon baked with lots and lots of brown sugar until it transforms itself into demonically fragrant slabs that bear more than a passing resemblance to pork-belly terrine. You want some of this stuff. Lou, a tiny, wonderful wine bar on the south end of Vine, serves a pretty decent range of artisanal cheeses, including the incredible 10-year-old Hook cheddar from Wisconsin, the garlic-laced salamis of Seattle's Armandino Batali, and house-made rillettes. The wine list is pleasantly oddball, thick with rustic bottles of obscure country wines and including as many ultraorganic biodynamic wines as Amdur can find. Lou has a minor specialty in both long-braised meats and tasty vegetarian soups, and the elaborate Monday-night wine dinners revolving around, say, choucroute, Alsatian baekehoeffe or the season's first Alaskan halibut have become legendary. Still, on cool nights there may be nothing better than a plateful of that pig candy made with Lou's house-smoked bacon, a bowlful of olives and a glass of organic Cotes Catalan. *724 N. Vine St., Hollywood.*

LUCQUES The California-Mediterranean cooking of Suzanne Goin, which is feminine in all the best ways, is profoundly beautiful in its simplicity, rich in beets, goat cheese, and squashes, and there is satori to be found in every bite of grilled fish, every herb salad. When she's on, Goin teases out the flavor from a tomato with the precision of a sushi master, making textural contrasts dance and playing with bursts of acidity and the resinous flavors of fresh herbs. Lucques, named for a vivid green variety of French olive, is located in Harold Lloyd's old carriage house; it boasts an ultrasleek Barbara Barry design and one of the nicest patios in West Hollywood, but on loud weekend nights the restaurant can sometimes seem as if it is about 90 percent bar. Sunday family dinners are not to be missed. *8474 Melrose Ave., W. Hollywood.*

MELISSE When Melisse opened a few years ago, it seemed as if Josiah Citrin was trying to create a Michelin-worthy restaurant by force of will alone, imposing luxury ingredients and luxury prices on a local public that seemed happy enough to eat its seared venison without the benefit of Christofle silver, velvet purse stools, or airy sauces inflected with fresh black truffle. The cooking was always good enough, but the effect was faintly ridiculous, like a teenager trying on his father's best sports jacket when he thinks nobody is looking. (What I remember best from my first several visits is not a particular dish, but the sight of Don Rickles and Bob Newhart at the next table insulting the waiters with material that would have killed at a Friars Club roast.) And the prices, $95 for an all-but-mandatory four-course menu, would be high even in Paris. But Citrin has grown into Melisse; he wears it like a custom-fitted suit. And his cuisine, which uses farmers'-market produce and the most modern kitchen techniques without calling attention to itself, has shed most of its baby fat—the cassoulet of white asparagus with morels, the melting Copper River salmon and the butter-soft duck breast at a spring dinner all brought out the soulful essence of the ingredients in the least showy way imaginable. *1104 Wilshire Blvd., Santa Monica.*

MICHAEL'S Back in its Nouvelle Cuisine days, Michael's may have been the first market-oriented restaurant in Southern California, a showcase not just of glorious art—Rauschenberg, Stella, Graham, Hockney—but of tiny vegetables, local meats, California wines, and luxury foodstuffs identified by port of origin. And this was the restaurant that taught Angelenos that California wines could be just as serious as French ones. There still may be no better afternoons in Los Angeles than those spent on Michael's garden patio, hefting Christofle silver, inhaling Dungeness crab salad, house-made gravlax, tweaked yellowtail sashimi, and an oaky, buttery Napa Chardonnay with just enough bottle age. Michael's still feels a little like an exclusive party that somebody forgot to invite us to. *1147 Third St., Santa Monica.*

NOOK Sometimes you get the feeling that the owners of Nook are running less an American bistro than a joke about an American bistro. As faithfully as they reproduce the fundamentals of the kinds of fancily unfancy restaurants that pepper every urban neighborhood from San Diego to Augusta, Maine, they are also poking fun at them with every dried-cranberry garnish and each day-boat scallop, each obscure Belgian beer and each boutique Oregon Pinot Noir, each crusty roast chicken and dish of iconic macaroni and cheese. Almost every aspect of the restaurant, from its double-height communal table to the admonition on the menu that cell-phone use interferes with the controls on the deep fryer, is as ironically pitch-perfect as the Neil Diamond songs on a Silver Lake DJ's iPod. *11628 Santa Monica Blvd., No. 9, W.L.A.*

ORTOLAN At a time when l'Orangerie is dead, and half the emigre chefs in California are putting their knowledge of Escoffier to work cooking pasta, Ortolan, which reflects Christophe Eme's Loire-trained palate, may be the most serious French restaurant in Los Angeles. If you are a fan of intimate, dungeonlike restaurant spaces, dining rooms so dark that diners are issued little flashlights along with their menus, and presentations that extend to mushroom soup served in test tubes and fish seared on hot river rocks, then Ortolan may be the restaurant for you. Actually, Ortolan's basic premise—high-level French cooking served in a supper-club setting—is an attractive one. And Eme, who co-owns the restaurant with his paramour, Jeri Ryan, who is often to be seen working the room, is remarkably skilled: the squab, served as a roasted breast paired with a leg confit, is exceptional, as are the crisp langoustines done in the style of Robuchon, and the complex tasting menus are among the most accomplished in town. *8338 W. Third St., L.A.*

OSTERIA MOZZA Almost anybody who has tasted Nancy Silverton's miracles in the media of bread, pastry, cheese, or pizza can attest to the power of the way she thinks about food. Silverton's osteria, a sleek, bustling restaurant in the same building as her Pizzeria Mozza, has at its center her mozzarella bar, a loose take on the mozzarella-centric cuisine at the chic wine bar Obika near the Pantheon in central Rome. And it is to her credit that her ideas, along with the skills of Matt Molina, the young San Gabriel native who is her chef, and the contributions of partners Joe Bastianich and Mario Batali as well as wine czar David Rosoff—that Osteria Mozza pulls together: the braised guinea fowl and the spoon-tender pork roast inspired by rural Umbrian trattorias sharing menu space with meat-sauced *garganelli* and *tortellini en brodo* from the most sophisticated restaurants in Bologna; the baroque, almost sashimi-like constructions of fresh mozzarella and exotic condiments co-existing with the simplest possible rendition of *linguine cacio e pepe*. (The standard disclaimer applies: Nancy is a longtime family friend and she co-wrote a book with my wife. You are free to discount any of my opinions, although you would be a fool to do so.) *6602 Melrose Ave., L.A.*

PIZZERIA MOZZA At Pizzeria Mozza, Nancy Silverton has people arguing over the entire paradigm of what a pizza might be. Her pizza is airy and burnt and risen around the rim, thin and crisp in the center, neither bready in the traditional Neapolitan manner nor wispy the way you find pizza in the best places in Tuscany. The crust is sweet and bitter, salty and chewy, circled by crunchy charred bubbles that may or may not be snipped off by the chefs as they inspect the pizzas at the pass. Every pizza at Mozza is a unique marriage of flour, salt and hot-burning almond wood, stretched into irregular disks, as individually lovable as children, topped with sausage and wild fennel, or squash blossoms and burrata, or fried eggs and pureed anchovies. Mario Batali is a part owner, and the buzziness and heat may remind you of Otto, Batali's pizza parlor in Greenwich Village, although Mozza's pizza is better than Otto's. The antipasti, which are mostly vegetables, include crackling, deep-fried squash blossoms stuffed with oozing ricotta cheese. David Rosoff's all-Italian wine list is short and obscure but loaded with delicious things to drink, and nothing is over $50. *641 N. Highland Ave., L.A.*

PROVIDENCE When Michael Cimarusti left the stoves at Water Grill to start Providence, his fans were expecting nothing less than the Los Angeles equivalent of fish palaces like Le Bernardin and Oceana in New York, with a book-length catalog of Burgundies and Alsatian wines to boot. At this glowing restaurant, he managed to fulfill even those superhigh expectations—this is among the best, most civilized kitchens ever to hit Los Angeles. It just doesn't get better than Cimarusti's tartare of live spot prawns served with buttery leaves of brik pastry, sauteed squid with piquillo peppers and meltingly soft slivers of stewed pig's ear, or a terrine of foie gras with muscat gelee that may be the best foie gras preparation in this foie-gras-happy town. The dessert tasting menu of pastry chef Adrian Vasquez is a five-course degustation demanding and ambitious enough to command the attention of an entire evening, a universe of pureed avocado and hot cider foam. *5955 Melrose Ave., Hancock Park.*

750ML Buenos Aires? 14th arrondissement Paris? It's hard to pinpoint exactly what the view from this bistro's picture window calls to mind, but the panorama of trees, century-old buildings and whooshing Gold Line trains is unlike any other in the Los Angeles area at the moment, a gleaming utopian vision that would bring a smile to any urban planner's face. 750ml, presumably named for the capacity of a wine bottle, is another venture from the owner of Malo and Cobras & Matadors. It is a tiny, expensive small-plates cafe with an equally tiny menu that works better as a full-on restaurant than it does as a wine bar. It's probably best not to come too hungry: hazelnut-dusted chanterelle ravioli are delicious, but there are only two of them in an order, and a portion of the mustardy hand-chopped steak tartare is small enough to qualify as an hors d'oeuvre. But the wine list, strong on choices from Spain and Southern France, is swell. And the clientele seems to average at least 20 years younger than the usual South Pasadena crowd, whose money tends to flow more toward bungalow restoration than to plates of beef shoulder with taleggio fondue. *966 Mission St., South Pasadena.*

SONA is an exquisitely Los Angeles restaurant, a serene bubble of luxury and refinement whose basic unit of consumption is the rippling, nuanced tasting menu, which changes with the seasons and with the whims of chef David Myers. Dinner here may include cubes of sansho-pepper-scented tuna married to sauteed sweetbreads, passionfruit cannoli stuffed with peekytoe crab, tiny Nantucket scallops flavored with dates and poppy seeds, and rare duck with red wine and pumpkin seeds toasted to resemble the exact crunch of its skin. Sona is the farthest thing imaginable from the Rabelasian assault of a brasserie. The morning after nine courses at Sona, it will already seem like a half-forgotten dream. *401 N. La Cienega Blvd., W. Hollywood.*

25 DEGREES The tiniest restaurant project from the O.C.-based team that brought us Dakota, Whist and Red Pearl is a bordello-style, flocked-wallpaper saloon with a big list of wines by the half-bottle, the chance to have Red Hawk or Crescenza on your cheeseburger instead of ordinary cheddar, and big Chinese takeout containers filled with herb-flecked pommes frites. The soundtrack is probably close to the one you played in your car on the way to the AC/DC concert, if you were into stuff like that, a grinding mix of '80s guitar rock played with enthusiasm and played loud. The single dessert is a slab of chocolate cake big enough to feed 10. *7000 Hollywood Blvd., Hollywood.*

UPSTAIRS 2 Just above and affiliated with the Wine House and within shrieking distance of the 405, Upstairs 2, a small-plates brasserie pushed to the postgraduate level, may neither serve the most refined food in town nor have the most startling wine list, but it very well may be the best place on the Westside to go for food and wine—small portions of Todd Barrie's Mediterraneanized New American cooking accompanied by Marilyn Snee's roster of wines by the glass, separated into categories that expertly match up with the food as if they were microengineered for each other. Really, after seeing what Snee can do with a half glass of fizzy Dr. Loosen Sekt Late Disgorged 1989, I'd hate to see what she could accomplish with a few scant grams of plutonium. *2311 Cotner Ave., W.L.A.*

VALENTINO and V-VIN Everybody's favorite Italian restaurants tend to serve perfected country dishes, rustic vegetables and grilled meats that replicate what a gifted grandmother might prepare for dinner in her Umbrian fireplace. But Valentino's food is as far from home cooking as any French chef's, and the wine book, one of the largest collections of Italian vintages outside Italy, contains as many adventures as any J.K. Rowling. Valentino has always been one of the most controversial restaurants in Los Angeles, loved by foodies who claim to have eaten the best meals of their lives in the dimly lit dining room and loathed by people who claim that the restaurant is a con job. It can be difficult to coax the best from Valentino. But although Valentino is quite expensive, the $85 tasting menu (and you're missing the point if you order anything else) seems almost reasonable. And if you plan ahead and discuss your wine desires with owner Piero Selvaggio, you will discover that the kitchen here works best when it is asked to cook to the contours of the wine. If you are in the mood to economize, a snack at V-Vin, the restaurant's wine bar, earns you a crack at the list. If you're going to hang out at a wine bar, you might as well head toward one that takes its wine seriously. *3115 Pico Blvd., Santa Monica.*

VERTICAL WINE BISTRO Probably the swankest wine bar in Old Town Pasadena, this high-design joint juts from a hidden courtyard on Raymond's restaurant row, all subdued lighting and gleaming surfaces and hidden corners. You will never, never feel out of place in an LBD or a pinstriped Thom Browne suit here, or lack for well-heeled admirers. But Vertical is more ambitious than that: it aspires to be nothing less than the Pasadena equivalent of A.O.C., with zillions of wines available by the taste, the glass, the bottle and the flight—three side-by-side Williams Selyem pinot noirs, for example, or New Zealand sauvignon blancs, or Argentine malbecs. Sara Levine, who opened the foodie-beloved Opus, is the chef here, and beyond the wine, Vertical is a showcase of artisanal cheeses and cured meats, Serrano-ham-wrapped fig poppers and meaty, grape-friendly small dishes like pulled pork with prunes and polenta, and duck confit with chestnuts. If you would rather look into the depths of a Barolo-braised brisket than into the eyes of an attractive stranger, at Vertical it can always be arranged. *70 N. Raymond Ave., upstairs, Pasadena.*

VINCENTI Valentino may be grander than Vincenti, La Terza flashier and Giorgio Baldi may draw a more famous clientele, but Vincenti is a showcase of Italian wine and the spiritual center of fine Italian cooking in Los Angeles, its hearth. And befitting a hearth, much of Nicola Mastronardi's food comes from the big, hardwood-burning ovens, flavored with the presence of smoke, of forests, stone chimneys and chilly afternoons—a scallop, say, sprinkled with bread crumbs and baked in its shell until it sizzles; a magnificent veal chop; soft curls of cuttlefish tucked into an herb salad; a whole, truffle-laced squab. The adjacent rotisserie turns out the best restaurant version of porchetta I have ever tasted in California—loin and belly are wrapped into a spiral, seasoned with fennel and spit-roasted to a crackling, licorice-y succulence. It is certainly possible to eat several mediocre Italian meals elsewhere in this neighborhood for the price of a single superb one here. At these times, it is good to remember that on Monday nights, pizza also comes out of these ovens. *11930 San Vicente Blvd., Brentwood.*

VINUM POPULI Adjacent to Ugo, Vinum Populi is a wine bar with training wheels, a place where you can try Chateauneuf de Pape or Puligny Montrachet without fear of mispronouncing the long foreign words, have a bit of *lardo* on bread if you dare, a pizza if you don't. Instead of ordering wine from a waitress or bartender, you recharge the kind of debit card you may remember from the laundry room in your college dorm, you thrust it into a machine, and you wait for a single ounce of the fluid to be dispensed into your glass. It is a good way to try high-end wines like Gaja Brunello that you would never get to taste otherwise, and a bad way to tie your drink on. An ounce of wine isn't a lot, and by the end of the night you will probably resemble the others, jabbing at the buttons like a chicken jabbing at the lever of a lab machine, waiting for that kernel of corn. *3865 Cardiff Ave., Culver City.*

VIOLET A pleasant, mainstream bistro, Violet has all the appropriate buzzwords on its menu: the harissa aioli, the braised veal cheeks, the rare ahi tuna with wasabi mashed potatoes— but it is also possible to drop in after a show at McCabe's up the block for a caesar salad, a decent pepper steak, or a dish of very nice macaroni and cheese made with Gruyere, slivered leeks, and chunked-up Serrano ham; or to stop by at lunchtime for a cheeseburger or a sandwich of that same Spanish ham turbocharged with sliced manchego cheese and breathtaking amounts of fresh garlic. Violet is a little restaurant that cares. *3221 Pico Blvd., Santa Monica.*

WILSHIRE Wilshire is an odd place, a handsome patio restaurant that seems unable to decide whether it is a farm-driven restaurant or a roaring bar and grill; a salute to the seasons, a paparazzi's stalking ground, or a celebration of the organic wine and food that can be purchased with an American Express card. Christopher Blobaum, who has run more high-end hotel kitchens than anybody else this side of Escoffier, seems to be running his dream restaurant, and he obviously spends some of his happiest hours at the Santa Monica farmers market. At Wilshire, there will always be jewel-like baby Nantes carrots the week that baby Nantes carrots hit the best farm stands; sweet satsuma tangerines in the duck confit salad at the time satsumas are at their peak; tiny purple artichokes when tiny purple artichokes are the thing—the stuff that defines Southern California as a great agricultural region, with a comprehensive wine list to match. Wine director Matthew Straus has a thing for chunky, rustic reds that go well with Wilshire's deceptively simple cooking. *2454 Wilshire Blvd., Santa Monica.*

WILSON FOODBARCAFE The new breed of Culver City restaurant has connections at the Farmers Market, the serious-casual vibe of a Prada sweater and a birth announcement on Daily Candy. Beer lists are as long and as carefully curated as wine cards. The chefs have usually escaped from well-regarded but mainstream restaurants, and their dining rooms are temples of personal expression. This high-design restaurant from Michael Wilson, set into the bottom level of the new Museum of Design Art & Architecture building, is a Culver City place right down to the eel on the BLT, the La Espanola chorizo flavoring the mussels, and the organic Semillon on the wine list. Wilson's appetizers tend to be small-plate modern-tapas things designed to be nibbled at the bar with a glass of sauvignon blanc. A smoky, slow-cooked pork shoulder does double duty as pulled pork at lunch and as an entree-size roast at night; tea-smoked whitefish is a dinner appetizer and the basis of a mayonnaisey whitefish-salad sandwich at noon. *8631 Washington Blvd., Culver City.* ➥

"HOW I GOT THAT STORY"

Jonathan Gold has won a Pulitzer Prize, been profiled in the New Yorker, *and earned legions of fans and followers on his* L.A. Weekly *food blog—all while pursuing an almost accidental food-writing career. Gold's emergence as the most readable, edgiest chronicler of southern California cuisine began as a lark: He decided to eat his way along the street he drove each day on his bus commute.*

Known for heroically long sentences, vibrant metaphors ("a wheelbarrowful of bechamel"; "the Montrachet-slinging equivalent of Willy Wonka's chocolate factory") and sentences so epigrammatic that you have to resist the urge to make them your new email siggy, Gold, like his favorite dishes, is capable of making readers salivate with desire. Here, he talks about how with Folio Editor and AAN Editorial Committee member Anne Schindler.

Traditional food critics offer restaurant reviews. Your pieces seem to both define and elevate the culinary scene in Los Angeles. I wonder if you view your role as aspirational in a sense— contributing to a better food scene generally? Or if it's just about getting your next great meal?

It sounds odd—I've been doing this a long time—but when I started writing, almost all the coverage was of mainstream restaurants, where a ninth-tier bistro would get covered, and the best Thai restaurant in the United States wouldn't. (I'm pretty good about covering the culturally and culinarily important places for the *Weekly*, mainstream or no, but I do sometimes worry that the best of the third-tier places are having more difficulty fighting their way to the top now.) The food is obviously what occupies me the most, but if I've done anything in the last 25 years it's to get Angelenos to realize the breadth and scope of the city they live in, and possibly to be a little less afraid of their neighbors. You may just be going to Compton to eat some barbecued brisket, but when you're there, you look around a little, chat up the people next to you in line, and perhaps begin to see it as a living place occupied by people not so different from you, not simply as the home of "the other."

And I think if you're a young chef in Los Angeles, it's much harder now to ignore the vast city around you. During the height of the Asian fusion thing, you used to see, for example, Thai noodles cooked by chefs who had obviously never tasted real Thai noodles. That doesn't happen any more.

Has working for an altweekly shaped your writing style? How?

People are surprised when I say this, but I basically write the same way for the *Weekly* as I do for the slicks and for big dailies. The references vary a little. When I was the restaurant critic for *Gourmet*, I assumed my readers knew what bechamel was but I had to explain Metallica; at the *Weekly* it's probably the opposite.

What writers do you emulate? What books or authors do you recommend that young writers read?

I'm probably a bit past the point of emulation. I love Balzac's microscopic ways of describing things, Walter Benjamin's *Arcades Project* is a continuing source of inspiration, and Luca Turin's perfume reviews are amazing. That being said, I was obsessive about Joseph Mitchell, A.J. Liebling, and especially Calvin Trillin when I started writing about food, and that is where I recommend any young food writer begin.

It seems like you eat more exquisite meals than most people. Do you ever eat just, like, a PB&J? Any mundane guilty pleasure?
PB&J, no. Even the default five-minute breakfast at my house—sourdough toast rubbed with garlic, a slice of proscuitto, a bit of fresh mozzarella, a tangerine from my tree, a plunger pot of Kenyan—is pretty twee. But I do make a lot of grilled-cheese sandwiches.

There has been a lot of politicizing of food in recent years. What is your take on this trend—does it affect what you do? Do you yourself have food politics?
I've been saying lately that food has become the new rock 'n' roll. It engages young people across all economic and social spectrums, it involves ethics of what's being fed to us, why, and from whom, includes issues of poverty, empowerment, industrialization, racial equality, global warming, air and water safety, species extinction, etc.—and that's not even including food as the engine behind so much social media. How could one not be caught up in it?

Your style is aggressively engaging—you pose questions, advance theories, and write in a very conversational in tone. Are you trying to demystify the rarified world of food criticism, or is that just your natural voice?
It's the way I write. I'm not sure how rarified food criticism is these days, but the critics whose myopia restricts their gaze strictly to the hint of chervil in the remoulade are becoming endangered, I think.

Do you write quickly? How many words in an average week?
I was just glancing at a journal of what I was doing in the early nineties, and it flabbergasted me: three concert reviews, an album review, and a restaurant review for the local daily in an average week, plus a few magazine essays, a tri-weekly column, and at least one cover story for national magazines each month. Now, it's just my three columns for the *Weekly* and what's supposed to be (but usually isn't) two blog posts a day, and it seems like a 24/7 job. Maybe 2,500–3,000 words a week, although I just finished a 13,000-word cover story.

The "Breaking Free" piece on L.A. wine culture was nearly 10,000 words, and included dozens of individual restaurant visits. How do you approach a large story like that? How long does it take to put together? What kind of expense budget do you have?
When I do a story like that, which I do about twice a year, it does entail an awful lot of time in restaurants—for a piece on L.A.'s Koreatown a few years ago, I visited 140

different places, many of them more than once. It's laborious, and takes months. Even the relatively simple one I just finished—"99 Things To Eat in Los Angeles Before You Die"—seemed to take the better part of six weeks. Expenses, I suppose, are higher than usual, but the pieces let me cover a lot of restaurants that I might not get around to in the course of regular coverage, especially high-quality places that have been around a while, and the issues seem to attract a lot of advertisers, so I think it works out. I make up for the high expenses by writing about street food!

What trends do you see ahead in food writing, particularly in terms of the impact of new media?
We are obviously in an area of great tumult at the moment, and I am the farthest thing from a sage. But it does seem as if there is an extraordinary amount of interest in the subject of food at the moment, and with the many thousands of people trying their hands at food writing at the moment—on blogs, on Yelp, on comment sections—most of them are, of course, quite unreadable, but some of them are going to turn out to be quite good.

The Jester's Quest

Christina Waters

JUNE 4, 2008

Randall Grahm has been called many things: Rhône Ranger, marketing Svengali, punster extraordinaire. Over the last quarter-century, the lanky, long-haired trickster-winemaker has reinvented himself enough times to make even Madonna blush.

After switching his attention to a handful of Italian varietals, Grahm went on to unleash dozens of proprietary styles, each with its own satirical label. To the high-end syrahs for which he was lauded, he added a low-end line with controversial screw-top closures. By the end of the last century, oenophiles were dizzy from all the spin Grahm inflected upon his postmodern empire. But he kept up the pace. And just when the empire had ballooned, some said out of control, Grahm pulled off yet another transformation.

As if to exorcize the lees of his youthful, "gonzo" wine-making style, Grahm radically cut back his operation last year (from 450,000 cases to 35,000 cases), sold off the popular low-end Big House and Cardinal Zin series and sent the Pacific Rim Riesling brand to the Pacific Northwest. He retired three-quarters of his employees. Maintaining production of the flagship "Cigare" series largely from sourced grapes, Grahm, viticulturist Nicole Walsh, and associate winemaker Jillian Johnson are focusing on a handful of estate wines made from the Ca' del Solo property near Soledad.

"Randall was born to project delight—to make people happy," observes John Locke, Bonny Doon Vineyard's marketing director for 17 years. "But there's also his Krakatoa and Vesuvius side—the need to create, destroy and then start anew."

This choice Nietzschean analogy sheds some light on the visionary modus operandi of Bonny Doon's "president-for-life." Having jettisoned his signature prankster approach to varietals, labels, and sales, Grahm is now reining in his former oeno-omnivore tendencies for a narrower, purer branding motif. "Purity of heart is to swill one thing," Grahm has frequently punned on the Kierkegaardian mantra. Only now he means it. Again.

The determination to will one thing—at least for the moment—has propelled Randall Grahm down this newest path. Like the hunt for a definitive New World pinot noir, laden with unique, site-specific *terroir*. Biodynamic vineyards currently fueling Grahm's elegant Ca' del Solo wines might guarantee the purity part.

But one more crucial piece is needed—an estate vineyard capable of yielding such a prize. A vineyard worthy of the rest of Grahm's professional life.

Doon-sizing the Empire

"I truly believe this. To make great wine, one must throw away the idea of making a profit," Grahm recently pronounced. "Pac Rim, Big House, all those were amusing. But it was like being in college too long. Enough already!"

Tightening his corporate belt, Grahm says, "I've given myself a kick in the butt. *Where* you do things is important—I need to find my own terroir. I need to feel at home."

That quest is made all the more urgent by the presence of a new family, especially his exuberant daughter, Amélie, five. She is helping drive what he calls "a different metric—it's about having the life I want to have." Legacy is always on his mind.

Donning his philosopher's hat, Grahm muses, "Wine knowledge is a road. Many people stop at certain points on that road—with New World wines, for example. They are easy to pronounce, immediately likeable. But if you go further—it's a story, but you want to go further—you'll find amazing wines, like the 2005 burgundies."

Ah, there's the rub again—Burgundy, the fabled wine powered by the sacred pinot noir grape. The grape that has eluded Grahm since those earliest days of winemaking on his own property in the Santa Cruz Mountains. "He literally trucked in hundreds of tons of limestone," recalls longtime colleague and wine educator Jason Brandt Lewis, "to try to create the right conditions for pinot noir." But the site proved too warm, too Mediterranean, to produce the pinot of his dreams, and so Grahm turned to other grapes, other styles, and the proliferation of the Bonny Doon brand began.

Risky Business

"It's presumptuous to set out to make a 'great wine,'" Grahm told me last month. "If I can only succeed in interesting wine, then I'll be happy. If I could only make good-but-banal wine—no!"

Taking the biodynamic gamble, Grahm is now focused on a few charismatic wines. "I want to feel that I've done my best. I'm taking chances—in fact more chances than ever. This is risky," he says of his latest biodynamic line. The risk, he explains, is "that nobody will buy the wine. The risk is that it will end up being far more costly than I can possibly recoup." Such risks, in the analysis of Lewis, are calibrated upon the current glut of highly rated wines on the market. Lewis sold wines with Grahm in the Wine Merchant days, and the two remained friends after moving to Santa Cruz.

"Back in the early '80s, we all knew all the other winemakers—it was a smaller community. We tried to help each other,"

Lewis says. "Now it's cutthroat. The advent of the 100-point system triggered a feeding frenzy of competition. Even 90 points is not as good as it once was."

Lewis believes "no journalist is going to waste a column on wine that is just 'really good.' Really good is just not good enough."

"Randall was taken very seriously when he started," recalls Locke. "[Robert] Parker called him 'a national treasure,' and said of the Cigare Volant that it was not only new, it was great."

The current executive editor of *Wine Spectator*, Thomas Matthews, agrees. "Randall has been an important figure in California's embrace of new grapes and new wine regions. We applaud his curiosity, his willingness to take risks and his ability to make good wines from many grapes and in many different styles," said Matthews. "It may be that his restlessness has sometimes worked against him. Making outstanding wines generally requires patient application."

Matthews explains what he means. "Randall has added and dropped grape varieties, vineyard sources, and even whole lines of wine." Grahm himself even describes the "old Bonny Doon," in his March tasting notes, as "a venue for exceptionally wacky marketing initiatives."

Outskirts of Eden

Grahm has been characterized as a cross between Shiva—the Hindu god of destruction and creation—and the Marx Brothers. Grahm's virtuoso parodies of *mondo vino* poohbahs managed to get the once-precocious maverick kicked out of celebrity paradise.

"He alienated a lot of people," Locke admits. Grahm himself bemoans this exile. But how many renegades grow up to regret their youthful excesses?

"There was a sense of us not being serious—people *still* don't know that we're serious. They treat me like an icon," he fumes. "But I'm not dead yet."

Others, like acclaimed Ridge Vineyards wine maestro Paul Draper, applaud Grahm's impetuousity. "His humor has been the greatest of gifts to an all-too-serious industry, as has the erudition on which it is so often based. He is one of the most creative of winemakers and wine marketers," Draper says.

"You need third-party endorsement," says Grahm. "And in this country, that means *Wine Spectator* and Robert Parker." Grahm believes that he has "totally alienated them—they either see me as a maverick, or an asshole."

Parker, the über wine arbiter whose approval can guarantee a winemaker's fortune, declined to address his opinion of Grahm. *Wine Spectator*'s- editor put it diplomatically: "I wouldn't say he has 'alienated' *Wine Spectator,* but since Randall appeared on our cover (in the April 15, 1989, issue), California has exploded with new wineries," Matthews pointed out.

And that too has accounted for some of Grahm's professional doldrums. "I think I compromised the brand by making so many different wines, and so many less expensive wines," he admits. Much like the Internet syndrome in which the glut of digitized information overwhelms the consumer's ability to process, so the expanding world wine web renders absurd any attempt to sort through all the product. Ergo, to the newcomer goes the spotlight.

Too Much Too Soon

"To be great, you have to have data, experience, and talent," contends Grahm's associate John Locke. "Randall has all that, plus a Promethean imagination." He also had fame. "Like a movie star suddenly vaulted to rock-stardom," recalls Lewis, "Randall got this amazing success. And while *he* didn't change, everything around him changed. His focus was always on small, but it got huge. It was no longer in his control." Lewis notes that California's "star system" of winemakers means that once you're on top, "if you slip in numbers, or in points, you're history." Grahm had to keep competing with himself. "Also some of the wines weren't as good as others," Lewis believes. "Very good, but not always great."

Locke agrees with this overall analysis. "The way it became just wasn't sustainable. We were goofing around too much," Locke admits. "He spent too much time doing too many things—it probably did distract from the wine itself."

Paul Draper applauds Grahm's restless experimentation. Calling Grahm "an old friend," Draper believes that, "as much as he loves the idea of terroir, I suspect he would be bored to tears if his creativity were limited to insuring that the character of a great terroir was carried through into the wine year after year after year."

The Biodynamic Turn

In 2003 Grahm began serious explorations into biodynamic viticulture, convening seminars, gathering experts, and hiring French biodynamic expert Phillipe Coderey to oversee grape management, and he began converting the Ca' del Solo vineyard to biodynamic glory. "The new revolution will be in the vineyard," Grahm wrote that same year, and immediately began romancing lighter alcohol, mineral-intensive wines, of which the very first to be Demeter-certified were released this year. "The choice to go biodynamic," Locke believes, "wasn't necessarily a tactical choice, but it was a happy one." In Locke's expert judgment, this choice not only helps place the winemaker/farmer back within the entire biodynamic loop, it creates arguably superior results. "These wines are alive," contends Grahm's associate winemaker Jillian Johnson, "unlike those made in the agrichemical style."

If his longtime colleague Locke is right and what Grahm needs now is "focus," the man himself contends that his focus has never strayed from the temperamental grape of Burgundy.

"Pinot noir is indeed always on my mind, and is in fact my most pressing viticultural ambition," he told me recently. "The problem of course is that finding a great pinot site in the New World is bloody difficult, if not nearly impossible." Grahm knows the score. "If you find a climatically very cool area, plant on very dense spacing (meter by meter), irrigate artfully and do a few other things right like keeping your yield down, you may produce a simulacrum of Burgundy, for which you will have to charge two to three times what a comparable Burgundy might cost. But at the end of the day, it is still but a facsimile." Grahm finds it "far more interesting to think about how one might produce a truly original pinot noir, one that could not be produced in Burgundy." In other words, a wine that expresses the unique terroir of this here and now.

Terroir, Baby, Terroir

How hard can this be? You grab a checkbook, bring your vineyard consultant, hop in the Citröen and drive around until the feng shui feels right.

Not quite. The quest for a new estate vineyard is fraught with complex issues. Zoning, environmental impact, climate, soil, the market, the ungodly expense of land anywhere near the Bay Area. "He wants to stay in Santa Cruz," Johnson believes, "but there aren't many places here that would work—and there are so many restrictions." Nicole Walsh, winegrower for the Ca' del Solo vineyard, saw a huge change in Grahm once the biodynamic decision was made. "He really focused on the vineyard. Whatever is inspiring for him at the time, he goes deeply into it—he's the most experimental, outside-the-box person I've ever met," she laughs. "Now it's a constant quest to grow grapes better, to be close to the vineyard. It's really a whole new identity."

With Ca' del Solo vineyard purring along with biodynamic white grapes, Grahm knows that it's crucial to locate the right vineyard to yield terroir-expressive red wines. But he's asking for a lot. Such a dream vineyard must offer "a perfect congruence between the objective factors," such as geology, limestone, rainfall, "and the hauntingly compelling subjective features." Grahm is looking for "a landscape that feels like home"—a personal sense of terroir that can yield a professional triumph. In other words, winemaking perfection.

"Randall's perfection thing," cautions Locke, "might be the biggest impediment to his future."

Full Doon Rising

"I'm not setting the world on fire right now," Grahm admits, lips pursed, eyes squinting thoughtfully. "I'm meeting new distributors, training their staff; I'm shlepping wine. My God, I'm doing the things I did 20 years ago! This is my baby-I have to preserve it and keep it going." Indeed, he is. There are loud rumors that the Bonny Doon Vineyard tasting room will come down from the mountain this summer and take residence on the West Side Santa Cruz winery property, along with a new tasting room cafe in the fall. Randall has just signed a book deal with UC Press, which means that his story, told in his inimitable way, will hit the bookstores next year.

Fit and brimming with ideas, Grahm looks convincingly born-again at midcareer. "What keeps it all going?"

He shrugs. "All stress, all the time."

The Biodynamic Revolution

Based upon principles articulated by Rudolf Steiner in the 1920s, biodynamic agriculture emphasizes the balance of all aspects of farming—soil, nutrients, animals, plants, climate—in a self-sustaining feedback loop. The farm (or vineyard, in this case) is viewed as a living organism. Including and surpassing organic farming methods, biodynamic agriculture utilizes precise herbal, compost, and mineral preparations, created and applied in conjunction with the astronomical calendar. The whole point is to create soil so healthy, so in balance with its companion plants and animals, that nothing else is needed to maintain optimum nourishment—and optimum productivity.

Steiner prescribed the use of special preparations believed to enhance fertility. While these often raise eyebrows among nonbiodynamic practitioners, the most important of these preparations are based upon the homeopathic ideal of "innoculating" the growing medium with certain vital ingredients. The preparations are numbered 500 through 508; the infamous preparation 500 involves filling a cow horn with manure, burying it at the autumnal equinox, and retrieving it six months later to form the nutrients for a "tea" that's applied to the fields. Other preparations, which are applied to the vineyards according to the seasons, involve ground quartz crystals, stinging nettles, chamomile blossoms, yarrow, dandelion, valerian, oak bark, and horsetail. The detail-intensive vineyard practice associated with biodynamic work yields what many winemakers consider a clean harvest. The land itself becomes cleansed enough of any prior toxins or negligent agricultural residues that it can be trademarked "biodynamic" by Demeter, the internationally recognized biodynamic farm certifying agency. The results in the bottle are believed to more fully showcase appealing minerality and express terroir, transporting the vitality of the vineyard itself into the finished wines.

A Brief History of Randall Grahm

The yellow brick road to Santa Cruz started at The Wine Merchant, an upscale Beverly Hills wine shop, where the young Randall Grahm sold, learned about, and drank great European wine. Smitten, Grahm resolved to try his own hand at making wine—after a stint studying philosophy at UCSC and ultimately taking a degree in plant science at UC-Davis in 1979.

Hoping to produce a great pinot noir, Grahm, with his family's help, purchased land in Bonny Doon, and soon discovered it to be "Rhône" at heart. Grahm replanted to syrah, roussanne, marsanne, and viognier. The results were inaugurated with the first vintage of Le Cigare Volant, a resounding New World homage to Châteauneuf-du-Pape. Setting a tone for the future, Grahm chose the French phrase for "flying cigar," an allusion to a 1954 prohibition against cigar-shaped UFOs decreed by the village council of Châteauneuf-du-Pape. This cautionary ordinance captured Grahm's fancy and was immortalized in the winery's logo.

In the late '80s and early '90s, Bonny Doon Vineyard became Grahm's oenotechnical playground/laboratory for a dizzying diversity of grapes and styles: there were eaux de vie and grappas; the celestial muscat canelli; the Italian and Spanish period replete with nebbiolo, barbera, dolcetto, malvasia, sangiovese, and albariño—each with its own irreverent and always colorful labels depicting priests, felons, angels, trapeze artists, UFOs, angry monkeys, fishermen, jesters, and exploding volcanos.

In 1989, Grahm joined Who's Who of Cooking in America, and in 1994 won a James Beard Award as "Wine and Spirits Professional of the Year." That same year the vineyard in Bonny Doon succumbed to Pierce's disease. The infamous Big

House series of wines created from Bonny Doon's Ca' del Solo vineyard in Soledad took off. Just after the turn of the millennium, Grahm recovered from a mysterious vertebral affliction. He became a father. He embraced Rudolf Steiner's biodynamic principles, in vineyard agriculture as well as in winemaking. In 2006, Grahm sold the Cardinal Zin and Big House lines, moved the Pacific Rim Riesling brand to Washington State, scaled back staff, sold his Ingalls Street winery facility—and leased it back—and slashed annual production from 450,000 to just over 30,000. The first Demeter-certified biodynamic Ca' del Solo wines were released this year. ☙

"HOW I GOT THAT STORY"

Christina Waters is a fifth generation Californian raised in Germany, France, and on the East Coast—which may explain her varied and specific knowledge of food and wine. A philosophy major at UC Davis, Waters has lived in Santa Cruz for the past 25 years, where she teaches and works as a freelance writer for Santa Cruz Weekly, *among other publications. Her 2009 AAN award is for a 3,000-word profile of Bonny Doon Vineyard owner Randall Grahm. The following interview was conducted by Folio Editor and AAN Editorial Committee member Anne Schindler.*

This story profiled gonzo winemaker Randall Grahm. How did you choose him as a story focus, and why?

Randall and I share a long media-centric history. We live and work in the same town, Santa Cruz, and [we live here] for many of the same reasons. I've written about Randall's evolution as a winemaker and entrepreneur for 25 years, and I recognized that he was entering a serious and new phase.

I decided to use my ease of access, which I have used sparingly in our long acquaintance, to advance the reader's grasp of what Grahm was creating.

Grahm has recreated himself several times over the years. Did his chameleon-like history affect how you approached telling his story?

Yes, absolutely. It meant that I had to start by ignoring this new phase as yet another re-invention, because he would be expecting that approach. Also, his most recent marketing hype and history meant that I now needed to reach way back and contact some of those who "knew him when," as well as skeptics about yet another so-called re-creation. The surprise was in finding their candid assessment, often harsh, and then weaving it into the story of who he wanted to be now, without cheap judgments.

Sometimes people who've been the center of some conflict—in this case, the wine industry rebel—try to control a story. Was that a challenge with this story? How did you manage that?

Randall is a virtuoso media manipulator and a man whose own promotional skills are legendary, so caution is always the strategy one uses in approaching him. But knowing his tactics so well, I approached him with an arsenal of unexpected questions and propositions, designed to disarm the virtuoso disarmer.

I pre-empted his tendencies to digress through a set of questions chosen to play to his self-styled strengths. I established my bona fides with an opening flourish of background knowledge, and then began to outflank his own agenda with another one.

I always intend to bring him into territory he hasn't yet fully packaged for public, i.e. media consumption. With Randall, this is always tricky. But possible. And in the case of this recent story, it seemed to have been successful.

Did you know much about wine going into this story? How did you educate yourself?

I have been nominated three times for James Beard Journalism awards, each time for feature stories about wine and wine-making, so I do feel comfortable thinking and writing about wine. That said, I am a research junkie smart enough to know that one can never know enough about a subject as old and passion-driven as wine. I read, tasted, consulted with other winemakers, and tried to stay poised somewhere between geekdom and innocence.

The story structure is split into several bite-sized sections and two sidebars, including one that is pure Randall biography. Why?

I shaped the sidebars to accompany the main text. Sidebars enrich, often adding concentrated handfuls of data, anecdote, history. I like the reader to be so smitten with the main story that they want more and more. The sidebars give it to them.

Grahm's biography is well-known to fans of his wine and followers of wine lore in general. Hence to braid it into the main fabric of the story might be to slow down the [story]. Putting Randall's colorful biography into a separate package lets the wine veteran chew on the central dish, while offering more juicy details to the less informed reader.

You've won other AAN awards before, for food and arts writing. What similarities are there between the two? What about them appeal to you as a writer?

Describing food, just as describing artwork, requires that you place your reader squarely within the experience. I always try to embed the reader within the experience I have had, so that they taste the meal with me, see the artwork as I do, always striving to heighten their enjoyment and deepen their perceptions.

I am drawn to both food and art, perhaps for similar reasons. They reveal everything about their creators and the cultures in which they flourish. Cuisine and art both feed the spirit, as well as the senses. Both force the writer to stretch, to invent, to attempt avenues of description that keep the writing fresh, without sacrificing depth or complexity.

INVESTIGATIVE
REPORTING

✿ ✿ ✿

CIRCULATION 50,000 AND OVER

Prescription for Disaster

by John Dickerson, *Phoenix New Times*

"A great investigation into a matter of life and death for the public. Good job of digging deeply into hard-to-get records and creating an original database to analyze the information. The story uses powerful and disturbing examples to show the dangers of a system that allows addicted doctors to continue practicing. The sharp writing made the series hard to put down. Bravo!"—Jon Marshall, Northwestern University

✿ ✿ ✿

CIRCULATION UNDER 50,000

"Might Makes Right"

by Jeffrey C. Billman, *Orlando Weekly*

"Well-chosen topic, thoroughly researched, compressed into one well-written and concise article."—Borzou Daragahi, Los Angeles Times

The Doctor Is Out

John Dickerson

MARCH 6, 2008

Laura Migliano was looking for some relief when she showed up for a doctor's appointment in April 2004. Ten years earlier, she'd herniated a disc while doing sit-ups. She spent a decade fighting the pain—with surgery, steroid injections, and finally with a battery-powered spinal cord stimulator. The stimulator helped, reducing the ache with electric shock. But then the battery died. Migliano, 41, was in agony when she saw Dr. Thomas Grade, a pain specialist at the Desert Pain Institute in Mesa.

It turned out she needed only a battery change. But Grade couldn't replace the battery for another six days, so he prescribed painkillers. Although a nurse by profession, Migliano had no idea that Grade's prescribed dosage of methadone—a narcotic usually reserved for heroin addicts trying to kick the habit—could interact with her other painkillers and kill her.

It did.

In his notes, Grade wrote that Migliano should take 5 to 10 milligrams of methadone. But on her prescription, he wrote 120 milligrams—a fatal dose when combined with her other medications, which Grade never determined before writing the prescription.

Migliano drove to the pharmacy and filled the prescription. Then she went home and drank the pills down with a large glass of water—just as the doctor ordered. She was expecting relief from her lower-back pain.

Instead, her best friend found her dead the next morning.

Accidents happen, even in medicine. Scalpels slip. Drugs interact unexpectedly.

Laws are designed to keep those mistakes at a minimum. But in the case of Laura Migliano and Dr. Thomas Grade, the rules in place weren't strong enough.

Migliano had no way of knowing it, but Dr. Grade was a recovering drug addict—practicing with the Arizona Medical

Board's blessing and without drug tests. Even after Migliano's death and multiple patient complaints, the board didn't learn of Grade's relapse into addiction for three years.

That wasn't soon enough to save Laura Migliano. An autopsy confirmed drug interaction as the cause of her death. Last year, Migliano's parents won a confidential legal settlement from Grade, who was still licensed to practice at the time.

Because Grade wasn't being drug-tested, it's impossible to know exactly when he relapsed. What is clear is that he finished the Arizona Medical Board's substance abuse rehab program in 1993 and practiced unmonitored for 14 years. Within 30 days of Migliano's death in 2004, the medical board received two more serious complaints against Grade. Both accused him of the same error that killed Migliano—prescribing narcotics without learning what drugs his patients were taking and failing to document their visits.

As a result of the complaints, the board restricted Grade's prescribing privileges but still didn't test him for drugs. It wasn't until 2007, when Gilbert police arrested Grade on charges of domestic abuse—and found him intoxicated—that the board pulled his license.

Grade isn't alone. Substance abuse was the leading cause of physician license suspension in 2007 in Arizona.

Arizona law requires that the medical board drug-test addicted doctors for only five years after they complete rehab. Then they're on their own. But that may not be adequate regulation. An examination by *New Times* of the records of 50 addicted doctors over a five-year period reveals that 45 of those doctors relapsed—and 15 of those relapses took place *after* the board stopped monitoring them.

And those are only the doctors who were caught. The pool is actually larger: if you, as a doctor in Arizona, voluntarily submit to rehab, your addiction is kept confidential. None of those doctors was examined in this investigation.

After the five years of drug tests have passed, addicted physicians are free to practice without monitoring. The board learns of relapse only when a doctor is arrested, self-reports, or is reported by a colleague. Some who completed rehab are caught when nabbed for drunken driving. One Glendale physician was even arrested for running a meth lab. Others avoid trouble with the law and continue seeing patients. In the past 10 years, at least two Arizona residents have died in the care of addicted physicians who relapsed.

In the information age, patients can research their physicians online, including on the Arizona Medical Board's website. But when it comes to a physician's addiction, the site can give a false sense of security. *New Times* found that some cases of addiction don't show up on physicians' profiles.

Arizona's look-the-other-way policy for rehab graduates is in line with the national standard, accepted decades ago. But after years of physician relapses, some experts think it's time to examine that standard. Last year, the state of California led the way in questioning its own rehab program for physicians. California's program was strikingly similar to Arizona's, particularly in its no-strings-attached graduation for addicted physicians.

Arizona's program has never been audited. But after California's program was audited, lawmakers forced the California Medical Board to scrap its rehab methods. That board met in January to create a new program, which will be announced in June. Alabama and a handful of other states now require life-long drug tests of some addicted physicians.

Arizona doesn't. But perhaps it should. Here's a reason why:

Phoenix residents may not recognize the name of Dr. Michael Mahl, but Tucsonans might. In 1997, Mahl, a child psychiatrist, was accused of molesting a number of boys at his Tucson group home for troubled teens.

According to medical board records and news media reports, Mahl's descent into drug and sex addiction started with prescription medication and then eventually included cocaine abuse. Mahl testified before the medical board that using cocaine drove him to sexual compulsion. Despite allegations of abuse from his employees and boys at his group home, Mahl was never criminally charged.

In August 2002 the medical board gave Mahl his license back and placed him on the standard five-year probation for drug use. Mahl moved to Chandler, where he's been working as a psychiatrist for adults. On August 9, 2007, Mahl's five-year probation ended, meaning that if Mahl screws up again, the Arizona Medical Board may be the last to know. Even though he testified that cocaine use launched his cycle of drug and patient abuse, he is free to prescribe drugs and counsel adults behind closed doors, without drug tests or accountability.

Mahl is among dozens of addicted physicians who've graduated from rehab and now practice medicine—including performing surgery and prescribing drugs—unmonitored.

At his office in Chandler, Mahl says he doesn't need drug tests anymore. "Five years is adequate. I couldn't imagine having to do it beyond five years," he says.

Mahl knows a number of physicians who finished the five years and then relapsed while seeing patients, but he's optimistic that he won't join them by relapsing.

Arizona lawmakers are, too. They aren't currently considering changes to physician-relapse laws. But at least one doctor thinks the existing system is broken. Cosmetic surgeon Stephen Locnikar wrote a book about his years in Arizona as an addicted doctor.

"I did the board's addiction program, but I never thought it actually applied to me. I thought, I'm just doing this because they're requiring it," Locnikar says.

He graduated from Arizona's rehab program, only to relapse and practice as an addict for years. He tells stories of snorting cocaine off his private bathroom sink between surgeries.

Locnikar believes addicted physicians should be monitored for the duration of their practice.

"After five years, they take the physicians off probation. It doesn't make sense," he says. "After my probation ended, I started drinking, picked up a few pills on the house. Then within a very short period of time—months—I was deep into addiction again. Whenever that probation period was up, and I had no gun to my head, I would relapse. If the probation had kept going, I don't think I would have relapsed. It's absolutely necessary for addicts."

✿

To be fair, no one's trying to let doctors in Arizona get away with murder. In the past decade, the Arizona Medical Board's rate of physician investigation and discipline has increased, and a number of policies have changed for the better. The board has more investigators and examines complaints twice as quickly as it did. But one practice hasn't changed—the board's Monitored Aftercare Program (MAP) for addicted physicians.

Local addiction experts Dr. David Greenberg and Dr. Michel Sucher run the MAP program. They did not return messages left at their office and declined requests through the board's spokesman, Roger Downey, for interviews. Downey said his agency is too busy to track the relapses of MAP graduates. Greenberg and Sucher report that 80 percent to 90 percent of MAP graduates do not relapse, Downey added.

New Times researched hundreds of medical board and physician records to see whether that success rate was accurate. It's impossible to determine because some doctors enter and exit the program confidentially. But 75 percent of the MAP graduates investigated relapsed after their drug testing ended. And those are just the physicians who were caught.

The investigation included records of 50 physicians who were disciplined for substance abuse between 2002 and 2007. Only 20 of the 50 doctors graduated from MAP. The board revoked the licenses of the 30 who didn't graduate.

But of the 20 addicted physicians who did graduate from MAP, 15 relapsed after the board stopped monitoring them— and while they were practicing medicine.

Many doctors who graduated from MAP in the 1980s and 1990s were not caught relapsing until 2002 or later. Because they weren't drug-tested, there's no knowing exactly when they relapsed or how long they practiced under the influence.

Based on a five-year records review, at least 200 addicted physicians have enrolled in Arizona's MAP program. Downey reports that an additional eight to 10 doctors self-report into confidential rehab each year.

Several legislators were contacted about the laws governing MAP. None was aware that legislation passed in the 1980s requires drug testing of addicted physicians for only five years.

Bob Stump, a Republican who chairs the state's House Health Committee, was surprised to learn Arizona's MAP program has never been audited. "I would certainly be curious to know, myself, what the relapse rate is," he says.

Stump says he has long supported malpractice reform and other physicians' rights but adds that public safety remains his highest priority.

"We can't allow physicians who are relapsed to be taking patients," he says. "If an audit of the board's Monitored Aftercare Program would be helpful to that end, then I would certainly be in support of that."

Sitting in a north Scottsdale Starbucks, Dr. Steven Locnikar looks like he walked straight off the set of *Scrubs, House,* or *ER.* At 40, he still looks the part of a suave, sophisticated young physician. But Locnikar has had his license revoked twice because of his drug addiction.

Locnikar wears a tight blue T-shirt that covers his well-built upper body and matches his eyes. He talks with the intelligence of a med-school whiz. His voice is calm and engaging as he candidly discusses his years as a drug addict and cosmetic surgeon in Scottsdale, detailed in his self-published book *Doctor Hyde,* released last year. The book gives a glimpse into the denial of an addicted physician.

In the early '90s, Locnikar was fresh out of his residency, and his cosmetic surgery practice was thriving. *Cosmopolitan* magazine even named him Bachelor of the Year.

And he was descending into his first bout with addiction.

"I started using casually, like anyone else, on the weekends," he says. "That went on for months. Then the weekends began on Thursday or lasted until Monday. You go to work tired and hung-over. To me, that is the absolute most impaired you'll ever be. Even if you didn't use on the way to work, you're cloudy, tired, impaired. You don't want to make decisions. Soon, I was using during work. There was a time where I'd run into the bathroom, nasal snort, and finish up the day."

In 1995, Scottsdale police arrested Locnikar for drunken driving. They found cocaine in his car and in his bloodstream.

Locnikar, a D.O., was responsible to the Osteopathic Medical Board, the cousin of the larger Allopathic Medical Board, which licenses M.D.s. The D.O. and M.D. boards share the same five-year rehab program.

The osteopathic board forced Locnikar into inpatient rehab and then onto the MAP probation, with its random drug tests. But Locnikar remained in denial.

"I played the game, went through the 'recovery,' but I didn't really get it. They wanted me to do it, and I did it. I still didn't think I was an addict," Locnikar says.

During his five years of MAP probation, Locnikar built another successful cosmetic surgery practice. At its height of success, he was making $5 million a year. He got married and bought a 10,000-square-foot home.

Five years later, he graduated. And the drug tests ended.

"At the end of my probationary period, once again, I'd achieved all this financial reward. But I never really felt fulfilled or happy or content. I casually started drinking, picked up a few pills on the house. Addiction progresses, even if you aren't using. You'll pick right up where you left off. I soon got to the point where pills or cocaine snorted didn't work. I started shooting, injecting heroin, Demerol, anything I could get my hands on."

Locnikar then practiced as an addict for three years.

"Even at that point, people were still hesitant to confront me because I was a doctor," Locnikar says. "We were in a $3- or $4-million house in Paradise Valley, with all the toys. When you see that on the outside, you think that somebody has it together."

At three in the morning on November 9, 2004, Locnikar was desperate for a fix as he sped downtown to buy cocaine. On the way, he totaled his Mercedes. Officers found syringes, vials of Versed, and other drug paraphernalia in his car, according to osteopathic board records.

The police notified the osteopathic board, which suspended Locnikar's license.

"Once I signed power of attorney, my wife sold the house and kept all the proceeds. I literally went from Paradise Valley to penniless," Locnikar says. "Within a very short period of time, I was homeless on the streets, pushing a shopping cart on Van Buren."

Months later, Locnikar's friends found him homeless, with no shoes or ID, in Tijuana, Mexico. "I don't even remember a lot of it. I was in a perpetual state of psychosis. I was finding spent needles on the ground, didn't eat for weeks at a time. Just shot up drugs."

Back in the States, Locnikar learned that his wife had divorced him. "At that point, no clothes, no shoes, as a homeless guy ready to die, I realized for the first time that I had a problem. I lost tens of millions of dollars, my family, every tangible thing in life. I watched all of it go away without even realizing what happened."

In January 2006, the osteopathic board revoked Locnikar's license for the second time because of his substance abuse. Under Arizona law, he was allowed to re-apply in January. He did.

Locnikar expects to have his license back soon. If that happens, the MAP program will stop testing him for drugs five years from now. Locnikar knows his propensity to relapse again and claims he'll continue paying $65 a day for random drug tests, even after the board stops requiring them.

"There's something about the thought of the random test that motivates somebody," Locnikar says.

Gary Blass was a successful emergency room doctor. He and his wife, Carlee, a ballet teacher, moved to Arizona in 1994, shortly after Blass finished his residency at Episcopal Hospital in Philadelphia.

On June 29, 2005, Glendale police raided Blass's Arrowhead home and uncovered, of all things, a meth lab. Blass and his wife were arrested for making and selling crystal meth. The Arizona Medical Board revoked Blass's license one month later.

But if the board had monitored Blass sooner, it might have saved the life of one of his patients.

Blass had graduated from his *third* MAP probation eight years earlier, in 1997.

When Colleen Lomax saw Blass's face on the front page of a newspaper after his arrest, she wasn't surprised. The Phoenix attorney knew the name Blass well, having represented the family of a man who died in his care. Doug Morton Jr.'s family won an undisclosed settlement in 2002, and that was without any proof that Blass had been impaired when he diagnosed Morton's heart attack as a sports injury.

"The nature of the malpractice was so egregious we thought all along, at some level, he had to be impaired," Lomax says.

Because the board wasn't drug-testing Blass, it's impossible to know when he began practicing under the influence, or whether, in fact, he was using when he saw Morton on the night of May 19, 1998.

That night, Morton, 36, felt a sharp pain in his left shoulder. Morton was a tough Midwesterner, a construction materials salesman who didn't much care for hospitals. After prodding from his fiancée and parents, he finally drove to the emergency room at Chandler Regional Hospital.

According to court records, Blass diagnosed Morton's pain as tennis shoulder—even though Morton had a full range of motion in the joint.

Lomax says Morton actually exhibited five of the seven classic signs of heart attack.

Morton tried to sleep that night, sitting upright in a recliner because of the throbbing. He assured his worried fiancée it was only a sore shoulder. That's what the doctor said. By sunrise, Morton had died a slow death from cardiac failure.

His son found him early the next morning, dead in his La-Z-Boy.

A heart attack killed Morton, less than 24 hours after his ER visit. Despite that grave error and four more errors in the ensuing years, the medical board still didn't submit Blass—an addict with a 20-year history of relapses—to drug tests.

The medical board instead mailed Blass a handful of disciplinary warnings for practicing sloppy medicine and keeping poor records. Then they allowed him to continue practicing, even after he unlawfully prescribed the narcotic OxyContin.

After the board stripped Blass's prescribing privileges, he apparently grew more desperate to secure drugs.

In 2006, Blass pleaded guilty in court to making meth at his house and was sentenced to probation. Two months into his probation, Blass allegedly pulled a gun on three Mesa police officers. According to court records, the officers subdued him without firing shots and then found marijuana on him.

On March 17, Blass's third drug-related criminal trial is scheduled to begin in Maricopa County Superior Court.

The deaths of Laura Migliano and Doug Morton Jr. have not been enough to get the attention of the Arizona Legislature, perhaps because of the lobbying power of the Arizona Medical Association.

Julie Fellmeth, a public interest attorney and law professor at the University of San Diego, says physician trade associations have been successful in limiting oversight on drug use among physicians. Fellmeth has been studying physician-addiction programs for more than 20 years. She was influential in the California Legislature's demand that the California Medical Board scrap its equivalent to Arizona's MAP program.

"Physician-rehab programs were all created years ago at the behest of physician trade associations. These are trade groups that want to protect physician licenses. Public protection is not their role," Fellmeth says.

David Landrith has been the Arizona Medical Association's chief lobbyist and policy expert for 17 years. Landrith wasn't a lobbyist 20 years ago, but he remembers the legislation from the 1980s that created today's MAP program.

And he is familiar with another bill he fought to make law 10 years ago. Dubbed the "Drunk Doctor Bill," it created confidential rehab for physicians who self-report their addictions. That law is the reason why certain cases of physician addiction don't surface on the medical board's website today.

"We're very supportive of the current program, and we do believe it falls within the effective standards in place around the country. We think it's great that the board would take the opportunity to mediate and return a valuable community resource back to the community," Landrith says.

But Jon Hinz of the Arizona Trial Lawyers Association says current laws favor the few physicians who are responsible for the majority of malpractice.

"Two percent of doctors are responsible for 75 percent of malpractice," Hinz says. "But if they keep passing these broad laws that protect all doctors, they're protecting the bad ones along with the good ones. By helping the very worst, they're lowering the level of the whole profession. They're literally opening the door for every quack who can't practice in another state to come here to Arizona."

Hinz says the laws can be traced beyond physician trade groups to malpractice insurance companies.

"There are countless measures to keep physician addiction as private as possible," he says. "They don't want monitoring because that protects them from civil liability. If the doctor was monitored and then hurt somebody while proven to be an addict, he would get sued."

Landrith disagrees. He says drug-testing physicians for more than five years would be cumbersome and unfair.

"We don't have any information to the fact that there's something wrong with the status quo. Lifelong monitoring would probably be unfair. We'd say, show us the data. Show us the studies that say it's appropriate. If you can show us the studies, then we'll talk," Landrith adds.

Dr. Greg Skipper, a national expert on physician addiction, heads Alabama's equivalent to the MAP program. He has studied thousands of addicted physicians and thinks lifelong monitoring would better protect not only the public, but also physicians.

"I think lifelong [monitoring] is a good idea," Skipper says. He adds that more state boards, such as Alabama's, are requiring some physicians to agree to lifelong monitoring. Arizona's is not among them. In fact, the Arizona Medical Board could not name a single physician who has opted into lifelong drug testing.

"The medical board can say you have to do this indefinitely," Skipper says. "Sometimes malpractice companies will require it. Actually, that's becoming more and more of a trend, where some third-party requires lifelong monitoring."

In California, that third party is the legislature. After California's physician rehab failed its fourth audit, state lawmakers there forced the board to scrap its MAP program and present something more effective by June 2008.

Audits of the California program revealed many of the same holes found in Arizona's: physicians practicing unmonitored and killing or injuring patients, and MAP graduates relapsing into career-ending addiction.

A full-fledged audit could dig much deeper than *New Times* did, simply because more information is available to auditors. A committee of state lawmakers can order the Arizona auditor general to perform such an audit. Fellmeth says that's the only way to evaluate the program's success or failure.

"An external audit is invaluable. Unfortunately, you cannot believe the medical board because most members of the medical board have no idea how that program works or how it's supposed to work. You can't trust the staff of the program to be straight with you. They never want to self-report, 'Oh, we're doing a bad job,'" Fellmeth says.

"We've had 27 years of spin about this program, of essentially lying with this false success rate, and every state program does it. I've seen it. Our program doesn't monitor any participant after they've left the program. They have no idea if this program is effective in the long term. To make any conclusions, you have to continue tracking them."

Downey, the medical board spokesman, says the board isn't cutting breaks for addicted physicians. "The Arizona Medical Board always keeps its mission in mind: Protect public health and safety. It investigates these cases completely, thoroughly, and fairly in a standard way with a formal process."

Downey admits that it's a tricky business to balance the doctor's right to practice with the patient's right to safety.

"We're trying to preserve the physicians we have. If we can rehab a physician and get him to take care of his problem, we don't lose a physician," Downey says. "The problem is, when you revoke a physician's license, you impact the lives of about 2,000 patients who are looking for a physician. That's not so easy these days. That doesn't mean we cut the doctor any deal. It's just, we're trying to balance public safety with the doctor's career here."

✦

Laura Migliano's story ended with her death after Dr. Thomas Grade over-prescribed methadone. But Grade's story continued.

After Migliano's death, Grade's partners voted him out of the practice and the office building he'd constructed. But Grade still held his license to practice, with a restriction only on the drugs he could prescribe.

Two years later, on March 4, 2006, Kathryn Curtis Campbell nearly died during a routine cervical epidural performed by Grade. According to a lawsuit and a medical board complaint, Campbell's heart stopped; she was legally dead. She was revived and rushed to a hospital. The lawsuit has since settled out of court for an undisclosed amount.

Grade continued to practice. Another complaint was filed, but because the board dismissed it in April 2007 the details remain secret.

Two weeks after that complaint was dismissed, Grade's wife, Emily, a radiation oncologist, arranged an addiction intervention.

On a Wednesday afternoon, Grade drove his black Mercedes SUV into the upscale Circle G Ranches neighborhood in Gilbert and parked next to his restored 1969 Camaro in his three-car garage.

At his home, Grade's family and friends, along with a professional interventionist, tried to convince Grade that he needed help for his addiction. The intervention didn't work.

According to a Gilbert police report, "Thomas became very angry and ordered everyone out of the house. When they all refused to leave, Thomas started screaming and yelling obscenities."

Grade shoved his wife, shouted at the interventionist, and retreated to the basement, yelling. Gilbert police arrived at the home to find Grade inebriated and barricaded in the closet of a basement bedroom.

Officers beat down the bedroom door and tried to arrest Grade. When he resisted, they used a Taser on him.

Grade was booked at the county jail. His wife soon dropped all charges.

In a phone interview from his home in Gilbert, where he still lives with his wife and four children, Grade is difficult to understand. He sounds like a fine-tuned machine that's been fed the wrong fuel, his complex vocabulary packed with four-syllable medical terms.

Grade says that after he was released from jail, he hopped a flight to the Ukraine to find a new wife.

"After Ukraine, I was paralyzed in Kiev, it turns out. I'm thinking that's what I might title my book, *Paralyzed in Kiev*. Well, I was looking for a woman to have another family with because my wife, also a doctor, is in the middle of a divorce with me," Grade slurs.

"It's a meaty story. I became so ill through the course of this. Post-traumatic stress probably instigated from a sporting injury in 1984. I started to get ill [at] the time when the medical board came after me. It's one of the worst boards in the country. I've been doing these hyperbaric treatments."

After Grade's arrest, the board ordered him back into addiction treatment, but Grade didn't show up for treatment or the required drug tests.

In September the medical board met to vote on Grade's license. Physicians usually bring an attorney to such votes and defend their right to make a living. But Grade didn't show.

On September 14, 2007, the board voted to revoke Grade's license, citing an evident relapse. It had been four months since Grade's arrest, one year since Kathryn Curtis Campbell went "code blue" during a routine epidural, three years since Laura Migliano died of a prescribed overdose, and 16 years since Grade graduated from rehab.

Grade still doesn't seem to understand that his license was stripped because of his addiction relapse.

Contacted by *New Times*, Dr. Emily Grade says her husband didn't practice under the influence.

"As physicians, we don't always get our records perfect," she says of the discrepancy between Grade's office notes and the actual prescription he wrote for Migliano. She thinks the medical board's strict discipline after Migliano's death drove him back into addiction.

"He had an amazing life until they took it away," Emily Grade says. "It's also a good lesson. Addiction is a lifelong risk." ●◆

Dr. Loophole

John Dickerson

APRIL 10, 2008

A Florida doctor lost his license after he was diagnosed as a sex addict—he claimed he could cure his female patients by fondling their breasts.

A Utah doctor lost his license after he illegally prescribed drugs over the Internet.

A California doctor lost his license after he was charged with hiding more than half a million dollars in profits, convicted of tax fraud, and sent to prison.

Another California doctor's license was suspended twice. The first time, he was accused of missing cancer in two patients. The second time, of misprescribing drugs.

Yet another California doctor went to prison and was ordered to pay $15 million in fines after he was convicted of defrauding Medicare by performing unnecessary surgery on the eyes of elderly patients.

And a fourth California doctor had his license suspended, then moved to Arizona and lost a patient. The doctor injected the patient with either cow hormones or sheep DNA (the doctor's given two versions of the story), which caused an infection. The patient died.

In the world of medicine, there are no second chances. A doctor makes a misstep, and a patient can die. That's why the boards that license allopathic and osteopathic doctors—M.D.s and D.O.s, respectively—are so tough, and often criticized for not being tough enough. Lose your M.D. license in one state in the U.S., and you may never practice medicine again. Certainly not in this state.

Unless you know about Arizona's Homeopathic Board of Medical Examiners.

For a few hundred dollars, some extra training (sometimes provided by the board's president himself, for a fee) and a test on the principles of homeopathy, an M.D. or D.O. who likely can't secure another medical license can get a license to practice homeopathic medicine in the state of Arizona. You'll be banned from some procedures, but for the most part, you can go back to practicing medicine—diagnosing patients, prescribing drugs, even performing minor surgeries.

All the doctors listed above—and more—are now homeopathic physicians, licensed to practice by the state of Arizona. (Except for that Utah doctor. He lost his homeopath's license last month after a patient died during a procedure he was not authorized to perform.)

And it's all perfectly legal under Arizona law.

Homeopathy isn't dangerous, per se. The alternative practice began in Germany in 1810. By modern medical and chemistry standards, it's a harmless pursuit because it dilutes chemicals almost to the purity of drinking water before injecting them into the body.

Classic homeopathy uses no prescriptions and is based on a theory that "like cures like" in sick patients. For example, if you're allergic to pollen in the air, a homeopathic physician might take that very pollen, dilute it, and inject you with it. The theory is that a small amount of the problem ingredient will cure you of your symptoms—sneezing, in the case of allergies. Modern chemists say homeopathic injections are so diluted that they have no effect, good or bad.

One popular homeopathic cure, oddly enough, is poison ivy oil. Because poison ivy causes a rash and can cause a fever, homeopathic physicians dilute the oil in alcohol, dilute it again, and use it to treat rashes and fevers. It may seem backward, but that's homeopathy. Homeopathic doctors track which substances help which patients, and then try the same treatments—pollen, poison ivy, or otherwise—to treat patients with similar symptoms.

But that hardly matters here, because Arizona's homeopathic license is not always used to practice homeopathy. In fact, none of the doctors in this story were practicing it when they killed or harmed their patients. And, as the Arizona Auditor General found last year, the real problem is that the board is lax when it comes to poor medical treatment, regardless of whether it's considered homeopathic.

Homeopathic doctors can get the D.E.A. authority to prescribe the same drugs an M.D. or D.O. can prescribe, and are allowed to perform "minor" surgeries (for example, a homeo-path can perform a vasectomy and administer local anesthesia, but can't perform a breast augmentation or give a patient an epidural)—which have nothing to do with homeopathic med-icine. That attracts doctors who can't get, or who are about to lose, their conventional licenses.

Only two other states, Connecticut and Nevada, issue homeopathic licenses. Those states have tighter guidelines for getting a license and give their homeopaths less prescribing and surgical power than Arizona does.

So Arizona's license is a unique opportunity. In effect, the law amounts to a loophole for doctors who've gotten in trou-ble, or know they'll soon get in trouble, to practice medicine with the initials M.D.h., as homeopathic physicians—even if they don't practice homeopathy.

The requirements for getting an M.D. license in Arizona are strict. You cannot even apply for an M.D. license if you've ever lost an M.D. license in another state. (And that includes California, which can "revoke" an M.D. license, then reinstate it. If your California M.D. license has been revoked, you can-not get an Arizona M.D. license.) You also cannot apply if you have a felony conviction.

It's a little easier to get a D.O. license. If you have lost your D.O. license elsewhere, or you're a convicted felon, you are eligible to apply—but given recent history, it is unlikely Ari-zona's D.O. board will let you through. An M.D. cannot apply for a D.O. license, or vice versa. The rules for M.D.s and D.O.s are similar in other states.

In order to apply for a homeopathic license in Arizona, you must be either an M.D. or a D.O. in good standing in Arizona or another state. If you have lost a license elsewhere in the past, that's okay. If you are a convicted felon, you're still free to apply. And most significant: once you are a homeopath, if you lose the license that got you in the door in the first place, you're fine. It doesn't affect your homeopathic license.

(Homeopaths in Arizona aren't even required by law to practice homeopathic medicine. That's a far cry from Con-necticut, where the homeopathic license is good for homeo-pathic treatment and little else.)

Doctors who've committed felonies or have had their licenses revoked in other states need only to listen to a couple audio CDs about homeopathy before applying for a homeopathic license in Arizona. (One $880 correspondence course is actually taught by board president Dr. Todd Rowe.)

A homeopathic license in Arizona costs $975, almost twice as much as a conventional M.D. license ($500). Since a conventional license allows doctors to practice classic homeopathy, there are only two reasons to pay more for the homeopathic license: because you're banned from getting a conventional license or because you want to experiment with treatments the conventional board doesn't allow.

The homeopathic board also fails to discipline the doctors it has already licensed. That's one finding from—amazingly—the first audit of the homeopathic board done since 1985. The report was released in August 2007 by Arizona's auditor general.

"The board appears to allow conduct that the other two Arizona physician regulatory boards have determined is unsafe or unprofessional," the auditor general reports.

Auditors concluded there may no longer be a need for the board, which was created in 1981 at the behest of alternative doctors, because many alternative procedures are now allowed with conventional licenses. They also found the board has:

- Sometimes waited for more than a year to look into complaints against doctors
- Licensed homeopathic doctors who weren't competent in homeopathy
- Licensed a revoked Arizona D.O. who failed the homeopathy exam three times
- Dismissed complaints against doctors without considering the accusations
- Allowed doctors to practice medicine far beyond the scope of homeopathy
- Failed to explain the difference between an M.D. and an M.D.h. to the public

Copies of the August 2007 audit were delivered to the 12 state senators and representatives who sit on the Joint Legislative Audit Committee.

And yet, legislation currently being considered by the state House of Representatives would rubber-stamp the homeopathic board for two more years. Another bill attempts to clean up the board, but it fails to plug the loophole that lets doctors with revoked licenses into Arizona. In fact, the second bill solidifies the board's power to license doctors who have had their licenses revoked.

Current homeopathic board members say they are addressing the concerns listed in the audit. But recent board decisions indicate otherwise.

New Times researched the licensing history of all 107 homeopathic physicians in the state and reviewed hundreds of pages of board records. Among the findings:

- One-fourth of Arizona's homeopaths have lost their conventional M.D. or D.O. licenses.
- The homeopathic board has licensed at least five convicted felons, whose crimes range from tax fraud to mail fraud. Four are now practicing. The other is on parole.
- The board dismissed a complaint against a homeopath after a patient died. Although a county medical examiner determined that the homeopath caused the death, the board ruled that the procedure did not violate the rules of homeopathy.
- One-fourth of the homeopaths licensed in Arizona don't live or practice in Arizona. Some practice with their Arizona M.D.h. in states where their M.D. license has been revoked. That is illegal in some states and legal in others.
- Other state medical boards pay professional investigators to study complaints against doctors. The homeopathic board uses volunteer alternative doctors to investigate their colleagues.
- Some doctors use their Arizona homeopathic licenses to perform face lifts, breast augmentations, liposuctions, and other surgeries that homeopaths aren't allowed to perform.
- Doctors who claim an interest in homeopathy need little training in the field to get an Arizona license.

Anna Prassa was a public member of the homeopathic board from 2000 to 2006. She says the board is flawed beyond repair.

"There's a reason why another state revokes a doctor's license," Prassa says. "For that to happen—and then they can waltz right into our state and get a license—that's a problem. It's a crime."

DR. GARY PAGE

In 2004, Dr. Gary Page, a dermatologist and M.D. from Utah, sent an application to the Arizona Medical Board. The Arizona Medical Board sent Page's application right back. Because his Utah license had been surrendered for Internet prescribing (and his California license revoked, as a result), Page wasn't eligible by law to apply for an M.D. license in Arizona.

If Arizona didn't have a Homeopathic Board of Medical Examiners, Page's story would likely have ended there.

Unable to practice medicine as a conventional M.D., Page sent an application to Arizona's homeopathic board.

Even though Page had no history of practicing homeopathic medicine, and though he'd been previously stripped of his medical licenses, Arizona's homeopathic board welcomed Page into the state.

Page was issued a homeopathic M.D.h. license. He moved to Gilbert with his wife and five kids—supposedly to practice alternative medicine.

But on July 3, 2007, Page was not practicing homeopathy, or any form of alternative medicine. He was performing a standard liposuction—a surgery not allowed under a homeopathic license.

According to records from the homeopathic board and the Arizona Medical Board, Page's patient, a 53-year-old woman, prepaid for liposuction on her thighs. Page injected the patient with anesthesia, which was allowed by his M.D.h. license, and then performed the liposuction, which wasn't.

The patient died shortly after surgery. The Maricopa County Medical Examiner cannot release the cause of death because board documents have concealed the victim's name.

That death—the third fatality at the Anthem cosmetic surgery clinic—was reported by the media. What wasn't reported is that Page walked right through the homeopathic board's loophole, securing an Arizona M.D.h. even after he'd lost his M.D. licenses in other states.

On March 18 of this year, Page surrendered his homeopathic license as the board was preparing to revoke his license because liposuction falls outside the scope of "minor" surgery homeopaths are allowed to perform.

He never could have practiced in Arizona, if not for the loophole that lets previously revoked doctors practice here as homeopaths.

Page did not return phone calls and emails seeking comment.

DR. GABRIEL COUSENS

In 1998, Charles Levy, 57, booked a flight to Arizona. Levy, an insurance agent, told his family he was in good health and planned to visit the Tree of Life Spa for a time of rejuvenation with a homeopathic doctor.

He looked forward to the live organic vegan diet and spiritual rest described by Dr. Gabriel Cousens, whose website promotes him as an M.D. and M.D.h.

Cousens is not eligible for an M.D. license in Arizona because his license was once taken away (but reinstated) in California and remains censured in New York. According to Arizona Medical Board spokesman Roger Downey, that makes a doctor ineligible for an Arizona medical license. If Cousens were a D.O., he would be eligible. But he's not. He's been practicing here as a homeopath for 15 years.

According to court records from a civil suit filed by Levy's family, Levy showed up at Cousens's secluded campus in the green hills of Patagonia, Arizona. He was hoping for a time of physical and spiritual rest. Cousens told him that injections of cow adrenaline and/or sheep DNA could energize his body. Levy agreed to five injections, which aren't a homeopathic treatment but are allowed by Arizona's homeopathic board.

Unfortunately, the injection site—on Levy's right buttock— grew infected, so he went to see Cousens about it. Cousens didn't recommend an antibiotic. Instead, he treated the growing abscess with acupuncture and massage.

The infected area became green and black. It spread down Levy's thigh, and on March 1, 1998, Levy did not wake up in his dorm room at the Tree of Life Spa. Cousens found Levy unconscious and attempted CPR, with no success.

Cousens did not call 911. Instead, he called an air ambulance, and arranged for a helicopter pickup on the football field of a nearby high school.

Cousens and a nurse carried Levy—draped in a bathrobe, bleeding from his mouth and groin—to a car and drove him five minutes to the field.

A Patagonia police officer was driving by the school when he saw Cousens and a number of spa guests gathered around an unclothed body lying on the grass.

Levy's buttock and thigh were black and swollen. His eyes were wide open. He was dead. After the helicopter took the body, Dr. Cousens told the officer that he'd injected Levy with sheep DNA. Later, Cousens contradicted his statement, saying the injection was actually cow hormones.

Whether the injection was cow or sheep didn't matter to Santa Cruz County Medical Examiner Dr. Cynthia Porterfield. She examined Levy's body and ruled that the injection and subsequent infection killed him. Specifically, she found that Levy died from Clostridium perfringens, a type of bacteria that grows in gas gangrene. During the Civil War, C. perfringens claimed thousands of soldiers' lives when it grew in their battle wounds. Modern antibiotics can kill the bacteria easily when used.

"I spoke with him the day before. The next day, I got a phone call that he was gone," Levy's son, Howard, says. "I pretty much haven't recovered since. He was not on any medication, didn't have high blood pressure, or a weight problem. He could go out and run three miles on the boardwalk."

Levy filed a lawsuit against Cousens, and Cousens paid an undisclosed amount to settle the suit after the medical examiner pinned the death directly on him.

The osteopathic medical board also examined the autopsy and ruled that the medical examiner was right to name the injection and infection as the causes of death.

But when Cousens's dead patient came up before the homeopathic board in 2001, the board dismissed the complaint—despite the medical examiner's findings.

The board ruled that, though a patient did die, the doctor did not violate any laws of homeopathic medicine.

In his October 11, 2000, court deposition, board member Dr. Garry Gordon says he served as the board's lead investigator into Cousens, but he also worked as an expert witness for Cousens in court.

Because the homeopathic board dismissed the complaint, the medical board in California—where Cousens holds his M.D.—has no way of knowing Cousens injected a patient with animal hormones. It has no way of knowing he treated a growing infection with acupuncture or that a county medical examiner named his treatment as the cause of a patient's death.

The Arizona board has since destroyed audio records from that meeting (technically, it did so legally).

"I think it's a travesty that he's still practicing in Arizona," Howard Levy says from his home in New York. "Those people who are allowing this to continue to happen are just as guilty. The simple fact that he can continue to practice medicine in any way, shape, or form shows that the system is failing the general public."

Today, Cousens still practices at his spa in Patagonia. He says he has "28 cubic feet of scientific literature" that disprove the medical examiner. He says Levy died of an extremely rare syndrome that strikes suddenly and kills in hours. Cousens also says Levy was sick when he arrived at the spa and had the gas gangrene infection long before his cow adrenaline injections.

"Dr. Porterfield, the pathologist, really was neglectful," says Cousens, who also says he thinks he would have won the case in court. (He says his insurance company forced him to settle.) "I believe that if we were in front of the medical board, they would have cleared me just as well."

DR. CHARLES CROSBY

In 2002 the Florida Department of Health forced Dr. Charles Crosby, a D.O., into the state's impaired-physician program.

Crosby had been kissing and groping female patients and staff, according to Florida records.

Crosby was diagnosed with a narcissistic disorder and with Frottuerism, a disorder "characterized by intense sexually arousing fantasies, sexual urges, or behaviors involving touching or rubbing against the body of a non-consenting person."

The surgeon and pain-management specialist's bedside manner included "touching patients' breasts in a way they found offensive (example, stroking their nipples) . . . kissing patients and staff . . . and using crass and sexual remarks that others found offensive."

Crosby told a psychiatrist he had "developed a special technique of manipulating women's breasts to treat pain in other areas of their body." That psychiatrist diagnosed Crosby with a breast fetish and ruled him unfit to practice medicine.

In June 2003 Crosby was still practicing medicine when he was caught manipulating the breasts and ribs of a woman at a medical trade show in Norfolk, Virginia.

On March 17, 2004, Florida's physician intervention program warned Crosby that it was restricting his practice and might suspend his Florida license.

Two months later, Crosby was standing before Arizona's homeopathic board, petitioning for a homeopathic license. Crosby didn't have enough homeopathic training, but the board voted to give him a license, as long as he took 40 hours of homeopathic courses. The homeopathic board licensed Crosby in Arizona—even as the Florida board was investigating him for groping his female patients.

Two months after Crosby secured his Arizona homeopathic license, the Florida board suspended his license. Crosby apparently never moved to Arizona. He lives and advertises in Florida, and his license is still suspended there. His Arizona homeopathic license is active, though he's on probation, which means Crosby has to submit reports that confirm he's seeing a psychiatrist.

Crosby declined comment for this story.

DR. MURRAY SUSSER

Dr. Murray Susser, 73, has been practicing alternative medicine for decades. The California Medical Board has taken his license away twice.

The first time was in 1997. According to California Medical Board records, Susser failed to identify some conventional cases of cancer. He failed to diagnose colon cancer in one patient, even though the patient had blood in her stool and complained of rectal bleeding.

For another patient, Susser prescribed natural vitamins in dangerous quantities, including "tannic acid, which is carcinogenic," and testosterone, which boosted blood pressure to unhealthy levels. According to California Medical Board records, Susser failed to see bowel cancer in that patient, too.

Susser's discipline culminated when he advised a patient who was jaundiced and experiencing severe abdominal pain to not go to the emergency room. Paramedics forced the patient to go to the ER, where she was diagnosed with severe liver and pancreas damage, due to the all-natural injections.

After two years of community service at 25 hours a week, Susser's California medical license was restored in 2000. His New York license is still surrendered.

In 2002 Susser secured a homeopathic license in Arizona. He's been practicing in Scottsdale ever since. In 2005, the California Medical Board again took away Susser's license (he's on probation again) for prescribing ketamine, an anesthetic and animal tranquilizer.

In 2006 Arizona's homeopathic board examined the same charges and dismissed them.

Known as "Special K" in the club scene, ketamine is similar to PCP. It can cause hallucinations along with extreme detachment from reality. The homeopathic board concluded that Susser was not in the wrong to prescribe ketamine to fibromyalgia patients—even though it falls outside the conventional standard of care.

In an interview for this story, Susser called ketamine the pain reliever of the future for patients with chronic pain.

The U.S. Food and Drug Administration begs to differ. The FDA approves ketamine only as an anesthetic and veterinary tranquilizer.

Susser also said the details in the California Medical Board's paperwork were charges and not facts. He says they weren't proved and that he signed the agreements only to avoid court fees.

DR. ELLIOTT SCHMERLER

On January 9, 2007, a physician stood before Arizona's homeopathic board and told his personal story of redemption. Too bad it wasn't all true.

It had been five years since Dr. Elliott Schmerler pleaded guilty to felony tax fraud. According to IRS documents, Schmerler funneled more than $500,000 through a corporation in the Bahamas and then used the money for personal expenses. He was sentenced to 15 months in prison and stripped of his Nevada medical license.

Two of Schmerler's cosmetic surgery patients had poor results, and he paid out money in lawsuits to two others, according to his homeopathic application and records from the Nevada Medical Board.

By December 2006 Schmerler had served his time in prison and finished his probation for the tax fraud case. He wrote the IRS a check for $96,533 to settle the score. That month the Nevada Medical Board issued Schmerler a restricted medical license that specifically banned him from performing cosmetic surgery in the state.

Because of his revocation and felony conviction, Schmerler could not perform cosmetic surgery as an M.D. in Arizona.

One month after Nevada issued him a restricted license, Schmerler was in Arizona petitioning for his homeopathic license. Standing in the basement boardroom at the state building for regulatory boards, Schmerler told the board a big lie.

"Since our previous meeting, I was issued a new, unrestricted license by the Nevada Allopathic Medical Board," he said.

None of the board members mentioned that Schmerler's printed license restricted him from ever performing any kind of cosmetic surgery.

Instead, the discussion focused on giving doctors second chances, particularly when their history involves felonies.

"I fully recognize we may take a little heat from the media because 'that homeopathic board is back to licensing felons again,'" then-board president Dr. Garry Gordon said as he made a motion to accept Schmerler's application. "But I take the full responsibility of recognizing everything I've seen and read about this doctor going forward."

The board members didn't ask Schmerler why Nevada banned him from cosmetic surgery. They didn't ask about the liposuction patient who ended up with an infected, oozing stomach or the breast augmentation patient who woke up with a lopsided chest—both documented in his own application and in Nevada Medical Board records.

Nobody asked Schmerler why the Nevada Medical Board disciplined him for "intent to deceive" or whether he would attempt to practice his specialties—liposuction and breast augmentation—in Arizona. Those procedures aren't allowed with a homeopathic license.

Instead, the board took Schmerler at his word. Gordon asked his fellow members to give Schmerler another chance at honesty.

"Physicians are really not well suited to digging ditches, but they don't have a lot of other things they're good at doing," he said. "They shouldn't be used car salesman. When I was in California, I was astonished how everyone who serves their time and does their probation is finally re-licensed."

Arizona law doesn't let the conventional board give M.D.'s such second chances. The only way Schmerler could bring his services to Arizona would be through the homeopathic board's loophole.

The board voted 5-0 to grant Schmerler a homeopathic medical license.

So how has Schmerler used his shot at redemption?

Schmerler advertises himself on the Web and at his Scottsdale office as an M.D. He is not a licensed M.D. in Arizona.

Homeopathic board President Dr. Todd Rowe says it's illegal for a homeopathic doctor to advertise as an M.D. if the doctor isn't licensed in Arizona.

According to Schmerler's office staff at A Surgical Art: A Cosmetic Surgery Group in downtown Scottsdale, Schmerler doesn't specialize in homeopathic medicine. He specializes in cosmetic surgeries—also illegal because his homeopathic license limits him to minor surgery.

A call to Schmerler's office confirms he specifically performs tummy tucks, breast augmentations, liposuctions, and facelifts, none of which is minor and none of which is legal to perform with only a homeopathic license.

There's no evidence Schmerler has harmed anyone in the year he's practiced here. But it's clear that he walked right through the homeopathic loophole to perform cosmetic surgery—the very thing he's banned from practicing in his home state of Nevada, and the very thing Arizona's conventional medical boards are designed to regulate.

Schmerler did not return phone calls requesting an interview for this story.

DR. RICK SHACKET

In 2003 Dr. Schmerler's partner in practice, Dr. Rick Shacket, shared the same page of an IRS press release, long before he shared the same office suite in Scottsdale. The press release detailed the felony convictions of both doctors.

Shacket secured his homeopathic license in 2001, before his conviction. The next year, he was sentenced to 33 months in prison after he pleaded guilty to creating a false identity so that he could hide $540,000 in profits, according to IRS documents.

A standard practice for nearly every medical board in the country, the California Osteopathic Board revoked Shacket's license. But Arizona's homeopathic board didn't. Shacket's Arizona license remained intact even while he was in prison and on probation. His profile on the Arizona homeopathic board website shows no discipline or letters of concern since his licensing in 2001.

In 2005, the osteopathic board also gave Schmerler an Arizona license.

Shacket did not return calls for comment.

DR. JEFFREY RUTGARD

In 1995, Dr. Jeffrey Rutgard, a San Diego ophthalmologist, was found guilty of talking senior patients into unnecessary eye surgeries so he could pocket the Medicare payments. He was sentenced to 11 years in prison and ordered to pay $15 million to Medicare. The California Medical Board revoked his license during the 1994 trial.

Rutgard was out of prison by 2004. He promised the Arizona homeopathic board he would move to the state to learn alternative medicine. A chiropractor even testified that he'd take Rutgard under his wing to keep an eye on him.

Four years later Rutgard apparently has yet to relocate to Arizona. The board hasn't penalized him, and Rutgard's license is intact. Despite his revoked California M.D. license, he practices part time in California with his Arizona M.D.h. and under the supervision of another homeopath, according to homeopathic board records.

California Medical Board spokeswoman Candace Cohen says Rutgard is breaking the law in that state if he is diagnosing patients or prescribing drugs, regardless of the Arizona license.

New Times could not confirm whether Rutgard has broken the law in California. He has paid his annual renewal fee of almost $1,000 for five years.

Rutgard did not return a message requesting an interview left on his home answering machine.

Dr. Todd Rowe has served on Arizona's homeopathic board since 2005. He took over as president a month after state auditors released their report in the fall of 2007. Rowe, a psychiatrist, holds a valid Arizona M.D. license in addition to his homeopathic license.

Rowe says he and his board members are working to fix the problems outlined in the audit.

"I do feel like there's cleaning to do, and we have been working on that. We thought the auditors did an excellent job and really listened to the issues," he says.

But Rowe disagrees with the audit's statement that the homeopathic board may not serve a purpose. He and others in the alternative medicine community say Arizona holds the unique position of protecting alternative medicine.

As for the audit finding that licensed homeopaths aren't practicing homeopathic medicine, Rowe says the board wants to change its name to the board of "homeopathic and integrative medicine." That way the board can continue licensing alternative treatments outside the scope of homeopathy.

Rowe adds that the board is prepared to protect and regulate alternative medicine and that it's cracking down. "We've been tightening our discipline, at least since I've come on board," he says. "All of our disciplinary actions have been at least [as stringent] if not more stringent than other boards."

He says the board is speeding up its investigations, too, by using volunteer homeopathic doctors to investigate complaints against their colleagues. Though that's a far cry from the professional, independent investigators the conventional medical board uses, it may be better than the recent system, in which board members investigated complaints themselves.

"We've made significant changes in the last year. There's a flow chart now that mandates we investigate every matter, at least since I've been president," Rowe says.

But three months ago, on January 9, the board failed to see an apparent violation of law right under its nose. Dr. Elliott Schmerler, the doctor banned from practicing cosmetic surgery in Nevada, stood before the board. It had been one year since the board voted to license Schmerler, a convicted felon.

The American Board of Cosmetic Surgeons had filed a board complaint that Schmerler was using their acronym, ABCS, on his business card and website—implying he's still board-certified, which he's not.

Schmerler showed the homeopathic board a new business card and said he had pulled the misleading acronym off his website. The board didn't discipline him, writing him a non-disciplinary letter of concern instead.

With that, Schmerler was off the hook.

The board had just been reminded, by the death of Dr. Gary Page's liposuction patient in July 2007, that it's illegal to use a homeopathic license for major cosmetic surgery in Arizona.

Still, none of the board members asked Schmerler why he's advertising as a cosmetic surgeon and M.D. when he isn't licensed as either in Arizona.

Rowe tells *New Times* he is aware that it's illegal for a homeopath to perform breast augmentations and tummy tucks in Arizona without an M.D. or D.O. license. He also confirms that "it's against the law for a doctor who isn't an M.D. in Arizona to advertise himself as an M.D."

So why didn't either issue come up in January, when Schmerler was before the board?

"We are only allowed to focus, as a board, on the complaint. We're limited in what we can explore outside of the initial complaint," Rowe says. But he adds that the board could open its own complaint, if it wanted. He says he's not sure why it didn't.

If Arizona lawmakers did disband the state's homeopathic board, it wouldn't be the first time that's happened in this country. In 1957, the state of Maryland disbanded its 80-year-old homeopathic board amidst controversy surrounding the doctors it was licensing. Other states have followed suit, forcing homeopaths to get licensed with the conventional board.

Some of Arizona's lawmakers say they have higher hopes for the largest homeopathic board in the nation. Despite last year's less-than-favorable audit, the state Senate voted last month to continue the board for two years.

The Senate also passed another omnibus bill that addresses a few of the problems highlighted in the audit. Both bills are expected to pass the House this month. But they don't plug the biggest loophole.

Barbara Leff, a Republican from Paradise Valley, and Paula Aboud, a Tucson Democrat, are members of the Senate Health Committee. Leff did not return calls for this story, but Aboud says she knows about the audit and that she and

Leff sponsored amendments to the omnibus bill that would affect the homeopathic board. One amendment touches more on the concerns of activist doctors than the concerns of the audit.

One new clause in the bill confirms the board's power to license doctors who've been kicked out of other states.

Aboud—who has sought treatment from homeopaths—says she's concerned about that very problem.

"If you're doing classical homeopathy, which is merely a spiritual practice of working on the level of the spirit or the body, there are not too many ways a person can be harmed," Aboud tells *New Times*.

"But this homeopathic board is allowing a homeopathic doctor to do surgery and acupuncture and treatments that do harm the public."

The bill passed by the Senate in March and pending in the House as of press time does take a step toward closing the loophole. It would require doctors who've been revoked to wait five years before applying for their homeopathic license. That doesn't stop doctors from applying months or weeks before their licenses are revoked in their home state.

Dr. Charles Crosby, the Florida sex addict, illustrates why the new legislation wouldn't close the loophole. The intent behind the new line is that a doctor like Crosby couldn't apply for a homeopathic license until five years after he lost his Florida license.

But Crosby didn't apply for his homeopathic license after Florida suspended him. He applied for it two months before they suspended him.

In all states doctors know when a medical board is investigating them. If doctors think they may lose their conventional licenses, they can secure an Arizona homeopathic license during the months of investigation in their home state.

Then, if their conventional license is stripped, they retain a homeopathic license. The bill that passed the Senate would not stop shrewd doctors from walking through the loophole. It still would allow them to keep a homeopathic license, even if they were stripped of the M.D. or D.O. license two months later—as Crosby was.

Conventional medical boards across the country rubber-stamp revocations. For example, when Dr. Gary Page surrendered his Utah license, California automatically revoked his license there.

Arizona's homeopathic board, however, doesn't have to follow suit.

The new legislation wouldn't affect the homeopathic board's ability to ignore revocations in other states—or even here in Arizona.

In fact, the proposed fixes would have let every single one of the problem doctors in this story into Arizona, though it would have delayed one doctor for two years.

If the House passes a bill that doesn't close the loophole, the governor could still veto it. Governor Janet Napolitano's spokeswoman, Jeanine L'Ecuyer, says she's surprised to hear the homeopathic board has licensed convicted felons.

"The governor has a general policy of not commenting on legislation until it's before her for her signature or veto," L'Ecuyer says. "But what you've described is of tremendous concern. We will begin the process of working with the board to see what's going on because public safety is paramount to the governor."

Dr. Kathleen Fry is one homeopath who doesn't think the new legislation would do enough. Fry is also an M.D. in good standing with the Arizona Medical Board. She testified before the Senate Health Committee in February that the homeopathic board is broken.

"I ask you not to continue this corrupt system because more people may end up maimed or dead." Fry said, then referring to Page's patient.

"It is this careless language that I believe led to the death of the unfortunate woman in Anthem last summer who underwent liposuction under local anesthesia. This language in this bill does not preclude another such tragedy occurring."

Chris Springer, executive director of the Arizona Board of Homeopathic Medical Examiners, is also the board's only employee. And she's a part-time employee. For 30 hours a week, Springer wears the hats of application reviewer, phone answerer, initial complaint investigator, and liaison between other boards and spokeswoman, among others. Before this job, she was the director of the state's board of nursing home administrators.

Springer has a few things to say about the audit and the potential new laws that would affect the board. She says there will be no more second chances for doctors who've lost their licenses elsewhere, regardless of what the legislature does this session. Her board is getting tough, Springer says. "The second chance isn't going to happen anymore."

As if the fallout from last year's audit weren't enough, Springer is fighting not just to keep the homeopathic board in existence, but also to keep her job in existence. This year, Napolitano is combining the staffs of several tiny boards. In Arizona, the concern seems to be more with consolidating office equipment and jobs than with regulation—at least, the regulation of homeopathic medicine.

In a lot of ways, Chris Springer represents the homeopathic board's six members. Down in the basement boardroom, cleaning up agendas after a recent board meeting, Springer gives her opinion of Dr. Gary Page.

She doesn't see Page as a formerly revoked doctor who found a loophole to practice in Arizona. She doesn't see him as a man whose patient died hours after a liposuction he wasn't licensed to perform.

"He has five kids and wife. Now he doesn't have a job," she says quietly. "It's sad."

Correction (posted April 24, 2008): It should have been stated that Dr. Rick Shacket surrendered his California medical license after a felony conviction for tax fraud. ✸

Blind Trust

John Dickerson

MAY 22, 2008

At 65 Paul Phillips was ready to retire. He'd raised his four kids, sold his Phoenix produce company, and even bought a 40-foot RV to drive across the country with his wife LuWanna. Phillips was working on his golf game, in anticipation of all the free time he'd have. Even more, he enjoyed playing ping-pong and catch with his grandkids.

But on March 13, 2001, Phillips found himself at the Mayo Clinic in Scottsdale, waiting to see an ophthalmologist. The vision in his left eye had suddenly gone blurry, and he was seeing floating specks of light in the same eye. Phillips has diabetes; he's had it for 18 years. He and LuWanna knew failing vision could be related, so she insisted he get the best help available. As LuWanna later recalled, she called the Mayo Clinic and scheduled an appointment with Paul's ophthalmologist.

Phillips fidgeted anxiously in the waiting room, wringing his hands—still leathery and calloused from 40 years of handling boxes of fruit and vegetables.

Then a nurse called him to examination room number 9, where she asked him to read an eye chart. After the nurse left, a man wearing the standard tie and suit coat of a Mayo physician—a trademark in the healthcare company's facilities— entered the room. He held an Executive Glaucoma Screening Form and Phillips's chart in his hand. He asked a number of questions and then examined both of Phillips's eyes.

That man, Paul Hughes, diagnosed Phillips on the spot with "K. sicca" or eye inflammation. He explained that the problem was simply dry eyes and Phillips need not worry about his left eye. Hughes recommended over-the-counter salve and drops, known as "tears." Then he walked Phillips to the billing desk, shook his hand and thanked him for visiting the Mayo Clinic.

On the way home, with LuWanna behind the wheel, Phillips wondered aloud why the doctor hadn't dilated his eye. He concluded the doctor knew more about eyes than he did.

He used the drops, but they didn't alleviate the blurriness or floating flashes of light.

Two weeks later, the Phillips were sitting in a movie at the Deer Valley Harkins Theatre on Bell Road when Paul's left eye went completely dark—as if somebody had dropped a veil over it.

The retina in his left eye had detached. The symptoms Paul Phillips reported at Mayo were classic signs of a tearing retina; according to the Mayo Clinic's own literature, if caught at that point when he'd visited the clinic, the condition has about an 85 percent chance of successful treatment with retinal reattachment. Once it had detached, it was much tougher. And today, after a series of surgeries, Phillips is permanently blind in his left eye.

So why did the Mayo Clinic fail to properly diagnose Phillips's run-of-the-mill malady?

Could be because Paul Hughes, the man who treated him—who held his chart and looked in his eye and recommended drops—isn't a doctor at all. He's not a physician's assistant or a nurse, either.

In fact, Hughes has no formal medical training and has never been licensed to provide healthcare or even sell glasses in Arizona. And yet, for almost 20 years, Paul Hughes "triaged" eye patients in the Mayo Clinic's ophthalmology department, deciding which doctor, if any, they should see. Some patients, like Phillips, never did see a doctor—or any other licensed practitioner beyond a nurse. Phillips says he wasn't told this. He assumed he'd seen a doctor; his wife had asked for an appointment with one; he'd been seen by a nurse, then by a man in a coat who certainly looked like a doctor and never said otherwise.

Even after Phillips's catastrophe, when the case had gone to court—where a jury would eventually award Phillips $3.5 million—Paul Hughes apparently had no contrition.

"I don't feel like I need to be certified in something I'm efficient at," Hughes said to the jury about the treatment he gave Phillips.

When Phillips learned that he was misdiagnosed by a non-doctor, he and his lawyer told the Mayo Clinic they could donate $2 million to the blind, or they could brace for a lawsuit.

Mayo chose the lawsuit, and lost.

In July 2006 a jury found in Phillips's favor; the judge lowered the medical malpractice judgment to $750,000, an amount that matches similar cases involving blindness.

Phillips says he has yet to spend a penny of it. (After the emotional turmoil of the trial, he's decided to keep the money.) Instead, he's spent the last year mourning the recent death of his wife of 50 years, as well as the loss of his depth perception.

Phillips's story is a case in point that when you visit the doctor, you can't assume you're seeing a doctor—or even a trained practitioner. Not at the Mayo Clinic. Not anywhere. *New Times* reported the details of this case mainly from interviews with Phillips, court pleadings, depositions, and transcripts from the trial.

It's hard to fault Paul Phillips for assuming that a practitioner in a suit and tie, holding his chart at the Mayo Clinic, was qualified to give a diagnosis. After all, Phillips had gone to the best. He knew of Mayo's international reputation for leading the way in cancer research. And Mayo had just been named the number one choice of hospital by consumers in the Phoenix area for the third year in a row, according to the National Research Corporation.

Beyond that, the Mayo Clinic—founded in Rochester, Minnesota, in 1888—is an icon, considered the gold standard of medical care. When the company opened an outpost in northeast Scottsdale almost 100 years later, in 1987, Mayo drew patients like bees to honey.

But the standards in place at the Mayo Clinic's ophthalmology department when Paul Hughes was hired—standards clearly not reviewed as the years went on—were hardly golden.

As revealed in court testimony, Paul Hughes was more than just a non-doctor who had his own office located between the spaces of Mayo physicians. Hughes came to Mayo as a convicted felon; his offenses included forgery and cocaine possession.

Not that Hughes was qualified to practice medicine in the first place; he doesn't even have a college degree.

If Hughes wasn't pretending to be a doctor, he was clearly allowed to see and treat patients in a way other non-doctors were not. (And in a way not allowed by Arizona law.) That's because Hughes was working for a longtime friend, then Mayo's director of ophthalmology, Dr. John Creasman.

Contacted for this story, Creasman says he trusted Hughes, regardless of his lack of official training.

"All technicians in our department become pretty good diagnosticians. You could take any one of them, and 95 times out of 100, they could tell the doctors what the patients had. They were right most of the time, so that was part of their responsibility," Creasman says.

Neither Creasman nor Hughes works for the Mayo Clinic now.

Creasman says that Hughes, still a close friend, was devastated by the lawsuit and would not comment for this story. Other attempts to reach Hughes were not successful.

Mayo employees testified that Creasman's trust of Hughes resulted in Hughes seeing 6 to 13 ophthalmology patients per day at the Mayo Clinic, usually without any physician supervision.

Hughes worked in that capacity at the Mayo Clinic for 18 years.

No other lawsuits against Creasman or Hughes surfaced in a search of lawsuits at the Maricopa County Superior Court and at Arizona's U.S. District Court. Creasman has a spotless record with the Arizona Medical Board, too. (At least, to the extent that the medical board keeps such records. For more information about the Arizona Board of Medical Examiners and other state-regulated boards, see the earlier stories in this series, "The Doctor is Out," March 6, and "Dr. Loophole," April 10).

Even if Creasman and Hughes aren't contrite, the Mayo Clinic certainly is.

Speaking publicly about the case, apparently for the first time, the CEO of the Mayo Clinic admits that Phillips's care was not ideal. He says it was a fluke that won't happen again.

"I've been in this position 6 years, and I've been with Mayo 31 years. Personally and representing the organization, I feel bad and take responsibility when things go bad. We see about 100,000 patients per year. We know this wasn't the optimal," Dr. Victor Trastek says.

"Today we have a lot more policies and procedures in place," he adds. "I hope the point comes out that these are different times, and we're all trying to give the best healthcare to every patient."

It goes without saying that a non-doctor shouldn't be seeing patients alone, says Katherine Hatwell, a spokeswoman for the American Medical Association. Hatwell says she's heard of optometrists (who fit patients for glasses) working as ophthalmologists (who operate on eyes), but she's never before heard of a non-doctor diagnosing patients in an ophthalmology department.

"We think people should practice to their education and training and not beyond it," Hatwell says. "If you don't have a medical license, you shouldn't be able to practice medicine."

Paul Hughes was officially trained to do one thing—fit people for lenses that an eye doctor has prescribed. That's equal to the guy at Costco who works the glasses counter filling prescriptions, not writing them. (In fact, even those salespeople at Costco are licensed by the Arizona State Board of Dispensing Opticians. Hughes has never been a licensed optician in Arizona, according to Lori Scott, that board's executive director.)

Even if Hughes were a licensed optician in Arizona, he couldn't treat or diagnose patients. He could only put their glasses together or order their contacts.

So why was Hughes allowed to see Paul Phillips? The answer starts about 40 years earlier, when Paul Hughes was convicted of his first crime.

Hughes was born in 1939 in the rural farming town of Friona, Texas—a panhandle community with a population of about 800, according to *A History of Parmer County*. To this day, the average male in Friona doesn't achieve more than a high school education. So Hughes's journey to the Mayo

Clinic, where he had an office and dressed in a suit and tie, was remarkable—in more ways than one.

In his deposition in the Phillips case, Hughes explained he flunked in an attempt to earn a degree at Southwest Junior College in Texas. He added that his medical training wasn't official, per se.

"I guess the rest of the education wasn't done in a classroom setting. I suppose it was mostly on-the-job training," Hughes said.

What Hughes left out was that his on-the-job-training started as an inmate at a prison in Sugar Land, Texas, as he would later confess to Judge Anna Baca.

Asked under oath whether he'd ever been arrested or served time, Hughes initially forgot to mention his years in prison. He answered, "Yes, speeding and changing lanes without a proper signal, and just everyday things that . . . I seemed to be in a hurry everywhere I went, so I accumulated a few traffic tickets."

Attorney: "Have you ever been to jail or in jail?"

Hughes: "Yeah. I went to jail because I didn't pay the fines."

Attorney: "How may times?"

Hughes: "One."

Attorney: "How long did you stay?"

Hughes: "One day. Actually, not a full day."

Attorney: "Anything else?"

Hughes: "No."

During the trial, it was revealed that Hughes hadn't told the whole truth. He had actually been to jail multiple times and prison once, and had been convicted of two crimes: forgery and possession of cocaine. The forgery conviction landed him a six-year prison sentence. Turns out that's when Hughes first learned about the human eye.

In the prison infirmary, Hughes met an ophthalmologist. He says he worked under him as a volunteer inmate for almost two years. When Hughes walked out of prison, he had one asset he didn't have before—a two-year prison education about the eye.

He applied for a job at Lee Optical in nearby Amarillo. "That's where I began my optical profession, in a store with something like five doctors and 60 people," Hughes said in his first deposition. Hughes was in charge of making and distributing the glasses that doctors prescribed.

Hughes then learned how to craft prosthetic eyes. He worked the Texas area as a "traveling eye salesman," selling (not installing) prosthetic eye implants to Vietnam vets who'd lost eyes in combat.

Hughes regularly solicited his prosthetic wares to eye doctors. During a cold-call sales pitch in Houston, he met an ophthalmologist by the name of Dr. John Creasman. The two became close friends.

Around 20 years later, the same Dr. Creasman got a call from an old medical school friend. Did he want to start an ophthalmology clinic in Scottsdale? Creasman agreed to assemble a staff at a for-profit business—the Mayo Clinic. The year was 1987.

The next year, Creasman hired Hughes to work as a technician at the brand-new Mayo Clinic's ophthalmology department in Scottsdale. Hughes apparently didn't even interview for the position.

"He just hired me and put me in charge," Hughes said in his deposition. For Hughes, it was a dream job. The Scottsdale region and the Mayo Clinic both enjoyed a decade of rapid growth. By 2001, Hughes was seeing between six and 13 patients per day, without any direct supervision from doctors, according to Mayo receptionist Cheri Chandler's deposition.

Attorney: "When you schedule [patients] with Hughes, are those patients seeing Dr. Creasman after?"

Chandler: "They are usually just scheduled with Paul."

That testimony aligned with Hughes's own words about his role as a near-doctor at Mayo. "The procedure is that the patient calls into the ophthalmology department, and they're triaged over the phone, best they can. And then they're scheduled with me . . . they're just scheduled on the schedule for either a doctor or myself."

Department head Dr. John Creasman also testified that Hughes was the only technician to see patients without a doctor present. He said none of Mayo's other six technicians saw patients alone, but Hughes did. According to Creasman, Hughes actually had a patient schedule.

It's that appointment schedule that Paul Phillips somehow landed on—even though his wife specifically requested an appointment with Dr. Thomas McPhee, an ophthalmologist.

On the night of March 11, 2001, Paul and LuWanna Phillips were watching TV. Phillips had never met Paul Hughes, but the two shared more than a common first name. They were both born in the late 1930s. And like Hughes, Phillips also grew up in a farming family.

Phillips spent most of his life picking oranges and building a wholesale produce business. He eventually sold his Phoenix-based Wholesale Produce and invested the profits into commercial property—mostly west Phoenix storage facilities built in the early '80s.

In 1979 Phillips had a 3,600-square-foot home built on the border of Glendale and Phoenix. When the Mayo Clinic opened in 1987, Phillips was one of their first customers. He and LuWanna knew the clinic's prestigious reputation. So they took their most serious concerns to Mayo—battles with cancer, other maladies, and, eventually, Paul's eyesight.

Phillips was first treated at Mayo's ophthalmology department in 1999. There he met Dr. Thomas McPhee, a reputable ophthalmologist who became his eye doctor. In 2000, Dr. McPhee left Mayo to practice on his own. Phillips says he would have followed McPhee to his private practice but didn't know McPhee had left.

As it turned out, Phillips's vision problems began a few months after McPhee left Mayo. Phillips recognized the symptoms as a possible detaching retina, only because his son once suffered the same serious problem. Phillips also knew his diabetes made him particularly susceptible.

LuWanna called the number for Dr. McPhee's office at the Mayo Clinic and booked the earliest available appointment, two days later. As LuWanna and Paul drove the 50 minutes from their home to Mayo, they both thought they'd be seeing Dr. McPhee.

They had been to enough appointments to know the routine at Mayo: fill out paperwork, get escorted by nurse to exam room, wait for doctor in a suit and tie, get diagnosis and/or treatment, and leave.

Phillips was soon called back by a nurse. The nurse asked Phillips to read the letters on an eye chart. Phillips couldn't read them with his left eye, he says. He answered some initial questions and then sat with LuWanna, waiting to see the doctor.

The next and last person to enter the exam room was Paul Hughes. (Mayo's records confirm that.) In his deposition, Hughes says he introduced himself simply as "Paul Hughes" and told Phillips that Dr. McPhee wasn't available.

According to the depositions of both Hughes and Phillips, here's what happened next:

Hughes tugged the sliding doctor's stool over to Phillips, took a seat and rolled within a few inches of Phillips. Then he examined both eyes. In addition to Phillips's medical records, Hughes held a form labeled Executive Glaucoma Screening.

Phillips and his wife assumed Hughes was a doctor because he replaced Dr. McPhee, dressed like McPhee, and performed an examination. Hughes then wrote a diagnosis of "K. sicca" and treatment of "tears." He explained that the problem was simply dry eyes. Records show no ophthalmologist or eye doctor saw Phillips at Mayo that day.

"Thank you, doctor," LuWanna Phillips told Hughes on the way out. Hughes, she testified, did not correct her.

In court, Mayo Clinic attorneys argued that Hughes only "assessed" Phillips. But medical records show Hughes wrote "K. sicca," the diagnosis for inflamed eyes, where the form indicates "Present Rx," the Latin abbreviation for prescription. With that, Hughes sent Phillips home.

Despite Phillips's complaints of severe blurriness and flashes of light, Hughes didn't dilate the problematic eye. Not that he should have known to; he isn't a doctor.

Hughes said he didn't dilate the eye because he thought Phillips was only in for a standard eye exam. But given the written diagnosis (in Hughes's handwriting), the documented complaint of symptoms, and the form that reads "Executive Glaucoma Screening," the jurors didn't buy Hughes's story. Even if Phillips had come for a standard eyeglasses exam, Hughes wasn't licensed to give one (and he documented the exam on a glaucoma screening form).

Two weeks after Phillips asked the Mayo Clinic to examine his eye, his retina detached completely. Doctors hired as expert witnesses for Phillips testified in court that Phillips's retina could have been fixed had it been diagnosed during his Mayo appointment.

The same doctors said the two weeks of additional scar tissue buildup made repair by surgery nearly impossible. That's why Phillips is blind in his left eye today.

Scottsdale attorney Mark Wesbrooks represented Phillips. He says his client's case against the Mayo Clinic is one of the most outrageous medical malpractice cases he's ever seen.

"This guy was a two-time felon. They actually created a separate schedule for him. Mayo tried to keep it hush-hush," Wesbrooks says. "It was a non-doctor who was allowed to practice medicine. He testified that he learned all about the eye while in Texas prison."

These days, it's common to go to the doctor and not see an actual doctor. That's not necessarily a problem. Many non-doctor practitioners are trained and licensed to diagnose patients. For example, physician assistants (P.A.s) and nurse practitioners (P.R.N.s) routinely see and treat patients. Both P.A.s and P.R.N.s receive years of medical training and residency before diagnosing patients in their area of specialty. They're also licensed and disciplined by state boards.

Even without any such training or certification, it's possible to legally work with patients, under Arizona law. There's a state law on the books that allows doctors to name anybody a "medical assistant." Medical assistants aren't allowed by law to see patients alone or to diagnose them.

Sometimes, however, they do. The state trusts physicians to be honest about the duties they give medical assistants, says Roger Downey, spokesman for the Arizona Medical Board.

For this reason, Downey says, medical care in this state is a swim-at-your-own-risk situation. "Patients may be offered a quicker appointment if they wish to see a physician assistant or a nurse practitioner at the doctor's office. Otherwise, patients should not assume the unfamiliar practitioner is a doctor. They should ask if they don't know. That's part of being an informed patient," Downey says.

"For elderly patients, most healthcare professionals recommend that an 'advocate' accompany them when they visit the doctor. An advocate in this sense is a relative or friend who can ask questions the patient doesn't think of asking. The advocate can also take note of the healthcare provider's instructions and information that the patient may not remember later."

That didn't help Paul Phillips.

Medical assistants sometimes go by the name "technician" in ophthalmology departments. The American Academy of Ophthalmology says technicians and assistants should never diagnose patients. Spokeswoman Christina Curas says ophthalmic assistants "are not licensed to practice medicine." Curas adds that it's a violation of the academy's bylaws and ethics to let technicians diagnose patients alone.

Despite those known standards, Creasman assigned Hughes to triage. Creasman knew Hughes was a convicted felon with no formal medical training when he hired him. But in an interview for this story, Creasman still says Hughes is qualified to work at the Mayo Clinic.

"Paul was the only one that did triage when [doctor's] appointments weren't available. He was the only one that had the expertise," Creasman says. "It's absolutely okay for Hughes to be working triage because he has more experience. In our department we don't have P.A.s."

Dr. Creasman also says the Mayo receptionist told Phillips he'd only be seeing a technician. (Phillips says otherwise, so it's his word against Creasman's. There's no recording of the conversation.) Creasman says Phillips was the negligent one, by assuming a technician was a doctor.

"There's no way Mr. Phillips could have misunderstood who he was seeing, because the secretaries make that really clear. Maybe he hoped he could see a physician after triage," he says.

National advocates say patients should never assume they're seeing a doctor, and patients shouldn't be afraid to ask for practitioners' credentials. Technicians and medical assistants shouldn't ever diagnose patients.

"One of the best ways for patients to help ensure that they receive safe and appropriate care is to be informed, ask questions, and make sure that they understand what is going on," says Diane C. Pinakiewicz, president of the National Patient Safety Foundation. "Patients and their families need to be viewed by all as part of the healthcare team and, as such, should be encouraged to speak up and actively participate in the care process."

Exactly two years after Hughes diagnosed Phillips with dry eyes, Phillips filed a lawsuit against the Mayo Clinic. His March 13, 2003, complaint alleged that the clinic overlooked his detaching retina and that they did so because Paul Hughes—a non-doctor—diagnosed his problem.

The case dragged on for three years, at a cost of tens of thousands of dollars. It was shaping up to be a boring malpractice case, packed with medical terminology and detailed time lines, but ultimately, it came down to one man's word against another's.

Had Paul Phillips actually complained of retinal symptoms? Had Paul Hughes really held himself forth as a doctor?

During the trial, Paul Hughes retired from the Mayo Clinic. It was June 6, 2006—exactly 18 years after he'd started. Days later, an anonymous tipster sent a mysterious fax to Phillips's attorneys.

The fax clearly tipped the scales. It came from a number inside Mayo and outlined the criminal past Hughes had hidden during his first depositions under oath. Judge Baca reviewed Hughes's sworn claims that he'd only been arrested for speeding.

"He clearly testified to the contrary, and it goes to his credibility. So he can be impeached with those," Baca ruled.

Baca called Hughes to the court, showed him the fax and told him to come clean. Hughes then said his first criminal conviction was for forgery. He explained that his eye education actually started in prison. Hughes then said his second criminal conviction was "a conviction for possession of cocaine, about 20 years ago."

Hughes was testifying in July 2006, making "20 years ago" about 1986—roughly when Mayo hired him to work triage and see patients alone as a "technician." Hughes then said that, among other things, he learned how to spell the word "ophthalmology" while in prison. "He gave me a real good training," Hughes said of the infirmary doctor.

To make matters worse, Hughes was caught in a second inconsistency. The medical record from Phillips's appointment was a one-page form. Hughes testified multiple times that he never modified or added to that record.

Phillips had requested and saved the same document back in 2001. When Mayo produced the same record—three years later—it had additional comments about Phillips's condition. Those comments were clearly in Hughes's handwriting and were obviously added some time after Phillips received his copy.

Between the additions to the medical record and the half-truth about his prison time, Hughes's credibility before the jury was obviously shot.

"It was never about the case beyond that point," Creasman says. "It was always about the personality of the individual."

Creasman thinks Hughes's criminal past should have been left there. "I practiced for 40 years. Never did I work with someone who had his expertise, his savvy, his honesty, his integrity. I've never worked with a technician that was as good as he was."

The jury disagreed.

March 19 is an obscure Catholic holiday, Saint Joseph's Day, honoring Joseph, the husband of Mary and foster father of Jesus. Paul "Joe" Phillips, his son Joe, and his grandson, Joe, consider it their own holiday. They celebrate together every year. And so on a Wednesday this past March, the three Josephs have gathered at Phillips's home to celebrate their holiday with cake, food, and a family party in the backyard.

Sitting at the kitchen table, Phillips describes the struggles of life with one eye. Some days he trips on the stairs in his home of 29 years. When Phillips's grandson Joe makes for the backyard, Phillips says he'd like to play catch with him. He can't.

Now 72, Phillips is otherwise healthy. He walks without a cane or other assistance. His hair is still dark, his skin tanned. His left eye is cloudy. Sometimes he wears a patch over it, particularly for reading, but he's not wearing a patch today.

"It takes me forever to read. You lose the line, and then you have to start the paragraph over again," Phillips says.

LuWanna, Phillips's wife, recently passed away after a long battle with cancer. Phillips says he regrets spending the last years of LuWanna's life fighting a court case. He says there's no price you can put on an eye.

Outside the house, Phillips's RV sits unused. He's tried to drive it twice. But after a minor accident each time, he decided it was too dangerous to drive the motor home with his damaged depth perception.

"We thought we were going to see Dr. McPhee. He's a good doctor," Phillips says. "Now I can't play golf. Some days I trip over the stairs in my own house. It's tough because the eye wants to see, and it takes away from the good eye." ➻

"HOW I GOT THAT STORY"

John Dickerson, a freelance writer and pastor, is a national winner of the $10,000 Livingston Award for Young Journalists, given by Tom Brokaw, Charles Gibson, and Clarence Page. In 2007 the Arizona Newspaper Association named him non-daily "Journalist of the Year," and in 2009 Arizona's Society for Professional Journalists awarded him with the "Sunshine Award," its highest honor for protecting public access to government records. In September 2009 Dickerson and Phoenix New Times *Managing Editor Amy Silverman participated in AAN's live chat series; the following is an edited version of that interview, which was led by* Folio *Editor and AAN Editorial Committee member Anne Schindler.*

John, the first story focused on drug and alcohol addicted doctors who may have relapsed while they were practicing. Can you start by explaining how you first learned there was a substance abuse problem among physicians in Arizona?

John Dickerson: Sure, it started with a handwritten press release. . . the kind of thing you throw in your personal slush pile and review on a slow day. The release came with a self-published book, an account of a Scottsdale cosmetic surgeon/millionaire who grew addicted to prescription meds, then cocaine and so forth. A sort of riches to rags deal. I contacted the former doctor, thinking it might make for a very short profile. We met at a Starbucks, and the guy looked like he'd walked right off the set of *ER:* very intelligent and well spoken. In the course of the interview, he began complaining about the state's "strict" monitoring of his addiction. I asked him to give me some details and, as he did, I realized that the story wasn't him. The story was the state's monitoring program. It seemed strict to him, but to me it seemed loose. I thought I'd check into it. So I did, and out came the first story.

Amy, when John first approached you about the doctor-addicts story, did you initially see it as an investigative series? How did you help him expand upon that story idea?

Amy Silverman: To be honest, I wasn't interested in the doctor's tale—at first. The more John and I talked, the more we realized there might be a pattern. I've been around long enough to know that Arizona's medical board has lax rules, so we had an inkling he'd find something. But really, the story came through John's persistent reporting once he got to the board's documents.

John, how were you able to find out which doctors had addiction problems, and how did you then try to determine whether they had relapsed?

John Dickerson: As a result of a public records request, the board did provide me with a list of physicians who had their licenses suspended or revoked as a result of substance abuse. I took those names, created an Excel spreadsheet, and then I worked backwards to trace their history of discipline and of malpractice lawsuits. Most of them had been known addicts to the board—long before their suspension or revocation. I began deducing numbers from the spreadsheet and saw a clear trend.

Amy, aside from exposing doctors for drug abuse, linking that addiction to possible harm done to patients is a dicey legal area. How were you able to find comfortable legal footing?

Amy Silverman: It is tough—but we did this all through records, backed up by interviews. And we were careful about legal review—and had no problems.

John, the second part of the series, 'Dr. Loophole,' reveals how doctors with serious allegations against them in other states are able to come practice in Arizona and essentially start over. Explain how this loophole works and how you learned about it.

John Dickerson: I'll explain how I learned about it first, then how it works. During the addiction story, I learned the lay of the land on Arizona's multiple medical boards. Arizona is one of only three or four states that have a homeopathic board. That seemed really curious to me, so I focused on that one. I then uncovered a state auditor report—just a few months old—that hadn't been covered in the news. The auditor report made some pretty serious accusations [and] was just a clear green light to really check this board out. Then I just reviewed the records of every single homeopathic doctor in the state. There were only about 130 at the time. I traced their backgrounds to see which states they came from.

Was is difficult to trace the out-of-state history of the homeopathic docs?
John Dickerson: It wasn't bad. The majority of state medical boards allow you to do basic searches on their websites.

Amy Silverman: John is being modest. He worked like a dog.

John Dickerson: Some states gave access to the entire disciplinary files. Others (like California) showed that there was a problem. Then I had to call their PIO and get it faxed over.

Amy, there was a huge amount of information contained in this second story— and a lot of explanations needed. How did you and John decide to structure the story to make it as clear as it was?
Amy Silverman: We went back and forth quite a bit and came up with an unconventional lead that gave a smattering of examples, then doubled back and explained them. I think it's always easier to write a story with too much material rather than the opposite.

The third installment in this series was very different in some respects—about a 65-year-old man named Paul Phillips who made a very unfortunate visit to the Mayo Clinic . . . There, a man who seemed like a doctor came in and examined him. Unfortunately, his diagnoses of "dry eyes" proved tragically wrong. Can you explain what happened to Mr. Phillips?
John Dickerson: The short of it is that his retina detached. The malpractice is that Phillips was diabetic, which, combined with his symptoms, made the diagnosis of a detaching retina very elementary. Mayo's own handbook—for consumers— describes it. Generally speaking, if a detached retina is diagnosed in time, it can be fixed with, I think, more than a 70 or 80 percent success rate.

He later learned the fellow that examined him was not a doctor, correct?
John Dickerson: Correct. The guy isn't licensed in Arizona to do anything medical at all. We got lucky with Phillips. A malpractice attorney I was interviewing for an earlier medical story told me about Phillips. I didn't believe him at first. Then I got my hands on the court records. (The lawsuit had gotten about a $2 million judgment by jury, reduced by the judge to around $750,000), and it all checked out.

Have there been any regulatory or legal changes since your series?

John Dickerson: I'm not aware of any legal changes since the stories. They won a national Livingston award, but I don't think our legislators want to deal with the lobbyists from the doctors.

Amy Silverman: I think if we hadn't immediately entered a budget crisis, something might have happened. But our legislature is stymied, to say the least.

Amy Silverman: John, I have a question. What would you have done differently if you had this to do over?

Hmmm . . . I probably would have kept going with a fourth part on yet another board, which I will leave unnamed, here in our great state of Arizona. Also, I would have trusted the advice of my seasoned editor more—for real though.

Might Makes Right

Jeffrey C. Billman

On April 12, 2007, Fernando Trinidad did something that would get most of us thrown in jail: he pushed a woman down the stairs at a downtown nightclub, injuring her ankle, and then lied to the cops about it.

But luckily for Trinidad, he is an Orlando police officer. His punishment? He lost a vacation day.

Trinidad abused his power and his badge, and he got away with a slap on the wrist. The woman he pushed lost her job and very nearly spent time in jail because he lied about what happened. If it weren't for a surveillance video, the reality of what happened that night would never have been known.

Trinidad was off-duty, working as a security guard for the now-defunct Club Paris. It was almost 3 A.M., and Trinidad and his colleagues wanted to get everyone out. According to Trinidad—a two-year OPD veteran who previously served in the U.S. Army—patron Jessica Asprilla was intoxicated and mouthy. She cursed at him as he tried to escort her out.

As he guided her down the stairs, Trinidad pulled out a whistle and blew. Trinidad says in his report that Asprilla spit on him. As he reached out to grab and arrest her, he says, she pulled away and fell down the stairs. Based on the report, she was charged with battery on a law enforcement officer, which is a felony, and resisting an officer without violence.

Later, Trinidad changed his story. In a deposition several months later, he claimed that Asprilla spit on him while mocking his whistle-blowing. He also accused Asprilla of faking her fall: "She was running down the stairs, and once she reached the bottom of the stairway, she took her famous belly-flop and landed on the ground."

Both versions were untrue. An unearthed surveillance video didn't show Asprilla spitting on Trinidad's face in the stairway. It didn't show her acting in any way threatening, posturing aggressively, or stumbling like a drunk. It *did* show Trinidad reaching out with his right hand and pushing Asprilla and Asprilla tumbling to the floor. Then it shows Trinidad walking right past her as she lay on the floor in pain.

On May 1, Asprilla filed a complaint with OPD's Internal Affairs Division. Internal Affairs investigators dug up the video and concluded what the tape made obvious: Trinidad was lying. According to an Internal Affairs report, "Trinidad pushed Asprilla" and "Asprilla's quick descent and subsequent fall resulted from having been pushed."

On August 29, Internal Affairs rendered its verdict. Section manager Dwain Rivers sustained the charge that Trinidad engaged in "conduct unbecoming an officer" for pushing Asprilla down the stairs. He found a second charge, that Trinidad didn't offer Asprilla medical help, not sustained—or inconclusive—largely because the tape had no audio. Still, the video "cast doubt" on Trinidad's version of events, Rivers wrote. He also concluded that Trinidad was guilty of falsifying police reports because his story was dramatically at odds with what actually happened.

You'd think that conduct unbecoming an officer and falsifying police reports would merit harsh punishment. Not so. An OPD memo dated September 27 recommended that Trinidad be suspended for 16 hours or lose two vacation days. On December 10, deputy chief Val Demings, who has since become chief of police, knocked that down to one day because no one told Trinidad he was being investigated for filing false reports before he was interviewed.

That may seem lenient, but by OPD's standards it's pretty harsh. In the vast majority of cases, officers accused of using excessive force get off with no punishment at all, even when there is compelling evidence the cops did what people say they did. Between 2003 and March 2008, 98 claims of excessive use of force were lodged with OPD's Internal Affairs Division. Internal Affairs sustained none of them. In every case, the accused cop was cleared.

It's likely that in many of those cases, that's exactly what should have happened. People being arrested do, of course, make complaints about the cops arresting them. Often the evidence is inconclusive, and the cops get the benefit of the doubt.

On the other hand, OPD's record suggests its cops are virtually never wrong, that charges of abuse of power are almost always a lie on the part of arrestees. OPD hasn't punished a single officer for excessive use of force in at least the past five years, despite pending lawsuits the city now faces and, in some cases, clear evidence the cops did exactly what people who filed complaints accused them of.

A three-month *Orlando Weekly* investigation, drawing on hundreds of documents and dozens of interviews, suggests OPD has a problem policing its own. The police department, it seems, is a place where rogue cops operate with impunity, and there's nothing anybody who finds himself at the wrong end of their short fuse can do about it.

"[OPD has] a habit of not imposing stiff punishments for egregious violations such as this one," says Adam Sudbury, Asprilla's attorney. "I will tell you of all police agencies, OPD [is] well-known in the criminal defense community as being, basically, an organized street gang with the authority to be street bullies. That's their reputation."

The Biggest Smack

The state attorney's office charged Asprilla on August 30. She was arrested a week later, following a routine traffic stop. OPD

Internal Affairs investigators, however, discovered the video-tape evidence that would ultimately clear her of all charges in May. They just never told anyone it existed, she says.

"If there were no video, I could have gone to prison for a long time," Asprilla says, adding that Internal Affairs never shared the tape with prosecutors or told her anything about its investigation. (OPD denies withholding the tape, and points out that Asprilla initially refused to cooperate with their investigation.)

She only found out about the tape in late December, when a witness mentioned in a deposition that OPD had spoken to her and showed her the tape. "Once we showed the video to prosecutors, they dropped the charges against her," Sudbury says, adding that the police were required to turn over that evidence. The two charges against Asprilla were dropped on February 8 and March 5, respectively, according to court records.

In the meantime, Asprilla lost her job as a social worker. She dropped out of graduate school because her arrest record—which included a charge of battering a cop—prevented her from landing a necessary internship. She racked up thousands of dollars in medical bills and began planning a lawsuit.

Sudbury says that the state attorney's office may yet press charges against Trinidad for pushing Asprilla down the stairs, lying about it, and falsifying police reports. If that happens, he may lose more than a day's vacation.

Meanwhile, Trinidad is still on the force, stationed at Orlando International Airport. The incident with Asprilla wasn't the first time he'd been investigated by Internal Affairs.

In June 2007 he was censured after leaving his department-issued shotgun and AR-15 in his squad car, which was parked on the street outside his Kissimmee house for four days while he was on leave. The cops found out about it when two teen-agers torched the patrol car, damaging the weapons. He was given a written censure.

Two months earlier, a home burglary victim accused Trinidad of refusing to take fingerprints at her house, despite her request that he do so. Another detective went to the house a week later and found nine prints, but they weren't good enough to use. The complaint against Trinidad was not sustained due to a lack of outside witnesses.

On February 18 of this year, a woman filed a petition for an injunction against Trinidad, who four days earlier—on Valentine's Day—had left her a series of profanity-laced voice mails threatening to beat her over a dispute involving Trinidad's wife. One example, found in court records, reads: "You fucking lesbian bitch. You better call this phone back. I swear to fucking God, if I ever fucking see you, [you're] going to [get] the biggest fucking smack in your face, the biggest fucking smack. . . . Keep fucking with me, you won't think I'm playing. . . . Prepare yourself, bitch. Prepare your-fucking-self."

A judge declared that the threats alone couldn't justify such an injunction. According to the petition, the woman also filed a complaint with Internal Affairs, though there is no record of such a complaint in OPD's 2008 Internal Affairs log.

Lies and Videotape

In several cases reviewed for this story, a pattern emerges: The cops arrest, and in some cases allegedly rough up, a "criminal." The person arrested is typically charged with resisting an officer without violence, but the charges are quickly dismissed. Meanwhile, the arrestee files a complaint with Internal Affairs, but the division ultimately clears the officer involved.

Because of the way Internal Affairs keeps its records, it's difficult to determine whether or not it is effective at policing the police. All Internal Affairs complaints with a finding of anything less than "sustained" are purged after one year. There is no paper trail.

The case of Officer John Seth James, however, does not inspire confidence.

In the early morning hours of September 2, James pulled over a pickup truck for an improper U-turn. As he approached the vehicle, he saw two men inside "jump from their seats in an attempt to change drivers," according to his report. He yelled at them and ordered them to stop resisting. Seeing one reach for the center console, James pulled out his gun and ordered Michael G. Wallace, 26, the man he thought was the driver, out of the car.

Wallace, whom James believed was drunk, continued to struggle, so James took him to the ground, arrested him and put him in the patrol car. In November the state attorney's office dropped all charges against Wallace. His attorney, Andrea Armas, says Wallace wasn't driving.

If the story ended there, the city of Orlando wouldn't have had to pay onlooker Josh Leclair $5,000 to keep him from filing a lawsuit.

Leclair was at a friend's house that morning and saw the traffic stop. He's a member of CopWatch, a volunteer group that monitors police activity, so he brought out his camera and began filming. A second friend videotaped Leclair videotaping the incident.

During the arrest, Wallace pointed out the cameras to Officer James, who didn't take kindly to their presence. He marched over to Leclair and demanded that he "go inside." Leclair refused. He was on private property, more than 30 feet away from the arrest. He wasn't interfering with anything James was doing. He had a right to film.

James gave the same order again. Leclair refused. James turned around and ordered another cop on the scene, "Detain him!" That officer, Paul Sanderlin, tackled Leclair like a linebacker on a Sunday afternoon.

When Officer Richard Studer—James's supervisor— arrived on the scene, he watched Leclair's tape and ordered him released. Leclair filed a complaint and turned over copies of both videos to Internal Affairs.

The tapes contradict much of what James told Internal Affairs about the incident. James said Leclair was one of a group of people only 10 to 15 feet away from the arrest, a group that he thought could pose a danger to him. In reality, Leclair was 36 feet away, standing alone. James told investigators Leclair was moving. He wasn't. James said he told Leclair to "get back." What he really told Leclair was to "go inside," an important distinction. James ordering Leclair inside is equivalent to telling him he can't film, which is not an order he is lawfully allowed to give.

Nonetheless, Internal Affairs exonerated James. Investigator Mathew Fleury interviewed an OPD firearms expert who excused James's behavior by saying that with all the swirling lights, it's possible James couldn't tell how far away Leclair was. (Sanderlin, the officer who threw Leclair to the ground, left the force soon after this incident and wasn't part of the investigation.)

In June, Leclair took his case to the Citizens Police Review Board, an advisory body that reviews Internal Affairs cases and makes recommendations to the department. After hearing his case, the CPRB did something it hasn't done in at least eight years, according to *Orlando Weekly*'s review of CPRB minutes since October 1999: it asked OPD to reverse itself and sustain the charge against James.

The decision, ultimately, is up to Police Chief Demings. As of press time, Internal Affairs manager Dwain Rivers says the department is awaiting a formal letter from the CPRB stating its recommendations, after which Demings will render her decision.

Leclair also threatened to file a lawsuit against the city, but after seeing the videotape, city lawyers sought to settle out of court. Leclair asked for $4,000 and an apology. The city made a counteroffer: $5,000 and no apology. He accepted.

The city paints that settlement as pragmatic, noting that it would have spent a lot more than $5,000 defending that case in court. "Just because we settle doesn't mean that the city thinks [the police] did anything wrong," says city spokeswoman Heather Allebaugh.

The city, meanwhile, is fighting another lawsuit alleging that its cops roughed up someone without cause—and again, videotape of the incident tells a different story than the police reports do. On Oct. 25, 2003, University of Central Florida tailgater Heather Hull was arrested for resisting an officer without violence and disorderly conduct. Charges against her were dropped a month later.

In his charging affidavit, OPD Officer Ira Morris says that as he and other officers were breaking up a fight outside the Citrus Bowl, a crowd gathered, swearing at the cops and throwing things. (He didn't mention why: according to a lawsuit filed by Jacob McCallister, one of the fighters, Morris and another cop knocked McCallister to the ground face-first, then Tasered him. Charges against McCallister were also dropped.) Morris said Hull jumped "on top of" another officer at the scene as the cops led one arrestee out.

Nothing of the sort happened. A video shot by a witness shows that as the cops dragged one of the fighters out of the parking lot, another girl—not Hull—walked up and touched one of them on the shoulder. An unidentified officer pushed the girl to the ground, hard.

Hull approached the girl, never touching an officer. But Morris and Officer Michael Burch reacted as if she posed a threat: They knocked her to the ground and Tasered her repeatedly. Here's how Hull, in her lawsuit, describes the event: "[Morris] pushed me over, punched me in the jaw with his fist or elbow and then he and [Burch] used Tasers on me and knocked me to the ground. After defendant Morris Tasered me, [defendant Morris] Tasered me directly against my abdomen while I was lying on the ground and offering no resistance."

The videotape backs up Hull's story and contradicts Morris's account.

A Familiar Pattern

Other cases tell a similar story. On October 29, 2006, Steven Zapf, then an employee of Emeril's restaurant at Universal CityWalk, was walking back to his car when he was followed by Officer Anthony Miller and two Universal security guards on bikes. The confrontation that ensued stemmed from a misunderstanding, says Thomas Luka, Zapf's attorney. Miller believed Zapf had struck his girlfriend on one of Universal's people movers. He had not.

Miller and the security guards formed a semicircle around Zapf. Miller demanded Zapf's ID. Zapf refused, and Miller Tasered him.

In his report, Miller says Zapf was belligerent, swearing at him repeatedly and pulling away to avoid being arrested. But Universal surveillance video (which does not have any audio) shows Miller and the security officers encircling Zapf. He walks backward very slowly in the video, still facing Miller, then Miller Tasers him. He isn't running, and he doesn't appear to be threatening Miller in any way.

In January 2007 the state attorney's office dropped charges against Zapf. Because he was issued a trespass warning from Universal, however, he lost his job. Luka says Zapf tried to file an Internal Affairs report, but was told that because Officer Miller was working off-duty, he couldn't. In May 2007 Zapf sued Miller and Universal Studios.

A few months after that, Karen Holbrook, then an *Orlando Sentinel* nightlife writer, had her own run-in with Miller. In October 2007 Holbrook cut through Wall Street Plaza a little after 2 A.M. on the way back to her car. A bouncer stopped her, assuming she was trying to enter a closed bar. Holbrook explained that she was just cutting through, and the bouncer let her go.

On her way, Holbrook says she saw Miller, who was working off-duty as a security officer, slam a male friend of hers against the wall. She pulled out her phone and dialed 911. Miller, she says, "ripped the phone out of my hands."

"Who is this?" she says he demanded to know. After discovering it was a 911 operator, Miller responded, "She's crazy," and hung up the phone, Holbrook says. Then she says Miller "drop-kicked me on the floor." She got up, and he "slammed me back on the ground again." He also doused her with pepper spray. "I felt it for days," she says. "I lost [some of my] vision."

Miller took her to the police station, but she was so bruised and bloody, the police had to wait three hours before they could take her mug shot. Pictures provided to *Orlando Weekly* show bruises to her arms, legs and face.

Miller said in his police report that he pepper-sprayed her because she was resisting arrest. His report doesn't mention the 911 call, and that call's existence is impossible to verify because the cops only keep 911 recordings for six months. The state attorney's office dropped charges against Holbrook in January 2008. Holbrook says she called OPD to file an Internal Affairs complaint, but "no one got back to me."

Luka, the attorney representing both Holbrook and Zapf, has filed his own lawsuit against Officer Miller. On September 21, 2006, Luka was arrested outside the popular downtown bar Casey's on Central after allegedly pushing Miller. At one point, Miller threatened Luka with his Taser, and Miller says that Luka responded, "I'm a civil rights attorney who fights the Taser. I would love for you to Tase me."

Miller arrested him.

Luka's and Miller's stories don't mesh. Luka says he accidentally touched Miller's arm, and Miller demanded to see his ID. After seeing his Florida Bar card, Miller unholstered his Taser and said, "I know you. You are going to jail."

Luka, a former Miami prosecutor and Orlando public defender, says Miller then took him to the downtown police substation, where he was placed in a holding cell for several hours. At one point, Luka says, two cops turned off the lights, entered the cell and beat him with their hands and batons, saying, "Do you want to take our deposition now, mother-fucker?" and "You have no idea what happens when you fuck with OPD."

Luka filed a complaint with Internal Affairs, but the division cleared Miller. According to the Internal Affairs report, several witnesses backed up Miller's version of the arrest, and for Luka's story about the beating to be true, he would have to have been arrested hours earlier than records indicate.

The state attorney's office declined to press charges, and Luka sued. "It's hard to tell what's going on," says Howard Marks, who represents Luka in his civil case. "The city is defending this thing vigorously. [The city] believes Tom is not telling the truth . . . [that] he's making it up. . . . We believe that Internal Affairs, 95 percent of the time, writes a report to support the officers' position. It's a joke here. It's an absolute joke."

Fun With Tasers

Between 2002, when he joined OPD, and August 2007, when he gave a deposition in the Zapf case, Miller admitted to using his Taser 42 times in the line of duty. According to Internal Affairs records, Miller has never been disciplined, which means that as far as OPD is concerned, all of those incidents were justified.

Falah Aljahmi would disagree. On September 9, 2006, the Dearborn, Michigan, resident was in Orlando visiting a friend. As he was walking to his car, two drunken white men spouting Arabic slurs accosted him, then jumped him. Aljahmi, who weighs 150 pounds, punched the first one and was wrestling the second when a third man tackled the whole pile, he says. During the fracas, his contacts were dislodged.

Aljahmi ran. Unfortunately for him, the tackler was Officer Morris, who gave chase. Other cops—Miller, Mark King and Michael Faulkner—ran after him as well. They cornered Aljahmi, who says that as soon as he realized the people chasing him were cops, he stopped running.

What happened next, as outlined in a lawsuit Aljahmi filed against the city and the officers, is chilling. Over the next few minutes, the four officers beat him and Tasered him at least four times while he was on the ground. "They were laughing and stuff," he says. "They thought it was a joke."

The cops say they had to use their Tasers because Aljahmi was, in Morris's words, "continuing to violently resist our attempts to subdue him." Morris drove his arm into Aljahmi's chest twice. After Aljahmi was on the ground, Miller Tasered him again. King slammed his knee into Aljahmi's shoulder. Faulkner Tasered him again while Aljahmi was on the ground because his arms were under his torso, the cops said, which made it hard to handcuff him.

Aljahmi was arrested and charged with battering a cop, resisting arrest with and without violence and disorderly conduct. As with the other cases, the state dropped all charges in April 2007. In February, Aljahmi filed his lawsuit against the officers and the city.

The city declined to talk about these pending cases, although it did issue *Orlando Weekly* a statement of support for its officers. "Our police officers face tough, split-second decisions everyday and it is common for them to err on the side of public safety."

Toothless

OPD's Internal Affairs department is, by design, cops investigating cops. If you have a problem with the inherent lack of objectivity in that system, you have one avenue of recourse: the Citizens Police Review Board. The CPRB is a volunteer advisory board that reviews Internal Affairs investigations. It toils in obscurity. Its meetings, once a month early on Wednesday mornings in City Hall, are sparsely attended. The local media seem hardly to know it exists. The board has no authority other than to recommend that Internal Affairs change its findings or reinvestigate. A review of CPRB minutes since October 1999 indicates that happens only rarely.

Of the hundreds of cases the board reviewed in that time span—about 40 per year—the CPRB has asked Internal Affairs to reverse its findings or reinvestigate eight times, and in two of those cases the board later changed its mind and approved Internal Affairs' findings. That leaves only six incidents in which the CPRB challenged Internal Affairs' decisions (although in some of the cases the CPRB has backed up Internal Affairs' finding of charges "sustained").

One of those cases was Josh Leclair's. Another came from two strippers who said that two OPD cops, James Carlies and James McGriff, had fondled them—and allegedly, one of the cops showed off his erect penis—during an undercover operation. In that case, Internal Affairs dismissed the results of a polygraph test the two women had passed and cleared the two officers.

In December 2006 the CPRB asked Internal Affairs to reopen its investigation and to take its own polygraph of the two women. OPD said no. In January 2007 an assistant city attorney stated more tests would be a waste of time.

The CPRB's impotence is spelled out in the city's contract with its police union: "The city may establish a Citizens Police Review Board . . . however, no such board shall have the authority to impose or modify disciplinary actions against employees."

The CPRB has no say in how an officer is punished; that is up to OPD management. Like Internal Affairs, the CPRB cannot take into account prior allegations or even sustained charges against an officer when considering a case, meaning that if a cop has been repeatedly charged with abusing his authority, it doesn't matter. The CPRB can't require accused cops to show up at meetings, so they almost never do.

The CPRB is, in the words of former member (and *Orlando Weekly* music columnist) Bao Le-Huu, "toothless." Le-Huu, in fact, says he decided to leave the board after almost two years of following the Carlies and McGriff case. Despite the long hours board members put in reading case files, he says, their efforts amounted to a show "to make people feel good."

In fact, Internal Affairs manager Rivers admits that of the six cases in which the CPRB either requested a reinvestigation or recommended that IA change its findings, there's no record of anything actually changing.

The board couldn't do anything to change the system, Le-Huu says, so it was a waste of time.

Outraged

Rivers says an analysis that assumes wrongdoing "because of the sheer numbers, not because of the fact," is flawed. In other words, he says you can't assume that just because every cop who has faced an excessive force complaint over the last five years has gotten off, that means that Internal Affairs isn't doing its job.

He also warns against using Internal Affairs' logbook to determine that his division goes easy on abusers. In Trinidad's case, Rivers notes that he was charged with an omnibus violation of "policies and procedures," rather than use of force. The logbook doesn't record what violations of policies and procedures officers are charged with. And given OPD's purging policy, such information, particularly in older cases, is almost impossible to come by.

So, Rivers says, abusive cops could be punished for abusive behavior, but it might be recorded as a violation of a rule other than "use of force." He also defends the CPRB process. The board, he says, has made a number of suggestions that OPD has adopted. But he doesn't think it's a good idea for the board to take an officer's credibility into account.

"If they are judging our cases by something we don't [use], it wouldn't be fair," he says. "If we start looking at credibility and not evidence, we're treading in serious waters."

Rivers points to the different viewpoints of cops and civilians to explain the high number of cases that his agency clears. In short, what some civilians see as abuse is completely appropriate under the police department's use-of-force matrix. Cops can use increased force as the threat increases, so even the *perception* of an increased threat can merit increased use of force. Even when videotape seems to be at odds with officers' stories—as in the Leclair case—Rivers says police reports might not match "because of perception, not untruthfulness."

Questioned about Trinidad's lackluster punishment, Rivers says that his agency's "hands are pretty tied." The level of an officer's discipline is determined not by Internal Affairs, but by that officer's superiors. And the superiors base the punishment largely on precedents that are listed in two large binders of records OPD keeps. If OPD doled out more severe discipline than it previously had for a similar offense, Rivers says, the officer might have cause to file a grievance.

Consequently, Trinidad lost a vacation day. "The public was outraged and so were we," Rivers says.

Stacked Deck

The deck is stacked in the accused cop's favor. That fact is codified in state law. A section of law known as the "Police Officer's Bill of Rights" says that before Internal Affairs can interview a cop, they must first let the cop see all the evidence and witness statements against him, a privilege not extended to the public during criminal investigations.

Use-of-force rules also give the cops the benefit of the doubt. "There is great leeway left for use-of-force discretion," says CPRB member Jeremy Markman. "It's there purposefully. Officers on the street have discretion."

There is a premium placed on keeping cops safe. Proving that an officer used excessive force, or did anything else, is difficult. For instance, if a complainant says a cop abused him, the cop denies it, and there are no witnesses, Internal Affairs usually returns a "not sustained" finding. Markman and Le-Huu also point out that, if the incident happens around downtown bars, witnesses are often bouncers and club employees. And since many cops work while off-duty providing security to these clubs, these witnesses are essentially the officers' co-workers.

Le-Huu also notes that the investigations CPRB members review are conducted by Internal Affairs—and thus, the CPRB relies on Internal Affairs to report on itself.

The lack of independent oversight isn't limited to Orlando. Orange County's Citizens Review Board has even less authority.

State law mandates that any investigation into a police officer be done by his or her employer. In Orlando, police officers are city employees. In the county, sheriff's deputies are employed by the Orange County Sheriff's Office, a separate constitutional office, which severely restricts what its oversight board can do. (It only reviews cases of abuse of power or excessive force, and like Orlando's board, only makes recommendations to the sheriff).

However, Orange County's charter does grant its board one power Orlando's board doesn't have: the subpoena. The county's board can require that deputies show up (although that authority is pending the outcome of a lawsuit, says county senior paralegal Jack Dougherty). The city's board cannot.

The city *could* grant its board that right. Because OPD cops are city employees, the city could empower the CPRB to do independent, thorough investigations of alleged police misconduct. If the city altered the language in its union contract, it could even give the CPRB real muscle.

Or the city could keep doing what it's doing now: letting the cops police themselves. ●◆

"HOW I GOT THAT STORY"

Jeffrey Billman was formerly news editor and senior writer at Orlando Weekly, *where he worked from 1999 (as an intern) to 2009, when he left to become the news editor at* Philadelphia City Paper. *Billman has a degree in journalism from the University of Central Florida and a master's degree from UCF in political science with an emphasis on public policy. Billman and his wife Adri have two dogs and no children, and, he writes: "We like it that way." In addition to his journalism, Billman writes, "I drink beer, read books, and occasionally play music." In October 2009 Billman and Orlando Weekly Editor Bob Whitby participated in AAN's live chat series; the following is an edited version of that interview, which was led by San Francisco Bay Guardian Executive Editor and AAN First Amendment Chair Tim Redmond.*

So this is an amazing story, Jeffery, tell us how you got started on it.
Jeffery Billman: Well, one element of the case—that Fernando Trinidad pushed that woman down the stairs and lied about it—had gotten some play in local media, so I can't say that I sort of developed it all on my own. I was originally looking into that particular case, pulling records and talking to people involved and such, and it sort of mushroomed.

Take us down the trail. Tell us how you followed that lead and where it led.
Jeffery Billman: I got the sense that this was way more pervasive, and way more fucked up, than met the eye. So we decided to pull all of Orlando Police Department's Internal Affairs records, at least the ones we could get our hands on. I also pressed a few lawyers who handle these sorts of claims, and each of whom either had prospective cases or knew of cases that all revolved around a similar story. And in many of these cases, despite a lot of evidence of wrongdoing, OPD declined to act. But the real kicker lay in the data: Out of the 90-some-odd abuse complaints that had gone before Internal Affairs, that department had rejected all of them. Every single one.

Did you have trouble getting any police records? How did you get the list showing that none of the 98 excessive force complaints were sustained? What about records on individual IA cases?
Jeffrey Billman: OPD, as I recall, keeps a log on the basics of all of its IA cases, and their eventual dispositions. However, under Florida's state law, if a cop is cleared—which is basically all the time—the file gets shredded. So, for most of the cases, there was little to no paper trail. We only could get a select few, and OPD wasn't exactly what you'd call helpful, no.

Bob Whitby: If I remember correctly it was an OPD policy to shred the records after a year if the complaints weren't sustained.

Jeffrey Billman: You're right, Bob. In many cases, we ended up relying on lawsuits that were filed, which included some elements of the complaints encapsulated in those IA files, because the IA stuff itself was gone.

Did you have any helpful sources inside the department?
Jeffrey Billman: Sources inside? Not really. *Orlando Weekly* had something of a row with the local authorities a few years back. They didn't like us all that much. No, this

was done with completely exterior sourcing. Some OPD guys, especially the IA manager who was desperate to show that he wasn't a tool of the guys with badges, were willing to talk, but nobody inside was up and volunteering anything.

Bob Whitby: Having sources among people who had claimed to have been abused was probably more important than having sources with the cops, because that's where the videotape came from, which was the strongest evidence.

How did you get onto that CopWatch videotape?
Bob Whitby: CopWatch was from Billman's favorite source, local ACLU guy George Crossley.

Jeffrey Billman: My favorite source, indeed. As for retaliation, I can't say that I remember hearing anything credible. I know the OPD brass wasn't particularly fond of me after that, but had I heard anything about specific retaliation, we would have printed it.

How about follow-up? It seems that the city's contract with the cops is part of the problem. Any action on changing that contract?
Bob Whitby: You are referring to how there is little oversight on the part of the citizen's review board. Nothing has changed.

Jeffrey Billman: Not a chance in hell. The mayor had some inkling about getting the cops to renegotiate during the budget crunch, but that was all about cuts and so forth and he folded like a lawn chair when the union flexed its muscle. He wasn't about to make something this unsavory part of the deal. In Orlando, the police chief is, after all, a mayoral appointee. He's not about to piss her off.

One of the challenges a lot of investigative reporters and editors face is when the story is done—that is, at what point did you decide you had all you were going to get—or at least, all you needed for the story?
Jeffrey Billman: Tim, I think at some point Bob just told me to write what I had, and then we filled in the necessary gaps and ran with it. It's one of those things you could work on forever, but at some point you have to pull the proverbial trigger. I'm the sort of compulsive type that would sit on something until I felt it was perfect, so I guess I need a little prodding to wrap these things up.

What would you suggest for other reporters looking at similar stories in their towns?
Jeffery Billman: See what's available in terms of records. Depending on the state and the jurisdictional laws, you may have access to a lot more IA data than you think. And also, look at these things quantitatively. The real story often lies not in an anecdote or two, but in establishing a pattern of behavior.

Tell us what other lessons you've learned from this story that could help the rest of us as we pursue police issues.

Jeffery Billman: Well, I'd say that it's always worth seeing who's watching the watchers. Each city has unique elements, but I'd bet more often than not the 'oversight' agencies that cops set up to give people peace of mind tend to be paper tigers, and that's definitely worth pointing out.

MEDIA REPORTING / CRITICISM

CIRCULATION 50,000 AND OVER

"One Mission, Two Newsrooms"

by Erik Wemple, *Washington City Paper*

"Thorough and definitive, Wemple shows absolute command of his territory. He uses bright writing and specificity to make unique observations on how internal turf battles shape the ways that large newspapers are adapting to the new media environment."—Gabriel Snyder, Gawker.com

CIRCULATION UNDER 50,000

"On Air, On Edge"

by David Koon and Gerard Matthews, *Arkansas Times*

"Well-reported, in-depth examination of an important topic following a tragedy. Does an outstanding job of questioning the cult of personality that is encouraged and promoted by television news operations."—Jason Salzman, Effect Communications

One Mission, Two Newsrooms

Erik Wemple

FEBRUARY 18, 2008

The *Washington Post* knew it had a hot story on the Walter Reed Army Medical Center. For months, ace reporters Dana Priest and Anne V. Hull had been rounding up horrifying anecdotes about the center's treatment of soldiers and Marines wounded in action in Iraq and Afghanistan. One recovering soldier had a cluster of black mold in his room; another was left to walk, disoriented, around the center's campus; hundreds were essentially forgotten by the Walter Reed bureaucracy.

The blockbuster investigative series debuted in the *Post* on Sunday, February 18, 2007. But an information-hungry public got a preview the night before. In a video, Priest described life in Walter Reed's Building 18: "Conditions here are far from ideal: mold and peeling wallpaper, shower rot, mice, and cockroaches."

That kind of multimedia pre-story hype is just why the *Post* invests so many dollars in washingtonpost.com, the dynamic site that tallies about 9 million unique visitors per month and regularly ranks among the top news sites in the country.

One problem, though: Priest's report was on NBC Nightly News, not on the paper's multimedia pipe. Priest had a contract with NBC and occasionally collaborated with the network on her stories. Several weeks before the Walter Reed package was slated to run in the *Post,* she approached her NBC producer about the project.

How much notice did she give washingtonpost.com? "Anne and I basically didn't tell them anything about the project until two days before it was going to run," says Priest.

Priest's editors had passed word along to washingtonpost.com. But weak partnerships yield underwhelming Web presentations, and the Priest-Hull stories had little of the dressing that commonly accompanies the paper's big investigative projects. "It was fine, but that was all it was," says Jim Brady, executive editor of washingtonpost.com.

In their defense, Priest and Hull didn't publicize the Walter Reed investigation in their own newsroom. The stories were a hush-hush proposition, rendered vaguely on story budgets and kept from folks who were routinely in the loop. Website staffers, though, occupied their own rung on the bottom of the ladder. "We kept [the story] from them because we hadn't worked for them that much, and we were really worried about any kind of leaking," says Priest, who worked more fully with washingtonpost.com on subsequent parts of the series.

Priest's candid words flesh out a melodrama to which just about every newspaper across the country is contributing a chapter or two. It's all about control—the news people and the Web people are grappling over who hires whom, who edits what, who pays for what, and who gets what first.

At the *Post,* those tussles pop up in just about every corner of the operation. Call your sources one day and hear about the national desk going toe-to-toe with dot-com over political coverage. The next, it's Style all pissed off that the section has no eponymous roost on washingtonpost.com's global navigation bar (it's called "Arts & Living"). And don't even ask about the out-of-control comments function or how the dot-com people (under)play stories on the home page.

The entertaining part of the drama lies in the pronouns. Whether the griper works as a newsie or a techie, the finger-pointing always targets "those people," "those folks," and other, less polite, designations. When the topic is washingtonpost .com, "we" generally takes a breather.

And why wouldn't it? The scrum for control of the *Washington Post's* future, after all, shuffles back and forth across the Potomac River. Priest, Hull, and hundreds of other *Post* editorial types work downtown. Their dot-com associates, meanwhile, do their biz in the Arlington offices of Washingtonpost .Newsweek Interactive (WPNI), the online publishing subsidiary of the Washington Post Co. (WPNI also manages Newsweek .com, Slate, BudgetTravel.com, Sprig.com, and TheRoot.com.)

Via subway, the trip spans five stops and a total of 20 minutes. By car, you're looking at 16 minutes over 3.4 miles in optimal traffic conditions. Whatever the mode, the trek deters all but dedicated Web-paper collaborators. "The way traffic is these days, it takes half a day just to get out there," says Lucian Perkins, a longtime photographer for the *Post.*

No wonder, then, that Priest hadn't worked with her Internet peers too much.

The geographic separation takes its toll on the *Post* in two ways. It causes frequent communication breakdowns whose remedies invariably involve costly investments in training and outreach, and it creates overlapping functions in which both the print and online operations assign reporters to the same beats. The result is waste, a luxury that no newspaper, including the *Post,* can afford in this era of slumping print circulation and advertising.

Last week, the *Post* made a gesture toward unifying the two operations: it created a new unit, Washington Post Media, and named Katharine Weymouth as its CEO. Weymouth, the granddaughter of legendary publisher Katharine Graham, promises to bring new vigor to the relationship between Web and print operations, in part because she has spent long spells in key positions on both sides of the river. The physical separation, however, will remain. "I don't think the river is the issue," says Weymouth. "If people decide that it makes more sense to have certain teams sit together, I'm open to that."

Other papers, meanwhile, have abandoned the *Post*'s separate-but-unequal model. A year ago, the *Los Angeles Times* integrated its news and Web functions after an internal report called the paper "Web-stupid." The *New York Times* began combining its Web-paper operations in August 2005 and accelerated the process when it moved to a new building last spring. "It's very much a two-way street," says Jonathan Landman, the *Times*'s deputy managing editor and top editorial voice on the website.

Post Executive Editor Leonard Downie Jr. brushes off talk about calling in the movers. The two operations, he says, are working together more closely than ever, and there's plenty of evidence behind the claim. Key newsroom editors have moved across the river to join washingtonpost.com; an estimated 15 percent of the activity in the *Post* newsroom goes to Web-only presentations; and Web producers are getting earlier and more complete involvement in print projects. The *Post*'s sports writers, too, have verily launched a downtown subsidiary of washingtonpost.com via extensive participation in blogs, chats, and videos.

"Our main message to the staff is, 'A merger is a non-issue,'" says Downie. "'The issue is how can we work more closely together toward mutual goals.'"

Yet in another breath, the *Post*'s top editor acknowledges that perhaps the clearest route to those goals isn't now an option. "We can't just walk into each other's offices all the time," he says.

Separate Pieces

In 2004 *Post* veteran Fred Barbash was working the early shift at the paper's Continuous News desk, an outpost established to funnel breaking news to the website. As he went about his duties, Barbash came across a fine piece of journalism by someone at washingtonpost.com. Fine enough, anyway, that Barbash felt compelled to send a compliment across the river, via email.

Barbash's words of praise bounced around a bit in the dot-com offices, as he was to discover. He later got an email back, but not from the person he complimented. It was from another dot-com staffer. "He said there was no call for the tone of voice," recalls Barbash.

Barbash picked up the phone and clarified that he actually meant what he wrote.

Just another exemplar of electronic mail's failure to convey nuance? Perhaps not. "People were easily misunderstood," says Barbash, noting that staffers had attitude problems on both sides of the divide.

By the time of Barbash's misadventure in morale-boosting, the two operations had already spent around eight years working on the same mission from separate offices. Washingtonpost.com launched on June 17, 1996, from Arlington, an "enterprise . . . driven by a sense of excitement at being at the forefront of a new medium with boundless possibilities," according to the authorized history of washingtonpost.com.

But why was this gung-ho group working so far from the *Post*?

The company line is that Don Graham, then the *Post*'s publisher, wanted the new online operation to innovate, to explore the vast Internet free from the retrograde tugs of a hidebound newsroom. "[He] believed, wisely, that this was a different medium, and this was an opportunity to create and take advantage of a new medium," says Douglas Feaver, who ran the editorial side of washingtonpost.com from 1998 through early 2005.

It's awfully convenient when a fancy organizational theory camouflages a cutthroat motivation for corporate behavior. And in this case, that would be union-busting. If Graham's only goal was incubation, he could have placed the Web people just around the corner from 15th and L.

Instead, he chose Virginia, a state with a right-to-work law and its attendant obstacles to union organizing. Remember—the *Post* is a company that earned its viability in part by crushing a 1975 strike by the pressmen's union, a grueling affair that involved standard old-school union thuggery and a bunch of *Post* execs doing menial chores to keep the enterprise running. Management still does battle with the various unions that represent workers in the downtown office, including the newsroom guild.

Why go through the same thing with the Internet operation? "The guild was the only remotely plausible reason to keep the two apart," says a *Post* source.

Post big shots generally change the terms of the conversation when asked about labor unions and washingtonpost.com. A common reply: *That's something you'll have to figure out yourself.* Or: *I think it's pretty clear why they're over there.*

As for on-the-record testimony, Feaver furnishes this bit of insight: "I never asked [Don Graham], and he never volunteered anything on the guild question."

At a staff meeting last week, Graham did acknowledge wide-ranging frustrations with the current Web-print structure. He declined, however, to comment for this story.

Perhaps the big boss isn't too eager to defend the thinking that's so often attributed to him. The stated reason for the separation, after all, is crumbling: washingtonpost.com has solidified its identity as an innovator in this medium and has the accolades to prove it too, including the first-ever national Emmy for Web video journalism, Edward R. Murrow awards, and a Peabody Award for "Being a Black Man," among others. The site is starting to pay off, too: in 2006 washingtonpost.com ad revenues were 14.5 percent of *Post* ad revenues.

So just what does the separation accomplish in the late'00s?

Well, it's still doing a pretty effective job of keeping people apart. At a meeting for all newsroom staff in mid-October, a *Post*ie pressed Downie on the prospects for a Web-paper merger. The editor repeated the company line that there were no plans either to come together or to remain separate forever.

Then came another question from the floor: Since Web issues often get discussed in these all-staff meetings, why aren't there any representatives from washingtonpost.com in attendance?

The answer was that the Internet people couldn't make it that day. They were out of town.

As for dot-com's inconsistent attendance at these get-togethers, Brady notes, "A lot of times we just don't know far enough ahead of time when those meetings will be."

Let the Competition Begin

The Going Out Gurus figure among the stars of the *Post*'s website. The team of specialists on fun is based at the dot-com operation, where they churn out a blog and a popular weekly chat titled "Got Plans?" Like their counterparts at many newspapers, the Going Out Gurus have a strong command of their region's food and entertainment scenes. Unlike their counterparts at many newspapers, they cover so much more than eating, drinking, and culturing. Readers know it, too. In an October chat, for instance, a visitor to washingtonpost.com posed the following question to the Gurus:

"Help'Rus, I need someone who can steam or press a thick satin wedding dress in the Chantilly/Vienna/Fairfax area. Thanks!"

The answer—Imperial Gown Restoration—came from Janet Bennett, the Gurus' very own shopping specialist. For that day's questions on music, food, bars, and where

Nightmare Before Christmas would be showing in 3-D, there were six Gurus on the case.

According to dot-com officials, "Got Plans?" regularly ranks among the top 10 most trafficked chats on the site, which pulls off 30 to 40 chats a week. The feature, which is part of washingtonpost.com's City Guide, pleases the site's money people, too, because it draws a young crowd of future brides and mobile professionals who have some big purchases in front of them.

Yet the Gurus' fandom lags in the Weekend section of the *Post*'s newsroom. That cluster has long complained about the prominent exposure that washingtonpost.com bestows on its in-house entertainment experts. On the other hand, Weekend content, goes the sentiment, gets buried.

An example: both Weekend and washingtonpost.com cover the Fringe Festival, the sprawling theater celebration that hits the city each summer. "Theirs takes priority," says a newsroom source.

In the words of another source: "They want to champion themselves and . . . they made it difficult to find Weekend. They did it at the expense of one of the most-read, self-sufficient, and profitable sections of the paper."

The ugly job of complaining to dot-commers about Weekend's Web visibility long fell to the section's former editor, Joyce Jones. According to various *Post*ies, Jones had a tense relationship with her washingtonpost.com counterparts, with the spats often centering on how hard it was to find Weekend content on washingtonpost.com. (Jones did not respond to numerous requests for comment.) In the eyes of her fellow Weekenders, Jones was sticking up for them, fighting the good fight.

From dot-com's perspective, Weekend blew its chance to chart its future on the Web. In the early '00s, reps from the website approached Weekend in hopes of crafting a partnership for lighting up the Internet. Howard Parnell, the Arlington operative who spearheaded the effort, says that the discussions followed a certain pattern. "I think that where the lively discussions took place was where they said, 'Why not just call this Weekend on the Web,'" remembers Parnell.

Like any self-respecting Webbie, Parnell said no—the Web required a different product, not just some repurposed print content.

With that, the two sides essentially retreated to their respective bunkers and did their own thing. "We sort of agreed to disagree in order to make progress with what we were doing online," says Parnell, who now works for the website of WNYC. According to Brady: "Some sections [of the *Post*] engaged with the Web, some didn't."

Years later, Weekend, like the rest of the paper, decided that the Internet was for real, a great platform for its cumulative work on Washington leisure. By that time, though, it had formidable competition from the City Guide and its Going Out Gurus.

Here's where *Post*ies learn the painful lesson that Brady and his people can arrange content on the website however they see fit. If the website's managers decide that the Gurus have something good cooking, they'll give them a nice foothold on the home page. They'll try to accommodate Weekend, but they're not going to do it at the expense of their own content providers. "Now that Weekend is working with us, I don't want to just throw the Gurus under the bus," says Brady.

True, the Gurus versus Weekend won't go down as one of the Washington *Post*'s great battles. At the same time, it's more than just another round of flannel-assed newsroom bitching. The little set-to shows just what happens when the dot-com people start acting like a news organization.

Many people in the *Post* newsroom would prefer that their peers at washingtonpost.com restrict themselves to technical stuff. Post the brilliant news stories that come from 15th and L, put together slide shows, edit the videos, and go home. But it doesn't work that way.

Of the 100 employees on the editorial side of washingtonpost .com, 10 provide content of one sort or another, a count that jumps to 20 if you add in contract writers and bloggers. Once their bylines go up on the Web, they become the competition.

These Arlington-based professionals work in a place that they commonly refer to as a "newsroom," a point that short-circuits longtime *Post*ies. "They have this thing called the news desk," says one. "I don't know what it is, but it's not what our news desk does."

Duplication of functions has a way of offending journalists who are feeling the pain of budget cuts. Why is dot-com paying for nightlife coverage and political coverage when the main newsroom does the same things—and is losing staff via early retirement offers and attrition? Such considerations merely stoke the outrage when *Post*ies see techies typing into their turf. The annoyance extends beyond just the Weekend pod.

- Style: After *Post*ies Amy Argetsinger and Roxanne Roberts launched their version of the Reliable Source in September 2005, the Web bosses approached them with a blog idea. They wanted wall-to-wall coverage of pop culture and celebrities on the site, the better to extend washingtonpost.com's national reach. The columnists did some prototypes before bagging the whole notion. A national celebrity blog, they said, didn't mix with the Reliable Source's usual grist of items on local luminaries.

The Web operation took the undeterred route, launching Celebritology, a gossipy blog written by Liz Kelly.

Enter rancor. Newsroom staffers have long deplored what they view as Celebritology's Tiffany-spot status on the site, scoffing at how the blog would often get "stripped across the top" of the *Post*'s home page, in the words of one staffer.

"The website has clearly decided that Celebritology is where it's at," observes Style writer Hank Stuever.

Other objections go to taste, or how Celebritology rarely does original reporting and links to tabloid-style sources that wouldn't meet dead-tree standards.

Brady returns the scoffing, noting that not even a Web force as formidable as washingtonpost.com can promote a blog into respectability. "The great thing about the Web is that it's a meritocracy," he says. "You can put something on the home page all day long and promote it, but if it doesn't connect with people, you're just not going to build an audience for it."

National Desk: Late last year, the *Post* hired washingtonpost .com congressional blogger Paul Kane to a full-time job downtown. At the same time that the move filled an important void in the paper's political coverage, it left one at the Web operation, where Kane's frequent online postings had built a following.

The captains of the print operation then proposed to dot-com's Brady that they manage the congressional blog.

Brady said no thanks—we'll deal with that.

A polite offer and an equally polite refusal: this is how power struggles are articulated at the contemporary *Washington Post*. Here, the paper's ranking editors were served another reminder that they controlled only part of the franchise. "They weren't happy," says a *Post* newsroom source.

Brady has a milder take on the matter. "It was a nice offer. I'm glad that they volunteered to do it, but I think for our purposes, we wanted to keep somebody who was still Web-focused," he says.

The Kane thing recalls the mythic flap over Dan Froomkin's Web column, a staple of washingtonpost.com whose origins lie with Graham. According to Feaver, it was Graham who argued that the site needed a regular feature "on the White House for the junkies," in Feaver's words.

From that discussion sprung Froomkin's "White House Briefing," an online-only column that launched in January 2004. The column's editorial approach, notes Feaver via email, was "newsy but not opinionated." When Brady took over in 2005, though, he decided to "just let it rip," writes Feaver.

Months of letting it rip touched off a backlash in the newsroom. By December 2005 John Harris, then the paper's national political editor, was telling the *Post* ombudsman that Froomkin's column would never pass muster in the newsroom. "It dilutes our only asset—our credibility," said Harris, who argued that the column's opinions tainted the paper's objective political coverage.

The tepid solution was to move Froomkin's work under the site's Opinion banner and change its name from "White House Briefing" to "White House Watch."

L'affaire Froomkin combusted in a newsroom enamored of the boundaries between itself and the dot-com operation. It's one of the pettiest chapters in the paper's digital adventure. Take the example of hotshot political reporter Chris Cillizza. He's a classic new-world journalist, active on his blog, "The Fix," as well as on regular old news stories. Occasionally he teams with a political reporter from the newsroom, and the resulting byline is a tribute to bureaucracy:

> Romney Homes In on a Message That Will Stick
> Michael D. Shear and Chris Cillizza
> *Washington Post* Staff Writer and washingtonpost.com
>   Staff Writer
> Thursday, January 28, 2008

Downie has quite an explanation for how this happens. First off, Cillizza is a washingtonpost.com employee, Downie says, and so the byline merely conveys the right information. Plus, leaving the ".com" in his byline accomplishes towering managerial imperatives. "[It's] also for the sake of psychic reward for the people who work at washingtonpost.com—to show them that it is valued in print in the *Washington Post* to be a washingtonpost.com person," says Downie.

Because of Downie's generosity—or perhaps in spite of it—the politics staffs at the two institutions work closely together on day-to-day coverage. Cillizza works from 15th and L on big primary nights to write the paper's critical "lead-all." Both crews work on "The Trail," a well-received diary of tidbits on national politics that appears both online and in the print product. "That's a sail that has very little drag on it," says *Post* Managing Editor Phil Bennett of the political cooperation. "It's working, and I think that the proof is in the journalism that's being produced which, from my point of view, is an extraordinary model going forward."

Questions of Taste

The Food section of the *Post* won't endorse just any old recipe. Whether the concoction is 12-Hour Tomatoes or Sausages with Cider Glaze, you can bet that a volunteer has rounded up the toasted, ground cumin seeds (for the tomatoes) or the Jonagold apples (sausages) and fired up a sample batch.

In December, for example, Food published recipes for more than 20 varieties of holiday cookies, each with its own testing disclosure.

This is the way it works: The tester buys the ingredients, hauls them home, and cooks. Expenses get billed back to the *Post,* an institution that has never shied from investing in journalism, be it investigative, spot news, fluff, online, or service. Eight full-time staffers plus a little army of freelancers produce coverage of the local dining and food scene—a robust national news desk in many papers around the country.

The generous newsroom budget funds not only comprehensive coverage but also an institutional seriousness of mission, of which tested recipes are just one small component. Dot-com managers learned this lesson in talks leading up to the March 2007 launch of washingtonpost.com's "Recipe Finder."

The *Post*'s Webbies were excited about building a virtual community of foodies through a recipe database. Let people throw recipes up there, the thinking went, and subject them to popular review. Unleash the power of the Internet to act as a giant self-cleaning oven, dissing the bad recipes for Sausages with Cider Glaze and elevating the good ones.

Newsroom folk weren't biting. There was just no appetite for mixing *Washington Post*-approved recipes with ideas thrown up on the site by any schmo with an Internet connection. "Yeah, great—just poison the readers," sniffed one longtime *Post* staffer when apprised of dot-com's ideas.

Bonnie Benwick, assistant editor at the paper's Food section, says the disparate visions for Recipe Finder weren't "anything that people stalked out of a meeting about." Interactivity, acknowledges Benwick, is "a lot of what draws people into the Web, but it became to me a matter of recipe quality."

The dead-tree squad won this particular battle. Recipes in the Finder carry the same "Tested by" tags that appear in the paper, a huge point of pride among newsroom food types.

Yet dot-commers apparently don't view this whole testing thing as a selling point for Recipe Finder. A kickoff announcement on washingtonpost.com stated that the tool "lets users search a growing database of more than 1,000 recipes that have appeared in The *Washington Post* newspaper and on washingtonpost.com."

No mention whatsoever that they all pass the vaunted *Washington Post* test.

Brady appreciates the newsroom's cooperation in putting together the recipe function. But he's not worried that a more interactive product would harm dot-com's precious users. "Sites have been doing this for a long time, and I have yet to read the first story about somebody getting botulism from them," he says.

The Virginia crowd is still pushing its vision on recipes, according to Nancy Kerr, washingtonpost.com's assistant managing editor of features. A first step, she says, is to provide users a space to comment on the recipes.

Oh no, reader comments!

No issue parts the two institutions like the ability of readers to hop on washingtonpost.com and post nasty, offensive messages. Washingtonpost.com was a pioneer in facilitating comments on all stories, and many newsroom staffers were slow to get over it. Internal newsroom message boards have repeatedly lit up over the hate speech that makes it onto the site. The debate flared up last November, following the racist comments that hit washingtonpost.com in the aftermath of the fatal shooting of Redskins safety Sean Taylor. Some *Post*ies have proposed bagging the comments altogether.

Newsroom staffers frame the clash as a question of tastes and standards. As in, those people have none, and we do. The cry from the other side of the river is that the newsroom doesn't get the Web. So long as the two organizations remain separate, those aspersions will continue crisscrossing the river, carrying more than just a nugget of truth with them.

It's hard, after all, to expect washingtonpost.com to soak up the journalistic culture of the *Washington Post*. Newspapers don't codify their standards and ethical sensibilities in a companywide memo. The process is far too sprawling and random: an editor kills a story over inadequate sourcing, a reporter makes a Jayson Blair joke on the elevator, a discussion breaks out in the cafeteria—can Woodward really reconstruct all those high-level conversations? Dot-com operatives, hunkered down in Virginia, miss out on all of it.

"We definitely spend a lot of time trying to educate the people at the Web about the culture of the newsroom and the people downtown in the ways and customs of the Web," says Liz Spayd, one of washingtonpost.com's top editors.

Reporters and editors at the *Post* have been making special trips just to understand what their dot-com counterparts are up to. By the end of 2007 website management had herded 75 *Post*ies through a special three-day training program for just this purpose. "It totally demystified the website for them," says Brady. "People came away saying, 'I didn't understand what you did.'" The news staff at the *Post* numbers roughly 800, so once Brady drags 725 more bodies through his offices, everyone will be on the same page.

The *New York Times* accomplishes the same end without stressing the subway system. "It's a great cross-pollination," says Landman of the *Times*' combined operation. "The producers get much more experience and journalistic depth that these [news] guys provide, and they give some great Web savvy and imagination, and you put that together and you're off to the races."

At the *Post*, Web and news personnel tend to spend a bit more time stuck in the starting gate. The downloading of institutional memory from one place to another occasionally runs into bandwidth problems.

Last July, *Post* gossip columnist Amy Argetsinger was making some calls on David Vitter, the Louisiana senator whose phone number had shown up in the phone records of the famous "D.C. Madam." After the story bounced all over the country, a New Orleans madam spoke up with allegations that Vitter had been a client of her brothel.

Argetsinger was all over it, nailing an interview with the Southern madam and pushing it toward publication. But her editor, Steve Reiss, spiked the story on sourcing grounds, arguing that the *Post* account rested precariously on the word of the New Orleans madam. Says Argetsinger via email: "Reiss was aware that everyone else was writing about her but said that we can't use that as an excuse—in essence, that the *Post* had to take the higher moral ground." Argetsinger rushed to find a replacement item.

The next day, the columnist set out to "revisit" the Vitter issue. She pumped "New Orleans madam" into Google and found that the first story to pop up came from the *Post*. Turns out that washingtonpost.com had piped into the website an AP version of the very same story that a Style editor had just killed.

Argetsinger wasn't mad; she was encouraged. Now she had an argument for her editors: hey, if we have the AP story on our site, why can't we publish our own version? "I guess I was arguing, 'look, the *Post's* already tainted here,'" writes Argetsinger via email. Not tainted enough: when the issue reached the desk of top editor Downie, he sided with Argetsinger's editor.

"Two different companies and two different standards operating under the same rubric"—that's how Argetsinger sums it up.

The Web leadership acknowledges promoting the story of the New Orleans madam. "I've been doing this for 12 years," says Brady, "and there's still a lot of things we're still trying to figure out."

An Image Problem

The photography department of the *Post* and the multimedia division of washingtonpost.com never got along well. The competition between operations, the struggle for control, the fights over standards, the sneering—every aspect of the *Washington Post's* digital dysfunction pops up in photography-multimedia.

This control drama featured key managers on both sides of the river: Joe Elbert served as the *Post's* assistant managing editor for photography since 1988 before stepping down late last year. Tom Kennedy has served as washingtonpost.com's managing editor for multimedia for 10 years.

For as long as they worked together, they fought. "Tom and I are both strong-willed control freaks that are like two dinosaurs going at it," says Elbert. Kennedy cops to being strong-willed but denies the control freak and dinosaur charges.

The top dogs at the *Post* have no qualms about acknowledging the conflict. "There was an enormous amount of tension between the two," says Downie.

But the explanation steers away from the systemic: "It was
a classic personality clash," says Downie. "Elbert and Kennedy's personalities clashed—I'm not saying whose fault it was
and, believe me, we tried to find out so we could chastise the
right person."

The real story, as always, is a bit more complicated.

Elbert, 60, and Kennedy, 57, are both franchise names in
the business of newspaper photography. Their career paths
crossed around 30 years ago, when Kennedy was working at
the *Gainesville Sun* and Elbert at the *Miami Herald*. From
there, both moved on and up, with Elbert joining the *Post* and
Kennedy landing big jobs at the *Philadelphia Inquirer* and
National Geographic before moving to washingtonpost.com.

In this riverine rivalry, Elbert had the manpower advantage. As the *Post*'s top photography editor, he bossed around
a staff of approximately 30 photographers and editors, compared to Kennedy's 16-member dot-com staff (which includes
part-timers).

Elbert did his job with flair. Under his watch, the *Post*
hauled in three photography Pulitzers. Prone to colorful newsroom outbursts, he was the type of manager who motivated
with candor and brevity. Former *Post* photographer Juana
Arias recalls sending in some work she'd done tracking Hurri-
cane Mitch in Central America. Elbert took a look at the pictures and had a simple message: "Juana, if you don't get better
images, don't come back," according to Arias.

Skepticism figured big in Elbert's shtick, a quality that he
applied not only to his colleagues' work but also to technology trends. "Joe doesn't just jump on the newest, latest band-
wagon. He waits it out to see what sticks and what doesn't,"
says Michael Lutzky, a former *Post* photographer.

Adapting to the Web, accordingly, went pretty slowly inside
Elbert's shop. Photography sources say he clung to an ideology that favored still photography as the Web matured. Elbert
says that dot-com's embrace of the latest in Web technologies
afforded him that luxury. "[Tom] was going to do one medium,

and we were going to feed him our stills, so from a really self-ish point of view it was fantastic. I really didn't have to worry about the website," says Elbert.

Elbert's loyalties to the legacy of the *Washington Post* were clear to anyone trying to manage images at washingtonpost .com. The two operations exchange photos through a program made by MerlinOne, a Quincy, Massachusetts-based software outfit. As an image works its way through editing, it passes from one "basket" to another in the Merlin program. The largest basket in the software is the first in the chain of editorial custody. Known as the "staff basket," it's the hopper into which *Post* photographers on assignment toss their photos.

Photo editors in the *Post's* newsroom had full access to the staff basket; their counterparts at the dot-com operation had none. They could glimpse the roster of images only when staffers at 15th and L sent the green light. Sometimes that wouldn't occur till the wee hours of the morning.

Thanks to basket protocol, the supposed guardians of the *Post's* future couldn't even get a look at the present.

One former *Post* insider calls Elbert's setup a "technical barrier" stopping washingtonpost.com from choosing photos. Whatever the characterization, the frustrations that it caused aren't hard to fathom. An Internet news site, after all, is an image-devouring machine. If the look of the site doesn't change visibly throughout the day, visitors will simply click off and try a competing site.

The arrangement caused its share of snafus over the years, most commonly when it was time to cover high-profile events, like a State of the Union address. The *Post* photography department, of course, always sends shooters to such occasions. But washingtonpost.com couldn't access their work quickly enough to put together a timely presentation on the site. And so the website managers cobbled together a workaround whereby they'd use wire photos to keep the site fresh until they could finally pull down some *Post* images. "The hard thing about it at times was that the *Post* photography was strong and rich, and certainly better than what we'd been working with at the time. But they couldn't alter their rhythms to accommodate us," says Kennedy.

Those rhythms, says Elbert, accommodated institutional priorities. Before the images could be released, they needed to be culled and edited. Sometimes photos had to clear legal and ethical reviews, for instance. "It really was kind of a hold queue," says Elbert. "Some of our photographers turn in eight or ten pictures and only two or three of them are any good. It's kind of a protection for the photographer. But it turned into *we were hiding the good stuff.*"

If sending photos across the river was a tension-laden activity, so was trekking over to the dot-com operation. Several current and former photographers say that the very act of visiting washingtonpost.com's headquarters was almost an authority-defying step. That is, Elbert wanted them producing for the newspaper and taking time out from work to go across the river was either frowned upon or worse. "It was not fun," says *Post* shooter Lucian Perkins.

One dot-com source says that meeting with *Post* photographers often required a diplomatic touch. The website on several occasions arranged rendezvous with photographers on the sly, complete with an explicit agreement that Elbert would not be notified, according to this source. "Whatever game people needed to play to feel secure," says the source. Brady says, "Photo staffers were rarely here, even though a lot of other people from the newspaper were starting to make their way over."

Elbert insists he never laid down any rules regarding trips to Virginia. The "genesis" of the problem, he says, "was that a couple people always wanted to go over there and it was more fun to go over there than to take assignments."

Given those quirks, the two sides struggled to reach the operational intimacy necessary to produce mind-blowing multimedia presentations. "Basically you have a whole photography department that has almost no connection to the website," says a *Post* editor.

In an April 2006 online chat, Elbert wrote, "we're really two separate operations and we haven't sorted out what to do down the road, stay tuned. . . ."

Some business school would do well to examine *Post* photography versus dot-com multimedia as a case study in runaway "soft costs." Brady, the top dot-com editorial manager, spent about a year trying to bridge the differences. Spayd also sunk untold hours into the project. Here's Downie on the subject: "It was a serious problem, and we tried to deal with it in many different ways. . . . It drove us crazy, and it drove the senior editors at washingtonpost.com crazy."

A bus ride accomplished something that high-level attention couldn't. Last year, virtually the entire photography department of the *Post* piled in for a trip over to dot-com. By all accounts, the ensuing discussion broke little ground, but at least both sides gave lip service to the imperative of working together. "I came back shaking my head and said, 'We could solve all these problems if we were in the same location. What do you say we all work together?'" recalls Dayna Smith, who formerly worked on the *Post*'s picture desk.

Months later came a breakthrough, at least in the eyes of dot-com: longtime photography ace Michel duCille attended the congressional hearings that featured testimony from General David H. Petraeus and beamed photos to washingtonpost .com. "That was tremendously helpful," says Kennedy. "It was the first time we were really able to work a situation like that in real time."

DuCille, however, isn't assigning watershed status to the moment. "To me that wasn't any kind of big breakthrough," he says. Look here: the two sides can't even agree on *compliments.*

DuCille is now running the photography department, following Elbert's departure from that position in November.

Barriers have fallen, too. Washingtonpost.com, for starters, can now track the staff basket. "I got so sick of it," says Elbert, referring to the pressure from Virginia. "I said, 'Just open it up, just open it up, I don't care if I get sued.'"

Day-to-day communication has improved in the Kennedy-duCille world—proof that if you give the *Post* about a decade, it can begin solving its website problems.

As for Elbert, he says that a lot of good intentions got lost in the space between the two operations. "If you can look eyeball to eyeball, things don't get out of control like they have," he says. "You're able to read people." He has returned to his roots as a photographer, and he's learning to shoot video. ❧

Erik Wemple was the editor of Washington City Paper *from 2002 until 2010, a period in which he wrote extensively on D.C.-area media, especially the* Washington Post. *Prior to becoming editor, he worked in other positions at the paper, and also was a reporter for the short-lived online media news site Inside.com. In 2010 Wemple left the* Washington City Paper *to edit an online local news startup in Washington published by Allbritton Communications Company, the founder of Politico. Wemple discussed his award-winning story in October 2009 as part of AAN's live-chat series. The following is an edited version of that interview, which was led by Tucson Weekly Editor and AAN Editorial Committee member Jimmy Boegle.*

What spurred you to write "One Mission, Two Newsrooms?" Was there a specific event or catalyst?
Actually, it was a bunch of events. Things were happening every day over there—people were so pissed on both sides of the river, and every time I picked up the phone to do some reporting on the *Post*, I'd get complaints about those bastards on the dot-com side or those old-media bastards at the print paper.

What made you finally decide to go with the story?
Well, after hearing that photographers were being discouraged from even going over and meeting with the dot-com folks, that pretty much sealed things. I mean, the *Post* is a very open place, traditionally. So the fact that they were trying to stifle communication and collaboration was a bit astonishing to me.

I'm amazed at the access you got to people at the *Post*. In many places, daily folks won't even talk to altweekly reporters. How'd you get such amazing access?
I don't think that was anything that I did. As I say, the *Post* under Executive Editor Leonard Downie was quite the model of transparency. People's default mode was to pick up the phone and explain their side of whatever story I was writing. So I found only a few people who failed to return my calls. Sure, the photographers were tough to pin down, but everyone else helped quite a bit and sat through really long interviews about all this stuff.

I wish other dailies were half as open as the *Post*. What kind of response did the piece get?
I think very little. I mean, there were like 20 comments on the site, and I heard some talk about it here and there. But, you know . . . it was a lot of "inside baseball"-ish material, so it didn't have a mass audience. The good thing is that for the few who did care about it, it sort of lives in their memory. I guess that's not much impact, but it's something.

Has the relationship between the *Post* and Washingtonpost.com changed since you wrote the story back in February 2008?

I will say that after it was published, the *Post* made the decision to fuse the Web and the newspaper. Now, I am not making a *post hoc ergo propter hoc* sort of claim here, but at least the story came at a time of change at the *Post*, at a time when the *Post* was looking at this setup very closely.

Wow. That option seemed off the table in your piece. Any idea what made them decide to fuse the operations?

Well, it may have been cost. Funny thing: just as the piece was headed toward publication, Katharine Weymouth, granddaughter of Katharine Graham, became publisher. I interviewed her about this and she declared her support for the separate buildings for dot-com and the newspaper. Then, just weeks later, you started to hear rumors about the merger that has now pretty much been accomplished. I'd love to think it was because of the story, but I really don't think so. I think the reason goes to a more compelling cause, and that's budget: there was a lot of duplication under the separation of dot-com and the newspaper, and cost savings have been realized through merging them.

You've been an old-fogey reporter doing media criticism for a while now, Erik. (Not that you're old . . . just sayin'.) What advice do you have for newer media critics in the altweekly world?

Pick up the phone, arrange interviews with people, get face-to-face. Journalists at whatever publication love to dish dirt about the bad things that their bosses are up to. You just need to approach them. Everything will flow from there. If that sounds too simple, too easy, then perhaps it is. But do this: read your local daily and zero in on someone's work; then call the writer and ask to speak to them about their work. Whether you say flattering things or nasty things about their work—that doesn't matter. Journalists love attention, and once they get it, they'll blab like no tomorrow. Just read people's work.

On Air, On Edge

David Koon and Gerard Matthews

NOVEMBER 19, 2008

It was, by anyone's estimation, an unspeakable crime: On October 20, Anne Pressly—a vivacious, fun-loving young woman with a smile for everyone she met and an up-and-comer at

KATV Channel 7 who seemed destined for TV journalism's big leagues—was found badly beaten and near death in her own bed, in her tidy house, in one of Little Rock's quietest neighborhoods. Though she hung on, lingering in a coma for five days, Anne died in a Little Rock hospital October 25.

As of this writing, the motive behind Pressly's murder is still unknown, and her killer is still at large. Police say they have found nothing to indicate that Pressly's assault was at the hands of an obsessed fan or stalker. It may have only been cruel fate that a murderous intruder chose the house of a local celebrity to invade.

But the crime and the inability of the police to quickly catch who did it has many people in Little Rock television news more worried than ever—and they were, as a lot, pretty worried to begin with. Behind the camera, local news directors are thinking deeply about security, and the way they push their on-air talent. Meanwhile, some of those in the harsh glare of the spotlight speak of a newfound sense of fear. The question is: in an age when you can find out almost anything about anybody if you've got five minutes and an Internet connection, where's the line between promotion and privacy? Can a person be both well-known and safe?

If this was any other moment in Little Rock, it might strike some as ironic that the woman on the cover of this newspaper—a consummate professional who spends at least six hours of her life every week working live in front of a camera—didn't want her face photographed for this story. It's just one example of the wall of caution, if not outright fear, that has imposed itself around local news stations since Pressly's death, a barrier we hit again and again in writing this story.

Of the local news anchors that we talked to, only one agreed to discuss the issue. Honoring her request for anonymity, we'll call her Jane.

Jane said that since the assault on Pressly, she has lived in an almost constant state of fear. "My whole life has changed," she said. "I lived on my own for 10 years and now I can't spend a night alone because I'm fearful to even walk out to my car."

Jane said that almost everyone she knows has a theory about the motive behind Pressly's murder. Hearing rumors circulate only heightens her frustration and anxiety. She said that while she was always cautious about her privacy—she didn't join the popular online social networking sites like Facebook and MySpace for that reason—Pressly's killing has made her much more cautious about what she says and does, both in front of the camera and in her personal life.

"I don't talk about personal stuff on the air," Jane said. "I keep my life very private. I'm not necessarily responding to requests for autographed pictures or anything like that. . . . We were all issued pepper spray, and I carry that with me all the time."

Jane said that while getting letters and gifts from viewers is just part of being in local, community-based news, even the fans are more mindful of potentially crossing the line. "Most of them are harmless," Jane said. "But it's funny, because now a lot of people will preface their letter with 'I'm not a stalker.' They'll say to you: 'I'm not a stalker, but I really enjoy watching you on the air.'"

Jane said the stations could do more to protect the privacy of their on-air personalities. Especially troubling for her are some of the things that can be found on a typical station's website. While Jane didn't mention it specifically, a good example of this might be KATV's "Choose Your News," a streaming website feed that features reporter Kristin Fisher working at her desk in real time—typing, chatting on the phone, rushing out to cover stories. Viewers choose the stories she works on, keep in contact with Fisher through email and Twitter, and watch the reporting process unfold. The station is trying to cash in on new technology and pioneer a new type of journalism, but it raises questions about the voyeuristic nature of the project. Before Pressly's assault, the feature could have rightly been called smart and innovative—a great way to give viewers a glimpse into the inner workings of the station, not to mention a golden opportunity for one of KATV's rising stars. These days, however, it's hard not to think about who might be watching. Fisher, however, says she's comfortable with the process and KATV has made efforts to protect her safety.

"Of course there were conversations about my safety. But we decided that I'm not taking a risk that's any bigger than any other reporter. I'm always with somebody. A lot of times I'm in the newsroom so people can watch the desk camera. If I need to say something, or if I need to make a personal phone call, I have a mute button," Fisher says.

Stations are taking measures to beef up security. Ed Trauschke, news director at Fox 16, says the station has hired an armed guard to come in every night. But some doubt that promoting on-air talent will change.

"I don't think they're going to change any policy," Jane said. "I really don't. I think putting our email address right underneath our faces on the air—that probably shouldn't be as readily available. But I don't feel any change."

Until a suspect is arrested, Jane's anxiety and the fears of the broadcast community as a whole are unlikely to recede. From the minute she wakes up until she goes to bed at night and nearly every moment in between, Jane said she finds herself thinking about whether someone might be out there who would do her harm. "It has made me more guarded," Jane said. "But that's more when I'm not working. I feel the most safety at work. I feel so unsafe at home. Home, where it's supposed to be your little nest—I dread it."

Though word of the crime against Anne Pressly hit the Little Rock news business like an earthquake, nowhere has it been felt so deeply as Pressly's home station, KATV Channel 7. "Everyone's still in shock," said news director Randy Dixon. "Nothing like this has ever happened at this station or in this market. It rarely happens anywhere in the country. There's a heightened concern, of course . . . the police department has spoken to some of our staff about personal safety, and we're going to have some self-defense classes."

Dixon said that the safety of KATV employees and on-air talent has long been a concern. While he didn't want to comment on specific new security measures the station has implemented, he said that the building and its parking lots have had surveillance cameras in place for years. As for how the station handles letters, emails, and other communications with fans—especially those whose tone or language causes concern—Dixon said he has always been "wary and careful" in dealing with that, including keeping a correspondence file and informing police about those who send suspicious or repeated emails. As did many we talked to in the news business, Dixon said there's a line that can be crossed when communicating with a television personality. Where that line is, he said, is often a "gut thing" for a news director.

"You get the typical letters saying, hey, I hate your hair and other things like that where the viewer is just trying to get some input," he said. "If someone says, 'I want to come meet you,' then it's easy to tell when they cross that line. We err on the side of conservatism, especially in cases like that." Several of those the *Times* talked to also rely on gut feeling when determining when a writer or caller has gone from being a fan to a potential hazard.

Rob Heverling, news director at KARK Channel 4, said that every communication has to be judged on a case-by-case basis, but when a fan does say or do something that crosses the line, intervention by a third party usually stops things from escalating, especially if that third party is the police.

"Most of the time it's harmless, but it is scary when you have somebody calling repeatedly or saying they want to come by and meet you," Heverling said. "But you have to be aware of it, because we want our people to be safe." Heverling said that shortly after the assault on Anne Pressly, he held a meeting in which he told staffers to be "a little more wary" and call and check up on each other. In addition, he said, the station combed through the talent bios on their website and removed anything that might be potentially dangerous or too personal, including whether a person was unmarried or lived alone. "It makes you stop and think," he said, "that it could happen here."

Bob Steel worked for more than 18 years in Little Rock's TV news business, serving as news director at both KARK and KATV. Like others the *Times* interviewed, Steel kept files on any communication that raised a red flag. Most of the letters the talent received were harmless, he said. Several, he recalled, were from mentally challenged people who saw an anchor on TV and innocently thought they were in love. Still, Steel said, it's hard to know who is a threat and who isn't, which makes it important to keep things on file.

"Then if somebody crosses the line, you have a record that they have made contact and you can probably find out who the person is pretty quickly. . . . If there's a lot of vile language, if there's a lot of sexual talk, I'm going to notify the authorities right then," Steel said. "If it's just a guy who thinks she's beautiful and he's in love with her, I'm not going to worry too much about that, but I am going to save the letter."

Though Steel said male anchors under his watch received threatening calls or letters from time to time—usually in protest to a story they had reported—females bore the brunt of the sexually explicit and potentially violent communication with fans. In rare cases, face-to-face encounters left them shaken for weeks.

"I remember one instance in which one of our anchors—and I wouldn't want to say who—was followed by a gentleman in a Jeep to a local mall. She went into the mall, and when she came out, the gentleman had his pants down and was masturbating as she got into her car. It scared her literally to death." Steel said the man was apprehended days later when he did the same thing to the wife of another on-air personality at the station. In another case Steel recalled, a man sent a videotape to a female anchor in which the man disrobed.

To alleviate the uneasiness among staff, all stations have made counseling available in either group or one-on-one sessions. More than one has arranged for an expert in personal security to speak to the staff. "The other thing we've tried to do is put some perspective on [the] crime," Heverling said. "At some point, you want to say, yeah, this is serious, but let's not overdo it. Let's not live our lives in fear."

One thing Heverling said he has specifically talked to his reporters and anchors about is their participation in online social networking sites. While there are restrictions on who can look at a MySpace or Facebook page—the owner of the page usually has to designate a visitor as a "friend" before that person can view their page—it's common for users to have placed a trove of private information, from family photos to daily diaries to their cell phone number, on the other side of that rather flimsy barrier.

"We've counseled our reporters, especially after the Pressly event, that this isn't a two-way communication," Heverling said. "Somebody might be viewing a MySpace page and they get the sense that they know you. We've cautioned them to lock those sites down and suggested it might not be a good idea to have a page at all."

For viewers, possibly the biggest question in all this is: how much will the anxiety over the Pressly case change what you see on the local news and at the news stations' websites? The answer, most in the business say, is not a lot. The industry rises and falls on the perceived connection between the talent and the audience. If a reporter or anchor is seen as approachable and friendly, ratings tend to go up. If an anchor or reporter is seen as distant and cold, ratings go down. For most local stations in America, that means making sure the talent comes across as a friend and neighbor, be that via umpteen trips to county fairs and parades, or just by that certain knack for likeability that some gifted personalities seem to have. The goal is simple: make the viewers feel like someone they never met is part of the family.

"If you're looked upon, whether by design or just naturally, as someone approachable, you're going to get better numbers," said Doug Krile, anchor at KARK from 1986 to 1997. "One of the questions they would use when they were talking to viewers was: If Doug Krile knocked on your front door right now, would you, A) Let him in, B) Let him stand in the front hallway, C) Let him into the living room, or D) Let him into the kitchen? If you got to the kitchen, you were golden."

Jeanne Rollberg is an associate professor in the School of Mass Communication at UALR. A former reporter and news anchor, Rollberg said news stations—especially those in smaller markets like Little Rock—rely on their ability to create a relationship with the public, especially when it comes to morning show anchors like Anne Pressly.

"It only makes sense that the news teams that lead those newscasts so early in the day portray themselves as friendly, personable, and lighthearted as well as competent," Rollberg said. "Viewers are often engaged in multiple tasks as they prepare for their day, so they're not as likely to be paying the level of attention to news stories per se. . . . Personalities matter there."

This relentless promotion of anchors and reporters as friendly and approachable can lead to a "false reality" for certain viewers, Rollberg said. "It is easy for viewers to come to feel that they know anchors [and] reporters personally when they do not. . . . I'm personally uncomfortable with much of the previously private information that shows up in promos or online. Not only do I think it isn't wise to have much of it available for safety reasons, but I also think it elevates the personality factor far too much and takes away attention from the real, meaningful news of the day."

Anne Jansen would agree with at least some of that. A reporter and anchor with KTHV Channel 11 for over 25 years, Jansen retired earlier this year to become a full-time mom. She said that stations have always pushed the personality angle, but believes that some have taken things to a new level in recent years. "Even back in the 1970s, they did stupid promos to make you think the anchors were one big happy family and went sailing together on the weekends," Jansen said. "But the industry has changed so much. It's almost like the person saying the news has become a celebrity. The modern day anchor has an aura of fame around them."

Jansen said she never had anyone she'd consider a stalker or obsessed fan during her days on the desk, but added that concern for her family's privacy was one factor that figured into her decision to step out of the spotlight. There were times when she felt the station sought to delve too far into the details of her personal life. When she was pregnant with her first child, Jansen said, station officials approached her about doing a series of promotional spots to coincide with a drive to get women to take folic acid, a vitamin necessary for proper fetal development. After some thought, she kindly refused.

"I always felt kind of strange about that," she said. "They came to me when I had my first son and they wanted to do some kind of promotional thing and tie it to my pregnancy. It was for a good cause, but I just didn't feel right about it. That's not to say that it isn't the right thing to do, but it just didn't feel right for me."

Chuck Maulden, news director at KTHV Channel 11, said the public's appetite for details about anchors' lives is nearly limitless. "There's such an insatiable appetite for the people who are in your living room every day," Maulden said. "They get married or have children, people want to know: What happened? Are they OK?"

While stations have a heightened concern for their on-air talent in the wake of Pressly's murder, they are also uniformly—albeit a bit reluctantly—unapologetic about the issue of promotion. As KTHV's Chuck Maulden put it: "You do have to have people represent your brand, and obviously in television that's the way it is."

KATV's Dixon doesn't expect any change in the way stations present their talent to viewers. "That's what we do for our business," Dixon said, "and if you don't do it, you're not doing your job. That's the nature of what the business is."

"We do want people to bond with and appreciate our anchors," said KARK's Heverling. "Basically we're going into their living rooms and bedrooms and kitchens and we want people to be comfortable with them and relate to them. Now, having said that, while that's very, very important, I think if you pay attention, you won't really learn that much about them."

Steel doesn't see the industry moving away from personalities to sell the news programs. He does, however, believe that the crime against Pressly will remind stations to protect their talent.

"I have a saying that there's not a story worth your life," Steel said. "Be cautious at all times—and I'm talking about storms, fire, pestilence, and stalkers." ➥

"HOW I GOT THAT STORY"

Gerard Matthews is an associate editor and reporter at the Arkansas Times *in Little Rock, Arkansas, where he covers local politics, environmental issues, the media, and just about everything else. Gerard joined the paper in September 2008 after earning a master's degree in media and public affairs from The George Washington University. He also has a degree in political science from the University of Central Arkansas. David Koon is an associate editor at the* Arkansas Times. *In addition to being an award-winning reporter, David is a fiction writer whose work has appeared in Crazyhorse, Glimmer Train, and the* New Stories from the South *anthology. He is a graduate of the Iowa Writer's Workshop, where he was the 1999 James Michener/ Copernicus Fellow in fiction. He lives in Little Rock with his wife, Lisa, and his son, Sam. In December 2009 both Matthews and Koon participated in AAN's live chat series to discuss their coverage of the tragic murder of television news talent Anne Pressly; the following is an edited version of that interview, which was led by former* Las Vegas Weekly *Editor and AAN Editorial Committee member Scott Dickensheets.*

Where did this story begin for you guys? A tip? A hunch? Or . . . ?

David Koon: This story began for us where it did for just about everyone in Little Rock: we got to the office on October 20, 2008, and heard that Anne Pressly had been assaulted. That morning, my editor actually ended up sending me to the hospital emergency room where doctors were still working on Ms. Pressly, trying to stabilize her. As far as I know, I was the first reporter there. I saw Ms. Pressly's friends and KATV colleagues all gathered outside the emergency room, and when they spotted me they rushed inside. I think it might have been kosher for me to follow them inside at that point and see if they had any comment, but it was really a moment for me where I said: 'Do I want to be a reporter, or do I want to be a human being?' Ultimately, I ended up coming back to the office without a quote. It was the one time in my career as a reporter when that didn't necessarily feel like a bad thing.

Gerard Matthews: That morning, we got a tip, I think it was from one of our sales people, that there were some cop cars around Anne's house. I went over there to check it out and, sure enough, everybody's worst fears were confirmed. We got something up on our blog very early and just continued to follow the story from there. I think our spot coverage that day was just as good, or maybe even better than anyone else's.

Did your newsroom have any kind of "are we doing this because it involves TV people instead of, say, insurance agents?" discussion beforehand?

Gerard Matthews: As far as any discussion in the newsroom went, we just thought there was something larger that none of the other outlets were going to cover. Yes, you had a high-profile person that was involved, but there were also some bigger questions that the TV stations weren't going to cover. For example, is there any blame to be placed on the stations themselves for over-promotion of their on-air talent? In TV, it's all about personality, and local news stations, not just here but everywhere, really promote the heck out of their people. Nobody else in town was going to be asking questions.

How did the TV folks respond when you started poking around?

Gerard Matthews: We were getting stonewalled a lot. It's really weird when you're reporting on people you see at press events and news conferences. The whole dynamic kind of changes. I don't think media personalities and those that are in the biz are used to being on the other side of the questions.

David Koon: I think the main thing was that a lot of them were worried about revealing too much about their personal fears—of giving the impression that they were afraid of the viewers. Local news is such an odd environment. In order to be successful as an anchor or TV personality in a market like Little Rock, you have to be approachable, you have to be likeable, you have to be somebody who—as the veteran Little Rock anchorman Doug Krile told us—people would invite not just into the living room, but into the kitchen. For a lot of stations, that means pressing the on-air talent to lay a good bit of their personal lives out on the table for viewers to peruse: engagements, weddings, pregnancies, births, children. Viewers see all that, and—if all goes well— they begin to trust the anchor the way they'd trust a friend. Win that trust, you win the ratings. The problem is, that 'I'm Your TV Friend!' image doesn't really square too well with the idea that a news personality might be afraid that a fan might take something too far.

After about the fifth or sixth "no comment," I started to really suspect that was what we were dealing with. And when we finally did get a very well-respected Little Rock news anchor to open up to us on condition of anonymity—"Jane" from our story—our suspicions were largely borne out. What we heard from her was that her anxiety over revealing too much of her personal life for the sake of ratings, when coupled with what had happened to Ms. Pressly, had really turned her into a person who was afraid a lot of the time.

What was the response from readers and from other journalists?

David Koon: We got a lot of great feedback on this story, both from the public and other journalists. At the time the story went to press, Little Rock was consumed with curiosity and dread about the murder of Ms. Pressly and the idea that her killer was still out there. At the same time, as I said, the news anchors in a small market like Little Rock really do become a part of peoples' lives, and I think a lot of our readers just wanted to know what the folks they watch every night on the television news were really, deep-down-in-their-guts thinking about all this. We managed to deliver a warts-and-all glimpse behind what is usually a fairly tightly drawn curtain. I think the readers appreciated that.

What was the story with the person police ended up arresting?

David Koon: Only a few days after our story went to press, the LRPD arrested a man from Marianna, Arkansas, named Curtis Lavelle Vance after linking him to the crime scene through a single hair. Mr. Vance was a small-time burglar with a 76 I.Q. He apparently entered Ms. Pressly's house looking to steal her computer and television. Vance eventually confessed to the murder, telling police that he'd never seen Ms. Pressly on television, and didn't know she was a news anchor. In November, Vance went on trial for the crime, with prosecutors seeking the death penalty. The jury found him guilty of capital murder, residential burglary, rape, and theft of property, but deadlocked 9–3 on the issue of whether to put him to death. As a result, Vance was sentenced to life in prison without the possibility of parole.

Do you both cover media on a regular basis?
Gerard Matthews: I had only been working at the *Times* for about a month and a half before this story broke. David had been doing a media column for about three years. I took over that column right after this incident. So it was kind of weird because David knew a lot of people in the media community. Some would talk, others wouldn't. This was really my first big media story. First big story period, really.

What's your general approach to the media column? What's the reason to have one in the first place?
David Koon: For the media column, it's kind of cool to look in on this little microcosm of a media network or market. You can kind of tie smaller things that happen here to larger issues, or vice versa.

Gerard Matthews: Yeah, and it's not really a column, it's more newsy. There's not a lot of straight opining on whatever you want. We try to ask some important questions and comment on how things are being covered here because it can get kind of insular sometimes.

MUSIC CRITICISM

CIRCULATION 50,000 AND OVER

"Ride the Plastic Lightning"
"Guns N' Roses"

by Rob Harvilla, *Village Voice* and *L.A. Weekly*

"What alternative journalism music writing is all about. I especially like that he takes popular subjects then glazes them with the alt journo flavor. Game over."
—Todd Inoue

CIRCULATION UNDER 50,000

"The Metal and Mr. Kenney"
"Dissonance Directives"

by Luke Baumgarten, *Pacific Northwest Inlander*

"Informed, entertaining, smart without being snarky."—Cynthia Joyce, msnbc.com

Ride the Plastic Lightning

Rob Harvilla

SEPTEMBER 17, 2008

I have not yet had occasion to actually hear Metallica's totally badass new album, because I am way too busy *living* it, tearing off magnificent spider-fingered runs during the manic breakdown in "My Apocalypse" on my doofy-looking plastic guitar, which corresponds to the on-screen actions of one Lars Umlaut, a morbidly obese face-paint-and-spiked-leather gentleman who summons a vicious flock of bats when he gets *really* excited. Yes, in keeping with the band's longstanding, unflagging embrace of modern technology, *Death Magnetic,* the band's first release since 2003's disastrous *St. Anger* and the following year's even more disastrous Jesus-these-guys-are-wussy-lunatics documentary *Some Kind of Monster,* saw release Friday as both a plain ol' Virgin Megastore/iTunes product and, far more desirably, as a fully playable 11-track Guitar Hero III download. Innovation! You don't actually want to *listen* to a song called "The Unforgiven III," right? Wouldn't you rather merrily click 'n' clack through it while staring intently at a television instead? I agree. Let us make rock-criticism history together.

Actually, let us start off by noting that every tune on this album is, like, 10 minutes long; for those of us with early-onset arthritic tendencies, this creates the first-ever scenario where you'll find yourself saying, "Shit, I wish this Metallica record had more ballads." But long before your wrists start aching, when you first drop $17 or whatever (the Microsoft points system is deliberately confusing) and tear into opening salvo "That Was Just Your Life," there's an enormous, perverse pleasure in slithering through the slow, ominous opening riff, a barely masked "Enter Sandman" rip that eventually explodes, predictably and wonderfully, into that apocalyptic double-kick gallop and bombastic tirade of totally unnecessary and totally awesome *buddabrumpbumpbumpbump* drum fills that typify the Metallica experience. James Hetfield is still grunting testosterone-drunk inanities as though they're biblical prophecies, but this way, as you're otherwise occupied with the task of not getting your ass booed offstage, you only catch the occasional errant cliché ("fall from grace"!) and knuckleheaded aphorism ("Love is a four-letter word"!) as you struggle and sweat. "The End of the Line" is even better, a loose and tremendously *fun* mélange of seemingly unrelated riffs, especially the jabbing one-note (Which note, you ask? The red one.) blast that powers the chorus and eventually morphs into a daffy Kirk Hammett guitar solo that spirals off into delightfully atonal busted-fax-machine nonsense.

Yes, just in time for the Guitar Hero generation, Metallica has finally unmuzzled its own. *Some Kind of Monster* was a deranged, fascinating, brutally unflattering portrait of a once-terrifying band of boozing sociopaths reduced to impotent, simpering infighters, clearly artistically bankrupt as a 40K-a-month therapist sought to scam them all the way to actual bankruptcy, too. Only Hammett came off well, in a visionary tirade wherein he pointed out that the band's refusal to allow any bitchin' solos on the bludgeoning, joyless *St. Anger*—a decision based on the notion that bitchin' solos were totally outdated—would only make the record sound totally outdated when bitchin' solos returned to prominence. He was right, and *Death Magnetic* plays like a peace offering, giving Kirk ample opportunity to roam, and you, oh recreational Guitar Hero warrior, ample opportunity to dislocate a finger trying to keep up with him. "All Nightmare Long" is particularly vicious/loopy in this regard, and loopy in a lyrical sense as well, James grunting *"LUCK! RUNS! OUT!"*as though reading directly from Revelations (which he might be, actually). The chorus is "Hunt you down without merc-*aaaaaay!"* Fun stuff.

The ballads? One out of two ain't bad. "The Day That Never Comes" is super-easy (500-note streak, suckas) and finds James in fine bellow; it pleasingly recalls Lynyrd Skynyrd's "Simple Man," for whatever that's worth. True, after some top-shelf power-ballad catharsis, the tempo speeds up and some limp, aimless riff-bashing ensues, far more inexcusable a pander to the diehard *Master of Puppets*–coveting heshers than the first half is to the melody-loving mainstream. There's a fine line between "jamming" and "stalling." But it's nonetheless a hell of a lot better than "The Unforgiven III."

Oy. The song itself isn't terrible, but the way it's presented in video-game form is lethal. The track begins with nearly a minute of piano-and-string-section goop, and for that minute you, the fake guitarist, have nothing to do but idly stare at your fake band and the fake crowd, neither of whom has anything to do either, but are both strangely still acting like they're rocking out, the fake band strutting and stomping about, the fake crowd whooping and headbanging to what might as well be Yanni. It all feels very, very sarcastic. Hard to conceive of a song called "The Unforgiven III" as a fount of unintentional humor, but there you go.

The other major problem here is "Suicide and Redemption," an actually-10-minute dirge offered in the game as two separate tracks: James's part and Kirk's part. The former is painfully dull; the latter is painfully dull for seven minutes and then suddenly gets *incredibly fucking hard.* Endless blistering triplets that shut you down and get your ass booed offstage instantly. The third time I slogged through what seemed like a half-hour of quasi-melodic farting just to get abruptly vaporized and subsequently informed that I'd only made it through 70 percent of the song was awfully demoralizing. How can I accurately review this record without hearing that last 30 percent? What if there's a Balkan brass breakdown or a Lil Wayne cameo or something? You mean I have to downgrade and go through this bullshit on *medium* difficulty? That's even *more* boring and demoralizing! But finally, just once, with artfully deployed star power and an inelegant, button-mashing, hail-Mary fusillade, I emerged victorious on the other side . . . and endured another unremarkable three minutes of quasi-melodic farting. I've got a great idea for the plot of "The Unforgiven IV."

But *Death Magnetic,* and this truly bizarre way to experience it, is all about redemption, and for that we've got "Cyanide": a terse main riff, repetitive enough to get really good at but not tired of, coupled to James's typically dopey lyrics—"Cyanide! Living dead inside! Break this empty shell forevermore!" It's maudlin high-school poetry as always, but perfect in this context—every note assigned a candy-colored button, band and audience alike rendered as goofy cartoons. It's a toy, and a cheap thrill, and oddly perfect. When the loopy solo hits, tilt that plastic ax upward, deploy star power, and pray for the best. If you can't ride the lightning, maybe you can ride it out. ➜

Guns N' Roses

Rob Harvilla

NOVEMBER 26, 2008

We can all agree that Sunday's eons-delayed, punchline-defying, free-Dr. Pepper-triggering release of Guns N' Roses' *Chinese Democracy* marks the death of something—some combination of the music industry, "the album" as a unit of cultural import, old-guard rock stardom, irony, sincerity, free-market capitalism, hip-hop, the spread offense, and neoconservatism. Regardless, I feel comfortable stating that it's the last record I will ever buy just to read the liner notes. Holy shit. Do pop into Best Buy this week and have a gander.

(Deep breath.)

Fourteen studios in four cities. Twenty-two assistant engineers. Eight folks under the heading "Additional Pro Tools." Six more under "Logic." The phrase "initial production" recurring. Eleven musicians get their own personal thank-you lists; deranged mastermind Axl Rose's require nearly three columns of tiny-ass type. (Notable names: Mickey Rourke, Donatella Versace, Izzy Stradlin.) And these are just full-album credits. All 14 songs get their own personal bibliography: "There Was a Time" has six guitarists (five is more common) and five orchestral arrangers (Rose is cited as both); "Madagascar" boasts not just French horns but synth French horns, plus clips from two Martin Luther King Jr. speeches and dialogue from *Mississippi Burning, Cool Hand Luke, Braveheart, Casualties of War,* and *Seven.* Full lyric sheet, too: Within the first minute of histrionic piano ballad "This I Love," Rose rhymes why, goodbye, I, eyes, wise, try, inside, deny, die, mine, inside, why, goodbye, inside, light, bright, night, and deny. I look forward to re-reading these liners in *Best Music Writing 2009;* you will greatly prefer them, at least initially, to *Chinese Democracy* itself. For what has really died here is the word "overproduced." It will no longer suffice. So dense, so suffocating, so paranoid-android synthetic, so ludicrously engorged is Rose's magnum opus that you will have absolutely no problem believing it took dozens of people millions of dollars and nearly two decades to complete it. This is the mythical burrito microwaved by God, which is so hot, God himself cannot eat it. Upon first, second, third, quite possibly tenth listen, it's a deeply unpleasant experience. You'll warm to it. Maybe.

Cling to Rose's voice. He's still got it, that deranged shriek-to-moan bazooka of lust, contempt, pathos, and megalomania that made us love him—and a full stable of jilted bandmates, exasperated label minders and overworked lawyers tolerate him—in the first place. And though he frequently sounds like a cruise-ship *Phantom of the Opera* parody of himself, this record gets better the more ridiculous and self-absorbed it gets. Daffy guitar solos by gentlemen named Buckethead and Bumblefoot enliven fairly turgid compu-thrash riff-rockers; eye-rolling piss-and-moan heartbreak dirges ("You're the only one I have ever loved that has ever loved me," etc.) are mercifully eclipsed by distinctly meta I-did-it-my-way anthems of defiance. Rose toys with several metaphors ("Blame it on the Falun Gong," advises the title track) to describe the titanic improbability of this album's mere existence, often abandoning them in midsentence at his whim:

> Riad N' the Bedouins
> Had a plan and thought they'd win
> But I don't give a fuck 'bout them
> 'Cause I AM CRAZY

Indeed, the best one-line summation of *Chinese Democracy* is the "If I thought that I was crazy/then I guess I'd have more fun" thesis of the oddly exuberant piano-rocker "Catcher in the Rye" (seriously, it sounds like Journey). "Madagascar," the mournful MLK/*Cool Hand Luke* one, is meant to be the climax, with a luscious French-horn/synth-French-horn bed worthy of a Björk B-side, and though things have gotten way, way, way out of hand by the time we're in full-blown arena-rock mastadon-stomp mode and Rose is implicitly equating his stubborn purity of vision to the civil rights movement, the sheer audacity gives you hope. That you can now purchase and listen to this album—that heartless major corporations patiently waited years (one and a half decades!) for its fruition—makes a better case for the undiminished possibility of the American Dream than the election of Barack Obama. The subtext imbues otherwise pedestrian tunes with a gleeful self-help delight: "Scraped" bashes around gracelessly but means what it fuckin' says when it says, "You're stronger than the lies that they tell you" and "Nothing's impossible/I am inconquerable." That's not a word; it is now.

Again: three full listens and/or four full hours, minimum, before you reach this state of admiration. Inevitably, *Chinese Democracy* sounds like too many cooks following way too many recipes. Totally rad finger-tapped wankery aside, "Shackler's Revenge" is a charmless, grating butt-rock dud infinitely more tolerable as a Guitar Hero download (a dismaying recent trend). For fans of second-tier, vaguely funky mid-'90s industrial, "If the World" is straight-up God Lives Underwater. And "Sorry" is a plodding, sub-Daughtry knuckle-dragger wherein Rose accosts one of his myriad enemies (whether his foe wears a suit or leather pants and a top hat goes unspecified) with deeply lame gibes like, "You talk too much/You say I do/Difference is nobody cares about you" and "You close your eyes/All well and good/I'll kick your ass like I said that I would." You can fall in love with the idea of this album and eventually teach yourself to love the album itself, but nothing packs a tenth the vitality and exhilaration of, oh, let's say, "It's So Easy."

God, "It's So Easy." You put on *Appetite for Destruction* (in, like, 1987), cranked up "Welcome to the Jungle," and believed that no finer specimen of pure, vicious rock 'n' roll hedonism could ever exist, and then came track two: "It's So Easy." It's an objectively perfect song, and though objectively perfect songs aren't effortless, per se, they sound that way—the effort, the craft, the forethought, the money, the time and the personnel, they require is the least interesting and prominent thing about them. *Chinese Democracy* is the inverse: a hilariously painstaking attempt to synthesize that lightning, a lost cause taken to delirious extremes, a fascinating catastrophe inspiring equal parts awe and pity. A would-be Hollywood blockbuster upstaged by its own credits. ➟

"HOW I GOT THAT STORY"

The frenetic inventiveness of Rob Harvilla's music criticism—from the laugh-out-loud quality of his prose to his conceptual playfulness (reviewing a Metallica album by playing it on Guitar Hero)—derives from a simple personal mission statement: "Amuse yourself." Then he passes the fun on to readers of the Village Voice, *where he's worked for four years. Before that, Harvilla was music editor of the* East Bay Express, *in Oakland, Calif., and before that he was an arts writer/editor at the Other Paper in Columbus, Ohio. He's freelanced for* Spin, Blender, Entertainment Weekly, *and others. Age 31 at the time of this interview (conducted by former* Las Vegas Weekly *editor Scott Dickensheets), Harvilla lives in Brooklyn.*

Of Guns N' Roses' *Chinese Democracy,* you say "Upon first, second, third, and quite possibly tenth listen, it's a deeply unpleasant experience." How often did you have to subject yourself to the disc to say that with authority? More or about the same as a typical disc you'd review?

Generally if I'm writing 1,000 words about a record I'd like to listen to it 10-plus times, which was probably the case for *Chinese Democracy,* though it felt like way more than that, if you know what I'm saying. I think that particular week I was traveling, so I listened to it a lot while walking aimlessly around San Francisco eating my hotel's free chocolate-chip cookies. This softened my feelings about it to some degree probably.

Have you listened to it since reviewing it?

In its entirety, no. You kind of burn out on a record after listening to it over and over like that. Only the ones I really love tend to survive. Sorry, Axl.

After 15 years of buildup, mythology, hype, counterhype and so on regarding *Chinese Democracy,* did you feel any special pressure to rise to the, ahem, "occasion"? Or was there no sense that it *was* an occasion, other than in Axl Rose's mind?

As the buildup is/was technically older than my own journalistic career, yes, I suppose I was aware of the momentousness. It changes your thinking when you know every publication on Earth is obligated more or less to have a take on it. But even though I loved *Appetite for Destruction* (which my mom refused to buy for me when I was 9, on account of the profanity, etc.) I can't say I'd followed *Chinese Democracy*'s slow, painful genesis that closely.

How early in your writing process did you decide to review *Chinese Democracy* through the prism of its liner notes, and Metallica's *Death Magnetic* through its Guitar Hero version? And what was the secret to making those choices seem not at all like gimmicks—which could have easily been the case—but rather as the natural way to assess them?

Actually I'd downloaded *Chinese Democracy* somehow and was listening to that most of the week, but then right before I got on the plane to head from San Francisco back to New York City, I bought a retail copy (at Best Buy, of course) and read the liner notes on the flight, and wrote the whole thing then, so the liner-notes thing wasn't premeditated, no. In that case it's less a gimmicky review than just a review that gasses on about the liner notes for probably longer than it should.

As for Metallica, I actually hadn't heard *Death Magnetic* in normal record form when I wrote it—I decided going in to only review the Guitar Hero version. Which is a pretty goofy approach admittedly, but when you're writing about records every week you tend to look for new and fresh approaches, to amuse yourself if no one else.

Your writing is so distinctive that it begs the question of influences. Who or what helped mold your prose style?

I can't point to any specific writers, to be honest—I wanted to be a music writer after reading back-issues of *Rolling Stone* in my orthodontist's office. I haven't really patterned myself after anyone, but there's pieces of everyone, I'd imagine. "Amuse yourself" is my general creed, for better or worse.

The Metal and Mr. Kenney

Luke Baumgarten

JUNE 26, 2008

It's mid-evening and the maples are rustling gently. An early summer breeze has brought the first whiffs of chill to what has been a warm day. The dining area is shaded but bright, dappled sunlight still dancing off the tops of the century-old brick buildings to the north and south. With his back to Howard Street, Abe Kenney sits ensconced between a railing and his amp. Guitar in hand, he provides the tempo and melody for a half-full patio of diners as they tuck into their field roasts and fresh whitefish. As far as paved downtown alleyways go, it doesn't get more bucolic or serene than this.

It's the middle of a modest dinner rush at Mizuna. Kenney is dressed like the restaurant's servers, head to toe in dress casual black. His movements are economical. He's stoic and precise as he plucks his way though Mauro Giuliani's "Grand Overture"; stern as he wends his way through Isaac Albeniz' "Torre Bermeja." He seems the very model of a modern dinner musician.

He's meant to blend in, to become part of the scenery. Even a cursory glance, though, and things start to stand out. You notice his tattoo, a spurge of jagged arrows radiating out from a point on his forearm—more chaos theory than eight-fold path. Then you see his guitar case, leaning against the amp, bearing stickers with similarly jagged lettering arranged symmetrically to resemble bat-like wings or the whirl of quick sand. They are the telltale marks of a death-metal acolyte. If you hadn't already, that's about when you realize that the music Abe Kenney is playing has a darkness to it. "Torre Bermeja" is spry in parts, but feels forlorn, even panicked at times. Another song in Kenney's repertoire is based on Francisco Goya's late-eighteenth-century etching, "The Sleep of Reason Produces Monsters," a haunting scribble about what arises when men trade reason for superstition. When we invest our world with demons, Goya and Kenney suggest, we become monsters ourselves.

Kenney remembers driving through the mountains with his family as a child, while Edvard Grieg's *Peer Gynt Suite* played on the radio. The tale of trolls and witches as allegory for man's egoism gave him an interest in classical music—its storytelling and its ability to evoke the monstrous. He discovered guitar in his adolescence and was always attracted to disparate forms of music. At first it was punk and classical. Eventually, punk gave way to ever more technical and dark forms of metal.

Society tends to put these forms at odds with one another, with classical guitar placed among the most august and timeless high art while metal is filed among the depths of recent pop culture. And Kenney doesn't disagree with that totally. The two usually sound worlds apart, he says. The human conditions they tackle, though, are the same.

"There was a lot of dark, often anti-religious imagery," Kenney says, "mixed with pointing out society's exploitation of people and the horrors of war and the disgusting aspects of all of that."

He finds composers from hundreds of years ago using similar tones to work through the same human tragedies and evils. "When you have a minor[-key], dissonant, religious piece, you can't help but picture apocalyptic or hellish imagery," Kenney says, invoking Bach specifically. "You can't help but imagine [the author] dealing with sin and the turmoil of religious devotion."

Kenney characterizes his current band, Obstruktor, as a thrash metal band straining at the limits of that genre. The band's vocalist, Wade Hampton, handles the band's lyrical content. "He's trying to say something from a personal perspective that relates to larger views of society," says Kenney. "We're trying to make art that deals with more than just typical anger."

That leaves Kenney to weave stories of his own into the band's lightning-fast churn. "Anne Akiko Meyers said that by studying old music, you get a more intense interest in new music," Kenney says, paraphrasing the concert violinist. "By studying old composers, I get new perspectives on metal and what I want to do in the future. Technical ideas, musical theories—but also just the depth that classical has. There's always specific context for the music, an idea that represents image patterns. I'm always telling myself to make the music be more than just notes."

One of the bigger differences between his work in metal and classical is the attention he receives. "I don't exactly play concerts on classical guitar," Kenney says. "I'm always background music." But that might be changing too.

Kenney's session at Mizuna last Thursday became more concert-like as the evening wore on. Though he didn't get much traction with the early crowd, by the time 9 P.M. hit and the final wave of diners had begun to work its way through sea scallops and pasta Bolognese, about half the patio was visibly pleased their organic, pan-roasted chicken was being served with a dollop of pathos (lowercase pathos, that is. For selections from Kenney's defunct band, Pathos, you would need to have dined during the eight o'clock hour).

During his last set of the night, sandwiched between a few livelier pieces, the Sturm und Drang of an older metal composition retooled for acoustic guitar set the space a-chill. The happier fare got appreciative claps; the metal left the patio near-silent. "That," said one apparent regular to his companion, with a wide smile, "was one of the death-metal pieces I was telling you about." ➥

Dissonance Directives

Luke Baumgarten

NOVEMBER 5, 2008

No drones, no mixers, no laptops. The last thing you'd expect to find on a flyer advertising a noise show is a bunch of rules.

It's not unheard of, after all, for shows in the genre to feature someone playing a chainsaw or using percussion to rattle windowpanes. At this particular event—the International Noise Conference (INC)—don't be surprised if one performer convinces the prettiest women in the audience (or from a nearby bar) to take the stage with him and hack away on guitars for the entire set. Noise can't be described by Western musical notation. It's the kind of thing you feel pushing though your bowels—rearranging your organs—as much you hear it tickling past your eardrums. The name itself suggests patternless randomness, dissonance, chance, and cacophony. Glorious chaos.

How can there be rules when you're shooting for glorious chaos?

Well. . . . Thing is. . .

The rules, "they aren't hard and fast," Lewis Pardum says impishly. Pardum is curator of the Spokane leg of the INC, a traveling symposium that hit some 29 cities this year and will roll into Spokane on Saturday night. Pardum seems a little uncomfortable with the rules, and how to explain them in the larger context of noise, especially since his own love of the genre derives from "the formless nature of it." Some of his explanations involve statements against intellectualism and in favor of deconstructionism. The simplest answer he finds, though, is "Rat thinks it's boring."

There's no better way to put it. Rat Bastard—founder and cultural ambassador of the INC—thinks drones, mixers, and laptops kill a party. The way self-serious kids stand in front of their computer screens clicking a mouse, adjusting knobs, barely moving, faces bathed in green and blue light—it drives him nuts. "I call it suitcase rock," Rat says. "They started that crap in Detroit."

The rules, then, are a somewhat paradoxical attempt to create chaos from order. Or at least from onstage languor. To get artists to step away from the laptop and grab a guitar or a meat grinder—or a pretty girl who's never held a musical instrument before—and see what happens. To give aural art a visual component, and also to go nuts onstage, sending torrents of sound cascading off the walls, maybe hurting yourself in the process—all in the name of that great, deep, precognitive rush of sound.

You can label INC anyway you want, Pardum says. You can philosophize about it. "You might say it's an intellectual statement against everything else," says Pardum, "but more it's just these people going nuts and forcing people to watch."

It's about turning the audience into voyeurs of the most uncivil kind of musical act. Rat Bastard's rules, then, are meant to draw out the exhibitionist in every performer. For him, it's all about the show, the atmosphere, and so is his festival. Some people get it, some people don't. Certain segments of the noise community in Detroit don't. In his estimation, neither does most of Japan.

"It's a certain type of party," Rat says. "They have crazy bands in Japan, but they don't understand the party. They take it too seriously. It's like work."

Though they don't share his tastes in performance, Rat defers to these noise traditions. Detroit got an INC event this year. Japan would have, if he could have found enough bands and a venue. There's really only one scene that's completely metropolis-non-grata with Rat Bastard: Seattle f---ing Washington.

✼

Though it's not really a conference and is only marginally international (playing shows in Seoul, South Korea, and the barely not-American Toronto), the International Noise Conference is still accustomed to bigger cities than Spokane. In 2008, Nashville, Austin, Los Angeles, Chicago, New York, Baltimore, and San Francisco were all stops on the tour. Seattle, notoriously, was not.

"They just couldn't get their shit together," Rat says. "It was, like, three months I was calling people." The best the town could pull together was a tentative house show somewhere, but Rat is a person of principle. "I was, like, 'I'm not looking at a house show, man.'"

INC events sometimes have dozens of performers (and often that many fans watching). A house show wouldn't cut it. So the festival stayed in Portland an extra day and coordinators down there threw a noise barbecue (an idea absolutely ripe with food-based noise-generating possibility). And the next day, Rat drove to Minneapolis.

INC Spokane was born, in a sense, from a seed of annoyed disappointment with a town renowned for its music scene. Rat and Pardum saw each other at No Fun Fest in Manhattan this year. Because it was a noise event not given to INC's rules (read: it was rife with suitcase bands), Pardum and Rat had time to talk about the idea of a Washington show. If Seattle couldn't bring it together, maybe Spokane could.

Spokane would not be the smallest city to have an INC show. That honor falls to Easthampton, Massachusetts, population 15,994. Spokane is, though, far enough under the national radar that Rat commits to the frequently used, perfectly logical, utterly wrong "spo-KAYNE" pronunciation. Still Rat has a highly positive image of Spokane—"I don't consider SpoKAYNE a small town for music," he says. "A lot of musicians come from there—good ones." He's excited for an event that (with 19 acts playing at two per hour) could have Object Space bumping until 6 A.M. on Sunday.

Pardum is excited too. Having grown up in Cheney before moving to Phoenix for college, Pardum characterizes himself as a fan of most types of avant-garde music. Returning home and settling in the near reaches of Spokane Valley, he didn't expect to find any kind of noise scene here at all. Spokane's noise horde isn't huge, but it's lively. Half the bands at INC Spokane are from the area. The rest are coming from Seattle and Portland and Vancouver.

Both Pardum and Rat relish that fact especially. "I think Seattle has some residual guilt," Pardum says, smiling broadly.

●◆

"HOW I GOT THAT STORY"

For his winning trio of music pieces, Luke Baumgarten of Spokane, Washington's Pacific Northwest Inlander *covered a lot of ground: a death-metal guitarist with a love of classical music; a cheerfully profane girl-punk band; and the sonic chaos of the noise movement. Now 29, Baumgarten is the paper's arts editor, after serving as its music editor.*

"Before I got here, I had absolutely zero journalistic experience," he says. "After college I sold corporate liquidation on eBay for a year, then answered phones and blogged while failing to get into grad school, then gave away film and music reviews for free to a paper in the resort town Sandpoint, Idaho. Anything to build clips." He began freelancing for the Inlander *in May 2005and had a full time job there a few months later. "Pretty fortunate in that regard," he allows. In this interview, Baumgarten discusses his writing with former* Las Vegas Weekly *editor Scott Dickensheets.*

How did you come across Abe Kenney, the death-metal guitarist playing classical acoustic at an outdoor restaurant in downtown Spokane?
It was one of those knowing-the-players situations. I'd known Abe from (his band) Obstruktor and then saw him playing acoustic guitar for an art opening at this very mainstream art gallery. I'd heard about Malmsteen Metal and wondered if Abe was one of those guys—people who love the unique kinds of virtuosity possible in both metal and classical guitar—so that was kind of how I approached the story. Then, as always happens, I found out his love of both genres is much more conceptual and comes from a darker, more interesting place than just a love of guitar noodling.

How well-versed were you in classical music or noise before you wrote pieces on those genres? Did you have to bone up much?
I'm a pop guy by inclination and had basically zero knowledge of either classical or noise coming into either story—except in the former case, middle-school band and my dad's love of Chopin. For the Kenney piece I just let him take me on his journey. He told me about listening to "In the Hall of the Mountain King" in his parents' car

on family road trips and how that gave him a love of the form from an early age—but also specifically how composers like Grieg gave him this craving for the kind of dark-night-of-the-soul side of classical music. It led him to punk and hardcore and eventually harder and harder forms of metal.

He's a quiet guy, so letting him talk about his inspirations and motivations first got him to open up, and I just tried to keep up with all the names and compositions he was dropping, so that, once he was comfortable, I could go back and ask him about those things in more detail.

For the noise story I just let Lewis and Rat Bastard rant and rant and rant, and then afterward I went back and did my homework, watched YouTube videos, listened to poor-quality live recordings and tried to use that and their quotes to paint it as viscerally as I could. Noise—at least that kind—is all about viscera.

How large and varied is Spokane's music scene? What's it take for you to stay current with it?

I think the music scene is average to small for a city and region our size, but it has some interesting pockets of growth and diversification—metal and folky singer/songwriter-ishness, oddly enough. There's this Presbyterian college in the northern suburbs that's been churning out some really interesting music from kids who either (a) have a conflicted David Bazan-type relationship to Jesus or (b) are atheists and thus can't believe they ever went to a Christian college. There are maybe 10 clubs consistently hosting original music that court active, up-and-coming artists or established artists still pushing themselves artistically (not nostalgia acts, basically).

Having that small a scene is tougher than you'd think to cover—especially when you're not in a media market that has a ton of competition. It's easy to just call those clubs, do some research and just write whatever's playing. When music was my beat (I'm the arts editor now, and I've handed those reins over to a new music editor), I always wanted to challenge myself to look for art at the fringes, like shows in raw spaces or in people's houses. Court the avante garde or at least the underground, such as it is here.

When you write a piece like "Dissonance Directives" about a subgenre that, as you say, might attract a dozen devotees to a show, how do you imagine your readers: As people who might actually attend the show now that you've informed them about it? As serious local music fans who likely won't attend but want to know what's going on? Or as casual readers who might read because the subject is quirky, but who might also bail after a few paragraphs? How do these considerations affect the way you write the piece?

The *Inlander* is an interesting paper, insofar as we have the deepest market penetration of any weekly in America (this is media audit speaking)—somewhere around 33 percent of the 600,000 people in the area read us. That's a staggeringly broad demographic. So, week-to-week, your mindset has to be that there are potentially just as many grandmothers reading about pop music as there are tweens reading about *Waiting for Godot*. So for me, whether it's a story about how sprinkler laws affect clubs or Jess Walter's latest novel, I always answer the question: "Who's going to read this?" with "Potentially anyone." And as a result I try to write stories that will inform and edify stakeholders and at least entertain everyone else.

Obviously you shoot to inform and edify everyone, but leaving people entertained is a fine fallback position. So that's my mind-set going into any story for the paper. I want to write a hip-hop story that will be smart enough for fans but not so jargony as to alienate people. And I want to frame a story about the financial hardships of a downtown arthouse theater in a way that's going to leave suburbanites who've never seen a film there feeling a sense of loss. With music writing, that tightrope usually rests somewhere between the person who's making the music and the musical themes—the points where art and the artist interact. You don't have to know what syncopation is to understand the need for self-expression.

Self-expression is one of those universal human desires that can always make for great storytelling. In the case of something especially fringe-y, like noise, I expected most people to not go to the show I was writing about. I didn't expect my story to persuade them, either, because the takeaway really was, "You know that weird genre of music you might have vaguely heard of? It's even weirder than you think."

And I think that in no way invalidates the story. Altweeklies sometimes think of themselves as event-idea-generators, with each arts story being a variation on: "this is what's going on, this is why it's rad, go out and do something." And certainly that's a big part of the job.

I do, though, think that any time you tell a compelling story—regardless of whether an audience ultimately becomes the subject's number one fan—that story has the potential to humanize the mainstream to an unknown or misunderstood group.

It's kinda like what Abe was doing with his music at the upscale restaurant. When that middle-aged guy turned to his tablemate and said, "That was one of the death-metal pieces I was telling you about," I got the feeling that he'd maybe undergone an act of humanization and now he was passing that on. Not to get too "We Are the World," but it's that incremental understanding that makes communities better places. The majority of what we do in arts writing might seem like a story about a dumb pop band or the symphony's third flautist, but there's always (well, usually) passion there, and always a human story. I feel that if I can tease out those kinds of stories whenever I can, then I've done something to help.

NEWS STORY— LONG FORM

CIRCULATION 50,000 AND OVER

"Snitch"

by Ashley Harrell, *SF Weekly*

" 'Snitch' is a terrific story. This is show-don't-tell journalism at its best. The dialogue is wonderful. The problem of getting people to come forward in the case of these kinds of urban homicides is well documented. But the complexity of such situations is rarely explored. Harrell does it beautifully without ever hammering us over the head with the myriad reasons why people don't say what they saw. The story is also a beautifully structured narrative with the artful use of detail that one finds in good fiction. Harrell also effortlessly gained our trust with her clear authority over her material. Brava!"—Celeste Fremon, WitnessLA.com

CIRCULATION UNDER 50,000

"Courting Disaster"

by Gwynedd Stuart, *Folio Weekly*

"Fantastic work. A really riveting, outrageous, frightening story, the kind this category and this medium is all about. Well done."—Daniel Hernandez

Snitch

Ashley Harrell

MAY 21, 2008

It's 7 A.M. on April 16, and Deanna Johnson's alarm clock is going off. She ignores it, and lies so still she could be mistaken for a corpse. She does not open her eyes. She tries not to think about anything. If a woman refuses to acknowledge that one of the most terrifying days of her life has arrived, then maybe it hasn't.

But Deanna, a grandmother who lives in the most notorious housing project in San Francisco, who in her 48 years has been homeless, addicted to heroin, a prostitute, and a victim of domestic violence, is no stranger to reality. She knows that in two hours she will be on the witness stand sitting directly across from a murderer, breaking the most fundamental law of the projects: don't snitch.

With a grunt, Deanna hoists her swollen legs over the side of the bed. She has fluid in her knees and a full figure to carry, so she walks with deliberation to the south-facing window to smoke her morning Newport. It'll help her wake up a bit—it was tough to get a good night's sleep when every little noise had her scared for her life.

The jitters have killed any semblance of appetite, so Deanna walks and feeds her guardian pit bull, Nina, but skips her own breakfast. She dons a crimson suit and matching head wrap, which covers the red and black braids that sweep dramatically across her head. Finally, she secures a silver cross around her neck and sets off down the hill to meet Inspector Kevin Jones of the San Francisco Police Department. He doesn't come to her door because that would draw the attention of already-suspicious neighbors.

The unlikely pair swings by the methadone clinic at 1111 Market to retrieve Deanna's daily dose, then proceeds to the homicide department at 850 Bryant, where she watches the tapes of her police interviews to refresh her memory. Finally, Jones escorts her to a special waiting room for victims, where she can rest and steel herself for the prospect of taking the stand.

"I just want to get this over with," she says. "I don't like to have to look at him."

By "him," she means Junk. At least, that's what everybody in the Double Rock housing project in the Bayview calls Jamal Butler. He's a convicted felon on trial for the brutal murder of a junkie named Allen Broussard, whom everybody called Tigaboo.

Deanna's testimony might send Junk to prison for life, and she thinks that's about right. Because of Junk and her testimony against him, she stands to lose her home, her fragile relationship with her son, and even her dog.

Exactly nine months before, Deanna had been puffing her Newport at the window. She did this almost every morning because it relaxed her, and she liked the view from the perch of the Alice Griffith Housing Project, popularly known as Double Rock.

Gazing into the distance, Deanna could see Monster Park shooting up above the greenery in Candlestick Point. She scanned the faraway row of pastel stucco houses ensconced in the hills above San Francisco Bay, then refocused on the more immediate scenery.

Below her window, a chain-link fence had collapsed into a straw-colored embankment strewn with trash—rotten furniture, toilet-paper rolls, a crushed Milwaukee's Best can. Next door, water crept from under the door of a vacant residence, where someone broke in and stole a vital piece of plumbing. Dilapidated identical two-story townhomes peppered the landscape, which resembled some unholy amalgam of landfill and war zone.

Deanna didn't mind living here. In fact, it was the best life she had ever known.

She grew up in Hunters Point without either parent. Her father left when she was 3; her mother went to prison when Deanna was 9. Raised by an unaffectionate aunt with three children of her own, Deanna became pregnant at 17 and dropped out of high school. Then a guy introduced her to snorting heroin. A few years later, she was pregnant again. And again. And again. The last baby died of sudden infant death syndrome at three and a half months. Her oldest son was shot numerous times, then died of a drug overdose.

Deanna worked in a restaurant for six years, but eventually she quit and became homeless in the Tenderloin with her second husband, who beat her regularly for four years. She still has the scars on her forehead. Her aunt raised her surviving sons, Damian and Dominic. After her husband got beaten into a coma, she filled out an application for public housing and was accepted to a project in Potrero Hill.

That's when things started to turn around. Deanna got her boys back and become a regular visitor at the methadone clinic. There she was reunited with childhood friend Willie Hill, who agreed to drive her to and from the clinic. They soon started a relationship, but because of the domestic violence in her history, she refused to live with him.

In winter 2006, because of a plumbing problem, the Housing Authority transferred Deanna to Double Rock. There, she transformed her apartment into an immaculate but comfortable nook, tucked away from the messed-up world. She cooked her children's favorites—chicken tenders and french fries—kept a spotless house, took care of her sons, and walked her dog.

The morning of August 17, 2007, changed everything.

Deanna remembers puffing on her cigarette when she heard the gunshot. She had no way of knowing the havoc it would wreak on her life. She didn't even see the actual murder.

According to witness statements to police and the medical examiner's report, the story went like this:

Tigaboo had planned to sell a stolen car stereo to Melvin Priestly, who was known to his friends as Pumpkin. The deal was going down in front of Pumpkin's place at 69 Nichols Way, but Junk, who knew Tigaboo, seemingly had other plans. Wearing a black mask, he showed up behind Tigaboo and pulled out a black 9mm pistol.

"You think you're tough? You think you're hard?" Junk asked. Then he aimed the gun at Tigaboo's head and pulled the trigger. The bullet entered Tigaboo's skull, ripped through both hemispheres of his brain, and exited just above his left eyebrow, never to be recovered. He fell forward onto the pavement, dropping the stereo. Still spiked with cocaine, the blood of the emaciated 37-year-old addict rushed onto the sidewalk and slipped into the crevices. He was dead.

Seconds later, Deanna watched from her window as Junk ran up the concrete ramp between Nichols Way and Double Rock Street. This stretch is called the Cut. Junk's dreads bounced as he flew up the Cut and under Deanna's window.

He disappeared at the side of her home. Next, she heard a loud, furious banging at her door that sounded like the cops. Her older son, Damian, opened the door—and there stood Junk. He looked wild, Deanna remembers, which made her uneasy.

Junk was bad news. He would often come around to her home at 6 Double Rock with Big Carl, Damian's father. Though Junk was a convicted felon, Deanna had seen him with a gun before. And though her sons referred to him as Cuzin Junk, Deanna often reminded people that Junk was no blood relative.

Deanna crept halfway down the stairs; though her view was partly obscured by a wall, she says she heard everything. According to witness statements, Junk bragged to Damian about "taking a nigga out" on Nichols Way, and was "laughin' and shit" about the murder.

Junk then presented Damian with a balled-up camouflage jacket, and told Damian that he killed Tigaboo in retaliation for breaking into Big Carl's house 10 years ago. Deanna heard him tell Damian he owed him a favor and that Damian should guard the murder weapon.

"Make sure nobody touch that gun," Junk told Damian before racing back out to inspect the aftermath.

When the door shut, Deanna barreled down the stairs and examined the jacket with her son. Inside were two black gloves with white stripes on the middle fingers and a shiny black 9mm pistol.

"Get this gun out of my house," she shrieked. Damian wrapped it back up and stuffed it in the living-room closet, then went to his room and made a phone call. "Mom trippin'," she heard him say.

Minutes later, Junk came back to get his gun, and then he was gone. But Deanna was smoldering. She worried that her son might now be an accessory to murder. Beyond that, it terrified her that Junk could kill a man, then brag about it. Why were black people always killing each other?

She had seen some shit in her life: four drive-by shootings, in fact, one of which was fatal. But she had never considered snitching until now. Her son was involved. She was involved. Cuzin Junk, who wasn't really a cousin at all, apparently cared so little for Deanna and her family that he had brought a murder weapon into their home.

Later that day, Deanna made three phone calls to the San Francisco Housing Authority tip line. She felt comfortable calling only because a monthly newsletter from the Housing Authority promised the tip line was anonymous.

Though recordings of the messages were difficult to decipher, a few sentences were clear. "The shooter was a man named Junk . . . he had a 9-millimeter and he shot the guy in the head . . . I don't want to be involved. . . . Have a nice weekend."

The San Francisco Police Department has been struggling to stay on top of the city's well-publicized homicide problem. So far this year, 43 people have been murdered. Before April 1, the police had arrested suspects in only 8 of those cases.

In Double Rock, investigations can prove more challenging than usual, as police officers almost never get the information they need. Nobody in the community will talk. Everybody has reasons.

Sister Stephanie Hughes, the spiritual leader and unofficial matriarch of Double Rock, can tell you why. In her close-knit community, she says, everybody knows everybody's business. The streets talk. When somebody snitches, word travels fast and they die. Even when snitches opt for witness protection, they still die.

Everyone in Double Rock is familiar with the story of Terrell Rollins. Just two years ago, Rollins, the main witness in a gang-related killing, was shot dead in an auto body repair shop. He was in witness protection at the time, yet had come back to the city to fix his car. He was 22.

Then there was Justin Lee. The 40-year-old had been both victim and key witness in a 2005 attempted murder case, and on January 7—the same day Lee left witness protection—an assailant chased him through the Mission until he tripped and fell, then shot him dead.

But in Double Rock, it's not just the snitch who's in trouble, Sister Stephanie explains: it's the snitch's whole family. "The fear is not just for ourselves, but for our children," she says. "No police department is going to be right there with our children on a 24-hour basis."

Furthermore, Sister Stephanie doesn't like the cops' attitude. They're friendly only when they need something from somebody, she says, and otherwise, they've got no respect.

On the day Tigaboo got shot, Sister Stephanie brought a bullhorn to the murder scene with the intent of leading a prayer for the crowd that had gathered. "My heart was crying," she says. "I followed the spirit of God." Unfortunately, God led her across the yellow police tape, and Sister Stephanie found herself stuffed in a hot police car, windows up, for nearly a half hour. She knew what she did was wrong, and she apologized. But her detention was too harsh, she says, and cops were "on a power trip."

Not surprisingly, in their investigation of Tigaboo's death, homicide detectives were having trouble finding willing witnesses.

But on August 22—two days after Deanna placed her final anonymous call identifying the killer—there was a miraculous breakthough in the case. The police found drugs and a weapon in Deanna's home, which gave them the leverage they needed to enlist her as a named witness.

Police had purportedly received a tip that Pumpkin was staying at Deanna's place. Because he was on parole, they didn't need a warrant. And when they showed up, the door to 6 Double Rock was wide open. Deanna—who is on probation—wasn't home.

The cops searched the house. They found Pumpkin; his mother, Terri Priestly (whom everyone calls Auntie); Damian and his half-brother, Lil' Carl; some crack and powdered cocaine; and a gun (not the murder weapon).

When Deanna learned her home was being raided, she thought the police had traced her anonymous calls. They wanted more information, she reasoned, and to keep her son from getting in trouble, she would have to give it to them. "I love my little son to death," she says. "I did what I thought I had to do." Deanna called Homicide, identified herself, and said she had information about Tigaboo's murder. She would tell them everything, but could they please not arrest Damian at 6 Double Rock?

Auntie and Pumpkin were arrested. Lil' Carl and Damian were not.

The same day, Deanna sat down and told investigators everything she knew. In return for her cooperation, she hoped that the cops and the Housing Authority would let the drugs-and-gun-in-the-house incident slide. She worried that the Housing Authority would have grounds to evict her, and what she wanted most was to be able to stay in Double Rock. That was her home.

A month later, the Housing Authority taped an eviction notice to Deanna's door. The police report from the incident had landed on a desk at the Housing Authority, prompting officials to evict everyone involved: Deanna, Damian, Pumpkin, Auntie, and even a man who had illegally sublet a room to Auntie.

Auntie was gone within three days, as the eviction notice required. For his parole violation, Pumpkin landed at San Quentin. Deanna and Damian, on the other hand, were permitted to stay.

Deanna says she was told by Inspector Jones that her eviction had been "put on the bottom of the pile," and that she could remain in Double Rock even though the Housing Authority refused to accept her rent. She prayed she'd get to stay, and says assistant district attorney David Merin led her to believe that was possible. "He said, 'We're going to make sure you are no worse off than when you met us,'" she says.

That is, if she testified in court.

The D.A.'s office declined to comment on Deanna's case, citing risk in confirming an individual's participation in the witness relocation and assistance program, but Captain Larry Wallace, the head of the program, said the district attorney has no power to delay or overrule evictions.

Damian would also have to be involved, and investigators asked Deanna to get him to come to the station. Damian refused, but they eventually got him anyway.

On November 28, a hysterical Deanna called the cops to report that Damian had pushed her and told her that if she snitched, she'd be killed. The cops seized that opportunity and arrested him. They interrogated him for more than three hours and told him that if he didn't cooperate, his newborn son, who had been born prematurely and was in the hospital, might grow up without a father. Damian would need to come back to 850 Bryant anyway, they told him, because he was going to be subpoenaed.

Three months later, in the middle of the pretrial hearing, Damian began to testify, but left during a break and went into hiding. Deanna again pleaded with her son to turn himself in.

He refused. "I can't get involved," he told her. "What you are doing is hazardous to your health."

Damian was right. Just recently, a bullet had pierced Deanna's living-room window, and Willie's tires had been slashed. Maybe coincidences, maybe not. Investigators had urged both Deanna and Damian to sign up for witness protection, but they repeatedly resisted. The possibility of relocating to Sacramento was getting thrown around a lot, and neither had interest in moving far from everything and everyone they knew. Deanna was willing to try somewhere like Treasure Island. Or maybe go back to Potrero Hill. But Sacramento? No way.

On each day of the murder trial, Junk had an attentive audience. On important days, there were as many as 15 people on his side of the courtroom, including his mother, aunt, three of his babies' mamas, two of his six children, and plenty of friends. In the intermissions, they'd all smile and wave.

Nobody from Tigaboo's family showed up.

On the first day Deanna Johnson took the stand, Willie came to support her. Five of Junk's devotees, including his mother, glared at Deanna as she slowly made her way to the stand. To them, Deanna was a liar and a drug addict. She was doing all this, Junk's aunt speculated, because she simply did not like Junk.

Deanna is not what the district attorney would call an ideal witness. In 2005 she pled guilty to assault, attempted robbery, and illegal possession of tear gas. (It was illegal because she had previously been convicted of several felonies.) She takes Seroquel for bipolar disorder, and though she says she's off heroin and crack, her son told investigators in November that Deanna had smoked crack recently. Her memory, she admits, is not very good.

But there Deanna sat, a reluctant yet key witness in an all-too-infrequent Double Rock murder trial.

Assistant district attorney Merin began his examination with simple questions. Was Jamal Butler in the courtroom?

"He's sitting right there," Deanna said, pointing at Junk. But he looked different than he had on the day of the murder. Short, tight coils replaced his dreads. Instead of camouflage, he wore a smart black suit and an electric-blue button-down shirt, though he seemed ill at ease in it. On several occasions, Junk loosened his collar and dusted off his sleeves, though they were perfectly clean.

After a few basic questions about Deanna's family, Merin drew her family tree on the chalkboard. He then asked her to identify photographs of the inside of her closet and the view from her window.

That's when Junk's eyebrows shot up and his lips crept into a tight smirk that seemed to say, *how dare you.*

Though Deanna was shaky on the stand, she essentially told the same story she had from day one: Junk brought a murder weapon to her house. He bragged that he killed a guy. She had come forward to protect her son.

The cross-examination didn't go as smoothly. Over the course of all the questioning, Deanna had given three versions of where she was when the gun went off: in her bed, at her window, and on her back porch. Her recollection of who was in her house that morning also varied. She told investigators that Lil' Carl and Damian's girlfriend, Tiffanie, were in the house, but on the stand she said they weren't. In separate statements, Deanna said she remembered being in two different places when she watched Junk leave her home for the second time.

Defense attorney Floyd Andrews didn't let those inconsistencies slide. He frustrated Deanna by pointing out her memory lapses, but she kept it together: "I'm not good with times and dates, but I know what I saw," she told the jury without being asked.

The most compelling portion of Deanna's testimony was her recorded phone calls to the Housing Authority tip line. Because she made those calls before she was evicted, that ruled out the possibility that Deanna was lying to keep her home. "What have you gotten out of testifying?" Merin asked.

"Nothing," Deanna said flatly.

When Pumpkin—who had been brought down from San Quentin—was called to the stand, an eerie silence enveloped the courtroom. In the docket, Pumpkin was listed as a "hostile witness." As minutes ticked by, the judges, lawyers, and cops whispered to each other, as did Junk's family members. Junk folded his hands in front of him in what looked like prayer.

The first signs of Pumpkin were the clinks of his chains in the hall. Then, in a flurry of orange jangling, he took the stand. In prison attire, his short, round body matched his moniker; he sported light facial hair and a rattail. He looked directly at the floor and refused to take his oath. Judge Carol Yaggy advised the court that Pumpkin had taken the oath that morning, and asked the prosecutor to begin his questioning.

"Mr. Priestly, do you understand why you are here?" Merin began.

No answer.

"Where were you on the morning of August 17?"

Nothing.

"Could you please look at me?"

Nope.

Pumpkin was ordered to answer the questions, but refused. He was then found in contempt of court and shown out. The jury would never hear about how, after the cops found him at Deanna's home, Pumpkin was arrested and interrogated. According to police department transcripts, during the three-hour interrogation Pumpkin broke down crying and admitted that he watched Junk kill Tigaboo.

Next on the stand: Damian Bradley. His hiding plan hadn't really worked out. On the previous Friday night, Damian stuck his head out the window to find cops approaching his home. He tried to escape out the back door, but was tackled by an officer. They rolled down the hill and both were injured.

In court, Damian wore a giant bandage over a laceration on his shoulder. While lifting up his shirt to show the jury, he grimaced. "I'm kinda sore," he said. "I can't raise my arm all the way up."

Damian is lanky and handsome, with a baby face and charming smile. Though he exudes confidence, he doesn't hide his emotions the way many hardened 20-year-olds from the projects do. Vulnerability aside, he seemed to have little respect for his mother. He told the jury that Deanna was on medications for mental issues, and couldn't be trusted.

Then he directly contradicted her testimony.

"On August 17, did Jamal Butler bring a gun to your house?" the prosecution wanted to know.

"No, sir. No, sir," Damian said.

"You told the cops he brought the gun to your house wrapped up in a green camouflage jacket," Merin continued. "You told them it was a 9-millimeter."

"I said that because they were telling me I'd never see my son again," Damian replied.

The jury viewed the taped police interrogation from November, when the cops had responded to Deanna's distress call by arresting Damian. On the portions played in court, it appears the interrogators were doing their best to terrify him. They tell him that his cellphone can be tracked, that's he's in a big pile of dog doo-doo, and that they're disappointed he's calling his mama a liar. If he doesn't talk, they say, his baby will grow up without a daddy.

Damian resists for more than an hour, and explains to the investigators what becomes of snitches. "Niggas killing your babies over this kind of shit," he says. "Niggas kill they baby mamas over this. Niggas kill they best friends over this kind of shit. . . . This is not to be played with; this is some serious shit . . . excuse my language."

When the investigators tell Damian his mother loves him, and that they're upset he's calling her a liar, Damian shakes his head. "She don't love me, man," he says.

"Your mama is one courageous woman," one police officer says. "And she loves you, whether you want to believe it or not. Kevin and I just spent over an hour with her, [and she was] crying about you."

"Where she go?" Damian asks. "'Cause I ain't got no ride."

Eventually Damian cracks and admits that Junk brought him the gun. He asks if he can be a confidential informant, and maintains a firm position that he cannot be involved. All he cares about is his son, he repeats over and over. He doesn't want to bring his son into this. When he finds out that the entire conversation has been recorded, he gets very quiet.

But on the stand, Damian insisted he was threatened and that he said only what the inspectors wanted to hear so they would let him leave. Finally, he broke into tears talking about his son, who died shortly after Damian's interview with the cops.

That might have moved the jury, but it apparently didn't sway its opinion of Junk. On Tuesday, May 6, before a courtroom of Junk's friends, family, baby mamas, and children, he was found guilty of second-degree murder. The jury also found him guilty of illegally possessing a deadly weapon.

On June 11, the judge will sentence him to somewhere between 60 years and life in prison.

When the verdict came in, Deanna Johnson was holed up at the police department. Because the jury had deliberated for almost a week, an acquittal or a hung jury seemed within the realm of possibility. Investigators didn't want her unprotected, especially not in Double Rock, so they had asked her to come down.

Then again, a guilty verdict wouldn't be good news for Deanna's safety, either. However things went that morning, the cops planned to try to get her into witness protection one last time. The last thing they wanted was more headlines about a witness getting whacked for coming forward.

They had a pretty solid plan.

When the investigators learned the prosecution had won, they told Deanna for the first time that she would not be able to stay in Double Rock. (Tim Larsen of the Housing Authority says this wasn't necessarily true, and that she could have gone through an appeals process.) So on the day the investigators most wanted Deanna to leave town, they made her believe she had no home to return to. She felt manipulated and used. "All I wanted was to keep my home," she said. "I feel like they played me for a fool."

She had no idea where she would go. Willie said she could live with him, but with her history of domestic violence, she wasn't interested. She had saved almost no money, and the city wouldn't help her find new housing, unless it was hundreds of miles from San Francisco. And just like that, Deanna was facing two options: homelessness or the witness protection program.

The plan was not negotiable. Police would escort her to Double Rock, where she would have 10 minutes to collect her belongings. Then they would take her somewhere far away. She was not to return to San Francisco under any circumstances. She was not to tell anyone where she was.

The investigators handed her a pen.

Before Deanna could pick up her things, there was one additional stop. District Attorney Kamala Harris wanted to meet this brave woman in the flesh.

Officers led Deanna to Harris's office, where she was welcomed with a warm smile. Harris told Deanna how proud she was. How she wished there were more people like her who would stand up and do the right thing. Harris even gave her a housewarming gift—a large vase of white flowers Deanna didn't recognize. They looked like roses.

None of it made much of an impression on Deanna. They were nice flowers, but she had no home to put them in. As police guided her out of the office, she looked around. Everybody in this office will go home tonight, she thought. Meanwhile, she was going to a hotel. "I was feeling like my world was taken out from under me," she said. "Me and my son."

As police escorted her to an unmarked car in the basement, Deanna began to feel dizzy. "It was like a dream," she said. "Like it wasn't really happening."

When she arrived at her home, she noticed a number of black-and-white police cars. Officers were stationed at her front and back doors. She could swear there were more cops around her home than the day Tigaboo got killed. Her 17-year-old son, Dominic, still in his red 49ers pajamas, had gotten scared and sneaked out the back door.

Deanna called him back to give him the news. "My son was in tears," she said later. "He didn't understand what was going on. He didn't want to be yanked out of his room. It was like I was in another world from that time on."

Deanna grabbed a few changes of clothes and some toiletries, and said goodbye to everything she knew, including Nina the pit bull. In all the chaos, she had forgotten to ask whether the D.A. would help her find a temporary home for the dog. Turns out, they wouldn't. After the movers emptied 6 Double Rock, the dog remained in the vacant home until a friend from the methadone clinic agreed to take her, but wasn't sure he'd be willing to give her back. Two days later, he walked Nina off-leash and she got in a fight with another dog. Nina is now quarantined at the SPCA.

Aside from losing her dog, Deanna was rushed out of the life she had become comfortable with, and in the most embarrassing way she could imagine. "The whole neighborhood watched from across the street as me and my son put our belongings in the trunk of the police vehicle," she said. "It was awful. I wished I could just wiggle my nose and vanish."

As she got into the car, Deanna noticed a woman across the way, hanging her laundry on the line. The woman looked content. "I wished that was me," she says.

Since the day of Junk's conviction, Deanna has been staying at a faraway hotel with Dominic, who is "bored shitless." For nearly a week, Deanna was broke, and the District Attorney's office refused to give her cash. Just vouchers for food at Safeway. Deanna thinks it's because they didn't want her to have a way to get back to San Francisco.

She'll be looking for a home in which the District Attorney's office will put her up in for one year. Over that time, she plans to save as much money as possible and try to be a good provider for her sons.

As for Damian, he's in hiding. Deanna doesn't know when she will see him again, and worries constantly. She heard that her son is considered to be a snitch. ✏

Ashley Harrell, a staff writer with SF Weekly, *joined the paper in February 2008. She covers the crime and courts beat, but she notes that "in reality, the topics I wind up covering are totally dependent on what stories I can find. . . . The stories I'm most drawn to usually involve poverty." Before joining* SF Weekly, *Harrell worked for* New Times Broward-Palm Beach, *the* Point Reyes Light *(West Marin, California) and the* Boca Raton *(Florida)* News. *She also interned at New York* Newsday *and graduated with a master's degree in journalism from New York University in 2005. Harrell was interviwed about her winning columns by* Tucson Weekly *editor and Editorial Committee member Jimmy Boegle.*

How did you come across the story of Deanna Johnson?
I had gone over to the Hall of Justice in San Francisco to pull search warrants, and briefly stepped outside to smoke a cigarette. I never carry a lighter or matches, because I find it's a good way to meet people (for stories and not), and in this situation, the person who wound up lighting my cigarette was Deanna Johnson. She was there for a pretrial hearing, and was clearly agitated about it. She began telling me about how she had to testify in court, even though she didn't want to, and I slowly began to realize that she might be the subject of a story. I took her phone number.

What happened from there? And how did you get this woman—who clearly has many reasons NOT to trust people—to trust you?
I spoke with Deanna on several occasions after that, and did some research into the murder trial. As for winning her trust, it wasn't very difficult. Deanna was in a tough spot, and I think she believed that things couldn't get much worse. It was comforting for her to talk through the situation with somebody like me, who had no agenda other than to get her story.

You're white. Did the fact that the subjects were largely black, and the setting was these crime-ridden projects, create any challenges for you?
Yep, I'm white. And before this story, I had never been inside a housing project. Over the course of the story, I was warned repeatedly by the cops that I shouldn't be hanging out in Double Rock, because it was dangerous for someone like me. That was a little scary, but I chose to ignore the advice and spend hours wandering around Double Rock, taking in the scene and talking to everybody. The people I encountered, though sometimes skeptical at first, turned out to be extraordinarily kind and helpful.

The fact that you spent all that time in Double Rock really shows, especially in the detail, like in graph three: " . . . [Deanna] walks with deliberation to the south-facing window to smoke her morning Newport." How did you manage to glean such amazing detail? I mean, you weren't actually there when Deanna's alarm clock went off that morning.

I had wanted to be there that morning, but it didn't work out. So instead, I met with Deanna when she got to the courthouse and asked her to go over in detail what her morning was like. I must have asked her 30 questions about her routine and thoughts that morning, which she definitely found strange to be answering, but I knew I wanted to set that scene with lots of detail, and the only way to get it was to ask. I also made several subsequent visits to Deanna's home, where she demonstrated to me how she smoked at the window.

It seems like there are no real "good guys" in this story (except perhaps Deanna, who is quite troubled herself). The cops, the prosecutors—*everyone* comes off poorly. How did all this dreariness affect you emotionally?

It was extremely depressing, but I knew I had a good story, and I was learning so much. That kept me energized and motivated.

What kind of feedback did you get from the story? What eventually happened to Deanna?

Not too much feedback from the public, but a few things happened with the cops and [district attorney's] office. The cops complained to us that the story had damaged their ability to find willing witnesses, though they couldn't really give any evidence of this. They cut me off for a little while, but eventually we all had a meeting where we all talked about our feelings, and they agreed to resume talking to me. I also heard from a spokeswoman with the D.A.'s office that their people reviewed policies on witnesses going into the relocation program, and actually made changes to how they deal with witnesses' pets. It was too late for Deanna's pit bull, Nina, who had to be euthanized, because she had basically gone crazy in the days she was left alone. That pretty much devastated me.

Deanna disappeared into witness relocation, and I have not talked to her since. I'm really hoping that someday she gets back in touch with me.

What advice do you have for journalists just starting out?

To the young people considering journalism, I'd say there will always be a need for storytellers, and I'd advise you to ignore warnings about the struggling media industry. The more important question, I think, is over what kind of life you want for yourself. Journalism might seem like a glamorous profession, but it's actually really hard and really depressing a lot of the time. When you're doing it right, you don't make many friends, and it's not a lifestyle that most people would choose. Make sure you really want it.

Courting Disaster

Gwynedd Stuart

DECEMBER 16, 2008

Brenton Butler was on his way to fill out a job application at Blockbuster Video when his life changed forever. Picked up by police, accused of killing an elderly Georgia tourist in cold blood, the Englewood High School ninth-grader was interrogated, forced by police to sign a confession, and eventually tried for first-degree murder. He spent the next six and a half months in jail.

The 15-year-old had nothing to do with the May 2000 crime, as later became clear, but the case against him was strong. An African American teenager with few resources, he'd already signed his name to a document claiming he'd killed Mary Ann Stephens. The woman's husband had identified him as the killer. And a city, hungry for justice in the senseless killing, was eager to see someone punished.

Despite the apparent futility of the case, two leading attorneys in the Public Defender's Office believed their client when he said he was innocent. And slowly, they built a case that exposed the holes in the state's claim—showing that police had taken the teen out of jail to extract the confession in the woods in the dark of night, and insisting that Butler had been beaten by detectives—a claim backed up by photographs showing his badly bruised face. More importantly, they proved that the "confession" itself was pure fiction, a version of events dreamed up by police that bore no resemblance to the particulars of the crime.

It was a difficult case, one that meant casting doubt on the honesty and motives of police, including lead detective Michael Glover—the sheriff's son. But attorneys Pat McGuinness and Ann Finnell pressed ahead, and eventually won the case. Brenton Butler was freed.

The outcome was nothing short of miraculous. But what happened after was almost more astonishing. Both State Attorney Harry Shorstein and Sheriff Nat Glover publicly apologized to the boy, admitting their case against him was unjustified. Two other men—both repeat offenders—were later convicted of the crime. And a documentary film about McGuinness's and Finnell's work on the case, "Murder on a Sunday Morning," won an Oscar in 2002.

There are plenty of people who regard the work of public defenders with disdain, believing that the people they represent—poor, uneducated, often accused of heinous crimes—deserve nothing but a stiff sentence and a life behind bars. But the Brenton Butler case proved, irrefutably, that the office is sometimes all that stands between a monstrous injustice and the rights of the accused. It showed, too, that casting doubts on the veracity of police and the claims of the state attorney is sometimes essential in the pursuit of justice.

It's telling, then, that in the recent staff bloodletting at the Public Defender's Office, in which 10 attorneys with a collective 300 years of experience were fired, McGuinness and Finnell were among those let go. Observers in the legal community say the message is in keeping with the apparent mission of incoming Public Defender Matt Shirk: to drain the office of effectiveness and experience, and to take a less adversarial role with the prosecutors and police.

A close ally of incoming State Attorney Angela Corey—he's often called "her protégé"—Shirk made strong overtures to the law enforcement community during his campaign. Among other things, he promised to be less confrontational when dealing with police in court, ensuring his employees would never call a cop a liar. Shirk has also suggested that his primary goal after taking office will have less to do with seeking justice for his clients than making targets of them. In a November 6 interview with the *Florida Times-Union*, Shirk said he planned to use the public defender's diminishing resources to investigate whether his clients were truly indigent and deserving of free legal representation. (Shirk declined to be interviewed for this story.)

❖

For office veterans, the future of the public defender seems clear. "In some ways, it reminds me of an infant when you give it a new toy," says McGuinness. "Its first instinct is to destroy it."

If you don't know Bill White's name, you're not alone. Though he's been the 4th Judicial Circuit's public defender for the past four years and worked in the office for the past 34, he says that one thing was abundantly clear on the campaign trail: most people had no idea who he was or what he did. He says he was asked questions by constituents like, "Doesn't the state attorney appoint the public defender?" and "Is that even an elected office?" Others were under the impression that the state attorney and the public defender were the same person.

White admits he was ill-prepared for the campaign challenge. This election marked the first time in the office's 45-year history that a public defender drew an opponent.

Shirk's candidacy was a surprise, too, because of his relative inexperience. Though he's well-connected—his dad was a former GOP county chairman in Illinois, his father-in-law is former Duval County Undersheriff John Gordon, he's a member of First Baptist Church—his résumé is unimpressive. He graduated from Florida Coastal School of Law, an accredited but not highly regarded commuter law school on Jacksonville's Southside, and has minimal criminal defense experience. He graduated in 1999 and has never defended a murder trial. But Shirk had one clear advantage in the recent election: he ran as a Republican. In a race in which only one Democrat won election countywide (at-large City Council-member John Crescimbeni), White faced voters in an overwhelmingly red district with a tendency to vote a straight GOP ticket.

White says he felt a little like he was "crying wolf " when he tried to explain to people that he could lose to Shirk. But even he didn't fully realize how vulnerable he was to partisan voters. Although he won Duval, he lost overwhelmingly in heavily Republican Nassau and Clay counties. Shirk told the *Times-Union* he won because his message and policies resonated with voters, a view White calls "delusional."

"I think the 'R' won it," says White. "He won because he's Republican."

Sitting behind a wide desk in the office he'll continue to occupy until January 6, White still seems somewhat stunned by the outcome. "I think when you take an office that is essentially apolitical, and you put it into the political arena, anything can happen. A relatively unknown candidate with relatively little experience can win if the party affiliation is that strong." He adds, "I regret that I'm not that good a politician."

White never set out to be a politician. In 1967, having decided to concentrate on criminal defense as a law student at the University of Florida, White offered his services to a young, meagerly staffed Public Defender's Office. Not yet an attorney, he was tasked with investigating the case of a woman accused of murder. With the help of White's research, the woman was found not guilty, and all charges were dismissed. "I was hooked," he says.

White was hired by then-Public Defender Lou Frost in 1974, and over the past three decades, he has hired many young attorneys himself. He has a standard warning for them.

"When I talk to them, I say, 'There's no money, the whole world dislikes what you do when they find out what you do, your only thanks are going to come from your peers, and you're going to get knocked down every day. . . . So why do you want to work here?'"

Shirk was among the young attorneys White has seen come and go over the years. After graduating from Florida Coastal, Shirk worked at the PD's office for five years before entering private practice and eventually opening his own firm with another PD alum, William Durden III.

"I don't know that he stood out as a superior attorney," says White when asked about Shirk. "He did his job for the most part, he won some cases . . . but he never had a supervisory role."

Shirk's lack of trial experience has been floated as one reason he decided to fire so many senior attorneys. McGuinness believes Shirk is simply intimidated by the prospect of supervising a much older, more experienced staff.

White says Shirk told him the dismissals were made for financial reasons: the top-salaried attorneys were the first to go. But White disagrees with that premise. He says he'd figured out how to keep the office solvent—even with anticipated budget cuts—without laying off top talent.

The firings certainly weren't made based on performance, since Shirk didn't review any personnel files prior to announcing his decision. Indeed, his decision to fire such marquee names as Alan Chipperfield and Susan Yazgi, in addition to Finnell and McGuinness, seemed impersonal in the extreme. Rather than notifying the terminated staffers himself, or at least individually, he had a subordinate email a list of names to White. Two of the names—including McGuinness's—were spelled incorrectly.

"Matt obviously didn't have the good sense—or manners, I should say—to notify us personally," says Finnell. "He knows us all, obviously. I supervised Matt Shirk. Al [Chipperfield] or Susan [Yazgi] would have supervised him in county court. These should have been people he felt comfortable contacting personally."

If the attorneys weren't fired for financial reasons or because of job performance, the question of why they were fired remains. For some observers, the answer is State Attorney Angela Corey. Shirk and Corey are close friends and political allies. Corey encouraged Shirk to seek the seat and was publicly supportive of his bid. Shirk interned under Corey, a fact his campaign website noted with pride, saying he worked "under the direct tutelage of Angela Corey." One fired public defender who asked to remain anonymous said he was disturbed by Corey's references to Shirk as her "darling" during the course of the campaign.

Since Shirk's victory, Corey has remained a palpable presence. A Shirk spokesman referred questions from *First Coast News'* Donna Deegan to Corey, and White says she contacted at least one of his employees to discuss the "transition"—something akin to Obama making staffing suggestions for the Bush White House.

"She's apparently a close advisor of his," says McGuinness, adding that Corey contacted several people in the office prior to the announcement of the cuts. Asked why Corey would have a hand in personnel issues, McGuinness suggests it may represent a simple—if insidious—legal strategy.

"From Corey's [perspective], a less-experienced Public Defender's Office gives her prosecutors a target-rich environment." Homicide Division Chief Finnell has spent less time wondering about the "whys" of the dismissals, and more time reconciling how the hobbled Public Defender's Office will operate after their departure. She notes that Shirk fired five lawyers certified to try death penalty cases, leaving only one on staff in Duval County. Finnell fears the move will cripple the homicide unit. "I don't know if he's planning on hiring more death-qualified lawyers, but it would be impossible for one attorney to handle all death cases, especially because it's anticipated that Angela will file more death penalty cases."

"[The voters] have no idea what they've done," Finnell adds. "The indigent in Jacksonville will suffer as a result of this. . . . We're all going to suffer as a result of this."

Ronald Mallett is the chief executive officer of Thigpen Heating and Cooling by trade, but since the election, he's acted as Matt Shirk's unofficial spokesman. He's advised Shirk to avoid speaking to the press himself until he officially takes office in January.

"He's not the public defender yet," Mallett told *Folio Weekly*. "It's just not a good time to do [interviews]." Pressed for some clarification of Shirk's relationship with Corey, Mallett snaps, "This isn't a question-and-answer period." Though Mallett promised to distribute a press release addressing several questions *Folio Weekly* submitted, as well as questions posed by other news outlets, he did not produce the document by deadline.

Among the unanswered questions are several dealing with Shirk's campaign promises. Shirk ran on a platform of fiscal responsibility, promising to operate the office more cheaply and to establish a trust fund for the office to handle budget shortfalls. The office already has a trust fund, something White suspects Shirk is well aware of. And, at least in his personal life, Shirk hasn't exactly been a model of financial responsibility. As recently as last year, Shirk was sued by the collection agency H.F.C. for failure to make payments on an outstanding credit card balance of $6,544. A deal reached in February requires Shirk to pay court costs and attorney's fees of $1,035 on top of the original debt, and to pay $500 a month until the sum is paid in full. Also back in 2006, Shirk received a summons regarding an outstanding debt of $13,537 to Bank of America. (The case was later dismissed by the plaintiff.)

There are also questions surrounding Shirk's promise to investigate his own clients. He has said he plans to use the office's already overburdened investigative staff—a team that's traditionally responsible for investigating the state's cases—to probe the financial capabilities of clients. ("You know whether your clients have money. Either they drive nice cars or wear nice clothes," Shirk told the *Times-Union*. "We need to recognize that and at least bring that up to the court.")

Not only does it seem an odd use of diminishing resources, but it is a policy that conflicts with existing duties of the office. It's the job of the clerk of the Circuit Court, not the public defender, to determine if someone is indigent and deserving of services. That arrangement is both accepted and encouraged in legal circles. In a list of "dos" and "don'ts" for appointing defense counsel, the Brennan Center for Justice at New York University in September published a study that explicitly warns public defender programs not to screen clients' finances. The study, titled "Eligible for Justice: Guidelines for Appointing Counsel," says that such financial probes would constitute a conflict of interest, endanger confidentiality rules and pose a threat to the attorney/client relationship. "As a practical matter, many public defender programs do screen their own clients," the study concedes. "But as an ethical matter, they should not."

Shirk plans on demoting the office's current chief investigator in order to hire a retired police officer. Some contend that asking an ex-cop to investigate police procedure is an obvious conflict, and suggest that pro-law enforcement bias could prevent someone in that position from adequately carrying out an investigation.

"If you have too many [officers on the investigative staff], it can create a situation where you don't get the point of view that you need to have in a defense office," says White. He adds, "We have a very different role [than police] to play, which is zealously defending our clients. It's harder to change their mindset if they come in from law enforcement."

Although White was endorsed by the sheriffs in all three counties in his district, Shirk did very well in law-enforcement circles. The Fraternal Order of Police was among the organizations whose endorsement he earned. While debating White before the FOP's membership, Shirk made a pledge not to challenge the credibility of officers at trial. White says the statement was a political gambit to win the FOP support, but one with worrisome consequences. "The implication was that you wouldn't be going after police officers. Well, we don't 'go after' police officers, [but] we will challenge any witness when their testimony is incredible. If there's evidence to show that a police officer is lying, you have an absolute duty to bring that forward and tell the jury that the evidence supports your finding that this police officer is lying. And that does happen."

Still, Shirk's words resonated with the police union. FOP President Nelson Cuba concedes statements like that went a long way in earning his organization's support. "I think part of what helped Mr. Shirk get the support is that he was big on— no matter what—his office would . . . be professional with officers and never be disrespectful with officers." Cuba says that respect has been lacking in the current Public Defender's Office, and that he's looking forward to Shirk's tenure for improvement. Says Cuba, "That will only tell with time as we move forward."

Though Shirk isn't talking, his allegiance with prosecutors and police worries some in the law enforcement community. State Attorney Harry Shorstein says he maintained an "excellent" relationship with White—and Lou Frost before him— but emphasizes that it's always been, and should be, "purely adversarial."

"I don't know Mr. Shirk well," says Shorstein, "but I do know my successor [Corey], and there are people who take an unprofessional adversarial relationship, but that's prohibited by the rules of good ethical behavior." Shorstein agrees it's unusual for a state attorney to support a public defender in a political campaign, adding, "But, it was purely political and somewhat disconcerting because these offices should not be political. These jobs . . . should be nonpartisan, just like the judges."

Defense attorney Teri Sopp notes that Shirk's law partner Durden commented in open court one day that Shirk wasn't even interested in being the PD—he wanted to be a state legislator. "It's clear to me that this is just Shirk grabbing and running for an office . . . as a stepping-stone to greater political adventures," says Sopp. "I'm sickened by it."

Although Mallett was the Shirk advisor who referred Donna Deegan's questions to Corey, he dismisses any notion that she is too close to Shirk or in any way speaks for him. "He's his own man," says Mallett. "She's not on his transition team, nor does he go to her for advice. But she's a good friend, and I think they're going to work really well together."

One thing's certain: when Shirk takes office, he's going to have to deal with some transitional poison. The weekend following the firings, a flier was posted throughout the Public Defender's Office that read, "Dear Matt Shirk and the Republicans: Thank you for destroying our family, firing our heroes, and crushing the dreams of hope, justice, and freedom for the indigent accused." It was signed, simply, "We the people."

By Monday, they'd all been taken down and thrown away.

➥

What specifically motivated you to do this story?
When Matt Shirk—who was something of a nobody in local legal circles—won the election against veteran Public Defender Bill White, there was an undercurrent of shock and outrage in the Public Defender's Office. And then the firings began. One of Mr. Shirk's first moves was essentially to decimate the top tier of attorneys from the Bill White era, a move that was interpreted as being politically motivated. Anyway, there was widespread worry that Shirk was putting politics before the rights of the indigent accused. (I should mention that Shirk claimed he fired the office's veteran attorneys for financial reasons.)

And Shirk refused to talk to you for the story. How did that change the way you approached the piece?
I think that sometimes, a person's refusal to participate in a story becomes part of the story. The period during which I wrote the piece was between his election and the date he'd officially take office, and he wasn't speaking to the press at all. Instead, press inquiries were directed to his "Chief of staff," a heating and cooling executive with a very obvious lack of PR experience. That spoke volumes.

Do you feel that his absence from the story affected the fairness of the piece in any way?
I've always thought it ill-advised for individuals in situations like Shirk's (in his case, a newly elected politician making controversial decisions that the media is clearly going to latch onto) to refuse to avail themselves to reporters. I'd certainly want the opportunity to have my voice heard. That being said, I believe I did my best to tell the story in a manner that was fair, considering the subject's lack of participation.

What kind of feedback did you get when "Courting Disaster" hit the streets?
Good and bad, I suppose. Bill White's supporters were pleased with the story; Shirk's weren't quite as pleased. We received several angry letters about the way we represented the law school (Florida Coastal School of Law) Shirk attended. I believe we described it as "accredited but not highly regarded." Frankly, it's accurate. I don't recall hearing anything from Shirk's office after the story came out, but I did receive a congratulatory letter from him when he found out I'd won the (AAN) award. It says, "Glad we could help!"

That letter actually sounds kind of charming.
Ahaha. I thought it a tad passive-aggressive.

At least they're reading you. Anyway, you used some anonymous sources in the piece. Did that cause any concerns for you or your editor?
I think there was only one anonymous source, actually. I'm very conscious of keeping that to a minimum.

Talk a little more about that—why you keep anonymous sources to a minimum, and why you felt it was worthy in this case.

"According to a source who wished to remain anonymous . . ." sounds so tabloid to me. I just don't like it. Also, I think it's important to take into account why the source wants to remain anonymous, why they wouldn't want their name attributed to a quote or two. In this case, I was speaking with a trustworthy individual who didn't have anything to gain by being interviewed, but plenty to lose career-wise by going on the record. I had so many sources on the record in this piece that I didn't think one anonymous source would make the piece any less credible.

So, now that Matt Shirk has been in office for a while, we can ask: What's happened? Have the fears of Bill White and others proven justified?

Funny you should ask. I was (recently) contacted by a local attorney who discovered that Shirk placed an advertisement in the latest issue of the *Florida Bar News* for death-penalty-qualified attorneys, inviting them to "send their salary needs." If he hadn't canned the majority of the experienced, death-penalty-qualified attorneys in his office, he wouldn't be resorting to the want ads, would he?

Any advice for newbie reporters?

Being new to the field myself, I'm not sure I should be doling out advice just yet. But, what the hell. Always double- and triple-check the spelling of people's names and place names. Little mistakes can so easily drain writing of credibility. Also, don't be afraid to ask the uncomfortable questions. The harder the question is to ask, the better it probably is, and the less likely it is that other reporters have already asked it.

NEWS STORY—
SHORT FORM

🏅 🏅 🏅

CIRCULATION 50,000 AND OVER

"Local Couples Fight for Gay Rights in Wake of Proposition 8"
"Midwest Oil Mining a Crude Idea to Many"

by Beth Walton, *City Pages* (Twin Cities)

"Beth writes with the direct force of a battering ram, clear and incisive. Great stuff!"—Kevin Fagan, San Francisco Chronicle

🏅 🏅 🏅

CIRCULATION UNDER 50,000

"Turn Off the Radio"
"Taming the Wild West"

by Phillip Bailey, *LEO Weekly*

"Each story is strong and well-written. Best all around entry."—Eliza Barclay

Local Couples Fight for Gay Rights in Wake of Proposition 8

Beth Walton

NOVEMBER 26, 2008

Doug Benson and Duane Gajewski are marriage junkies. Like many gay couples, they have multiple anniversaries. Since they met in the 1990s—Doug was vacuuming at the DFL office in Duluth where he worked and Duane mistook him for a janitor—they have attempted marriage five times. In 1993 the couple was rejected for a marriage license in St. Louis County. In 2000 they traveled to Vermont for a civil union. Three years later they went to Thunder Bay, Canada, for a quaint, legal ceremony. Their last stop was in 2004 in San Francisco after Mayor Gavin Newsom issued a directive to the city clerk to issue marriage licenses to same-sex couples, claiming that the California Constitution's equal-protection clause gave him authority to do so.

For the first time, the couple had a marriage recognized, albeit temporarily, by some form of the American government.

"That was the best Valentine's Day ever," says Benson, 54, his smile peeking out from a thick brown beard.

The two waited 24 hours in line to exchange vows that February, and gave each other San Francisco tourist trinkets instead of rings. "We're not jewelry people," jokes Gajewski, 44, talking during a break from his actuarial job. "When we went through the ceremony, the officiate actually said, 'With this *thing*, I thee wed.'"

Today, the Robbsinsdale couple is hoping for a sixth marriage attempt right here in Minnesota. To them, marriage rights aren't about walking down an aisle in the church—there are a host of benefits, including tax breaks and end-of-life issues that are only legally protected by marriage.

"I have a resentment of having paid taxes in this state all my working life, being a citizen involved in my community, and then being discriminated against by the very government that we support," says Benson, who started the Northland Gay Men's Center in Duluth, a chemical-free meeting place for homosexuals. "We're being denied equal protection of the law, and that's not just a phrase from the Constitution—that comes with real ramifications."

For months Benson and Gajewski have been working with the Minneapolis-based law firm Mansfield, Tanick, and Cohen to file a class-action lawsuit against the state of Minnesota, arguing that its current ban on same-sex marriage is unconstitutional. They formed the nonprofit Marry Me Minnesota in an attempt to raise the $30,000 they need to go forward, and hope to file after the New Year.

The firm, notable for its work in overturning the state's concealed-carry law, plans to employ the same arguments that were used in Massachusetts and California to allow same-sex marriage—specifically, relying on the constitutionally recognized rights of due process and equal protection.

"There's never a good time to suppress freedom and liberty," says Marshall H. Tanick, who is overseeing the case. "Expanding rights doesn't just benefit some, everybody benefits from having broader rights. This is a case about freedom and the extension of the Constitution. The beneficiaries of this case won't just be gay and lesbian people. We think the beneficiaries will be everybody."

Not everyone shares his enthusiasm. With only 10 gay and lesbian couples on board, thousands more oppose the action. Out Front Minnesota, a nonprofit geared toward promoting equality among the state's GLBT population, has publicly come out in opposition to the suit. When rumors spread about the pending action, Out Front and other local GLBT organizations jointly issued a press statement arguing that to file now would be a mistake. Doing so "poses a significant risk to marriage equality," they opined.

Phil Duran has spent the last eight years as a staff attorney for Out Front Minnesota. To him, all of this amounts to an enormous problem of precedent. "In virtually no other state do you have the situation that we have in Minnesota, where you would in essence be asking the Supreme Court to reverse course," he says.

The Minnesota Supreme Court was the first to prohibit gay marriage in 1971 in the case of Baker v. Nelson. The state legislature later codified the ruling in 1977, and the decision was reinforced in 1997 with the Defense of Marriage Act, which clarified that "lawful marriage may be contracted only between persons of the opposite sex" and went on to specifically prohibit "marriage between persons of the same sex."

While it is true that in the last decade some states have been moving toward marriage equality, the bulk of the decisions that have been litigated have in essence agreed with Minnesota's approach, Duran adds. Marriage equality is not friendly terrain legally in Minnesota, and if a lawsuit is unsuccessful, there will be just one more obstacle for future activists to overcome.

"We would just assume the Baker decision would just grow old and wither away over time, as opposed to it being reaffirmed today and breathe new life into it," says Duran, who calls himself an "activist gay-rights lawyer."

Duran says that Out Front's position is justified but acknowledges it is deeply frustrating for him and others. "Why would I not want to support a lawsuit by well-intended people, particularly when the arguments are ones that in my heart I agree with? It's totally a matter of strategy and particularly a matter of timing."

But some couples don't have that kind of time. Tom Trisko, 63, and John Rittman, 66, have nestled into retirement in their picturesque brick colonial in southwest Minneapolis. Unfortunately, their time away from work hasn't been as relaxing as expected. They wanted to travel Europe together, but have postponed their trip after spending hundreds of hours with lawyers and insurance companies to make sure they are protected in an emergency. Their passports say American, but their marriage certificate is from Canada.

Trisko, a former CFO and corporate economist, worries about what issues may arise in a medical emergency or death. His parents are dead. He is an only child and he has no offspring. "The only person I have in this world is John," he says, adjusting his glasses in a way that makes him look like a college professor. If Trisko's last days are in the ER, he has no assurance that his partner of 34 years will be allowed to preside over his affairs.

Trisko's family has lived in Minnesota for seven generations. His father fought in World War II. "He knew I was gay and he would not have fought in that war if he knew how this country would treat his son," he says forcefully.

As he rants in his stately living room, where a framed certificate nearly two feet high marks the couple's 1999 marriage ceremony at St. Mark's Cathedral, he takes out a bound copy of the federal Constitution. He flips through the neatly marked pages, reading key phrases aloud: "No state shall make or enforce any law which shall abridge the privileges or immunities of citizens of the United States; nor shall any state deprive any person of life, liberty, or property, without due process of law; nor deny to any person within its jurisdiction the equal protection of the laws."

Having lived through the 1950s,'60s, and'70s, Trisko sees today's debate in the same light as the one over interracial marriages decades ago. He wonders why a country that rose up against the flawed "separate but equal" system would forbid gays the same marital rights.

"In this country, for some reason, we always have to fight for our rights," he says. "If we don't do it now, it's not going to happen." ➥

Midwest Oil Mining a Crude Idea to Many

Beth Walton

DECEMBER 3, 2008

Some 1,500 miles northwest of Minneapolis, the luscious green boreal forests that once lined the banks of the Athabasca River have been flattened. All that's left is an empty, lonely, gray moonscape. That, and the drills.

The machines push deep into the earth, farther than they ever have before, in order to extract a thick black syrup that sticks together with the sand and dirt to form a tar-like gritty dough. This is a dense and viscous form of petroleum called bitumen. It's oil, and the U.S. wants it.

A web of pipelines has sprouted up throughout the Midwest, following the Great Lakes, moving all the way from the Dakotas to Chicago and Detroit. The Canadians have stumbled upon an estimated 1.75 trillion barrels of crude, arguably the second-largest usable oil reserve in the world.

But it comes at a heavy cost, a price so large that one environmentalist remarked that in comparison to the nightmarish ramifications of the oil sands, offshore drilling is an "environmental yawn."

The land must be strip-mined and the petroleum heated with diluent hydrocarbons to melt the oil so that it is thin enough to flow.

"The key issue with these tar sands is that this is the bottom of the barrel, the last sludge of oil remaining in the world," says Michael Noble, executive director for Fresh Energy, a Minnesota-based environmental policy organization. "It's the dirtiest and most polluting oil by far, much more polluting than conventional sweet crude. Its mining, extraction, refining, and shipping would all essentially move the refining capacity of the Gulf Coast up to the Midwest Great Lakes region."

Even so, continued demand, the high price of conventional crude, and new technology have made it profitable to extract, and one Canadian company plans to make bank.

EnBridge currently boasts the longest crude oil and liquid petroleum pipeline system in the world and plans to add 16,000 miles to the Midwest region in an effort to exploit the recently available oil sand crude in Alberta.

"The U.S. needs a growing and reliable source of crude oil . . . EnBridge already transports 11 percent of U.S.-imported crude, and this will provide us even more capacity to tap into this very secure supply," says Denise Hamshere, a spokeswoman for the company. "We're not going to conserve our way out of using gasoline and jet fuel and asphalt tomorrow. So, meanwhile, this is the safest, [most] economic and secure way to meet both needs."

The oil sands issue came to a head in St. Paul last week when, after two years of negotiations, EnBridge appeared in front of the state's Public Utilities Commission for the necessary permit to expand pipelines.

Minnesota's share, 450 miles of pipe, would be composed of two different lines. The Southern Lights line would run north from Chicago, through Minnesota and back into Canada, and would transport diluent hydrocarbons from U.S. refineries to the oils sands so that the clumpy crude could be thinned for transport. A proposed Alberta Clipper line would run southeast from Alberta, Canada, to Superior, Wisconsin, crossing northern Minnesota and moving some 450,000 more barrels of crude to market.

At the meeting, Public Utilities Commission Chair David Boyd, a Republican, took a deep breath before starting the discussion. He told the other commissioners and the crowded conference room to be as succinct as possible; it was sure to be a long day.

Though the commission's staff and an earlier administrative law judge had approved EnBridge's plans, the Minnesota Center for Environmental Advocacy had challenged the projects with a flurry of legal paperwork the night before. It was now up to the commissioners to decide.

In order to acquire the necessary certificate of need to build the pipelines, the company must show that there is an increased demand for its product, said Kevin Reuther, staff attorney for the center. And, at the time of an energy crisis, when people are shouting out for alternative fuel, more crude pipelines are not what we need.

"It's hard to conclude that we're going to stay on the track of ever-increasing oil consumption," he reasoned. "Our governor, our new president, everybody agrees that we need to end this addiction to oil. It's pretty clear that Canadians are really trying to get access to major oil markets."

As he clicked through a PowerPoint presentation, Reuther pointed out that approval of the proposal would essentially double Minnesota's state pollution level. Between extraction, transportation, refinement, and use, the process would add an additional 132 million tons of pollution in the air per year.

In one year alone, the Alberta Clipper project would carry the equivalent of 230 times the capacity of the Exxon Valdez. And EnBridge doesn't exactly have the best safety record. In 2002, the company suffered an oil spill that put 252,000 gallons of crude into the surrounding landscape. Five years later at another location, a pipeline exploded, killing two workers.

The suited lawyers lined up behind representatives from EnBridge didn't seem fazed. As lunchtime neared, Republican Commissioner Dennis O'Brien told his colleagues to vote in favor of the pipeline proposals. He said he would rather have oil from our friendly neighbors up north than from our enemies overseas.

The vote was held. EnBridge's permits were unanimously approved.

All that is left now is for EnBridge to finalize the route, settling disputes with concerned farmers and members of the Fond du Lac tribal community over land issues. The company plans to have the Alberta Clipper line up and running by 2010, and by 2015 pump as much as 1.8 million barrels of crude per day to the U.S.

"It's just the most polluting new fuel we could bring into the economy," says Ken Bradley of Clean Water Action Minnesota. "It is horrible that we are even considering bringing it to the marketplace at all. We should be doing everything we can to stop it." ➼

"HOW I GOT THAT STORY"

Beth Walton came to City Pages, *Minneapolis's alternative weekly, in early 2008. Twenty-eight years old, Walton had already built a career in daily newspapers, with stints at* USA Today *and the* Las Vegas Review-Journal, *but at* City Pages *she was able to synthesize her reporting skills and her passion for storytelling. Walton holds undergraduate degrees in English and women's studies from Albion College and a master's degree in international development from Western Michigan University. This interview was conducted by Hank Sims, editor of* North Coast Journal *and a member of AAN's editorial committee.*

What was the difference between daily news and working at a weekly? What was the shift?

It was an incredible shift. As a daily reporter, you kind of grow up with this mentality: "I have to get a job at the *New York Times,* I have to get a job at one of the big dailies, because that's where the important journalism happens. I have to learn the inverted pyramid and find an anecdotal lead and I have to make it all fit in 10 inches."

To switch to this type of journalism that I had never taken seriously was an incredible challenge, and a quite rewarding one. Because when I did work for a daily, I was getting kind of burnt out and I was feeling like it was making me a worse writer. Once I abandoned that, I literally told myself, "Beth, you need to revert back to your creative writing classes in high school and college. Back when writing was fun." Once I could get to that, I found long-form journalism to be the most rewarding writing experience I've ever had in my life.

These pieces, though, aren't too much longer than a story you'd find in a daily paper, yet you pack a lot of thought-provoking and very emotional scenes into this smaller form. How do you go about that?
You have to think about your readers. You have to think about what interests them and engages them. And for me, that's often whatever interested and engaged me.

So with the oil story, I start out by talking about the "gray moonscape." Well, that's because they were showing us these pictures that I had never imagined the Earth looking like. So I wasn't paying attention to what they were saying at that moment, because *that's* where my attention was. And so as a journalist, I always try to trust my instincts—if that was what was drawing my attention that is what I would share with my readers.

That's very interesting. The things that distract you are the important things. That's what you tell.
Yep.

These are all stories with big, wide themes. They're kind of outside the staples of the weekly world—city government, politics, crime. Is that something you brought to _City Pages_?
I think so. I had no idea about the culture of alternative newspapers. I went in there completely blind. But we had to do pitch meetings every week, and that's something you don't do as a daily journalist. All of a sudden I was being asked to come to a meeting and have something to say, and I didn't know the city at all—I didn't know Minneapolis at all. And we didn't have beats.

I don't know if this is typical of all your work, but it struck me that these three stories have a strong sense of justice. That's what seems to drive them.
I'm not an environmentalist and I'm not an advocate for very many things, but I do really admire human beings who are activists. And all of those stories, for the most part, were about people who were saying, "Hey, this isn't right." They were trying to change something, and that, to me, is a very compelling subject.

I think fiction is really fun, and I think the challenge in nonfiction writing is to find those stories—to find those people doing things so incredible that it reads like a novel.

What attracted me to all of those stories were not the issues—family, environment, or gay rights—but rather the strong, impassioned characters. People make great storytelling, and good storytelling is an often overlooked but necessary way of disseminating information. I believe what I hope all journalists believe: making accurate information accessible and available to all is one of the most important things in any society. To do that successfully, you have to be in it for the story.

Turn Off the Radio

Phillip Bailey

SEPTEMBER 16, 2008

Arriving a recent Saturday morning five minutes before going on air, J.T. Woods, longtime host of "Views and News," a daily talk show on WLOU-1350 AM, found a memorandum from the station's management posted on the doors of the station. The same note was taped to the studio microphone, outlining three policies he'd never seen before.

Dated September 6, the memo was addressed to all broadcasters at WLOU-1350 AM and WLLV-1240 AM, which are owned by the same company, saying Federal Communications Commission and station policy prohibits anchors from endorsing, mentioning, or interviewing political candidates between now and Election Day. Alarmed by its content, Woods says once he read the memo, he immediately took the subject to the airwaves.

Since then, Louisville's oldest African American radio station has been in a stir. The memo issued by management falsely claimed that FCC regulations restrict the political commentary of its on-air personalities. After *LEO Weekly* made several inquiries with the station's owners and FCC headquarters, outcries from prominent members of Louisville's black community eventually led the station to clarify the memo, removing references to the FCC and acknowledging that the policy is all its own.

"I found this disturbing," Woods says. "You can't even mention the name of the people from the two major political parties."

LEO Weekly obtained a copy of the memo. It also said anchors are not permitted to interview candidates without prior approval from the station manager, and that if a conversation with a caller turns to talk of the candidates, it should be terminated. The memo adds that anyone who does not adhere to the policy will be immediately fired.

"If that's the case, Rush Limbaugh needs to shut down his show for the next 60 days," says DeVone Holt, host of Simmons Saturday Morning Solutions, a weekly broadcast on WLOU, sponsored by Simmons College of Kentucky. "There's no way you can do news and not mention politics."

Holt says implementing such a policy would silence an important voice of public opinion in the black community. Since 1948, the channels—basically one entity—have been broadcasting mainly to a black audience here. There is little other black presence on the airwaves in terms of substantive news in Louisville.

"We'll have fewer outlets," Holt says. "We can't compromise our ability to speak openly and honestly."

In a telephone interview last week, an attorney with the FCC's political office said none of the bullet points in the memo reflected official agency rules. He said the station could, however, adopt stricter policies than those enforced by the FCC. Local affiliates often do that in response to community complaints.

Peter Davidson, president of New York-based Davidson Media Group, which owns the stations, says broadcasters must understand that local management must be watchful custodians of the airwaves, which have rules about using racist language, being partisan, and endorsing candidates.

Late last week, Davidson said he hadn't read the memo. However, he admitted the same rules for talk radio stations such as WHAS-AM apply to WLOU/WLLV, but until he could discuss it with management, he stands by their position.

"If it was put up by the general manager, it's our policy," he says.

The idea that public opinion could be stymied didn't sit well with one of Louisville's chief black ministers.

"As long as we are paying for our time on the air we will exercise our constitutional right," says the Rev. Kevin Cosby, senior pastor at St. Stephen Baptist Church, Louisville's largest black congregation, and president of Simmons College. "If our show is pulled off because we are engaging our people to think about the critical issues of the day, we don't need to be on that station."

Cosby says the memo was deceptive because it claimed to be official FCC policy. He said last week he would encourage everyone to abandon WLOU/WLLV if the station enacted the memo's provisions.

The flexing worked.

"It was poor judgment on my part," Vivien Ogburn, acting station manager, says. "I was under the impression that the memo was FCC policy. I have since learned it is not."

Within days of Cosby's proclamation, Ogburn, who was named to the position in May, said it was a mistake to post the memo without reviewing its provisions more closely. She said it had been used under the former station manager, Argie Dale; she was the station's business manager at the time.

The intent was not to discourage commentary but to install a cautious protocol she believed was necessary after complaints during the Democratic presidential primary about hosts being partisan toward Barack Obama.

"We're here to represent the community," Ogburn says. "I'm worried about the reactions to the memo and plan to apologize for any misunderstanding."

Prohibiting anchors from mentioning the candidates by name was excessive, she says. Ogburn plans to write a new memo outlining the station's policies; however, she says WLOU/WLLV will maintain stricter rules than other talk radio stations because of its religious format.

"The focus has always been on conveying the gospel message. We do not want this to become a political battleground," Ogburn says. "As Christians, our focus shouldn't be on that."

The idea that broadcasts could be curtailed by the religious overtones of the programming troubles some of the anchors.

"They used the FCC to take themselves off the hook," Woods says. "Management knew what they were doing."

He says his show gives black audiences a venue to champion and address issues important to the entire community. However, he says complaints by the religious community have often plagued shows that are critical of heavy religiosity.

"It's good for some, but others may not like us," he says. "That's not a reason to take it to the degree they were talking about." ➡

Taming the Wild West

Phillip Bailey

NOVEMBER 5, 2008

Mariann and Wayne Dunkerley bought a home five years ago deep in west Louisville's Shawnee neighborhood. Two decades of living in Nashville was enough for Mariann, a Paducah native ready to return to the Bluegrass.

The new house was missing doors, and had significant flood damage and rotten wooden floors that had collapsed to the basement, making remodeling a laborious process.

"It was the worst house on the block," she says. "Only a light bulb was left. We got it for real cheap, but it needed a lot of work."

By the beginning of winter 2004, the Dunkerleys were just nestling into their home down the street from Shawnee High School when they first noticed an unofficial divide between their neighborhood and the rest of the city.

"People would tell me I lived in the West End," says Mariann Dunkerley. "I remember thinking, 'What does that mean?'"

The following summer, they found out exactly what that meant. In April 2005 a pregnant teenager, Romanique Thompson, 17, was murdered two blocks from their home. In June, Christopher Harrison, 20, was shot multiple times one block away. In July, Jacob D. Harvey, 23, was killed around the block, not far from his own home.

"It was tragic," says Dunkerley, adding that even before that bloody summer, she noticed drug trafficking on her street.

That's when she decided to contact the Metro Council to ask if there was a block watch she could join. "They said there wasn't one, but encouraged me to help start it," she says. "That's where it all started."

Not long after launching the block watch, Dunkerly and other concerned residents decided a key to cleaning up the neighborhood was eradicating the corner liquor stores, which seemed to be breeding grounds for drugs and crime. The group petitioned to hold a special election banning liquor sales in much of the Shawnee neighborhood.

The results of the September 2007 wet-dry vote: 86 percent favored banning liquor sales in four precincts (N104, N105, N107, and N109). The election results were entangled in litigation until a judge upheld the vote earlier this year. Dunkerley says voting the four precincts dry was never about putting anyone out of business, and had even less to do with alcohol.

"These liquor stores are set up for single-serving sales," Dunkerley says. "It promotes a lot of foot traffic and people acting as if they were at a bar. But instead they hang on the corner with their little brown bag."

Months after the ban was upheld, one of the corner stores, Bakhos El-Khoury, owner of Bakos Liquors, attempted to sidestep the ban by moving his store across the street into a wet precinct. The Louisville Metro Alcohol Beverage Control Board, however, denied El-Khoury's application for a liquor license, citing "community sentiment" in its ruling. El-Khoury appealed, but last month the Kentucky ABC upheld the earlier decision.

Attorney Ted Gordon, who represents El-Khoury, says there's no way to directly relate crime to liquor stores.

"It all depends on how it's managed," Gordon says. "If you go to 34th & Vermont, that's a nasty liquor store known for people drinking outside, loitering, drugs, and gambling. Just a nasty area—period."

But Major Yvette Gentry, who commands the police department's second division, says crime analysis reports show significant improvements in the Shawnee area. Patrol reports indicate a 24 percent decrease in violent crime, including a 57 percent drop in sexual assaults and a 27 percent drop in domestic violence.

"There's also a 47 percent drop in street robberies," Gentry says. "That's a big deal."

Crime statistics for the four dry precincts obtained by *LEO Weekly* through the open records law bear most of this out.

The department is neutral on the wet-dry debate, and Gentry wouldn't say if banning alcohol sales has reduced crime. But she says patrol officers do report noticeably fewer people hanging around liquor stores after dark.

"We're seeing less loitering around those places," Gentry says. "The opportunity for crime doesn't exist as much. It's not that the owners are bad people or that people who drink alcohol are the ones committing crimes, but there's less opportunity."

What's been effective, Gentry says, is the combination of diligent residents and prevention efforts.

"I would love to take credit for a lot of it," Gentry says. "But we have people in Shawnee who say, our neighborhood is too good of a neighborhood and we're not moving out. We're going to stay here and deal with our issues."

Councilwoman Cheri Bryant-Hamilton, D-5, who represents the Shawnee neighborhood, says the wet-dry vote was a victory, but what's going on in her district goes beyond the battle with liquor stores. The next step is drafting a comprehensive neighborhood plan, which west Louisville hasn't had since 1983.

Parallel to the neighborhood plan, Hamilton says her office also is working with the Metro Louisville Economic Development Department to conduct a West Market Street corridor improvement study.

"We're talking about making a neighborhood vibrant again," Hamilton says. "It'll probably be an 18-month to two-year process."

None of this would be possible, she says, if not for residents like Mariann Dunkerley. Luckily, Hamilton adds, "We have a bunch of Marianns."

One of the 28 recipients of the 2008 Mayor's Good Neighbor Award, Dunkerley is set to give a presentation at the Mayor's Neighborhood Summit on the success of the wet-dry vote. Back in Nashville, Dunkerley was a whispering Republican, never active in politics. Now she's neck deep in civic servitude as the communications chair for the Shawnee Neighborhood Association and member of the West End Crime Prevention Council.

"I just felt this need to do something," she says. "After putting blood, sweat and tears into this house, I am not moving. I refuse. I'm just not." ➥

"HOW I GOT THAT STORY"

Phillip M. Bailey was only 24 when he wrote the following stories, which were among his first as a full-time staff reporter for the Louisville Eccentric Observer. *He received his career calling at the* SOULution, *an underground monthly newspaper at the University of Louisville founded by black students frustrated by coverage in the school's official student paper.*

Bailey says that the SOULution *taught him his craft, and its success in changing the discourse on campus helped inspire his passion for reporting. "I truly believe journalism—if done correctly—is the last bastion of public intellectualism left in this country," Bailey writes. "I like to think in those grand terms about this work we're doing." Bailey also was a 2008 fellow at the for Alternative Journalism summer residency program at Northwestern University's Medill School of Journalism. Bailey discusses his journalism with* North Coast Journal *editor and AAN Editorial Committee member Hank Sims.*

There's a lot of shoe leather in these stories. But contrary to most conventional journalism advice, you always lead with a human being. No inverted pyramids here. Talk about your approach to telling compelling and complete stories in these short-form pieces.

I never believe in the "dumb it down" approach to news. I feel that we owe it to readers to give them basic respect—they're smart enough to understand complicated matters—but it's important for a reader to connect with a story first. And people love stories with compelling yet average folk who are like them. That's how you open readers up to the important details in government documents and national policies, which are admittedly a headache to read.

The string that connects these very different pieces would be three regular people being confronted with a problem. People do that every day when they face a daily grind, and their character often determines the rest. What counts is the story of how that person's conscience responds. Readers understand that everybody has a challenge to overcome.

If I have a personal story in a piece, I always try to describe the person's appearance, reaction, feelings and surroundings, because I want readers to think along with that person.

On a daily newspaper, these stories would probably come from three different reporters. In the weekly world, everyone has a broader beat. How do you pick which stories to pursue, and what made you decide that these three stories were worthwhile?

These stories were very different in nature, but were the easiest to select because their basic nut graph sparks a conversation. That's when I know I have a good story.

The "Taming the Wild West" story, for instance, was about how to combat crime in a neighborhood. We often hear those stories in terms of police initiatives, crime statistics, federal programs, and city promises, but in the trenches you need people like Mariann Dunkerley who will fight house by house. That's the story we ought to follow, because if she loses steam then it becomes a question of morale.

There are hundreds of people who know what it is like to want to reclaim their community from crime, drug abuse, poverty, or police brutality. And only people like her can unlock those stories.

Most alternative weeklies are all about the city, and in these pieces you come off like a metro reporter to the core. What makes Louisville a great city to write about?

Louisville is one of those cities going through the growing pains of shedding its Mayberry image. Usually we see that tension in our political or business coverage—for instance, in the efforts revitalize downtown and how its rubs up against a strong local effort to "Keep Louisville Weird."

We have a lot of growing up to do demographically—which means racially—as a "Gateway to the South" city. There is no viable black middle class that can sustain much of anything. African Americans are still economically, socially, and politically locked in this hyper-segregated city.

Still, there is an attempt to become more urban, youthful and more open-minded.

POLITICAL COLUMN

🎖🎖🎖

CIRCULATION 50,000 AND OVER

"Stimulus, Chicago-Style"

by Ben Joravsky, *Chicago Reader*

AND

"The Mayor's Press Pass"

by Tom Robbins, *Village Voice*

"Excellent, intensely local, explanative journalism."—Shawn Zeller, Congressional Quarterly

🎖🎖🎖

CIRCULATION UNDER 50,000

"Solo Ingles Derrotado"

by Jeff Woods, *Nashville Scene*

Stimulus, Chicago-Style

Ben Joravsky

MARCH 26, 2009

I swear, half the job of reporting on the city's tax increment financing schemes is learning how to read between the lines in the propaganda the city issues about them.

Last week the Community Development Commission OK'd plans to shower the MillerCoors beer company with $6 million in subsidies from the LaSalle Central TIF. According to the overview the city provided the CDC, the money will help MillerCoors rebuild the eight floors of offices the company will occupy once it moves its corporate headquarters to 250 S. Wacker, a 14-story building at the northwest corner of Wacker and Jackson.

The overview, drafted by staffers for the city's Department of Community Development, explains that one of the reasons Miller and Coors merged in June 2008 was to give consumers "more choice."

But as MillerCoors CEO Leo Kiely told the *Rocky Mountain News*, the merger also enabled the country's second- and third-largest beer companies to reduce overall costs by about $500 million a year, mostly by cutting an unspecified number of jobs. The overview doesn't mention that.

"In the spirit of creating a truly new company, MillerCoors had to select a location for their new headquarters," the overview goes on. Company leaders didn't want to stay in Milwaukee (home to Miller) or Denver (home to Coors) because "it was felt that location in either city would suggest that one of the partners had a controlling interest in the new company."

They flirted with Dallas but settled on Chicago because it's "a true international city" with "an attractive talent pool," "unique business resources," "good schools," and "easy commutes." (I guess no one with MillerCoors, or for that matter the Department of Community Development, has ever had to depend on the CTA.)

And, almost as an afterthought, the report mentions that "during the selection process, both the City of Chicago and the State of Illinois offered economic incentives" to offset MillerCoors's "considerable relocation costs."

I'll say. Our old friend Governor Rod Blagojevich, about six months before he was hauled out of his house in handcuffs, forked over some $18 million in state tax breaks and subsidies, and Mayor Daley agreed to chip in a little more, which we now know to be $6 million. By contrast, there's no record of Dallas offering anything on top of its already-lower property taxes. (Neither Dallas city officials nor MillerCoors responded to calls for comment.)

Once they settled on Chicago, MillerCoors execs narrowed their real estate choices to three possibilities: 250 S. Wacker, 33 S. State (the old Carson Pirie Scott building), and 350 N. Orleans (also home to the *Sun-Times*). In terms of warding off blight—the nominal purpose of TIF subsidies—pushing State Street would have made the most sense, as the eastern part of the Loop has a far higher vacancy rate than the west. But the city left the decision up to MillerCoors. As a result, our tax dollars are going to give the better-off part of the Loop a leg up over its poorer cousin.

But this problem goes back to the founding of the LaSalle Central TIF, where—thanks to gaping loopholes in TIF law—the city managed to stretch the definition of blight to cover one of the hottest real estate markets in town. By 2030, when this district mercifully expires, the city expects it will have siphoned off at least $1.5 billion in property taxes from the schools, parks, police, fire, and other needy public services. City planners have said they will use the cash to, among other things, renovate the old architectural landmarks on LaSalle that are becoming out of date.

Well, 250 S. Wacker is hardly an architectural jewel. Constructed in 1957, it's a steel and glass box that looks like it was squished to make it fit in its corner space. As even the plan overview dryly notes, "This building has not been identified as historically significant."

In 2005 the joint venture of Carnegie Realty and D2 Realty LLC bought it for about $16.8 million with plans to renovate it and convert it into offices and condominiums. "We are extremely happy with the property which is situated in an 'A' location for our prospective buyers," John Thomas, CEO of Carnegie, said in a press statement at the time. "We anticipate our buyers will be wholly owned or multi-generational businesses that foresee their real estate needs and investments for the long term."

By then Thomas had already been convicted of business fraud, and as part of his deal with the feds he became a government mole, according to a 2007 *Tribune* article by David Jackson. So maybe the building does have some historical significance after all.

At any rate, after renovating the building, Carnegie and D2 sold it in 2007 for about $57 million to AEW Capital Management, an investment firm out of Boston. But by last summer, the downtown office boom was dying, and AEW was desperately seeking new tenants, as the vacancy rate at 250 S. Wacker was about 82.5 percent. When MillerCoors moves in, 100 percent of the building will be occupied.

According to the city, the $6 million TIF subsidy represents about 27 percent of the $21.8 million MillerCoors will spend to rehabilitate their space. The project overview does not explain why it will cost that much to rebuild a structure that was rebuilt only two years ago—without any TIF assistance, which highlights the lack of analysis in the city plan of why this rehab qualifies for help. It's hard to see a Fortune 500 company that made a $54 million profit the last three months of 2008 as a hardship case.

Perhaps the argument is that without the $24 million in public dollars MillerCoors wouldn't have moved to Chicago in the first place. But so what? Who actually stands to gain from this deal?

Well, clearly MillerCoors. And it's also a good deal for AEW, which no longer has to worry about filling up its space. And the Walgreens and Panera Bread on the ground floor will probably pick up some new customers.

According to the overview, the "project will expand the tax base because the investment in the property will result in an increase in its assessed value." Well, let's hope so. At the very least, maybe AEW will drop its ongoing appeal to get the Cook County Board of Review to lower its assessment.

(The firm currently pays about $422,000 a year in taxes on the building.) But even if the tax base does expand, until 2030 none of those new tax dollars will go to schools, parks, or other taxing bodies; they'll flow into the LaSalle Central TIF fund, so Mayor Daley can hand them over to the next conglomerate that comes knocking on the city's door.

Then there's the matter of the 325 jobs that the city keeps saying MillerCoors will "create" with help from the city's "workforce development specialists." I don't know why they're even bothering. It's not like the company's producing 325 new positions for unemployed Chicagoans—they're relocating folks from Milwaukee and Denver. And they might not keep all 325 jobs in Chicago. According to the project overview, they'll only be penalized if they employ fewer than 293 here. None of these new employees will even be required to reside in the city. MillerCoors CEO Leo Kiely says he'll get an apartment in Chicago but keep his primary residence with his wife in Denver.

MillerCoors has agreed to give back to Chicago in another way: it says it will spend some of its money on fencing and landscaping for the river walk just west of the building. I don't think that will make up for the full $6 million either—but given the cost overruns on the rest of the river walk, you never know. ••

"HOW I GOT THAT STORY"

Ben Joravsky has been a Reader *staff writer and written a weekly column since 1990. "That's 20 years, people!" he writes. He also has four books, including* Hoop Dreams*, and writes a blog, The Third City, which covers "everything and anything except politics," he says. This interview was conducted via email by* Santa Fe Reporter *editor and AAN Editorial Chair Julia Goldberg.*

You're a political columnist, but your columns are more about investigative reporting than opining. Do you operate like a beat reporter when you're working on your columns?

I don't operate like a beat reporter. Beat reporters pretty much have to report what the bosses of their beats tell them. Instead, I often follow up on what the beat reporters write. I dig into a story to find out what has not been reported so I can explain to my readers what's really going on and how it impacts their lives.

Most daily papers cover local government. Do you consider what the dailies are covering when you are deciding what to work on?

Absolutely. As I said, I follow the news very closely. But in many cases I won't write about a political story even if it's really popular because I don't think it's very substantial. For instance, I didn't write about the city's ban and then un-ban of foie gras.

Your columns deal with some wonky stuff. How do you make something like TIF (tax increment financing) interesting and understandable to readers?

That's the million-dollar question. You have to take a deep breath and tell your readers—OK, readers, the following really wonky paragraph is like eating your spinach. You might not like the taste, but once you finish, you'll be really strong, like Popeye.

Then you take them through it step by step, giving plenty of examples. So, for instance, instead of just saying a TIF freezes the amount the schools get in property taxes for 24 years, I would write: for example, if the schools were getting $200 a year in taxes when the TIF was created, that's all they will get each year for the next 24 years.

Then once you've finished the explanation, you reward them with a wisecrack. Everybody loves a good wisecrack.

Has the online environment changed how you approach your work?

Not really—other than I don't get out as much as I used to. In the old days, I'd have to track down information by going to the library. Now a lot of that information is on the Internet.

What advice would you give aspiring political journalists?

As much as possible, don't take yourself too seriously, don't be afraid to put a joke or two in your coverage and don't believe everything the government tells you. In fact, it's a good idea not to believe anything the government tells you.

The Mayor's Press Pass

Tom Robbins

OCTOBER 27, 2009

One reason for the remarkably charmed life of Mike Bloomberg's administration as he sails toward re-election has been the waning of the city's news business. This is an odd blessing for a man who made his fortune as a media mogul. But just ask Rudy Giuliani, or David Dinkins, or Ed Koch, and they'll painfully explain.

When this city enjoyed four fat daily newspapers, editors clamored for strong, tough copy to fill them. Whenever scandal hit—make that even a mini-scandal—each one scrambled after the story. Local TV news, which gets its morning bearings from the dailies, gleefully joined the hunt as well. This happy combination produced many full-strength media pile-ons and visible shivers in City Hall.

There was a keen reminder of this changed world when a man named Raymond Harding put himself back in the news this month by pleading guilty to fraud at the state's pension fund. Back in 1997, Harding, the boss of something called the Liberal Party, was the city's top lobbyist, his law firm raking in millions from clients seeking favors from Giuliani's city hall. These were easy for Harding to arrange since he had personally invented Giuliani as a political player.

It took a while for the dailies to catch on to this scheme, but when they did, the effect was viral: they became a four-man tag team, taking turns serving up tales of greed and insider trading. Giuliani was then at the top of his game and delighted in telling off reporters. But he knew disaster when he saw it. Claiming ignorance that his mentor was making a fortune off his administration, he publicly chided his aides and ordered his pal to lay low.

These days, the papers are onion-skin thin, and exposés are catch-as-catch-can. *Newsday,* which once gave rival editors panic attacks every morning, doesn't even have a city edition anymore. When Dinkins was in office, the Long Island tabloid investigated even the type of fertilizer he used on the Gracie Mansion lawn. Nowadays, to fill their meager space, editors prefer colorful yarns to investigations. Until this month, one newspaper carried an entire column about empty rooms. We have the Web, with all of its many hardworking blogs, but most of these spend their energies keeping political scorecards with all the obsession of fantasy baseball addicts: who's on first, and what coaches are in the dugout? The business of government and its many failings goes largely unexamined.

Poor Ed Koch: he was trashed as a miserable miser in multiple front-page stories because he had some 2,000 homeless families sleeping in shelters. Mike Bloomberg has five times as many, and no one even knows about it.

It's not that there's no investigative spadework being done. What's missing is critical mass. Last week, the *Daily News'* Juan González delivered some excellent fodder for a full-scale media assault in city hall's Blue Room. He reported that the mayor's billion-dollar plan to relocate the city's emergency 911 call system has become a fiasco. Not only has Bloomberg's team blown its budget and deadlines, but it has also ignored the findings of its own consultant, which found the project was mired in mismanagement. Rather than dump its lead contractor, as the consultant recommended, Bloomberg's top aides insisted that the plan go ahead as is—defects be damned.

This type of project is supposed to be smack in the mayor's sweet spot since it involves computers and communications, the business that made him the city's richest man. It should also be one of those instances where he runs rings around old-school politicians because of his keen business acumen. Instead, here he is, tripped up by the same cost overruns and bureaucrats that plague ordinary humans. Another mayor in another time might have suffered many tough questions the day after such information surfaced. Instead, only the *News* chased its own story.

The same thing happened this summer, when the *Voice* reported a scandal at the city's NYC-TV operation, where the top executive was fired and his deputy arrested ("Inside the Mayor's Studio: NYC-TV's Secrets of New York," August 4). Unlike the perennially tainted buildings department that has plagued every mayor, the problems at NYC-TV came from Bloomberg's own supporters. He had repeatedly hailed the station as an example of his innovative approach to government. But instead of minding the store, his aides had traipsed around the world, making their own private movie. This tale also failed to trip the press alarm that scrambles the media into action.

The big story late last week was the stunning court ruling on the illegal Stuyvesant Town rent hikes. But you'd never know from the coverage that Bloomberg had praised the original deal cut by landlord Tishman-Speyer (headed by one of his strongest allies). Or that his top aides had scotched a plan to keep Stuy Town affordable. Or that a hefty chunk of the financing for the deal came from Merrill Lynch, the late investment firm that was a top Bloomberg LP client and which the mayor was barred from dealing with under a Conflicts of Interest Board ruling. That story—told here in detail by Wayne Barrett just last month—also died an orphan.

Bloomberg's biggest claim to mayoral fame as he grabs for the third term that he used to insist he would never seek is his success at the business of education. This is a debate worth having. But Bloomberg consistently wins by default because the other side never fully shows up. As the legislature was considering the renewal of Bloomberg's mayoral control law this year, Brooklyn Assemblyman Jim Brennan issued six lengthy reports on the law's impact on the schools. They were detailed and thoughtful critiques on student achievement, school organization, and contracting. Asked recently how much press he received about them, Brennan paused. "I'm not sure there was any," he said.

There have been scattered stories about instances of grade inflation and test-score manipulations (again, with the *News* in the lead). The startlingly poor results of national student tests this month prompted even the *Post*, whose news pages have steadily cheered Bloomberg's education policies, to suggest that fraud was afoot somewhere. But the big picture still escapes us, along with whatever role was played by the education bureaucrats at the Tweed Courthouse.

At the mayor's annual Gracie Mansion Christmas party for the press last year, those in attendance report that Bloomberg took the stage to offer his idea of a joke. "I see that my three best friends in the media—Mort, Rupert, and Arthur—aren't here," he quipped. Then he walked out, right past the grunts who cover him all year.

Actually, the joke's on us. Even as newspaper fortunes sank in recent years, Bloomberg diligently courted media barons like Zuckerman, Murdoch, and Sulzberger, who he understood could make his life difficult if they so chose. Minus their support, as Joyce Purnick's new Bloomberg biography proves, he would have never risked his end run around term limits. But he knew he had little to fear. As Purnick's book also tells us, even his weekend disappearing act to go to his mansion in Bermuda has gone unchallenged.

"He does his radio show Friday morning," a former aide told her. "At 11:05, the latest, he's in his car. At 11:30 he is at the airport. His plane is in the air at 11:40, he's in Bermuda at 2:10. He's on the golf course by 2:30. . . . Almost every weekend, spring and fall."

There's a photo op that's been even more closely guarded than military caskets arriving at Dover Air Force Base: Mayor Mike, golf bags over his shoulder, striding across the tarmac toward Air Bloomberg. ⟿

"HOW I GOT THAT STORY"

Tom Robbins has been reporting on New York City people and politics for more than 30 years, with stints, he says, ". . . at the New York Daily News, the New York Observer, and City Limits magazine. I'm on my second tour of duty at the Voice, having returned in 2000 after leaving with the late Jack Newfield in 1988 to go to the News." Robbins discussed his work with Santa Fe Reporter editor and AAN Editorial Chair Julia Goldberg via email.

"The Mayor's Press Pass" examines how the shrinkage of investigative reporting in New York has given Mayor Mike Bloomberg more leeway than his predecessors. Are you finding this to be the case for other beats you cover, or is local government being more specifically under-examined?
The everyday business of politics—the scrum of races, candidates, consultants, and polls—gets more focus than ever thanks to the proliferation of Web logs. The messier business of what goes on inside government—the powerbrokers, the deals, the contracts, and their collective impact on everyday New Yorkers—is increasingly off the news radar. Go figure.

What's your process for deciding what you are going to write about, and how much autonomy do you have in choosing your stories?
I aim for topics getting short shrift elsewhere, scoundrels who have evaded detection, heroes whose stars haven't shined, and issues that get my juices going—good or bad. Or just to tell a story. As long as I generally stay east of the Hudson and west of Long Island, I think I get to pick my spots.

When the *Village Voice* was acquired by New Times, there was proliferate concern that political reporting would get the shaft. Has the environment changed
for you in terms of how and what you report?

There are many fewer of us doing it, but my own local beat has stayed marvelously
the same. The loss of national political coverage was a tough hit, for paper and readers alike. And then there's this Seinfeld-esque, believe-in-nothing Web coverage
where the only goal seems to be to get as many giggles, sneers, and leers as possible.
That wasn't exactly the *Voice*'s founding mission. That part's pretty ominous, though I
guess we're just going with the industry flow. Maybe they're just doing what us muck-
rakers are supposed to do: following the money.

You're a veteran of this business. Has the online environment changed how you
approach your work?

Not really. It's the same deeds, contracts, payrolls, and campaign filings we always
dug out; they're just easier to get, and not our exclusive happy hunting grounds
anymore, which has to be good, right? I have to look over my shoulder a lot more to
keep up with the deluge, which is also fine. What's a little dispiriting in the brave
new world is so much anonymous venom generated at the touch of a keypad, and
the newsroom hush where so much of the interviewing and door knocking is done
in silent, digital fashion.

What advice would you give aspiring political journalists?

Go to meetings, climb stairs, find the people with passion and see what they're about.
Ask every question you can think of, especially the ones to which you think you already
know the answers. Find out who's picking up the tab.

Solo Ingles Derrotado

Jeff Woods

JANUARY 29, 2009

Given the opportunity, Nashville almost always plays into
the hands of national media types looking to portray us
as rubes and knuckle-draggers. Not this time. Against all
odds, the city rejected English Only last week with a solid 57 percent of the vote. Instead of a new dose of national mockery, we were held up as a shining example of what's
right with America during the week that we honored Martin

Luther King Jr. and inaugurated our first African American president.

As Tom Oreck, chairman of the Oreck vacuum cleaner company, told the *New York Times*: "People here said Nashville is a warm, welcoming, and friendly environment that celebrates diversity."

To hear our leaders talk, we're the new La Ville-Lumière. (That's "City of Lights" for all you rubes out there.) Mayor Karl Dean, who gambled his popularity on the outcome, declared: "From here, we continue to move forward as a city, and we do so with no barriers in our way."

Former Vice Mayor Howard Gentry gushed: "We refused to give in to the ugliness that something like this could create."

Let's not get too carried away here. True, it's heartening that the city's progressives seem able to stop daydreaming about love and harmony long enough to run an effective campaign. But not by any stretch is this the dawning of a new day or a crippling blow to intolerance in our city. In fact, had English Only been on the ballot in November as originally planned, it would have passed overwhelmingly.

It went down only because of low turnout due to a special election. That fact alone gave the English Only foes a fighting chance, magnifying the importance of their ability to educate and mobilize a small segment of voters. They spent $300,000 turning out 41,000 voters for their side. That was enough when only 73,000 of the county's 330,000 registered voters went to the polls.

K.C. McAlpin, director of ProEnglish—the hate group that bankrolled English Only—came to Nashville for the election and went sheepishly back to Arlington, Virginia, the next day. The lesson he learned? When you're selling ignorance, uninformed voters are your key demographic.

"We'll be a little smarter next time about staying away from special elections," McAlpin told the *Scene*.

The best news from this election? We might have seen the last of Eric Crafton. If English Only had won, the term-limited council member would have been emboldened to run for another office, maybe even mayor. Let's all hope he now just goes away.

Sex, Lies and a Secret Memo

During his first week on the job, state House Speaker Kent Williams has been called a lying double-crosser, a traitor, a nit-wit, and a sexual harasser. And that's just for starters. Guess the honeymoon's over.

Republicans have made no secret of the fact that they're out to put a whammy on Williams, who betrayed GOP leader Jason Mumpower and stole the speaker's gavel in a secret deal with House Democrats.

On his weekend radio show, right-wing windbag Steve Gill summed up the feelings by calling Williams "nothing but a lying, cheating, backstabbing, traitorous piece of scum."

And that was before Mumpower released a memo claiming that two years ago, a tipsy Williams approached Republican Rep. Susan Lynn in the legislative parking garage and told her, "I'd give a week's pay just to see you naked." According to the memo, Williams later apologized and promised Lynn he'd never sexually harass her again. Then he did it again eight days later, apologized again, and promised not to do it again. Really. No kidding this time.

Williams has issued a blanket denial but stonewalls reporters' questions, claiming illogically that he's prohibited from saying more because of a confidentiality provision in the legislature's policy against sexual harassment. It makes him look like a criminal lawyering up as the cops close in.

Republicans are feigning innocence about the memo's release, suddenly fearing the public will think their smear campaign has gone too far and they'll look like vicious bastards. But they can't seem to get their story straight.

Mumpower said at one point that Lynn contacted reporters who then demanded the memo under the state's open records law, and he had no choice but to release it. Lynn says Mumpower misspoke. She insists she always wanted the matter handled privately and reporters contacted her, not the other way around. It's enough to make your head spin.

We can't wait for the next poll of our lovable state lawmakers' approval rating. After all that's happened, we see them falling below Pol Pot and Bernie Madoff in public esteem, just ahead of Dick Cheney.

PUBLIC SERVICE

🎗 🎗 🎗

CIRCULATION 50,000 AND OVER

Heroin

by Robbie Woliver, Tim Bolger, and Michael M. Martino Jr., *Long Island Press*

"The epitome of public service reporting. Excellent."—Mosi Secret, ProPublica

🎗 🎗 🎗

CIRCULATION UNDER 50,000

Jackie Walker

by Betty Bean, *Metro Pulse*

"Well-written, engaging, and clear example of the article having an impact."
—*Angela Woodall*, Oakland Tribune

Long Highland

Robbie Woliver, Tim Bolger, and Michael Martino Jr.

JUNE 26, 2008

They had all the proof they needed that they were fighting a real war.

Recently, two detectives from the Nassau County narcotics/vice squad went for a quick bite at a county line area bagel store. Both are seasoned veterans, having fought the darker side of suburban life for some years. Among other duties, of late, their time had been spent dealing with an increasing heroin problem in Nassau County, one they know is very real and very frightening.

Across the store, they noticed a young man sitting at a table falling asleep, or nodding off, into his lunch. Moments later, another young man exited the men's room with blood trickling down his arm. The detectives moved in to investigate. The young man snoozing in his bagel was arrested after the cops found heroin in his pocket. In the confusion, the bleeder got away.

This was in the middle of the day, in a typically white, middle-class American suburb. And it is becoming a familiar story.

A Typical Teenager

Jessica* seems like the nicest girl in the world. She's soft-spoken, bright-eyed and as sweet as can be, the kind of girl you'd want your kids to hang out with.

For years, she'd find the kind of kids *she* wanted to hang out with on the streets of Levittown. That's where the former Island Trees High School student would wander to buy her heroin—from fellow students. That is, until the night her stepmother found her in bed unconscious, blue-faced, with saliva dribbling down the side of her mouth, OD'ed.

"I almost died," remembers Jessica.

In the hospital, she was shot with adrenaline through a needle in her heart, an instant detox. She remained in the hospital with a collapsed lung for a week, going cold turkey.

*Not their real names.

"I was convulsing and thrashing, trying to get out of my body," she recalls. "I weighed 100 pounds and eight people had to hold me down. I look back at it now and cringe. I had no concept of how I was playing with death."

She started using heroin at 15 and stayed on it for four years. Now, five years clean and 24 years old, she says, "I desire it all the time. I liked the rush and release. It was an exciting, thrilling, and new experience that you just cannot feel unless you're high."

That's what authorities are up against.

In The Trenches

Going to the offices of the Nassau County Police Department Narcotics/Vice Squad (NCNVS) makes you feel like you are up to no good. There, they don't look like cops, and there's a degree of mistrust in their eyes that cannot be shaken. It is the product of dealing with liars for a living.

Detective Lt. Andrew Fal's face does not carry the lines one might expect from a cop who has been on the job almost 40 years. As the commanding officer of the NCNVS, Fal has a lot on his plate. His day consists of dealing with some of the darkest aspects of the human condition, including human trafficking, prostitution, and drug dealing. He has seen the drinking age change more than once, several police commissioners and county executives come and go, and crime stats go up and down in Nassau. Nothing should surprise him, really. But recently he has been shocked by something he never thought he would see again: heroin, once again taking root as a popular drug, on LI's manicured streets.

When heroin began to show up in arrests around Nassau, especially with young people, Fal was stunned.

"I said, 'No, this can't be,'" says Fal, who remembers when heroin began to claim lives in Nassau 30 years ago. "I mean, how stupid are these kids?"

There is no denying that the drug is a big problem among kids in their late teens and early twenties, says Fal. Across Nassau and Suffolk, more and more arrests, overdoses, and, most disturbingly, casual use, are related to the drug that is perhaps the most hardcore of all illicit substances.

According to Detective Lt. Peter Donohue, deputy commanding officer of the NCNVS, the numbers don't lie. In 2003 in Nassau, he says, there were 102 heroin-related arrests. Last year, there were 151—a frightening increase of almost 50 percent. But those numbers can be misleading. Many people who are arrested for petty crimes, rather than drugs, are committing them for one reason—to get more heroin.

Although Suffolk police were unable to make heroin arrest statistics available as of presstime, the *New York Times* reported 95 fatal heroin-related overdoses in 2005 in Suffolk, compared to the 47 in 2004. Rehab clinic admissions for opiate abuse from a criminal justice referral source rose in both counties, by 32 percent in Nassau and twice as much—66 percent—in Suffolk between 2000 and 2007, according to the New York State Office of Alcohol and Substance Abuse Services.

"Heroin is emerging as a threat," says Suffolk County District Attorney Tom Spota through his spokesman. "Over the past few years, a significant rise in the drug's purity coupled with a greater supply on the streets has resulted in an increase in the frequency of heroin overdoses," the spokesman added. As a result, in 2005 Suffolk County police responded by creating a special unit in the county police narcotics bureau, to track and investigate heroin overdose cases.

Detective Lt. William Burke, commanding officer of the Suffolk Police Narcotics Section, points out that there has been a shift in the heroin-abusing demographic since his rookie days three decades ago.

"When I first came on the police department, I always came across heroin junkies who were 40-year-olds. Now you will see younger kids using heroin," he says, attributing the change to the new, stronger wave of smack. He gives another reason for the resurgence: today's heroin is cheaper.

"It's a trend that's been going on over the last several years," adds Burke. "We have issues with heroin everywhere."

"Obvious And Out In The Open"

According to the NCNVS, the hotbed of LI's heroin community seems to be the South Shore communities of Massapequa,

Bellmore, Merrick, Seaford, Wantagh, Copiague, Linden-hurst, and Babylon.

But the epidemic does not stop there. Tony North Shore towns are also facing their own problems, Fal warns. Economics may play a role in why the rest of the Island may not hear of these issues on the Gold Coast.

"On the North Shore, the problem is well hidden behind money," says Fal. "When a kid gets in trouble, [he or she] is sent off to rehab quietly."

And many teenagers and young adults do seem to be in trouble. Students at Syosset High School say that there's a pocket of seniors who have $400-a-day heroin habits. High school kids in Copiague say that their town is home to dealers who service teens. Massapequa High School students say heroin use is rampant—"obvious and out in the open"—in their school and town. At Ward Melville High School in East Setauket, the commons is called "The Pharmacy." At Sachem North, there's a part of the school openly known as "The Drug-store." Lindenhurst High School students brag that they're the "Heroin Capital of Long Island." And in Bellmore, kids from Calhoun High School say heroin is so prevalent that in some families, it's an intergenerational thing. Several sources from different towns report that some middle- and upper-class kids have junkie parents, and they steal their stash.

Most of the students and heroin users interviewed for this story warn that young heroin users aren't the stereotypical-looking strung-out junkies we know from the movies. These are white middle-class kids who pass for normal, looking sweet and typical—like Jessica—but who often suffer and die silently.

"Parents need to know that their goody-goody child could be doing heroin," says Jill*, 25, a seven-year crack and heroin user from Babylon, "and unless they pay very close attention, there are very few telltale signs until it is too late."

"Weekends and parties are the places where most of these kids use heroin," says one Syosset High School senior, who takes drugs but not heroin.

Across the board, the consensus is that the increasingly common path to heroin starts with what users call "pharm parties," where kids take whatever opiate-based prescription drugs are in their parents' medicine cabinet—Vicodin, Percocet, oxycodone—perhaps going so far as to crush the pills into a powder and sniff them. Teens who abuse prescription drugs are 12 times likelier to use heroin, according to a 2005 Columbia University study that also found that prescription drug abuse by teens tripled between 1992 and 2003.

Smackonomics

There is something very wrong when heroin is more affordable than gasoline. But, say police sources, that is exactly the situation. NCNVS's Donohue says that heroin is cheaper and easier to get than ever before.

Users agree that it does not cost much money at all to get into the game. A small bag could cost as little as $7. Once the heroin habit really begins, junkies may start to buy in "bundles," which could be as many as 11 or 12 bags, but usually an even 10. That could cost about $200 or less. The typical user buying in that quantity would get about two bundles, or 20 bags.

Fal says that the drugs are being sold primarily by neighborhood kids who start out by going to Brooklyn, Queens, or the Bronx to buy heroin for themselves. As word begins to spread, they start to pick up heroin for friends. Suddenly, they are dealers.

"They find their trade expands exponentially," says Fal. "They never see themselves as dealers when they are arrested. They just think they are picking up for their friends."

"Brooklyn's the cheapest," says a Syosset High senior. This is confirmed by most of the junkies who find they have to go off the Island to buy their heroin after they graduate high school.

"It's so easy to get heroin in school," says Jessica. "When you graduate, you graduate to Brooklyn or the Bronx, and things start to get seriously dangerous."

Most heroin users remain under the radar until their addiction causes them to commit petty crimes to support the habit. At first, they're stealing from parents and friends. Then they get more desperate. When caught, if they don't have heroin on them, they could be off the hook for the drug charge.

Being caught with a small amount of heroin, say, a small bag or two, is treated as a misdemeanor possession charge. The addict could be back doing the drug in just hours—or even less.

But getting caught with multiple bags could result in an intent-to-sell charge, which is big trouble for the suspect. They could wind up in custody at the worst time: when their withdrawal begins. Then it is a completely different nightmare altogether.

Not Just Horsing Around

Heroin is a hell of drug. Few substances have its immediate addictive qualities. Heroin is derived from the poppy plant, native to Southeastern Europe and Western Asia, but now is cultivated in many other parts of the world. Cops say the majority of the heroin that makes it to LI comes from countries such as Colombia, via Mexico. A member of the opiate family, which are the most addictive drugs, heroin goes right to the brain. It's that first hit that a heroin addict will chase after, forever. It is a futile chase, as most addicts will tell you.

It's been said by junkies that heroin is better than sex. While most would probably disagree, it makes scientific sense. In the early 1970s, scientists found that the human brain has receptors that seem to welcome opiates with open arms. Morphine, heroin, opium, and other similar substances affect the part of the brain that releases endorphins, those sweet, natural brain chemicals that provide a "rush."

Some have said the initial rush of heroin is like an orgasm, complete with flushed skin and heavy limbs. But as the drug begins to settle down and travel through the body, it acts like morphine, numbing and calming the nerves. The feeling is so pleasant that users want to do it again. And again—well, that is, if they don't mind vomiting every once in a while. Welcome to the Terror Dome.

"Users develop a tolerance, so you need more and more heroin to feel the euphoria that is associated with the first heroin high," says Dr. Joseph Rio, the chief toxicologist for the Nassau County Medical Examiner's office.

Consequently, the brain urges the addict to do whatever is necessary to get that high. Of course, along the way the body begins to develop a dependence too. Rio says that, not unlike substances like tobacco, the physical hook of heroin becomes a painful, nagging feeling.

But that tolerance is phony, because it is only the brain that is getting used to the opiate effect of the drug. The body continues to take a pounding, and there is no real tolerance level to achieve. Organs like the liver and kidneys will be damaged. And once a sniffer graduates to the needle, a host of other issues present themselves, including hepatitis B and C, HIV/AIDS, abscesses from repeated punctures not being cleaned, and other infections. Once someone begins doing heroin, there really is no upside.

Fal says, though, that this dependence works to the advantage of the cops.

"Addicts don't want to get sick," says Fal. "They get what we call diarrhea of the mouth."

That is when the cops can start to break down the walls of silence built up by drug addicts.

"When we arrest addicts, they know they only have a certain amount of time before they start to sneeze, get chills, and eventually be lying on the floor in the fetal position in withdrawal," says Donohue. And don't forget the insatiable itching, parodied by non-users but feared by junkies.

And a junkie will do anything to get a fix. That desperation has led to recent arrests in both counties. Sources confirm a recent bevy of arrests in the Massapequa area, which they believe will continue to lead to more information.

Recently, a married couple was arrested for a string of robberies in Massapequa. The man and wife were robbing school-aged kids, tearing chains from the kids' necks or grabbing whatever they could to fund their heroin addiction. Beyond south Nassau, on June 25 in north Suffolk, 21-year-old Victor Chunga of Smithtown was sentenced to 35 years to life for stabbing to death 70-year-old Martha Watson in her Nesconset home last December. Chunga stabbed Watson while trying to steal heroin from her grandson, Matthew Watson, who had stopped supplying Chunga with heroin. Matthew Watson was also stabbed repeatedly, but lived.

Fighting The Fire

The problem is so alarming that Nassau Police Commissioner Lawrence Mulvey and County Executive Tom Suozzi hosted a May 8 conference organized by the Nassau County Police Department for Nassau's school administrators.

A multimedia presentation opened the eyes of school officials, for many had no idea that heroin was making such a comeback locally.

The police department announced that it was holding the meeting with school personnel from districts "located in the south corridor of Nassau County, where an increase in the use of heroin amongst teens has made a significant resurgence." And yet, many insist that the drug is not a problem within their schools.

When asked about heroin use at Massapequa High School, Massapequa Public Schools administrators responded to the *Press* with fervor.

"The Board of Education and administration have never been informed of any use of heroin within the high school by our supervisory staff," said Acting Superintendent of Schools Charles Sulc in a letter faxed and mailed to the *Press*. "Furthermore, the Nassau County Police Department has never been in contact with the Board of Education, nor any level of the high school or district's administration, regarding heroin use by Massapequa High School students."

Sulc did not return calls from the *Press,* relying only on the letter.

Robert Schilling, executive director, assessment, student data and technology services for Massapequa Public Schools, flatly denied any heroin incidents with Massapequa High School. He did, however, attend the police department's conference. So what did he do with the information gleaned from such a dramatic presentation?

The school district had no comment on that question. Neither did officials from both the Copiague and Lindenhurst school districts, according to an email from their publicist, Kathy Beatty.

"We had no specific [incidents] at Massapequa High School," says Fal. "But, in general, there is a problem. And, it's a conclusion you can make, that it is in the schools.

"We are not about mincing words," Fal continues. "We made that presentation so all the school administrators knew that [heroin] could be coming. It's an emerging problem. We have to create an awareness. You can't just wait until you have a problem."

On a recent walk through downtown Park Avenue in Massapequa Park, Massapequa High School students were observed spending their newfound summer freedom hanging out on benches lining the street. When asked, one 16-year-old boy admitted to heroin use. "It's a good drug," he said, while trying to persuade passersby to purchase cigarettes for him and his friends.

At nearby Brady Park, a small, informal 18th birthday remembrance for a boy from Massapequa who died unexpectedly this past March was taking place. His friends were open about the boy's heroin use.

"Plain and simple, [Massapequa High School] has problems with dope," said the dead boy's 20-year-old friend from Levittown. The friend admitted that he himself is a former heroin user, right after the group at the table finished smoking some marijuana. "I don't think [the school district] wants to admit they have a problem," said the Levittown friend. He would know—he did heroin with the Massapequa teens.

Ask any junkie in high school, and they will probably laugh at the idea of the administration not knowing that heroin is being used by students in the school. Often, these kids do not hide the fact that they use.

Edward, now 24, took heroin while at Lindenhurst High School. He says, bluntly, "They knew who we were. It's this generation's drug of choice." This sentiment is echoed by many young heroin users.

Jessica, who once trolled the streets of Levittown for drugs as a high school student, agrees. She says, "Teachers are well aware of the heroin use. I had one girl in my English class announce to the whole class, in front of the teacher, 'I was up all night doing heroin.' I thought the teacher was going to flip out."

But Alice Andersen, a licensed social worker who serves as the drug and alcohol counselor for Levittown Division High School, says she has never seen a student with a heroin problem at the school.

"Alcohol and pot have always been the drugs of choice," she says. "We have not had one child [on heroin], or one report of heroin abuse in the school."

Ask someone who has used, though, and you get a very different answer.

"I knew I could always get heroin from a student from Levittown," says Jessica.

But it's not just administrators who disagree that heroin is becoming more prevalent. Some students do as well.

"I don't think it's really that bad—it's just certain kids," says Andrew Carroll, 17, who graduated Massapequa High School in June. The former hockey team captain, taking a quick break from his job at a local deli, described the news coverage focusing on the school as "exaggerated." Others see any trace of heroin use as something to be concerned about.

Abusing heroin leads to obvious addiction, but too often that habit will end in death. Dr. Rio explains that heroin affects the brain as it is communicating with the body. So, the brain might tell the heart to stop pumping blood, or the lungs to stop breathing. Too often, when someone who is high on heroin goes to sleep, they never wake up.

By all accounts, the heroin that is being used today is immeasurably more potent than in the past. The potency allows users to sniff heroin as opposed to shooting it at first. That is a mind trick that Fal believes gets the ball rolling in the wrong direction.

"Kids think it's no big deal if they sniff it," says Fal. "It takes the stigma away from the drug. The image of someone using a needle is not reality to them."

But no matter how it's taken, heroin use is a harsh reality. A hit of heroin that is sniffed or snorted can take up to 15 minutes to affect the brain. A subcutaneous injection—one that goes just under the skin—will make its way to the shooter's system in about 10 minutes. But an intravenous shot, one straight into the vein, is almost instant.

"We've been in a little bit of an upswing," says Kevin Leonard, clinic manager with the Suffolk County Department of Health's Division of Community Mental Hygiene. He is careful not to term the increase a trend, describing opiate abuse as "cyclical in nature," and noting that in his three decades in the rehab field, he's seen lots of ups and downs in terms of heroin use.

Meanwhile, though, Fal, Burke, and the rest of the cops across the Island remain steadfast in stamping out the flare-ups before they become an inferno. Fal remains astounded that heroin use is even an issue.

"With all the technology and information at their fingertips, how could these kids do heroin?" he wonders. "I mean, heroin is not just recreational. It is highly addictive. It causes problems. It increases crime."

Fal pauses.

"And, it causes death," he says. "They just don't understand the consequences." ➥

—With additional reporting by Heather Burian

Junk Bonds

Robbie Woliver

JUNE 26, 2008

Carol Whelan, a nurse, sits on her couch in her cramped, middle-class Cape home in Lindenhurst, occupied by a laughing parrot, two dogs, and a monkey. She shakes her head sadly. "The truth is," she says, "I'm getting tired of going to so many funerals of young people."

The young people she is talking about are her son Edward's friends. They were around his age, 24, when they died, and the death count is now about 10. The most recent was the worst—Thomas, Edward's best friend.

And what are they dying from? Heroin.

Edward is an imposing young man, 6-foot-2-inches tall, 195 pounds, a good-looking Penn Jillette with long hair in a partial ponytail and one of those great giant-dimpled smiles that lights up the room. That's not the only thing that's lit up in Edward's basement studio on this unusually hot June evening, where several of his friends are gathering. There's also Ricky and Lorraine, a 27-year-old married couple from Bellmore. They are junkies and they have just gotten high.

Edward, too, has been on heroin. That is, until this past April, a month after Thomas OD'ed.

"I just stopped," he says. "In honor of [Thomas]."

Sitting amongst the heavy metal posters, drum sets, electric keyboards, and assorted other instruments where Edward's heavy metal band InRed practices, are Jill, 25, and Ryan, 25—two of Edward's friends who also were heroin users, but who have since gone to rehab and are currently sober. Jill and Ryan have been clean since January of this year, and Ryan has been out of rehab since early May. Ryan came close to using heroin a week and a half ago, but a friend stopped him, and Ryan is very thankful his friend did that.

"It's a day-to-day struggle," admits Ryan, who looks like the clean-cut jock-next-door.

While Ryan and Jill discuss their successes, Ricky, with an almost cliched hangdog look, is nodding out near his wife, who has such a sad aura about her it is palpable. When showing the needle marks on her black-and-blue arms, the scars of recent cuttings are also obvious. Ricky looks helpless as she shows her bruised arms—even though he does help shoot his wife's battered veins with heroin.

Tonight Ricky—who seems like he might once have been a sharp, interesting young man—is, shortly after shooting heroin, zombielike. Edward, Jill, and Ryan seem absolutely radiant compared to him. He is their past.

"I can end any time I want," says Ricky, obviously not believing his own empty words. Ricky, Edward says, is unusual. "He can stop for a day and be OK. That's very hard to do," Edward says, almost in awe of his slumped-over, droopy-eyed, sallow friend. OK is a relative term here.

Jill and Ryan, who are not too far past that life themselves, agree. Jill, for example, was shooting up heroin several times a day. And that was just to bring her down from the crack cocaine she was smoking.

"I had a 95 average in high school," she says, wistfully describing her past. "I had a lot of dreams, but now I just make fucking $7.50 an hour in Waldbaum's." Unlike the others in this group, Jill started drugs late, at age 18. Coke was her drug of choice, and she had been an addict for close to seven years, first taking ecstasy, then snorting coke and then smoking crack and finally shooting heroin to come down from the coke and crack. She started late, but she made up for it big time.

She was shooting up all day, but no longer getting high, so she needed more and more. For a while she worked three jobs and says she kept up her appearance, but that all came to an abrupt end. She lost about 30 pounds (as did Ryan when he was using) and fell to 80 pounds. She now weighs a healthy 110 pounds and looks fit. She also collapsed a vein and now can't get blood taken from the arm.

The wake-up call? There were several. OD'ing was a biggie. "I almost died," she says. "My heart stopped." At this point her skin was yellow, she had black eyes, and her back teeth fell out. She also couldn't breathe. "The doctor told me I had such a large hole in my nose [from snorting drugs] that it would kill me," she recalls.

So she stopped snorting. And she started injecting.

Jill, who never smoked pot, says she was oblivious to the degeneration of her circle of junkie friends. "They had no teeth. They were dirty like bums," she says in retrospect.

Remember, while these users are now in their 20s, they all started using drugs as teens, some as young as preteens.

It was rampant in school, they all say. "You can count the people who aren't on heroin," says Edward, "as opposed to the ones who are." And Lindenhurst, they all say, is "the heroin capital of Long Island." That is, until Bellmore and Massapequa and Copaigue and Levittown and countless other towns come up.

"It's wherever you go, and the kids are getting younger and younger," says Edward, who attended Lindenhurst High School (partly at the Alternative Learning Center [ALC]).

"We'd smoke weed in the classroom. In ninth grade, kids would have coke and heroin on the table in the classroom.

"A lot of kids from the high school and ALC would get sent away for a year or so, their drug problem would be so bad," Edward says. His best friend Thomas was one of those kids.

Why Heroin?

"It's a social drug, and everyone was doing it," says Edward, who, like many of his friends, first began experimenting with drugs at age 11.

He started heroin when he was 14. His entire crowd was doing it. (There are some, who, 10 years later, are still on heroin.) It was cheap and very easy to get. Their stories are similar—they started by sniffing it and eventually turned to shooting it.

"It makes you not care what anyone says. It makes you an asshole," he says. "But I liked the feeling. It was amazing."

There is no stigma, nor a badge of honor. It's just what everybody does. No big deal.

"It was cheaper than marijuana, coke, pills, and alcohol, and one $10 bag would do the trick," says Jill. The coke high is only 20 minutes. Heroin would last longer, until the tolerance would build.

And where are the parents in all this? Jill says her parents "thought something was up. It was obvious, I wasn't holding down a job, I wasn't going to school.

"When my mom would go to work, I would shoot up and it would last two to three hours and then I'd have to get high again. I had to get high two or three times a day.

"I'm getting sick just talking about it," she says.

"Toward the end, I felt like I was tripping out. I was having anxiety attacks. I was hot, cold, throwing up, very emotional. I kept trying to leave signs, leaving needles around, stuff like that."

Jill's mother, who had been addicted to cocaine herself, finally said, "That's it. I know something's up. I want to take you to a funeral home. I want you to see your funeral. I don't want to find you dead." Jill's uncle OD'ed and her brother is a recovering addict.

Jill: "It was disgusting. You felt dirty no matter what you'd do. You lied to everyone. Drugs ruined my life."

So she got clean. "I took a long hard look," she says, starting to cry. But it's not easy.

She is now in a drug and alcohol program three to four days a week.

"Sometimes when I get frustrated and think about my shitty job, I ask myself, 'What am I clean for?' I know it takes a year to get really clean. But I smile again now. My family is trusting me again, and my friends are trusting me again."

At this point, Edward's cell phone rings, and he tells Jill that it's a friend of hers. Jill gets in an animated discussion with her friend, who informs her that Jill's mother is frantically searching for her, angrily saying things like, "I know she's up to no good. I know what she's doing. I know she's sneaking around."

"Fuck that," Jill says, "I told her where I was going," and with that she calls her mother and angrily reminds her that she is being interviewed for a newspaper story.

"I have no car. No phone. I live in a cubicle with no door, no privacy," she says. "They are treating me like I am 16.

"There are so many things I could have done with my life," Jill says.

Edward's situation is a little different. His parents are more trusting. They were very supportive when he came to them last January and told them that he was a junkie.

"I suspected something," says his mother, who is a methadone nurse.

"It's better when you have their support," says Edward, the soft-spoken rocker.

Part of why so many young people are junkies is the ease with which they can obtain the heroin, says Edward. "We'd go to [the dealer's] house and there would be cars lined up— sometimes 10 cars on each block. We had to wait hours almost every day." Ryan laughs at the memory. What they don't address is the danger inherent in these deals. These dealers, who sometimes have their much younger siblings deliver the goods, are dead serious, and they have the firearms to prove it.

But these dangers are of no significance to a junkie, when caught up in heroin's web. "Everyone seems to be doing it," says Edward. "In high school it seemed like 80 percent of the kids were doing it."

"And then there's the environment," Ryan adds. "Every commercial says, 'Take this pill.' Society is feeding you with drugs and saying, 'This will solve this problem.'"

What's the effect of school programs like DARE? These heroin users say, for them, the programs did more harm than good.

"They lied to us about marijuana, so we didn't believe them about heroin," says Edward.

And then there's the cheap cost. "I couldn't afford weed and alcohol," says Edward. "Heroin was a snap: $10 a bag."

But that $10 has a greater cost.

Married to the Drug

Ricky and Lorraine have been married for three years. Ricky has been sniffing heroin for about six months, and has been shooting up for the past six weeks. "You need more when you're sniffing it and it's more expensive," he explains.

Ricky's reason for using heroin is somewhat startling. "I install carpets," he says, "and I am in pain a lot. Tylenol will do nothing."

That's the problem. Heroin is no big deal.

"It takes away the pain," Ricky says. "It takes away the physical muscle pain and the mental anguish. You're just not aware of anything. I want to stop doing it. I am trying to get off it now. I know it's bad. The addiction is just uncontrollable."

Jill shakes her head and responds, "When you're on it you always make plans to quit. It's not that easy."

Lorraine, slouched over as she speaks, wears a pretty brown ribbon in her hair, making her seem girlish and innocent. But that couldn't be further from the truth. She's been on opiates for four years, and was hooked on morphine. She has been doing drugs since she was 13.

"Heroin addicts don't last very long . . . a year," says Lorraine, who has been doing heroin for the past seven months. She's been shooting up for the past six weeks.

"I can't imagine a good life," she says, head down, about her future.

What about life with each other now? "[Ricky] seems a little more zombielike, secretive, when he uses [heroin]," she explains. "I don't believe a word he says. He does six bags, two needles, sometimes before he even really wakes up."

Besides mistrust, there is no intimacy amongst junkies. Ricky, who started drugs at 14, says, "We don't think about sex. It's not an option."

"We know it's bad," says his wife Lorraine. "We just encourage each other. We say, 'This is ridiculous, we have to stop.' Then the other one says, 'You want to get high?' We're never in agreement."

"I don't care if I do it by myself. I don't really care. I'll do it in a parking lot, on the side of the road," Ricky says.

"Are you afraid of being arrested?" he's asked. He looks back with a blank stare.

"Maybe that would be good," someone adds.

"Our families are really concerned," Lorraine says dead-eyed, with no emotion.

Quittin' Time

How do you get the strength to quit?

"You have to be tired of the life, because you'll never get tired of the feeling," says Edward.

Ryan, who's been friends with Edward since kindergarten, has been on drugs since his early teens. He started off with painkillers—Vicodin, OxyContin—and then moved to heroin a year ago, "because it was cheaper," he says. "You'd get higher and it was a cleaner high." He entered rehab in January of this year and got out on May 2.

All five say they stole from parents and friends to support their habit. Some worked.

"Our money situation is hard," complains Lorraine, in the same tone she would use to say she was wearing a ribbon in her hair. Of course it's hard; there are two junkies who need to satisfy their addictions.

"I remember what that is like," says Ryan. "I would have rather taken $80 and spent it on drugs than eat three meals. I always said, 'I don't have a problem.' Just like Ricky is doing now. I remember coming here [Edward's house], puking. I didn't give a shit."

Ryan returns to the recent incident, when he almost used again. "After all the effort I put into it, it would hurt my family," he says. "They were so proud of me. One of the best feelings was finishing the program."

Jill looks at Ricky and tells him he's beginning to look like a junkie. "What does a junkie look like?" he asks. "Your skin is yellowish," she responds. "It's the way you carry yourself. Your facial structure. It changes from weight loss. You look like one," she reiterates.

"Have you noticed the changes in him?" Lorraine is asked.

"I guess," Lorraine says.

Jill shakes her head. She's been there.

Edward knows there's no talking sense to the two. They need something to scare them, or to inspire them.

An inspiration like Thomas.

Thomas died from a heroin overdose on March 5, 2008. Edward stopped shooting heroin a month later.

"He promised me he would never die," says Edward about the friend he had known since they were both eight. "He emailed me the day before he died, saying that."

Two weeks after the gathering in Edward's basement, Jill was in a local Applebee's, where she noticed the clientele staring at a particular table where a couple was sitting "facedown in their food." It was Ricky and Lorraine.

At presstime, Edward notified us that he had just learned that two more friends died of OD's. He called back soon after to also inform us that Ricky and Lorraine had been arrested for possession. They scored some heroin and on the way home, Lorraine suggested they shoot up in an abandonded parking lot in Bellmore, close to where they live. Ricky suggested they go home and do it. Lorraine won out, and they quickly were discovered by a cop on patrol. Lorraine is out on $2,500 bail but Ricky remains in jail. Ricky says that this is a good thing, and he hopes it will help him clean up.

Some of the names used in this story have been changed. ➥

Heroin Claims Another

Michael M. Martino Jr.

JULY 10, 2008

Natalie Ciappa was a pretty 18-year-old cheerleader from Mass-apequa with an honor roll GPA and a voice so beautiful that she was asked again and again to perform at her school, Plainedge High School. She was, according to her mother Doreen, "ev-erybody's kid, not the kid they would have to worry about."

The talented teenager was also a heroin addict. So when she did not return from a party on June 21, Natalie's mother and her father, Victor, went looking for her, fearing the worst. It had been a rough year for the Ciappas. Natalie had devel-oped a serious drug problem in the summer of 2007, and on Memorial Day 2008, she overdosed on heroin.

Three weeks after the holiday, every parent's worst night-mare confronted them. Their daughter, a recent high school graduate, was gone, a victim of heroin. Suddenly, a life full of promise and joy became another statistic in Nassau's battle against the dangerous opiate that is making a troubling resur-gence across the region.

On July 9, Nassau County District Attorney Kathleen Rice joined Nassau County Police Commissioner Lawrence Mul-vey, Nassau County Executive Tom Suozzi, Natalie's par-ents, and members of the Nassau County Police Department (NCPD) and district attorney's vice/narcotics squads at a press conference announcing the arrests of at least one dozen peo-ple on a host of heroin distribution charges. The representa-tives stood feet away from two tables holding huge stacks of cash, hundreds of bags of heroin, packaging equipment, and a handgun.

Among those arrested was Philip Ordaya, an ex-boyfriend of Natalie, and, according to her mother, a chief reason Nat-alie was addicted. Natalie is among several dozen who have died in Nassau County this year from the devastating drug.

"You know, 37 [suspected heroin] deaths [in Nassau County] is too much," says Rice in an interview with the *Press*. "It doesn't take a rocket scientist to say that it is a problem."

Police sources have told the *Press* that others were caught in the recent sting that nabbed Ordaya. According to Rice's spokesperson, Eric Phillips, "There are more coming."

"It definitely makes a dent, but it doesn't eliminate the threat," says Detective Lt. Peter Donohue, deputy commanding officer of the NCPD narcotics/vice squad, which oversees the Heroin Investigation Team (HIT).

As some predicted, the confirmation that heroin killed Natalie is beginning to rip the lid off the unseen lives of suburban heroin addicts. And her death also underscores the problem in that South Shore community of Massapequa, which police say is a hotbed of heroin activity among young people. In a recent *Press* cover story ("Long Highland," June 26), officials from the Massapequa School District vehemently denied any heroin-related incidents at Massapequa High School.

But a police source has confirmed to the *Press* that on October 5, 2007, a Massapequa High School student was indeed caught in heroin's web. According to the source, the student, a minor, was incoherent during school hours. After her condition was brought to the attention of school administrators and police were called, she was found to be in possession of 28 bags of heroin and subsequently arrested. A spokesperson for the district, Kathy Beatty of Sayville-based Syntax Communications, did not return requests for comment.

Doreen Ciappa also said that Natalie had told her there was no shortage of drugs in the hallways at Plainedge High School. When Doreen asked the school for help, she says, she received none, and when she tried to talk to Natalie's guidance counselor about her daughter's weight loss, the counselor said she thought Natalie "looked great." As was the case with Massapequa, a call to Plainedge Superintendent of Schools Christine P'Simer was not returned.

"School administrators need to wake up," says Rice. "It is a real problem."

Rice, who has made a name for herself as an Eliot Ness-type of prosecutor since entering office, believes that this is a start, but a lot of work is to be done. "At any given time, there are numerous investigations going on in this office," says Rice. "We keep track of the OD's in the county, and we saw the trend."

Rice applauded the bravery of Natalie's parents, who only weeks ago lost their daughter. She hopes their story will help parents identify the signs of heroin abuse early on so no more young people are lost.

"I hope it brings awareness to parents," says Rice.

Supported by her husband, Doreen took the podium at the press event and told the heartbreaking story of a fallen angel and a mother's desperate fight to keep her daughter alive. Doreen had poked and prodded through Natalie's belongings, questioned her and even joined MySpace and Facebook—posing as another person—to gain insight into Natalie's troubled life.

"Before you knew it, I was even the dealer's friend," she says.

Ciappa recalls that Natalie began dating Ordaya in 2007—although she later learned that Natalie knew him before they were a couple. He visited the house, and was even invited to a family function. Doreen did eventually discover that Ordaya was dealing heroin.

She also chronicled a futile attempt to get help for Natalie, who refused rehab, even after the Memorial Day incident. She recalled her horror when, after that overdose, she was told by authorities that the little glassine bags she found in Natalie's room were from heroin. Well before the Memorial Day incident, Doreen and Victor compromised, and sent Natalie to therapy, still not knowing the full gravity of her addiction. But when Natalie turned 18, they became completely powerless over her. In fact, Doreen remembers, she was so desperate that she planned on going to authorities to either gain control over Natalie or have her arrested. But it was too late.

"I would like to see the laws changed," says Ciappa about not being able to make decisions to get young people help once they turn 18.

According to Donohue, it was a connect-the-dots game in the aftermath of Natalie's death. The family, whom he describes as being "very helpful from day one," turned her cell phone and computer over to the police, who discovered some familiar names and numbers in her records. One name that did pop up was Ordaya's. Police realized he was one of those being recorded on one of the wiretaps that had already been secured. Ordaya's cell phone was subsequently tapped, too.

According to police sources, investigations that led to the arrests have been going on since late fall of 2007, but in February 2008 they went into full gear after the HIT squad gathered important information. Police had noticed an increase in a long-standing drug trade at the Hempstead Bus Terminal.

"Hempstead Bus Terminal has been a known heroin-buying spot for years," says Donohue. "There are lots of people who are functioning [heroin] addicts, and they will buy their drugs before they go to work, getting just enough to keep from getting sick during the day."

As the investigation continued, the police found a stash house—a place where drugs are packaged for sale and kept until street dealers pick them up—in nearby Roosevelt. The police obtained a search warrant and found 804 bags of heroin ready for sale.

A search of that house also revealed that the main suppliers of the drugs were allegedly Alexander and Edward Fontanet, both of Queens. Police said that they were working with Donald Kurth of Merrick and Patrick Graf of Massapequa. Rice had successfully applied to Nassau County Court Judge Frank Gulotta for an eavesdropping warrant on two cell phones used by the Fontanets, and information gathered led to the court allowing Graf and Kurth's phones to be tapped as well.

The resulting investigation netted evidence against Alexander Fontanet's wife Lorraine Cianciulli, Queens-based Jose Demench, Kurth's girlfriend Heather Wahl, and Graf's wife Melissa. Evidence also piled up against Damon Marinacci, of Syosset, and eventually Ordaya, of Seaford. With the exception of Ordaya, who was arrested July 7, the rest of the suspects were taken into custody on June 17. Additional searches at the Fontanets home revealed more than 1,000 envelopes of heroin and tools used to package and sell the drug.

A search of Graf's Massapequa residence and vehicle also turned up heroin, with cops finding about 500 bags, and Kurth's Massapequa home had more than 100. Ordaya was found to be in possession of bags marked with an "XX," denoting a particular heroin often discussed among the suspects.

According to Nassau County Assistant District Attorney Teresa Corrigan, chief of the district attorney's narcotics bureau, Graf was responsible for the street sale of up to 700 bags of heroin every one or two days before he would get more supply.

Rice, like most law enforcement personnel, is shocked at the popularity of heroin on LI's sleepy streets. But she has grown accustomed to being surprised when it comes to drug offenses.

"First, it was the prescriptions that kids were getting out of medicine cabinets," she says. "Now it is heroin."

Before Doreen left the press conference through a back door, she pleaded with parents to be more realistic about their children's private lives.

"Look in their eyes," she said. "Don't be fooled." ➥

Shame On Massapequa

Robbie Woliver

JULY 10, 2008

On June 26 the *Long Island Press* ran a cover story, "Long Highland," that touched a nerve with many Long Islanders. It was about heroin use among young people. Preteens and teens—that young. What we learned in our investigation was that heroin use is pervasive among LI's youth. No longer the province of inner-city gangbangers, the drug is now in up-scale schools like Syosset High School, where students have $400-a-day habits. It is often out in the open, and it is destroying many young lives and families.

After the article was published, we were swamped with calls and emails from parents who were battling this demon drug, fighting for the very lives of their addicted middle- and upper-class children.

Heroin use means nothing to the young people who are addicted to the drug. The users we spoke with were more than happy to provide their real names for the story (without regard for future repercussions, when, let's say, a prospective employer Googles them). And in a rare move, it was the Press that decided to keep our sources anonymous. Heroin use means so little to them, they do it in out in the open, in their homes, in the local bagel shop, at school.

It is so inconsequential to them. They start off sniffing it—what's the big deal with that, right?—and they quickly turn to shooting it. They're not looked down upon, because all their friends do it. And even when their friends OD, and even die, they'll still do it. One addict told us he started heroin because Tylenol stopped working for his aches and pains.

We can understand why these users don't take the drug very seriously—they are addicts. Beyond their addiction, it's hard for them to take anything seriously.

But there are people who should be taking this problem seriously who aren't. And there is no excuse for their behavior.

The *Press* rarely runs editorials like this—we usually say what we need to say in our stories. When we have someone to call out and take to task, we usually let our reporters do that in their objective forum. But the anguish of so many LI parents has moved us to respond in this manner.

In our countless interviews with cops, addicted teens, and frustrated parents, Massapequa came up, as much as any other town, as a region with a heroin problem. The Massapequa school district, more than any other we've attempted to communicate with regarding our heroin coverage, has been the most uncooperative. While they are hiding behind publicist-driven statements flatly denying any heroin problem in their schools, the students, police, and police blotters tell a different story.

In fact, Syntax Communications, the PR firm that handles Massapequa Public Schools, represents many of the other districts that we have had documentation on regarding heroin use, and when districts use these spin doctors to protect their reputations rather than using these firms to aid in awareness in cleaning up a problem, it outrages us.

This is the letter we received, dated June 23, 2008, from Charles Sulc, acting superintendent of schools in Massapequa, when we contacted him to discuss the heroin situation in his school district:

The Massapequa School District is very concerned about the article you are evidently writing regarding an alleged "increase" of heroin use at Massapequa High School, as indicated to us by [Syntax] spokesperson Kathy Beatty. This is a serious matter that is, to our knowledge, without foundation, and we ask as a matter of health and safety of our students that you inform us of the nature of your source data so that we may assess its credibility.

The Board of Education and administration have never been informed of any use of heroin within the high school by our supervisory staff. Furthermore, the Nassau County Police Department has never been in contact with the Board of Education, nor any level of the high school's or District's administration, regarding heroin use by Massapequa High School students.

It is the district's intention to reach out, through our attorneys, to the Nassau County Police Department's Vice Squad in order to identify the source of your information and to correct any misinformation that may have been provided. If, in fact, there is no source within the department who can attest to the conclusion you have relayed to Mrs. Beatty, we would expect the matter to be dropped. If there is reliable information provided, we would be more than happy to provide comment for the record.

Drug abuse among teens is a serious matter to both the school district and to the community. This district is proactive in its efforts to educate students starting in kindergarten and continuing through twelfth grade about the dangers of substance abuse. Publicizing inaccurate information will jeopardize your credibility, and do irreparable damage to the Massapequa School District's reputation. We respectfully ask that you treat this matter with the utmost care.

Sincerely,
Charles Sulc
Acting Superintendent of Schools

Mr. Sulc's threats, of course, are unfounded. But his misstatement of facts is something serious that needs to be addressed. His smoke-and-mirrors response—blaming the messenger, and diverting attention from the problem he has in his district—is outrageous. And one of his comments deserves repeating: "Furthermore, the Nassau County Police Department has never been in contact with the Board of Education, nor any level of the high school's or District's administration, regarding heroin use by Massapequa High School students." That's not true, say police sources. In fact, on October 5, 2007, a student who was a minor was arrested in the dean's office at Massapequa High School with 28 bags of heroin on her. Beyond that, on May 8 the Nassau County Police Department, along with County Executive Thomas Suozzi, held a conference for school superintendents and principals from schools located in the south corridor of Nassau County (including Massapaequa), where, the police say, "an increase in the use of heroin amongst teens has made a significant resurgence." So Sulc's denial is either unacceptable cluelessness or worse, since Massapequa was represented at this conference by Robert Schilling, Massapequa Public Schools executive director, assessment, student data and technology services.

Fact after fact proves Sulc wrong, and the district, as of presstime, continues to refuse comment on what steps they are taking to combat the growing drug problem that was discussed at the conference they attended. Beatty once again referred the *Press* to the above statement by Sulc. Another client of Beatty's, the Copaigue Public School District (a town cited by many sources for being home to drug dealers), had "no comment," and Lindenhurst Public Schools (which numerous addicts called "the drug capital of Long Island") was unable to be reached, she told the *Press* (duh, isn't that her job as a publicist—to reach them?). Shame on you all.

On the other hand, Principal Jim Nolan, of Sachem North High School, in Ronkonkoma, a school also mentioned in the "Long Highland" story, contacted us unsolicited and proactively after reading the story, to find out how, in any way, he could help his students.

Residents of Massapequa, you are being done a disservice. It's simple logic: Before you solve a problem, you have to acknowledge it. Sulc, who received a $44,418 raise July 1, is the proverbial ostrich with its head in the sand. (Sulc's salary is now $240,000, plus an annuity of $13,000 and a car allowance of $7,500.)

Massapequa, there is a terrible drug problem in your town, and in your schools. Nothing is more important than the well-being of your children—certainly not the "Massapequa School District's reputation." These heroin-addicted kids are a peril to themselves, to their families, and to the community around them, especially their non-user fellow students and peers. If your acting superintendent doesn't think there is a problem, and is willing to go on record with that, then you have work ahead of you. Maybe it's time for him to resign, before that 44K is spent. •◆

Save My Kid

Robbie Woliver

SEPTEMBER 11, 2008

This is not a story about statistics, with quotes from cops or government organizations, and neither is it an opportunity for institutions and professionals discussed within to be given equal time. This is the story of four sets of parents who have taken on the full-time job of trying to save their children's lives, attempting to pull them back from the cunning and seductive grip of heroin. There are many commonalities in their stories, but two things become evident from the start: no matter how hard the parents try, there are roadblocks at every turn; and once heroin becomes part of a child's world, it takes hold so tightly that it strangles the life out of the entire family. The names of the heroin users and their families have been changed in all the stories except for the Ciappa section.

One lesson all the parents tell is this: If you think your child is immune, you are mistaken.

In Edward Whelan's Lindenhurst yard, he hands me a small plastic packet of heroin. His smile, which I've written about before—the one that lights up the room—is tinged with doubt. It's a nice almost-fall day and the sun has already forgotten how to scorch, but Edward, who has been shooting heroin again after stopping for several months, is sweating slightly. He's not the derelict kind of junkie we've become used to; he's a decent kid from the suburbs, and he looks it, despite his habit. His crisp, white Sean John shirt glistens in the morning sun, the way his eyes did when we first met about a month ago when he introduced me to a group of his friends—some of whom were high on heroin, others who were in recovery—for a previous story I wrote about heroin use among Long Island's high school students.

You might remember them:

Ricky and Lorraine, both 27, who were high when we met (although "high" isn't exactly an accurate term: they were actually pretty low, depressed and lethargic. OK, zombies). They were busted a day later because they couldn't wait to make the short trip from their dealer to their home, and they stopped off in what they thought was an abandoned parking lot. It wasn't quite abandoned—there was a cop there. And they were arrested. Ricky went into rehab.

Edward, 24, tells me they are using again. The others, he says, are still clean.

I kind of knew Edward would start shooting junk again. He had stopped cold turkey on his own and was pretty adamant about not needing any type of rehab, a theme you'll find common among all the junkies in this story. But really it was when he told me that there is a constant tug toward the drug and that he "think[s] about it every day," that twinkle in his eye gave his future away.

Today is the day after 48-year-old actress Mackenzie Phillips, a former teenage junkie who has been proselytizing the sober life for decades, was arrested at an airport for heroin and cocaine possession. The lure, I'm reminded, is enormous.

This morning, Edward has a plan he's about to sneak on me. Junkies are very wily, if nothing else. He wants to move the interview away from his parents' house, where he lives, so I can bring him someplace where he can shoot up. When I say no, he just laughs. "Oh, well," he says amiably, "I'll just do it when I go to work." It turns out he couldn't even wait for that. He did it as soon as I left.

"I have no idea how to save my kid," says Edward's mother, Carol, sitting in a comfortable-looking armchair in their home, beginning to weep. "I don't know where to go at this point. I had a feeling he started drugs, and then he told us he had, but he says he'll stop. I've tried to stop him, but I don't know what to do at this point. I called one counseling center yesterday and they couldn't help me.

"Rehab won't help. All his friends went to rehab and they ended up going back on drugs or dying."

Unlike the other parents in this story, Carol is trying the laid-back approach. She has faith in her son. "I'm very concerned," she says. "I stay on top of it. But what am I going to do, put a gun to his head?" Carol's whole life is about worry. "My biggest fear is that he will not wake up in the morning," she says, crying again. "Every morning, it's a relief to see him."

Edward promises that this day—the day of our interview— will be his final day of heroin use.

Tomorrow, Edward Sr. will take his son away for an extended weekend, away from his dealer, away from his friends who encourage him to use, upstate to the country.

Carol, a retired methadone nurse, wipes her teary eyes and says, "I just don't want him to die like all his friends did."

Serenity Now

In their Nesconset home, brothers Steven and Bobby Clark, fresh-faced and blond, are sitting at the kitchen table. It's Bobby's birthday and a small cake sits before him on the table. Their mother is beaming at their side. If this were painted, it could be a Norman Rockwell *Life* magazine cover: the all-American family. The irony is, it is the all-American family, 2008 style: mom, dad, kids, dog, and heroin.

Steven, a wiry, good-looking 18-year-old, was the kind of teen that anyone would look at and say, "What a nice, sweet kid." And he was—at least, before this past June, when he got sickly skinny, with sunken eyes and an uncontrollable temper.

Steven was using heroin.

When his parents first noticed track marks on his arm last year, Steven said he had been scratched. He had an excuse for everything. But his father, Kenny, a recovering alcoholic, was not taking any excuses, especially after he found hypodermic needles in his driveway. Kenny immediately began trying to find help, starting with Stony Brook University Medical Center. They were unable to care for Steven. The track marks weren't fresh, the hospital workers said, so it was not a medical emergency. "Even if he came home now and overdosed?" Kenny asked incredulously.

"At the hospital, they said that there was 'nothing in their arsenal of resources to help,'" Kenny explains.

There are barriers along the way when a parent is seeking help for a child on heroin, Kenny complains: the high cost of rehab; insurance companies refusing coverage; centers determining whether the child is going through withdrawal and what stage they're at. Or parents can go the legal route, family court, which the Clarks opted for. Because of Steven's "menacing behavior" and his reluctance to get help, they took out an order of protection, which Steven violated the following day. The Clarks took the next painful step of having their young son arrested. At this point Steven was shooting three to six bags of heroin a day.

Kenny describes his interactions with his junkie teenage son: "His verbal outbursts take manic energy into a realm where anger is displayed by fits of cursing, projectile verbal crap coming at me as his face is pressed against mine. Threats like 'I'd love to knock you out' are viciously given in these face-to-face confrontations after short rational discussion has driven off the cliff. From zero to 90 in three seconds. The explosive anger, usually a day after his drug use, takes on ugly dimensions and leaves me emotionally exhausted and stuck in a hopeless place. I look to make sure that the windows are not open, and the neighbors have not seen and heard the drama. My pride and embarrassment have long ago evaporated into the dark void of my not-so-private distress."

Imagine this being your day-to-day life. Now double it when you find out your second child is also addicted to heroin. Kenny's older son, Bobby, 21, was hiding under the radar while all eyes were on Steven. And heroin was his drug of choice, too.

But Kenny didn't know, and since Steven was the obvious problem at hand, it all but consumed him.

"I sometimes think I will lash out at [Steven]," says Kenny. "I was never violent with my kids. Perhaps I should have been. On more than one occasion I did call the police. The disease of chemical dependency has taken much of my serenity and peace."

So because Steven broke the order of protection, Kenny thought that he'd get his son into the legal system, which would help place him into a mandated rehab program. The next day, on June 26, Steven went before a judge in criminal court in Central Islip for violating the order of protection by stealing money from Kenny's checking account and exhibiting aggressive behavior. "The judge was good. He knew I needed help," says Kenny.

Steven had taken his parents' ATM card and stolen more than $1,000 from their account.

Kenny stood before the judge, and with his voice cracking, said, "I am on a mission to save my kid."

On June 27, Steven was going to go through withdrawal and voluntarily admit himself to Nassau University Medical Center, in East Meadow for treatment. In order to be admitted, an addict has to be in active withdrawal. So Steven and his parents packed up and drove to Hicksville and checked in at the Econo Lodge. To pass time, Kenny and Steven went fishing while waiting for the withdrawal symptoms to kick in. At 5 P.M., when Steven was sick enough to be taken to the hospital, they packed his bag and drove toward hope—NUMC.

When they arrived at the ER, there were four other kids going through withdrawal, Kenny says, and one adult. After waiting almost four hours, Kenny says they were finally seen by a counselor.

"I need your driver's license," the intake counselor said to Steven.

"He doesn't have one," answered Kenny.

"We can't take him without it," said the counselor.

"He' a goddamn junkie," yelled Kenny, losing his patience. "He lost his license. He has a birth certificate, a social security card and two parents with him! We can't take him home, he's going through withdrawal."

"But these are the rules."

"Screw your rules," Kenny said angrily. But it was Steven who was screwed.

The counselor made a call to Flushing Hospital Medical Center detox unit to see if they had a bed for Steven, and they did. So the family drove right over. On the way they stopped so Steven could get a slice of pizza. While he was waiting for his slice, a girl entered the pizzeria and bought a bag of heroin from the man behind the counter.

When they arrived at FHMC, they were informed that the center couldn't accept their insurance. "How much will this cost?" Kenny asked.

"One thousand dollars a day," they said.

"Bottom line," says Kenny. "I'll do whatever I have to do."

Steven went through the six-day program and returned home. The Clarks were not satisfied; they had to get him more inpatient treatment. So they brought him to Seafield Center, in Westhampton, on the Fourth of July. Out of pocket: another $3,000 for a week at Seafield.

Imagine Kenny's surprise when he was called the next day and was told that another patient had smuggled some heroin into the center, and Steven was using again.

Seafield—despite letting this happen under its watch—was going to kick Steven out, but eventually let him stay. Unfortunately, Steven was evicted soon after, for fraternizing with a female patient, passing notes back and forth, which was against the rules.

Drugs finding their way into rehab is a big problem, Kenny says. He says that after Steven scored at Seafield, Kenny was told that addicts should have the tools in place to be able to reject it. "I don't buy that," says Kenny angrily. "How can they reject that while they're in the throes of addiction?"

Two weeks after leaving Seafield, Steven attended an anniversary meeting at Alcoholics Anonymous for his father's first year of sobriety. His father's sponsor, a reformed addict and now an addiction counselor, began mentoring Steven. It seems to have made a difference. "He's much better," says Kenny. "All the way, better. That man is a godsend." Then, Kenny, the weary realist, admits, "Well, maybe [Steven's] used once or twice."

While all this was going on, Bobby was getting heavily into heroin. He had already had several years of trouble with alcohol addiction, then moved on to Vicodin and then heroin.

Bobby had been a mellow child. But now the cursing, drama, and fighting were rearing their ugly heads in the Clark household again.

Bobby started physically wasting away. Although he maintained his employment at Applebee's in Lake Grove, his father calls the work environment there "a pharmaceutical center," and Bobby continued using.

But Kenny isn't so naïve that he completely blames others. "We parents enable these kids," warns Kenny. "We buy and pay for their car. We buy them clothes. We give them money and these lifestyles they lead. We let them have cell phones, which they end up using to buy drugs. When I was a kid, I used to think heroin addicts were the scum of the earth and would come from broken-down slums and from the boroughs. But now it's in Smithtown, Stony Brook, Massapequa . . . because kids have everything they want at their disposal.

"And the schools are no help either," complains Kenny.

"Snorting heroin is a socially accepted addiction," he says. "Like marijuana."

The fact that Bobby was using in the same house as the recovering, vulnerable Steven caused another level of concern.

Three weeks ago, Kenny found a looped belt in the back of Bobby's car. When he searched the glove compartment he found a bag filled with about eight hypodermic needles, and in the car's side pocket he found a half "buckle" (five to seven bags) of heroin—some of it already gone.

When confronted, of course, Bobby—with his broken-out face and gaunt appearance—denied drug use. "If we would have caught him with a needle in his arm, he would have denied it," says Kenny, who opted to call the cops. That would lead to mandatory rehab, he hoped.

But in this never-ending world of false starts and false hopes, the cops were unable to do anything. "Unless we find it [heroin] on him," they said.

Things escalated. Bobby stole his mother's wedding and engagement rings—rings she had inherited from her mother.

After an emotional confrontation, Kenny and his wife finally forced Bobby to comply—he was now their prisoner and he was going to go through withdrawal, away from his friends. But, sneaky as he was, Bobby managed to get some heroin from a neighbor friend—the son of a cop.

All hell broke loose, and Bobby ended up wrapping a dog leash around his neck in a half-hearted suicide attempt. Kenny called the cops and Bobby ran away with his 49-year-old father in hot pursuit. A mile and a half later, an exhausted Kenny caught up with his son after the boy collapsed in a stranger's backyard. Kenny collapsed later in the cop car, where he was given oxygen. All the while their neighbors watched—neighbors, Kenny says, who are blind to the fact that their kids are heroin users as well. Their kids were doing drugs with his son. He tried to warn them, but some refused to listen.

The journey of junkies that is familiar to most parents was just beginning: the wild ride from one hospital to another, one rehab center to the next, for short stays or being rejected for any number of reasons.

Bobby was first brought to Stony Brook University Hospital's emergency psych department. They determined that there was no active withdrawal, so they were unable to help. "They didn't want to deal," says Kenny. Eastern Long Island Medical Center, in Greenport, has very high criteria for admission and they too rejected Bobby, saying he was not exhibiting proper symptoms. Opiate addiction is not considered life threatening.

Kenny and his wife then took Bobby to a Riverhead hotel so the withdrawal process could begin. While calling rehab centers from his cell phone in the parking lot of the $300-a-night hotel, Kenny found empty bags of heroin on the ground. There is just no escaping this, he thought. Bobby had not yet gotten into deep withdrawal, so they moved on to Kenny's AA sponsor's home in Port Jefferson, where they crashed on his couch for two days. As Bobby's withdrawal symptoms worsened, they felt he was ready to go for an intake at the Seafield Center Amityville facility. But Seafield rejected Bobby because of his earlier suicide attempt. At this point Kenny started driving to the alcohol recovery-based Matt Talbot

Retreat Center, in Bohemia, but on the way there Seafield called back and said they had reconsidered and that their center in Westhampton would admit Bobby. The crazed traveling road show was about to come to an end.

After 21 days of mandated rehab at Seafield, Bobby shows signs of improvement. His skin has cleared up, his eyes are clearer. He was released this past Sunday, but on Monday night he tested positive for drugs. Bobby says it was from a painkiller he received at Seafield.

"It's important to tell parents who might have similar problems with their kids that the hope of recovery can be found in the rooms of Al-Anon, Family Association (Day Top Family Assoc.), Families Anonymous, Alateen, Narcotics Anonymous, and AA. If it were not for [this], my sons' addictions would not be addressed the way in which they have, and potentially, they would be dead.

"Tough love also helps," adds Kenny, who knows better than to believe this is the end.

"I have to do everything I can to save my kid," he says, crying. "I'll do everything I can and more."

The Never-Ending Story

In Sachem, Charlotte Mason has been fighting what she calls "a 20-year battle" to save her son, Brett, who has been an addict since he was 15. He is now 35, and he is still her baby. In many ways.

"I searched for any way to help. When he first started drugs it was before the Internet. I was calling 800 numbers and reading every book I could read," she explains.

Charlotte didn't waste any time when she realized her oldest son was on drugs. It was September 1989, the start of Brett's ninth-grade year, and she went to Principal Charles Cardillo at the former Sachem South High School.

"Listen," she recalls saying to Cardillo, "I understand that [Brett] is doing drugs and dealing drugs in school. I need help." Cardillo's answer: "There is no drug problem in this school."

She then brought Brett to his pediatrician, Marvin Leiber, M.D., of Holbrook, who had a brief, private meeting with

Brett and said, "He doesn't have a drug problem. He has an attitude problem."

And so it went. No one would listen to her.

Brett never finished ninth grade.

Things came to a head when Brett got in a physical altercation with his stepfather, George, who was devoted to helping his stepson. Brett called the cops on his stepfather and Child Protective Service caseworkers were eventually called to the Mason house. According to Charlotte, as soon as they arrived and met Brett and spoke with Charlotte and George, they realized what the situation was—parents dealing with a drug-addicted kid. Charlotte asked them, "Where can we go for help?" They had no answer.

"Nobody could help us. We sought out every kind of help. Al-Anon meetings didn't work; it was just people sharing their misery. I wanted action. I wanted to be proactive." That was two decades ago, and Charlotte and Brett are still fighting the same demon.

In between? Here's a sampling: in 1989 Charlotte tricked Brett and left him at South Oaks Hospital in Amityville for treatment, when he was 15. He was there for five months. Doctors there suggested that he be sent away for more long-term rehab, but Charlotte refused. "I couldn't let my baby go for 18 months," she says. She now desperately regrets that decision.

"From that point on, it just never stopped," Charlotte says wearily, about trying to help Brett recover from his ongoing heroin habit.

Because of his addiction, for the past 10 years Brett has been in trouble with the law. In 1999 he was arrested in Vail, Colorado, for possession and placed on probation in New York. With Brett now on heroin, things began to escalate. In September 2003 he completed 28 days of rehab in Seafield in Westhampton and was living in a halfway house. He was arrested for shoplifting in Queens and sent to Rikers Island, then extradited back to Colorado for violating his probation. He served approximately two years in prison in Colorado, where he remained sober and healthy.

He got out of prison on May 25, 2006, and returned to Long Island, still on probation, which recently ended this past

August. He was clean for a while, but began shooting heroin again. Even on probation.

That's how it was . . . on and on and on and on, for 20 years. It's amazing that Charlotte can joke about anything, but she is a strong woman. What she thinks about in the deep of night, no one wants to know.

"Why can't I stop?" he asked his distraught mother. "Help me. Help me. Help me."

How can a parent respond to a request like that?

"My son is going to die. Help me save my son," Charlotte cried to anyone who would listen, this past July, during a road trip similar to the Clarks.' Brett went through withdrawal in the car for four days as he was bounced between hospitals like the tennis ball at the Federer-Murray U.S. Open match.

It began with phone calls on July 18 to the Long Island Center for Recovery in Hampton Bays, Queens Hospital, Beth Israel Medical Center in Manhattan, Cornerstone Drug Treatment Center in Jamaica, Southside Hospital in Bay Shore, and Mather Hospital in Port Jefferson—they all refused to take him. Either there were no available beds or they didn't accept their insurance, Medicaid.

On July 20, Charlotte brought Brett to Eastern Long Island Hospital—you remember them, the ones with the high criteria. As with Steven Clark, Charlotte was told Brett was not detoxing enough. They brought him back the next morning and were told that his insurance wouldn't cover it.

"You have to take him. You have to save my child," Charlotte cried. But to no avail.

They kept calling hospital after hospital and no one was able to take him.

There was no choice but to detox him at home, with his brother, parents, and recovering-addict friends at his side.

The detox was "violent," Charlotte says. From July 21 to 23, Brett had a high fever and was sweating profusely, vomiting, and unable to eat or drink.

"I never left his side," says Charlotte. But she did leave to go to the bathroom. She says, "Unfortunately he could no longer take the suffering and snuck away from me for minutes, snuck out of the house and got high."

After he returned high, Charlotte and Brett's brother drove Brett from their Sachem home to NUMC in East Meadow, where, after hours of evaluation, he was turned away because they had no beds. Someone from NUMC called Mary Immaculate Hospital in Queens, and Charlotte was advised that there were two beds available. They rushed to MIH to learn that those beds had been taken in that short period of time it took to get there. There's no shortage of junkies.

"It was just heartless," says Charlotte. "Was I supposed to leave him on a doorstep?"

They brought him back home and the next morning they took him to South Oaks, where he detoxed for the next five days.

Medicaid would not pay for any more time, despite desperate pleas from Brett's doctor and therapist for long-term rehab. Medicaid suggested he try outpatient services.

Currently, Brett is an outpatient at Seafield, in Medford, and he sees a therapist and attends daily Narcotics Anonymous meetings.

Charlotte has spent the past 20 years consumed by fighting with doctors, negotiating with insurance companies, arguing with Medicaid, searching for medical help, paying legal costs, and wondering if her son would be alive by the end of any given day. There was hardly ever a minute of peace. For 20 years, and still going.

"I'm always waiting for the shoe to drop," she says.

"My biggest fear is getting that phone call that he OD'd. I hope no one has to go through this with their child."

"I'm Gonna Save Her"

Here's a cautionary tale for all the invincible kids who think that if they take a snort of heroin they can stop when they want. Ever hear of Natalie Ciappa, the 18-year-old from Massapequa who died of an overdose this past June 21? She only snorted heroin; she never shot up.

Natalie was that knockout beauty who attended Plainedge Senior High. You know all about her: the cheerleader, the great singer who sounded like Mariah Carey, the honor student with a 113 average. The girl with everything to live for. The one whose father found her on her acquaintance's couch, unconscious, her jaw so stiff with rigor mortis that her father's attempts at CPR were futile.

It's amazing that one small little packet of powder can do so much damage. One quick sniff can change so many lives in such an irreparable, tragic way.

The life of Doreen Ciappa, Natalie's mother, was not supposed to turn out this way: a mother burying her teenage daughter. It was not the way things turn out in the vampire romance novels Doreen writes. There is no death in that world. Just everlasting life.

What was everlasting for Doreen and her husband, Victor, was their nightmare watching their daughter waste away and their continual fight to keep her alive.

"We hit every roadblock there was," says Doreen. "They were pretty much everywhere." A suspicious Doreen asked a doctor of Natalie's to run a drug test. She was told they couldn't do it without Natalie's permission because of privacy laws. "They can't do it when they're underage, and they can't do it when they're over the age," complains Doreen. "It's at their discretion." Doreen, now on a mission, is attempting to change those laws.

She eventually went to Natalie's pediatrician and desperately pleaded, "I have to know what's going on." The doctor understood the seriousness of the situation and ordered a urine test that ended up showing marijuana and opiate use. "We were concerned at that point with OxyContin," says Doreen. "Heroin never entered my mind. In my generation [a girl like Natalie] never did heroin."

Natalie's behavior began to change. "She became very volatile," says Doreen. "She shoved passed us. She missed curfews. She didn't care about anything. She tore the house apart. Oh my God, it was completely unlike her." Before this, Natalie was the dream daughter. "It's the kid you feel good about that you have to worry about," Doreen warns.

Natalie was certainly the child that everyone wanted their kids to hang around with. She was in All County Choir, in the National Honor Society, a cheerleading coach, and she was employed at a local pizza place. All that soon fell apart when she began dating Phil Ordaya, 21, who was busted for possession a month after Natalie died. The Ciappas have since learned that Natalie began experimenting with heroin when she attended a party with Ordaya, and his ex-girlfriend gave Natalie a drug to sniff that Natalie thought was cocaine. It was heroin.

"When we first met him," says Doreen, "he was so quiet, shy, polite. He wasn't really like the other boys Natalie dated." Of course he wasn't. He was a heroin addict.

The once-beautiful Natalie was now losing a lot of weight and developing dark circles under her eyes. She was moody, violent even, and in school, her eyes, with those beautiful long dark lashes, fluttered shut in mid-class as she nodded off.

When confronted by a teacher about her behavior, clever Natalie told the teacher that she might be depressed. So in 2007—in the spring of 11th grade—Doreen says that Natalie's guidance counselor, Lisa Madison, at Plainedge Senior High School, called her to inform her that Natalie had a "depression" problem. Doreen had her own suspicions, and when she told Madison and the school psychologist, Lauren Marcano, her concerns, Marcano later got back to Doreen and told her, "I just met with Natalie and told her she looks great."

That following summer of 2007 Natalie really started to fall apart. Her weight fell dramatically, her behavior was deteriorating, and her overall appearance was even sicklier.

At the beginning of Natalie's senior year, Doreen, again, asked the school officials to check out her daughter. Natalie had already missed a few days of school because she was ill.

"I can't get her to go for therapy, so maybe you can see her once a week. I need you to see her," she pleaded to Marcano.

Doreen says that Marcano reported back that Natalie explained away her appearance by saying that she had a good exercise and diet regimen.

"Yeah, it's called drugs," Doreen angrily responded, in disbelief.

"She says she's happy, and she looks fine," Marcano said.

Fine? Natalie had lost 30 pounds, dropping from around 135 pounds to 105. Maybe it was the dark circles under

Natalie's sunken eyes that looked so good to the guidance counselor.

To make matters worse, Madison, Natalie's counselor, suggested Natalie apply to Arizona State University, a notorious party school far away from her parents' jurisdiction.

Things continued to deteriorate for Natalie, culminating on Memorial Day 2008, when she OD'd. Her parents found her on her bed in the morning when they woke; she was cold, blue-lipped and not moving. They touched her arm and she let out an otherworldly sound—it was Natalie trying to breathe. Victor attempted CPR, and hysterical Doreen called 911. Incredibly there was an ambulance already on the corner of their street. The emergency crew was unsure about which treatment to perform because they didn't know what drugs the young girl was on.

"This is what I've been finding," said Doreen, handing them small packets of powder. "What is this?"

"Heroin," they answered.

Natalie, whose heart had stopped, was revived at the house and then brought to New Island Hospital in Bethpage, in what Doreen was told was "very bad condition."

Five hours after Natalie was brought back to life, the hospital sent her home.

Sorry—did you think you read that wrong? I'll repeat it.

Five hours after arriving at the hospital from a heroin overdose, the hospital discharged Natalie.

The hospital psychiatrist, Faiza Khan, M.D., had briefly examined Natalie.

"If she spent five minutes with her, I'm being generous," says Doreen angrily. Bipolar disorder was the diagnosis.

"That psychiatrist had everything in her power. They had it in their hands. They could have turned this around," says Doreen, starting to cry.

"Keep her here for psychiatric evaluation, if nothing else," she pleaded. Natalie was a cutter and had a deep gash on her wrist. Doreen told the doctor, "This was a suicide attempt, keep her here." The hospital refused. She had to leave.

"We were crying. We were saying, 'Please keep her here,'" Doreen recalls. "You have to save my child. I'm begging you, please, please. We don't know what to do anymore."

Natalie, embarrassed, said to her mother, "You should have just let me die." Well, that was the last thing Doreen was going to let happen. But it was a constant struggle.

Three days after the overdose, Natalie came home high. She and her mother had a talk.

"You think you love me, but you don't," Natalie said to her distraught mother.

"But I do," said Doreen, crying while recounting the conversation. "I do."

"No, you love the girl you think I am. The girl I used to be, but you can't possibly love me now. You can't love this girl," Natalie said, arms outstretched to her mother.

"I love you," Doreen told her. "I'll always love you."

That night, Doreen stayed up watching Natalie from 11:30 P.M. to 5:30 A.M., making sure she was breathing.

During the following days, Doreen began calling rehab center after rehab center, across Long Island and around the country: YES, in Massapequa, South Oaks, Seafield, Eastern Long Island Hospital, Caron Treatment Center in Pennsylvania ($53,000 for three months), and centers in other locations such as Florida, for information and help. By now, you know the routine, and the result. No help forthcoming. Plus, Natalie didn't want help. She, like the other addicts interviewed for this story, believed she could do it herself.

Doreen even threatened Natalie with arrest: go to rehab or go to jail. Nothing worked.

It was downhill after that. Natalie fought Doreen at every turn. "You're going to have to pick me up and knock me out," Natalie threatened.

"If I didn't have two little kids at home, I would have knocked her out and dragged her in," Doreen says now with a hint of regret. "But I was afraid I'd lose my [younger] kids." "Don't touch me," Natalie warned her. "You're not allowed to touch me." As with most of the other parents trying to intervene in their child's addiction, things finally did get physical, and there was at least one incident when Doreen had to physically fight and wrestle Natalie to obtain her pocketbook. When she finally got it and checked it, she found heroin in it. And that became a bargaining chip— "Go to rehab or go to jail" now had some weight behind it. Doreen did one other thing, which she recommends to all parents of addicts: Copy your kids' telephone contact list.

"That was how we were able to find her the morning she died," Doreen says.

Doreen never gave up fighting to save her daughter. But doors were shutting closed on them wherever they went.

Natalie gave in and chose to check out South Oaks. But that took weeks, with overdue returned calls and in-the-future appointments. Finally, she was evaluated and was given two more appointments. She never lived to see them.

One day, Natalie's then-13-year-old brother, Nick, told Doreen, "Ma, I'm gonna save her."

"I told him, 'Don't put that on your shoulders,'" Doreen said. "I'm an adult and I don't know how to save her.'"

On May 25, 2008, five hours after arriving as an overdose patient, Natalie had been discharged from New Island Hospital, despite the protestations of her parents.

Overdosing again, one month later, on June 21, she was pronounced dead at New Island Hospital. ➣

Natalie's Law

Timothy Bolger

DECEMBER 18, 2008

In a standard show this week at the Nassau and Suffolk Legislatures, a teenaged choir serenaded lawmakers, high school dancers flaunted their moves, and whiz kids paraded their academic awards. Any of them could have been Natalie Ciappa, the late 18-year-old Massapequa girl who was equally gifted, but instead became the new poster child for the Long Island heroin epidemic when she fatally overdosed in June. The talented singer, beautiful cheerleader, and above-average honors student received awards similar to the citations that legislators handed out like Santa—a far cry from your typical junkie. Yet in death, the Plainedge High School graduate, who was awarded a scholarship to SUNY Old Westbury, starred in the role of her life as two bills that aim to root out the spreading heroin scourge were named in her honor.

Spurred by a special series of reports by the *Long Island Press*, the Natalie Ciappa Law passed nearly unanimously in both legislatures after much debate. Nassau County Executive Tom Suozzi is expected to sign the bill into law, although a spokesman for Suffolk County Executive Steve Levy would not commit, saying he has yet to review the legislation. Under the law, IT (information technology) staff with police departments in Nassau and Suffolk counties would have until March 16—Natalie's birthday—to start mapping heroin possession and sales arrests on the Internet. There are talks of the counties pooling resources to create a regional website, since both bills mandate that the information be updated monthly with the date, time, location, and defendant's age. The ultimate goal of the website is to pinpoint heroin "hot spots" and inform concerned parents to make sure their kids avoid those areas, proponents say.

Without the planned website, here's what we know: heroin-related arrests are up 30 percent in Nassau with 198 through November of this year, compared to 152 in all of 2007. Suffolk has a 28 percent increase, with 766 arrests, up from 597 for the same time periods, an increase attributable to Island-wide police efforts to investigate overdose cases. In May, Nassau police held a summit for school officials and alerted the public to the increase in heroin use among young adults, especially in the county's southeast corridor. State mental health officials report an increase in opiate overdose-related emergency room visits on LI, while national anti-drug advocates report the mean age for first-time heroin use fell from 26 to 21 years old. And as the *Press* investigation into high school heroin use ["Long Highland," June 26] revealed days after Natalie died, new users often start in their teens nowadays.

"The pain and anguish that this family is feeling could have been prevented," says Legislator David Mejias (D-Farmingdale), who proposed the bill on November 18, of Doreen and Victor Ciappa, Natalie's parents, who are now on a mission to pass a similar law statewide. "Had [Doreen] known that there was a heroin epidemic in the Massapequas, she could have done something about it," Mejias says, blaming school districts for what has been described as "ostrich-like behavior." Mejias charged the schools as being more interested in protecting their image than alerting parents on the issue.

Legislator Wayne Horsley (D-Lindenhurst), who proposed Suffolk's version of the bill the same day as Mejias, says that the plan is "putting a light, opening a window, on this issue that has caught so many by surprise." School denials—combined with the fact that younger users snort or smoke the increasingly potent, highly addictive opiate instead of shooting up— make it more difficult for parents to notice, a pattern that has proved deadly.

If the Ciappas knew that there was a student arrested with 28 bags of heroin in Massapequa High School in October 2007—a fact that the school district was caught lying about to the *Press*—they would have considered heroin a possible cause of Natalie's troubles and sent her to rehab, says Victor.

With the information to be provided on the website, Natalie's family hopes fewer parents will have to suffer as they have. "There is no excuse for anybody saying they didn't know," says Doreen, urging parents to put the information to use. "This law will mean nothing if people don't take action, so I am pleading with parents to go on this site and check it regularly. We want to make sure that other people have every opportunity to save their children."

Smack Down

Although the bill passed, it did not come without a fight and some compromise. The original draft did not include the website and instead required police to directly notify school districts when there is a heroin arrest within their district. But officials from the Nassau-Suffolk School Boards Association (NSSBA) were adamant that direct notification would leave school districts open to lawsuits—a position that received mixed reactions on either side of the county line.

Mejias maintained the direct notification portion of the bill was necessary and chastised the NSSBA, while taking the suggestion to also notify PTAs, civic groups, and houses of worship. To not notify schools directly "takes away completely the spirit of the bill," Mejias said following a December 1 public hearing on the proposal. His final version still included the notification, but added an amendment meant to prevent schools from being sued, which led to hours of debate before the final vote on Monday, December 15. If a school received information but did nothing with it because they felt that the information was too vague, but then a student died, the district could be held liable, the association argued.

Jay Breakstone, vice president of the Bellmore-based NSSBA, was not pleased with the fact that the direct notification to schools remained in the Nassau bill. "What I feared two weeks ago has come to fruition: The impression seems to have been left that the school board association is in favor of heroin use on Long Island," he testified in what became a loud back-and-forth with Mejias. After assurances from an official with the Nassau County Attorney's office that any lawsuit brought against a school district under the law would lose, the legislators voted unanimously in favor of the bill, with one abstention because that legislator represents a school district in his law practice.

"So what that a school has a liability to tell the parents that there's a drug dealer in the school?" Mejias asked rhetorically, noting that districts notify parents when there's a sex offender in the neighborhood or lice in the schools. The bill does not mandate that the school do anything with the information, just that they be notified.

Horsley, on the other hand, dropped the notification amendment to avoid the liability issue and redrafted the bill to establish what is officially called the Suffolk Drug Mapping Index, modeled after the Parents for Megan's Law website. "Isolating a responsible party may end up being a short-sighted, narrowly focused approach that does little more than consign blame, and relieve other parties of enduring responsibility," he explained in a statement following the change, suggesting that schools are not solely responsible.

Then in the week prior to the final vote in Nassau, Mejias quietly came around to the website idea, amending the bill to create the Nassau Drug Mapping Index. Both lawmakers spoke of possibly merging the two into a regional website. Still, the website wasn't favored by everyone.

Suffolk Legislator Thomas Barraga (R-West Islip) said he has dealt with parents of heroin-addicted children before, and the story is always they same: "Never my child." That is why he believes parents will continue to stick their heads in the sand and, in effect, only help make criminals better prepared. "Dealers and pushers will use the information to their advantage," he said in explaining why he was the only lawmaker on Long Island to vote no, yet still praising the intent. The website "will not remove one drug dealer from the street," he said, because "the pushers will be on the move" if they know where the hotspots for arrests are.

The concern had been echoed by police sources speaking anonymously, but there is a clause in the Nassau bill to prevent against heroin investigations being compromised. Detectives will not release arrest information until the investigation is complete, the same way that some drug possession arrests do not make it into police blotters immediately, so as to not tip off the dealer.

"This particular law, we feel, will aid in identifying areas where heroin usage is prominent and as one of the proactive approaches this department supported in this increasing epidemic," says Detective Sgt. Anthony Repalone, a police spokesman for Nassau. He notes that other crimes such as burglaries and bank robberies have been linked to heroin and that there have been additional fatal heroin overdoses among teens that have not been made public because of medical privacy laws, although he could not provide a number.

According to Detective Lt. Peter Donohue, deputy commanding officer of the narcotics/vice squad, the department has recently established a new process to track any heroin-related incidents encountered by patrol officers. Different codes are affixed to different incidents, such as a heroin possession, sale, or if an officer finds heroin on his or her patrol. When a patrol officer is involved in any heroin-related enforcement, the information must be shared with narcotics.

"There has been payoff with the new system. It enables us to get a real handle on things," says Donohue. "The junkie wants to get out of jail. They will sell out their connection in a heartbeat to get out to get more."

A spokesman for Suffolk police did not return repeated calls seeking comment.

Natalie's Law Beyond LI

A website is by no means a silver bullet to an issue this complex, but continuing to raise awareness is a good start, officials say. "This bill is one piece of a puzzle," Mejias says. Horsley has mentioned amending the bill next year to include other hard-drug arrests, such as cocaine, methamphetamines, and prescription drugs.

That would prove useful as kids often are introduced to the opiate world at "pharm parties," in which they raid their parents' medicine cabinet for high-strength pain killers such as Vicodin, OxyContin and Percocet. It not uncommon for kids to crush up the pills to sniff them, opening the door to intranasal drug abuse, and since today's heroin is easy to get and can be found for as cheap as $5 a bag on Long Island, that next step is easier than ever before, drug counselors say.

Yet despite the undeniable prevalence, denial still runs rampant. "This bill imposes no obligation on the school to add heroin awareness curriculum or to educate its administrators, teachers, and staff on the dangers of heroin," testified Oscar Michelen, a lawyer, professor, and anti-drug lecturer. As the founder of the Law Squad, Michelen offers drug abuse and criminal justice seminars to schools, but often finds that "they don't want the tough ones" about hard drugs. "They ask for more of a fluff piece such as how to protect yourself at prom," he says.

But with the website, involved parents can cajole unresponsive school boards, not that school officials say they'll need it. "Once we find out that we have hot spots, we have an education forum that we can move forward with," says Fred Langstaff, area director of the New York State School Boards Association. But the local pressure will have to be up to other parents, as the Ciappas have their sights set elsewhere.

"What's happened here I think is the first step in proving that there's enough people out there that that law is wrong," says Victor while planning the next Natalie's Law benefit concert to help lobby for a federal law that they hope to get passed. "We're financially responsible for them until they turn 21, but we can't check them into rehab when they need it, if they need it, when they're 18," he says. He learned the reason behind Natalie's unusual behavior two months after her 18th birthday, so she was able to refuse rehab. Only a judge could force her, provided she was arrested.

"When a kid is in their darkest hour, a parent is probably their last line of defense, or their last help, and when you take that parent's right away, it's really not helpful to the kid and they're still 18—as far as I'm concerned they're still kids," he says.

Generation Junk

Natalie's family had no idea she was abusing heroin because she sniffed it and didn't have the track marks from using needles to shoot up, the most obvious sign of heroin abuse. To cover up the physical signs of drug use, kids will try to hide themselves. Here are the more subtle signs for parents to look for:

- A hat being used to cover the eyes or long sleeves worn at inappropriate times
- Persistent blank expressions and increased lethargy
- Changes in temperament; lethargic or aggressive behavior
- Excessive sniffling and nose-blowing
- Avoiding conversations by giving short yes or no answers
- Falling asleep mid-sentence, in their food, or at other inappropriate times ➴

"HOW I GOT THAT STORY"

In April 2008 the Long Island Press *got a lead that turned into an incredible story— and a true public service, since it exposed a deadly increase in the use of heroin at local high schools. In this interview with* Westword *editor and AAN Editorial Committee member Patricia Calhoun, News Editor Tim Bolger recalls how a tip grew into AAN's Public Service award winner.*

This project started out as a human interest story—at what point did you realize that you had a much, much bigger story on your hands?

We initially got a tip from a methadone nurse who told us that many of her son's friends had fatally overdosed on heroin and that her son was addicted as well. We sat on her phone number for a couple of weeks while we tried to do some research on the topic. Then about a month later, when the local police department in the neighboring county held a big conference with school superintendents warning them that there was a new alarming trend of teens being arrested for heroin, that's when we realized this source was for real and we had to start digging into this full throttle.

How did you find the time and resources to tackle this project?

This was a rare story in that the then-Editor–In-Chief, Robbie Woliver, the then-Managing Editor Mike Martino, and I all teamed up. Usually we were all working on our own thing, but we realized early on that this was too big for just one of us to take on alone. At the time, I was a staff writer, so I was the only one out of the three of us who really had the freedom to pound the pavement and talk to the kids in the streets in affected neighborhoods. That's not to say that Robbie and Mike didn't get out of the office, but for the angles they covered, they relied on interviews at set times and places. It was also a bit of a role reversal for Mike and me. I'm the crime beat reporter, but he got in good with the cops for this story. He was the political reporter, but I was the one hounding the school districts to find out what they were doing with the information that the police had given them. At times it almost was like a "too many chefs in the kitchen" situation, but in the end it paid off.

What were the particular challenges working on a piece that involved not just minors, but such personal stories?

Seeing Doreen and Victor Ciappa, the parents of Natalie Ciappa, who became the poster child of this epidemic, out at press conferences crying before the cameras with such frequency after this thing became fully exposed can be tough to watch. They are just so angry that the school did not alert them to the fact that there was evidence of this going on in the community and they had to find out by their daughter overdosing. On the one hand it is inspiring to see them turning this tragedy into a teachable moment and getting out there and sounding the alarm, but on the other hand their story brings the room to tears every time they tell it, and I can't tell if it's cathartic for them or just pouring salt in the wound. It's been two years now since they lost their daughter and still, for them it's like yesterday.

When authorities put up their roadblocks, what did you do to get around them?

When Massapequa sent us the letter suggesting their lawyers contact our sources to ensure the accuracy of our story, we were both pissed off at the suggestion that they thought we or the police were wrong and excited that we were going to get to show the world that this was how far the school was going to protect its image. I handled the initial call from the publicist who suggested that we were putting our credibility on the line, but once there were threats of lawyers getting involved, Mike took it from there and spoke with the publicist and the school superintendent. Having someone with a background in PR who knows the tricks of the trade proved essential in cutting through their no-holds-barred spin.

How closely did the lawmakers who proposed new rules in response to this story work with you?
This was not the first time we've inspired some local government action, but this was the first time a story of ours prompted a law to be passed. Mike is probably too modest to tell it this way, but he was the one who told the county lawmaker who represents the neighborhoods most affected to propose a law that would make it impossible for the schools to continue denying there was a problem. The police now send a letter every time there is an arrest in their district. In Suffolk, the neighboring county, I was working on another piece after the heroin story came out when a lawmaker there brought up heroin and how he was trying to figure out a way to address the problem. We didn't really get into specifics, and it wasn't until later that he teamed up with and then later parted ways with the Nassau lawmaker who first proposed the school notification law. Suffolk opted instead for the drug-arrest-mapping website.

Now, almost two years after the initial tip, how has the situation changed at local high schools?
It's a mixed bag. We have a lot of schools that are hosting heroin awareness meetings with parents and it is getting a lot of attention in other local media who all have since started doing their own heroin series, yet a recent poll one of our competitors did found that there's still about a third of the local population that doesn't think heroin is a problem. Even one of the local county executives told Mike in an off-the-record conversation that he didn't think heroin was that big a problem—this after he announced his first anti-heroin initiative about a year after the story of this epidemic first broke. Personally, I've had people say right after hearing a lecture on heroin that they don't believe it, and I can't tell if they mean they're shocked or they literally don't believe it. Maybe it's a little bit of both. But even if awareness has increased, that didn't solve the problem. And funding for a lot of these anti-drug school programs is now at risk due to the economic climate.

Since AAN papers are often considered to be community irritants, what did it mean to win a public service award?

The only other AAN award we've won was a second-place prize for a former freelance Iraq War correspondent, although we've received honorable mentions for investigations and media criticism as well. So for our staff to finally break through with AAN was a big boost for us, but especially for it to be in this category. This story also won public service awards from the Society of Professional Journalists/Press Club of Long Island and the New York Press Association, so when we got word that it was also winning a national public service award, that was about as good as it can get. But these awards, combined with the Casey Medal we won for the story, really put us back on the map and gave us the altweekly street cred we've been striving for since we started publishing eight years ago. It also opened a lot of doors for us in terms of high-level sources who were now more eager to speak with us because they saw us doing seriously important journalism and that we have the ability to get ahead of the curve and write what no one else is talking about. And those doors that it opened also made it more likely that we will continue to be able to stay ahead of the curve and not let this one story be a flash in the pan.

Anything else?

The only other thing I can add is that personally, this story had an odd, completing-the-circle scenario. Seven years earlier, in my last semester of college, I was editor of the newspaper and we exposed the fact that a kid overdosed on heroin in a campus bathroom—but instead of alerting the students, the school just swept it under the rug. An editorial I wrote calling out the administration and warning that there might be a new trend brewing won me a school journalism award that helped get me the internship here, which later led to a job. Looking back, I wish I had thought to keep an eye on this issue before this parent approached us.

The Jackie Walker Story

Betty Bean

NOVEMBER 22, 2007

Has UT's first black All-American been denied hall of fame honors because he was gay? Jackie Walker's brother is on a mission to see that the Vol linebacking great is remembered.

October 16, 1971
Legion Field
Birmingham, Alabama

It was the third Saturday in October, and the Tennessee Volunteers came rolling into town on a four-game winning streak over Alabama's Crimson Tide. Bear Bryant awaited, intent on reversing his fortunes with a new wishbone offense, a retooled team, and a plan so brutally simple that it could be summed up in three words:

Stop Jackie Walker.

The Tide was gunning for Tennessee's senior captain, an outside linebacker whose fearless play had gotten him named an All-American as a junior, despite his slender physique. As a sophomore—freshmen didn't play varsity in those days—Walker and his teammates Lester McClain and Andy Bennett had become the first blacks to play against Alabama on Legion Field, and Walker had returned a bobbled pass for a touchdown. He'd pretty much owned the Tide in the teams' last two meetings, but this game, he would receive the full attention of Alabama's massive offensive line, which was anchored by 265-pound guard John Hannah, who later became a 10-time Pro Bowler in the National Football League and was named "Best Offensive Lineman of All Time" by Sports Illustrated.

Tennessee junior linebacker Jamie Rotella was an eyewitness to the mayhem, and the memory of Walker's valiant, hopeless battle in the 32-15 loss still burns bright.

"Jackie literally knocked himself out trying to stop Alabama's offense," he says. "He bore the brunt of their attack, and they kept coming after him . . . I'm telling you, Jackie took them all on. We didn't really care about concussions then, but he probably had one and continued playing. I was shocked. I couldn't believe Jackie was wearing down, because every game up to this, he'd been Superman. And every game after this, he was Superman."

Rotella's recollections are borne out in East Tennessee State University professor John David Briley's book, *Career in Crisis: Paul "Bear" Bryant and the 1971 Season of Change*. Alabama lineman Jimmy Rosser paid Walker a supreme, if backhanded, compliment:

"There was a nose guard on Jimmy Grammer, but his primary blocking assignment was on Walker. It was Jimmy's responsibility to stand him up on this play. After that, I would hit him on the right side, and then either Kraft or Hannah would come in and hit him from the left side. It was kind of like a sandwich. We did this on other people that year, but it was called the Jackie Walker Play after that."

Rotella didn't know the play had a name, but he's not surprised.

"Jackie weighed 188 and these guys weighed 275—so come on—three on one? It was the only time Jackie Walker was ever neutralized," he says. "Can you understand how shocked I am to hear that he's not in a single hall of fame?"

Rotella, who was elected captain and named an All-American the year after Walker left, is not alone in his shock.

Jackie Walker's talent, success, and historical significance are undeniable. He was not the first African American to play in the Southeastern Conference, but he was the first African American star. In a time when captains were elected by their teammates, he was the first African American to captain an SEC team (one of his alternate captains was offensive lineman Phillip Fulmer). He was the first African American in the SEC to be named an All-American—a feat he would repeat his senior season. His NCAA career record for interceptions returned for touchdowns has been tied, but remains unbroken. He led Tennessee to a record of 30–5 from 1969–1971, winning the SEC Championship in 1969 and the Liberty Bowl in 1971, and his quiet intelligence and winning personality made him a media favorite. The *New York Times* noted that he'd had a singing, dancing role in a campus production of *Fiddler on the Roof* the summer before his senior year, and the Fellowship of Christian Athletes flew him to Miami to sing at one of their national meetings.

While it might be a cliché to say he was the Jackie Robinson of SEC football, it's not a great exaggeration. It would also be true to say that his teammates were shocked to learn that he was gay. Marshall Walker says that's why his brother isn't in a hall of fame.

Jackie Walker has not been named to the National Football Hall of Fame, the Tennessee Sports Hall of Fame, the

Knoxville Sports Hall of Fame, nor has his picture hung on the Wall of Fame in UT's Black Cultural Center.

"They've tried to wipe Jackie's name out of history because of his sexual orientation," says Marshall, who is on a quest to keep a promise he made to Jackie before he died of AIDS in 2002, even though Jackie was dubious about it.

"I told him I was going to get him into the hall of fame or die trying, and he gave me that little smirking laugh, like 'Yeah, right.' I can see him now, just sitting there laughing at me."

Rumors that Jackie Walker was gay started circulating after his senior season and just before he was drafted by the San Francisco 49ers in 1972. Rotella refused to believe what he was hearing."I've always tried to be open-minded, and when the rumors first broke—remember, it was a different time back then, and ballplayers were protected, insulated from a lot of things—when I heard it, I thought 'What is it with these people? They'll make up anything to gossip about.'"

But it was no surprise to Marshall, who had known the truth since the year before, when he'd run into Jackie in the lobby of Hess Hall, where both their girlfriends lived. Jackie was sitting on a rail looking forlorn.

"I asked him what was wrong, and he said 'I told Melanie.' I said 'You told Melanie what?' He said, 'I told Melanie that I'm gay, and, man, she's upset. She didn't take it very well.' Jackie had this secret life for a long, long time," Marshall says. "The girlfriends? That was just a show. At that point, he could NOT let most of his teammates know. I promise you, it was ugly."

Their sister, Norma Jean, who has since died, told Marshall she'd known it all along, and although older members of the deeply religious Walker family struggled to understand the "new" Jackie, Marshall says the revelation never caused a real break.

Campus rumors persisted, and Rotella came to the realization that they were true.

"I was absolutely shocked. There was nobody tougher than Jackie Walker. How could I imagine him being gay? And really, whose business was it anyway? It didn't change the way

I felt about him. I admired him and respected him and looked up to him. There was nobody like him—he was just unparalleled. Statistically, he was probably the greatest defensive player Tennessee ever had. I cannot imagine why he's not in every hall of fame there is."

The rumors reached the ears of UT linebackers coach Lon Herzbrun and UT head coach Bill Battle. Herzbrun coached both Walker brothers at Fulton High School before he was hired at Tennessee. He had been close to the family for a decade, but recalls that as he and Battle were driving across town to the east-side YWCA to attend a party celebrating Jackie's being drafted into the NFL, they were worrying about what they were going to encounter.

Battle told Herzbrun he wasn't going to stay if Jackie showed up in a dress. Herzbrun offered to go in first and look around. The head coach waited in the car while Herzbrun looked for Jackie. When he spotted an attractive woman who looked a lot like Jackie, he tapped her on the shoulder and asked, "Who the hell are you?"

"She said 'I'm Jackie's sister.' It was pretty embarrassing."

Jackie didn't find much success in the NFL. Herzbrun believes that the 49ers weren't patient enough while trying to convert him into a defensive back. Jackie told Daw-U Smith— a friend in Atlanta, where he moved after giving up his NFL dreams—that he was cut from the team when the organization found out he was gay.

Marshall says Jackie found peace in life after football. "When I visited Jackie in Atlanta, I met a lot of prominent people in his environment. Would he bring his partners around? Yes. But he was still discrete. Did I ever see him holding hands, sharing hugs and kisses? No, I never saw any of that. He always had a certain reserve about himself, and he had a lot of pride. I never knew Jackie to intentionally want to harm someone, even as an adult. If you crossed the line, he would settle it right then. Could those rumors about cross-dressing have gotten back to the Athletics Department? Yes."

Born April 14, 1950, to Norman and Violet Wilson Walker, Jackie Eugene Walker's Knoxville was typical of most Southern cities of the day—strictly segregated by race. If he and Marshall went to town, they rode in the back of the bus. If they got thirsty, they drank from a colored fountain. If they wanted to see a movie downtown, they couldn't. They could have visited Chilhowee Park, but only on Thursdays.

"It never crossed our minds to go to Gay Street for anything," Marshall says. "We probably wouldn't have been able to afford it anyway."

The Walkers lived in Austin Homes until Norman and Violet divorced when Jackie was five. Norman got custody of the children: Evaline, Norma Jean, Marshall, Jackie, and Rosalind. Norman was a hard-working, God-fearing man who was the custodian at Fulton High School and a deacon and a trustee at Greater Warner AME Tabernacle. Violet, who worked for the city schools and was a local and regional PTA president, was a Pentecostal and a lifelong member of the God Gospel Singers. Violet later married the Rev. Lewis Thompson. She was a beautiful woman with a sense of style and a fine singing voice, traits Jackie inherited in abundance.

"Jackie was always a sharp dresser," Marshall says. "He got that from our mother. She could make a $5 dress look like a $100 dress."

After the divorce, Norman Walker and the children moved in with his parents, who lived in a house on Delta Avenue that was eventually taken by the city for the construction of Walter P. Taylor Homes. The Walker children were raised to be respectful and polite and never to call adults by their first names. Childhood friends remember Jackie as a fun-loving, joke-cracking kid who was good at sports, but who would just as soon stay home and play with his sisters.

Baseball, played with makeshift bats and taped-up balls, was the sport of choice among the boys in the Walker's Park City neighborhood— "Before everything got 'urban renewaled' away," says Marshall, who remembers the uprooting of neighborhood doctors and a dentist and a library, clubs and restaurants and stores and businesses. "Maybe it was considered 'progressive' at the time, but the individuals making the decisions were not the ones being affected."

Norman Walker left the house early on winter mornings to stoke the boilers at Fulton. Marshall, who sometimes helped his daddy shovel coal in the basement of the big, whites-only high school, remembers that he and Jackie often tagged along so they could play basketball in the school gym, never dreaming they'd ever be able to attend the school where their father was to spend his entire working life. But in the early '60s, a desegregation lawsuit forced the city schools to integrate. It began in the first grade, and was to proceed one grade per year. Austin High remained the only option for black high-school students until the court ruled that the glacial pace of Knoxville's plan didn't meet the "all deliberate speed" mandate of the Supreme Court's 1954 *Brown v. Board of Education* decision.

Marshall was in the first wave of minority students to attend the formerly all-white city high schools. It took the threat of a lawsuit to get him into Fulton (which he was told was overcrowded), but he was finally admitted to take vocational classes. He became an outstanding player for Herzbrun, and graduated in 1966, a year before the University of Tennessee started recruiting black players. He got a scholarship to play at historically black Florida A&M University (FAMU) for the legendary—and supremely quotable—Jake Gaither, a Knoxville College graduate who produced many of the first black NFL players and famously declared that he liked his boys "agile, mobile, and hostile."

Jackie followed Marshall to Fulton, where he excelled at basketball and was a member of the Madrigal singers. But football was where he won acclaim. His senior year, he was voted "Most Athletic," named to the All-State team, and played a key role for the Falcons' undefeated 1967 "Mighty Mites," piling up astounding numbers, including a 33-tackle performance against traditional rival Central. He's best remembered at his alma mater for "The Hit."

Fulton assistant coach Russell Mayes, who graduated from FHS in 1995, grew up hearing about the night Jackie Walker knocked out an Oak Ridge running back.

"As long as I've been in school, I've heard the story about the night Jackie Walker hit the guy from Oak Ridge," Mayes says. "'It sounded like a cannon going off.' 'They had to cut the guy's helmet off.' It was without a doubt the most famous play in Fulton history."

Jackie did a lot of soul-searching over where he should go to college. UT, which had only one black player, Lester McClain, was recruiting him hard. Tim Priest, who became the Vols' all-time interceptions leader as an all-SEC defensive back from 1967 to 1970, was a freshman that year and remembers his first impression of Jackie Walker.

"We were looking for something to do since we were freshmen and weren't playing the next day, and we'd heard about this guy at Fulton that was probably going to come to Tennessee, so we went out to see him. He was amazing. He was flying all over the field, tackling people. I still remember his number: 83."

But Jackie may not have been as sure a thing as Priest thought.

"Jackie called me at school and asked me how FAMU was, and he wondered if he should come there. He was talking about Tennessee, and said 'Man, I don't know about that place. . . I am fearful of playing in the SEC,'" says Marshall Walker.

Specifically, Jackie Walker, who played football with what Herzbrun calls "utter disregard for his physical safety," was afraid of playing in places like Georgia, Mississippi, and Alabama, land of George Corley Wallace and the city blacks had sardonically dubbed "Bombingham."

"He was scared. He didn't know what to expect. He knew he'd probably have to deal with racism, and that had never been an issue for him at Fulton—they probably wore out all that N-word stuff on me," Marshall says. "He was doing a lot of reading, and was well aware that there were no blacks there. But we knew he was at home and would have that family support. We also knew he was good enough to play."

Someone else in Jackie's corner was Herzbrun, a tough and compassionate man who played fullback and guard at UT, graduating in 1958. He coached both the Walker boys in high school, played a pivotal role in their college careers after UT hired him to coach linebackers, and maintains lifetime connections with many former players.

He remembers meeting Jackie in 1965.

"He was there with Marshall and their dad, who was the janitor at Fulton. My earliest recollection of him was that he was talented. He had good speed, quickness, and tremendous courage. I played him at linebacker because he was in a position to hit people, and I also played him at tight end when we got near the goal line so he could help block.

"He wasn't very big and he wasn't very strong, but he had great timing on his explosion. I knew he could be a great football player. I recognized his potential from the very beginning. At Tennessee, I had the privilege of coaching more All-Americans than anyone in the country at that time—Jack 'Hacksaw' Reynolds, Steve Kiner, Jamie Rotella, Ray Nettles—and there aren't many who meet those qualifications."

Herzbrun cared about Jackie Walker:

"He was important to me. That doesn't just go away. I asked an awful lot of players, and he responded as much as anyone I've ever had. A lot of times, when a person has a lot of talent, they really don't do the hard work it takes to be better than anybody else. That's why he was a winner. He had both. He should have been in the hall of fame long before I was.

"If you met him, you wouldn't have guessed he was as aggressive as he was on the football field. He was very quiet, but friendly, and was a guy that everyone liked. He was really talented in many ways—he could sing, had a great voice. Sang in the church. Most people really liked him. I think more than anything, he was so respectful, and he got back that same respect from everyone. I lived in Blount County at the time, and he'd come over to the house all the time, and we'd have spaghetti. He was dating some gal in Alcoa.

"He probably got his physical build from his dad. Everybody at Fulton loved Norman, and Jackie probably got his conscientiousness about accomplishing the task at hand from Norman. Whatever they did, they wanted to be the best at it, and Jackie just had the kind of warm personality that made people care for him."

Marshall has high praise for Herzbrun, whom he says " . . . put his job [at UT] on the line so Jackie could play as a sophomore. He said 'If he's not successful, you can have my job.'

And the first time Jackie hit his man and stood him up, and the other team didn't get the first down, [his teammates] realized Jackie could play. And once they saw that, they were in his corner."

When Jackie finally suited up his sophomore year, his father was waiting anxiously in the stands for his son's home debut. The Vols played Chattanooga, and Jackie picked off his first interception. Afterward, Norman Walker, who had watched white athletes from Fulton like Ron Widby and Bill Justus grow up and win scholarships to UT, talked to the *News Sentinel*'s Marvin West about how it felt to see his son in a Tennessee uniform. "I can't tell you what a good feeling it was to see him playing for Tennessee. . . . There's no better place on earth, as far as I'm concerned." Norman said he "got a thrill out of the interception."

Meanwhile, Marshall, who suffered a serious knee injury at FAMU, transferred to UT and started working out with the team with a conditional promise of a scholarship if his knee held up. It didn't, but Marshall earned two degrees anyway, and is now a social worker with the Knox County Schools. He says few people know the adversities Jackie had to face down to play in the SEC—particularly at away games in Georgia, Alabama, and Mississippi.

"My father and my mother and stepfather made a point of going to all of Jackie's games—especially the away games. They went to every game, everywhere he played—but not me. I never set foot in Mississippi or Alabama."

Noted sportswriter Keith Dunnavant's book *The Missing Ring* tells the story of how Bear Bryant's 1966 team was denied a national championship because of the racist record of Alabama Governor George Wallace. Dunnavant, who writes about the nexus of social issues and sports, doesn't think Marshall was wrong to worry about how Jackie would be treated.

"In terms of the tenor of the times—resistance to integration—there had been a 'gentleman's agreement' among schools of the SEC to not recruit African American players," Dunnavant says. "It was not written in stone anywhere, just kind of understood. Bear Bryant frequently talked about how he had wanted to integrate in the '40s, but was rebuffed because the [university] president at the time believed such an act would risk their membership in the SEC."

Dunnavant echoes the sentiments of every single person who was interviewed for this story:"I cannot imagine, given Jackie Walker's landmark role as a pioneer at the University of Tennessee and in the SEC, that he would not be honored in the state hall of fame. You're talking about a guy who took a step into the darkness, not only for UT, but for the state of Tennessee."

Unfortunately, racial problems didn't stop at the campus borders.

Ralph Boston, winner of three Olympic medals in the long jump (a gold in 1960 when he broke Jesse Owens's record, a silver in 1964, and a bronze in 1968), was UT's coordinator of minority affairs and an assistant dean of students from 1968 to 1975. He got on a plane in Mexico City and came directly to Knoxville after the 1968 Summer Olympics, which were held during the depths of the Vietnam War and are best remembered for the Black Power salute given by sprinters Tommie Smith and John Carlos, who accepted their medals, but stood barefoot on the podium and raised black-gloved fists as the national anthem played.

"This was a sign of the times, really," Boston says. "Not a lot of African American students were comfortable with the way things were happening for them on campus. You could periodically get called the N-word, and a girl who wrote for the *Daily Beacon* got a cross burned on her door. Dick Gregory came to campus and spoke in the old gym, and a group of white guys came in and wrapped themselves in Confederate flags. Marshall Walker got involved in that, and in another protest when Jackie wanted to play Othello. He auditioned, but they gave the role to a white actor, who played it in blackface. The excuse was that Jackie wasn't tall enough."

Meanwhile, the black football players wrestled with issues of playing time and style of play. Jackie's roommate, Andy Bennett, a two-sport athlete who was the "other" black recruited in the class of '68, got in trouble for outrunning his blockers on kick returns and for sporting a mustache.

He says he was able to survive because a black chef sneaked him food out of the kitchen, and because he, Jackie, and Lester McClain created their own support system.

"We were the Three Musketeers. We were teammates and friends and brothers. Jackie was always the peacemaker, and his family 'adopted' me while I was in Knoxville. They fed me and took me to church with them. It would have been hard to make it without them."

In the spring of 1971 someone called a closed meeting of black athletes to discuss a boycott. Football players, members of the track team, and representatives of a group called the African American Student Liberation Front attended, and they were on the verge of calling for a walkout. Boston was there, too.

"The few African American athletes there just kind of decided that they were going to boycott," he recalls. "They had students supporting them who were very much in favor of that, but Marshall Walker came in and said 'Hey, look guys—Jackie feels that he has a chance to be captain of the football team, and if that happens, it could not only help change things here, it could help throughout the SEC.' And they voted to stand down."

The next fall, after Jackie temporarily lost his starting position for talking back to an assistant coach, Marshall wrote a letter to the editor of the *Daily Beacon* that ran December 1, 1970, under the headline "Racial Discrimination in Sports."

He called out the father of Tennessee football, Robert R. Neyland, as a racist and said white coaches believed that "black athletes are supposed to use their bodies and not their minds." He said Lester McClain and Andy Bennett had been unfairly denied playing time, and that "Jackie Walker played only because they didn't have another white player with half his ability." He said discrimination "not only existed on the football field, but it likewise existed in track—and especially in basketball."

The Beacon editorial staff held the letter for awhile, and then ran it with an editor's note quibbling with some of

Marshall's secondary points, but agreed "in essence" with his larger conclusions.

When Jackie's playing days were over, he moved to Atlanta in 1974. Nicknamed "the city too busy to hate" during the early years of the civil rights movement, the Georgia capital had become a mecca for gays from all over the South. Marshall says Jackie needed to get away from Knoxville and its wagging tongues. Daw-U Smith thinks he just wanted to live in a bigger city with more opportunity and more diverse cultural activities. By all indications, Jackie thrived.

He came back to Knoxville frequently to visit his family, and when Norman Walker died in 1995, Jackie wrote a poem and read it at the funeral.

Daw-U Smith, now an artist living in Jacksonville, met Jackie in 1976 when they were both 26 years old and worked for the city of Atlanta in the parks and recreation department. Daw-U, whose name was David Smith in those days, said Jackie not only became a brother to him and an uncle to Daw-U's children, but badgered him into going to adult literacy classes when he found out Daw-U was dyslexic and could not read.

"Knowing Jackie Walker changed my life," he says. "He's the reason I learned to read, and it was Jackie who encouraged me to pursue my art. He believed you should do what you love.

"By the time I met Jackie, he was really comfortable with who he was. He was the captain of our tennis team, and was such a great athlete but was so humble that he didn't even talk much about the things he'd done. One day, we were walking home from Piedmont Park talking about football and he told me he'd played in college. I asked where, and he said Tennessee. I asked if he meant Tennessee State [then a historically black school], and he said 'No. The University of Tennessee.' And then it clicked in my mind, and I remembered watching him play.

"Jackie could do so many things, and he was so respected by so many people. I like to say he was a renaissance man. He lived a full life, and he touched a lot of people. Anywhere he'd go, Jackie had dignity. People knew his lifestyle, but he brought dignity and respect and honor. You can judge a person not just by how he climbed the mountain, but by how he helped other people up the mountain. Jackie made the people around him better.

"He was a really handsome man, too. I used to tell him that when he walked into a room, the women got weak and the sissies got meek."

When Jackie learned that he was HIV-positive in 1998, he cashed in some of his life insurance and traveled the world.

When he began to be desperately sick, Daw-U became his caregiver.

In June 2002 a 20-year-old man in a Lincoln gunned it at a Knoxville side street, jetted across Western Avenue and crashed into Violet Thompson's car, killing her as she was on her way home from church. Both Daw-U and Marshall say that her death broke Jackie's heart and made him lose hope.

Daw-U accompanied Jackie to Knoxville for the funeral and watched as he got up and spoke to the overflowing crowd at Rodgers Memorial Baptist Church. A videotape of the service captures a thin, frail man in a summer sports jacket standing at the podium sharing memories of his mother.

He told of going to PTA meetings with her, and how she'd take his hand and other kids would ask, "'Who is THAT?' And I would say, 'That's my mother!' And I was proud."

He paid tribute to her sweet potato pie and her church work, and promised to see her "on the other side." He closed with a gospel song, his once-rich tenor hoarse and whispery:

"In times like these,
you need a Savior,
In times like these,
you need an anchor.
Be very sure, be very sure,
Your anchor holds
And grips the Solid Rock."

"It took a lot out of him to sing that song," says Daw-U.

Jackie returned to Atlanta, and his health declined sharply. Andy Bennett, who lives in Tampa and owns a high-tech security business, visited him there right after he'd started dialysis. Bennett was shocked at his old friend's condition, but says Jackie tried to stay positive.

Jackie's youngest sister Rosalind and her son were able to spend Thanksgiving with him, and afterward, things went downhill. Daw-U says Jackie was constantly vomiting, and had wearied of the fight. Finally, he fell into a coma from which he never awakened, although Marshall, who drove down from Nashville when Daw-U called him, believes that Jackie knew he was there.

Jackie Walker died December 5, 2002. His family honored his wishes and cremated his remains. There were two memorial services: one at GSN Ministries, which serves Atlanta's gay community, and another at House of God Holiness Church in Knoxville. Herzbrun and Priest attended the Knoxville memorial, and Herzbrun presented the family with an official All-American portrait of Jackie in an orange-and-white frame.

Marshall Walker, who spent a lifetime watching out for his little brother, still has one last thing he wants to do for Jackie. When Jackie's kidneys failed, Marshall had wanted to give him one of his own, but had to abandon that notion when faced with the reality of the situation.

"Jackie said 'It won't do no good, man!' He told me that the virus would kill the new kidney within 24 hours."

So Marshall started working on getting Jackie into a hall of fame. It has been a solitary task, but now it appears that he's no longer alone.

Tim Priest, who is now a Knoxville attorney and a color analyst on Vols' radio broadcasts, is a member of the board of directors of the Knoxville Sports Hall of Fame. Shocked to learn that Jackie has not been inducted, he says he's going to do something about it.

"I've never nominated anybody, but Jackie Walker is certainly worthy in my eyes, and I don't have a clue why he hasn't been included. He's qualified for the National Football Hall of Fame, too. I'll tell you this: His name will be put in nomination. It's time."

Until then, Marshall can take comfort in the certainty that as long as they play football at Fulton, when new freshmen suit up for practice and get that talk about Falcon tradition, somebody's going to tell them about Jackie Walker and the lick you could hear all the way to Broadway. ➥

Local Hero

Betty Bean

APRIL 23, 2008

Jackie Walker, the first African American to captain a University of Tennessee football team and the first African American to be named an All-American from the Southeastern Conference, will be inducted posthumously into the Greater Knoxville Sports Hall of Fame July 17.

Last Thanksgiving, *Metro Pulse* told the story of Marshall Walker's quest to get his brother honored for his gridiron accomplishments, which included not only being a two-time All-American (in 1970 and 1971), but setting an NCAA record for interceptions returned for touchdowns that still stands today. Despite his distinguished career as one of the best of Tennessee's fabled linebackers, Jackie Walker died in 2002 without having been honored by his alma mater nor named to a single sports hall of fame.

Marshall believes Jackie was shunned because he was gay. Many friends and former teammates agree. Jackie Walker moved to Atlanta after college, and died there after a long struggle with complications of AIDS. One of the last times Marshall saw his brother alive, he made him a promise:

"I told him I was going to get him into the Hall of Fame or die trying."

It wasn't that Jackie asked Marshall to do this. "Football didn't define who Jackie was as a person," Marshall says. "Jackie wasn't really much concerned with his lack of recognition."

But that didn't stop Marshall from trying to do this one last thing for his brother, and last week, the long wait ended when the Greater Knoxville Sports Hall of Fame announced that

Jackie Walker will be inducted on a weekend that coincides with an annual family reunion. Walker's family will be in the house for the celebration.

"We haven't really had a chance to digest it yet, but we're all just happy, and real elated," Marshall Walker says. "I'm glad it's finally happening for him. We're just giving thanks to God. I'd been hoping for this for so long."

Since the Jackie Walker story appeared in Metro Pulse last November, it has been told in several media outlets, including a story last week in the *New York Times*. Many of his former teammates have been interviewed, including his classmate, UT's head football coach Phillip Fulmer, who served as an alternate captain the year that Jackie was named captain and is also being inducted this year. Fulmer remembers Walker fondly.

"Though he was always undersized, he was a great player—smart, great speed, and toughness," Fulmer told *Times* correspondent Chris Wohlwend. "And he was a great person." He called Walker "one of the best athletes ever in Knoxville."

Marshall recalls that his fearless little brother was "scared" when Tennessee started recruiting him, and the family was worried about Jackie having to play in stadiums in the Deep South. One of his teammates, Steve Kinder, told WBIR-TV that he remembered resistance to integration within the team, and "the N-word" raining down on Jackie from rival fans.

Jackie Walker's former teammates say that his sexual orientation was never an issue while he was playing, and they were surprised to learn that he was gay later on when he made the decision to live openly. He was drafted by the San Francisco 49ers, but was cut before he ever had a chance to play—maybe because of his small stature (5-11, 178 pounds), maybe because he was gay.

But by all accounts, he moved on with his life and spent two happy, productive decades living in Atlanta. When he learned he was ill, he cashed in his life insurance and traveled the world, reporting back to his family the wonders he had seen. Jackie held on until December 5, 2002. There were two memorial services: one at GSN Ministries, which serves Atlanta's gay community, and another at House of God Holiness Church in Knoxville. Lon Herzbrun, his linebackers coach at

UT, his high school coach at Fulton, and already a member of the Greater Knoxville Sports Hall of Fame, was there, along with his UT teammate Tim Priest, who is being inducted this year along with Fulmer and Walker. Herzbrun presented the family with an official All-American portrait of Jackie in an orange-and-white frame. ➥

A Promise Kept

Betty Bean

JULY 23, 2008

The Greater Knoxville Sports Hall of Fame's annual induction banquet at the Knoxville Convention Center last Thursday was a bittersweet reunion for Jackie Walker's teammates, family, friends, and coaches who came to see him posthumously honored. Many of them were pioneers in their own right. There was Lester McClain, who enrolled at the University of Tennessee in 1968 and was the school's first black football player. And there was Walker's classmate Andy Bennett. The three of them formed their own support system. At the banquet, Bennett and McClain represented sort of a Missing Man formation, Two Musketeers.

Lon Herzbrun, who coached both Jackie and his brother Marshall Walker at Fulton High School, was there, along with FHS legend Bob Black, who loves to tell the story of perhaps the most famous play in local high school football history—the time in 1968 when Walker hit an Oak Ridge running back so hard the lick could be heard all the way down to Broadway.

And there was Fulton teammate Oscar White, who, along with Marshall Walker, helped integrate FHS football and became a career military man. He reached the rank of colonel before he retired, and he lost his wife, Sandra, in the September 11, 2001, terrorist attack on the Pentagon.

Herzbrun, who moved on to become Tennessee's linebackers coach during Walker's freshman year, was flanked by All-Americans Jamie Rotella and Ray Nettles. Under his tutelage,

Rotella and Nettles, along with Walker, Steve Kiner, and Jack Reynolds, established UT as "Linebacker U." Marshall Walker credits Herzbrun with laying his own career on the line to help Jackie. Two more Walker teammates, Tim Priest and Phillip Fulmer, were among the 2008 inductees as well.

Nettles—a fiery, fearless player who invented the team tradition of celebrating defensive touchdowns by greeting the scorer with a flying tackle on the sidelines—is fighting cancer, but in a demonstration of the same gritty resolve that characterized him as an athlete, he flew to Atlanta from his home in Jacksonville, Florida, and caught a ride to Knoxville with Rotella. The banquet turned into a weekend of remembering the good times, like the way they used to wish each other good night through the walls from one room to the next, Waltons-style, when they were on the road.

"Good night, John-Boy," Nettles said. "It was just like tucking the team into bed, and the linebackers, we kind of hung together . . . that's normal. I played ball nine years up in Canada, and Jamie and I have stuck together all these years. With some teammates, all of a sudden it's over and you lose track of people, even though each of them have had something to do with shaping your life. It's like Lon (Herzbrun) always said: 'Choose your teammates wisely. Surround yourself with champions.' And that's what we did. You know your teammates are going to be there for you."

Condredge Holloway, the Alabama prep star who signed with Tennessee in 1971 after Bear Bryant told him, "Son, Alabama's just not ready for a black quarterback," is one of those teammates Nettles talked about. Now an assistant athletics director at UT, he was at the banquet sporting an orange tie. At the meet-and-greet before the dinner, he was reunited with an old rival—Thom Gossam, a Birmingham native who grew up dreaming of being Bryant's first black football player, but instead became a three-year starter at Auburn who has built a career as a screenwriter and actor. Gossam, the first black athlete to graduate from Auburn, was in Knoxville researching a screenplay he plans to write based on the Jackie Walker story. He didn't know him personally, but remembers Walker as a ferocious foe.

The 2008 inductees into the Greater Knoxville Sports Hall of Fame were introduced in alphabetical order, and Walker's was the last name to be called. When Marshall stepped into the spotlight in Jackie's behalf, there was an extra dollop of applause and some audible murmurs of "Hell, yeah." A well-dressed man at a table in the rear pumped his fist and said "About time!"

And what would two-time All-American Vol linebacker Jackie Walker, who entered UT in 1969 and became Tennessee's first black football captain his senior season in 1971, have done if he had been able to attend his induction into the Knoxville Sports Hall of Fame? Most of his old friends, colleagues, and teammates think he would have said very little beyond a simple thank you. They say that he would have flashed his big signature smile. And he wouldn't have had to pretend that he wasn't gay. On this night, it wasn't an issue.

Marshall Walker thinks Jackie would have had a tough message for today's young Vols:

"Jackie'd say, 'Study hard. Go to class. And don't make sports your only goal.' When athletes at UT, especially African American athletes, take these scholarships for granted, they're not showing any respect for history. Jackie and Lester and Andy went through a whole lot to give them this opportunity."

The night represented a promise kept for Marshall. Jackie Walker died of AIDS in 2002 without ever having received any of the post-career honors normally conferred on players of his stature and historical significance. During Jackie's final illness, Marshall promised him that he'd find a way to get him into a hall of fame. Jackie was skeptical, and sure enough, the years went rolling by and nothing happened, despite Jackie's having been one of the most outstanding Knoxville high school athletes ever, the first black All-American in the Southeastern Conference, the first black captain of a Tennessee Volunteer football team, and the holder of an NCAA record for defensive touchdowns that still stands today. Marshall wasn't the only one who believed this was because Jackie had come out as a gay man after his senior season at UT.

Tim Priest, who captained the 1970 Vols when Walker was a junior, is a Knoxville lawyer and UT's official radio color analyst. He probably had as much to do with Walker's induction as anyone, although he is too modest to claim credit. He was given the task of introducing the honorees, and he summed up the team's feelings about Jackie Walker:

"When you looked up and saw number 52 our there, you just felt better about our chances. You couldn't knock him off his feet. On his sophomore team, he played with Kiner and Reynolds. The next two years, he played with Nettles and Rotella. And Jackie was the equal of all of them. I am proud to be part of the class that has Jackie Walker in it. There is nobody that deserves to be part of it more than Jackie Walker."

Jamie Rotella, who was elected captain the year after Jackie, was thrilled to see three players from the 1970–71 teams honored.

"That had to be one of the best teams Tennessee ever had. And there was no question who the leader was.

"That was Jackie.

"Something Coach Herzbrun has been talking about this weekend is being involved with people who are willing to pay the price. The team records, individual records, and all the people who were involved in that team, including the people who didn't letter, the people who weren't blessed with as much talent as the starters, the people who came out and helped us—that was love. There were some very successful people who came from that team, and it's just very rewarding to recall everything that team did. And when I tell you Jackie was the leader, the star, I hope the NCAA Football Hall of Fame is taking notice. I'd like to see them come up with a better ballplayer than Jackie Walker." ➖

"HOW I GOT THAT STORY"

In the late 1960s, the University of Tennessee finally began integrating its storied football team, the Volunteers. Jackie Walker was one of the first African American players on the team, a hometown star who decided to risk playing the sacred game of Southern football in front of the white crowds of the Southeastern Conference. He became the first African American to captain an SEC team, the first in the SEC to be named an All-American. Yet he was never inducted in any hall of fame, and passed away in 2002 largely forgotten in his own town of Knoxville. Was it because Walker was gay? Betty Bean, a freelance writer with deep roots in Knoxville, decided to look into it. Westword *editor and AAN Editorial Committee member Patricia Calhoun conducted this interview.*

Did people know that Walker was gay?
I am from here, as we say around here. So I always knew about this story. There were rumors. I am a football fan, and I remembered Jackie Walker from when I was young. It was always in the back of my mind that I wanted to catch up with him.

How did you decide to do the story now, after Walker had passed away?
I was doing a story for a little weekly about a 40th reunion football game at Walker's old high school—his dad had been the custodian there—and people kept talking about Jackie Walker. In the final story, I devoted a couple of paragraphs to Jackie, and I got a phone call from his brother, Marshall Walker—I call him Marshall X. Jackie was kind of a shy, soft-spoken person, and Marshall was his hammer. He wanted to thank me for the story.

So you decided to tell the whole story of Jackie Walker. Did you have trouble getting people to talk?
It was just one of the best stories I'd ever run across. The more I dug, the more I found. People were pretty open to talking. It was very interesting to talk to his black teammates, his white teammates. And I ran into some unexpected gems. His high school football coach moved on to Tennessee about the same time Jackie did. He and the head coach, Bill Battle, were going to a party that Jackie's family had for him when he was done with Tennessee and going to the NFL. As soon as the football season was over, Jackie came out, he flamed out. Battle said, "If he walks in wearing a dress, I'm out of there." They walked in and saw a big, good-looking woman, and he tapped her on the shoulder. "I'm Jackie's sister."

Did it help that you were writing this for an alternative newspaper?
There's no other publication in this town that would have done this story. We don't do a lot of sports writing or sports stories, so finding one that had a really strong human interest angle that looked into some less-than-favorable history in the sports scene was really interesting to us. The Volunteer sports machine is just huge. It generates lots of money and lots of tourism; it's an icon in town that no one really wants to mess with. So nobody else would really tackle it, nobody else would be interested in showing the prejudices of the athletic department or the boosters. It hit on all cylinders for us. It wasn't just a forgotten heroes story, but told how the athletic department had tried to keep him in the closet—as a gay, black football player.

How was the story received?

It was picked up by the *New York Times*, and I was very pleased that they gave us a credit. Even more so, I was pleased that the sports figures around town realized that this was an injustice. It was a story that needed telling. I'm glad Jackie's finally getting his due.

SPECIAL TOPIC: ELECTION COVERAGE

🎖 🎖 🎖

CIRCULATION 50,000 AND OVER

"Moles Wanted"

"Police Raid Anarchist Homes in Advance of RNC"

by Matt Snyders, *City Pages* (Twin Cities)

"This is why we need alt-weeklies and why we'll miss them if they disappear."
—Ryan Grim, Huffington Post

🎖 🎖 🎖

CIRCULATION UNDER 50,000

"John McCain's Gramm Gamble"

by Patricia Kilday Hart, *Texas Observer*

"I actually remember this piece from the election, as it became a blogosphere-wide sensation when it was released. Solidly reported and researched, this piece broke critically important news just as the debate over the economy—and Gramm's role in destroying it—started to dominate the campaign. If I had the choice of selecting the best piece of election coverage—for ALL publications regardless of circulation—this would be it."—Markos Moulitsas, Daily Kos

Moles Wanted

Matt Snyders

MAY 21, 2008

Paul Carroll was riding his bike when his cell phone vibrated.

Once he arrived home from the Hennepin County Court-house, where he'd been served a gross misdemeanor for spray-painting the interior of a campus elevator, the lanky, wavy-haired University of Minnesota sophomore flipped open his phone and checked his messages. He was greeted by a voice he recognized immediately. It belonged to U of M Police Sgt. Erik Swanson, the officer to whom Carroll had turned himself in just three weeks earlier. When Carroll called back, Swanson asked him to meet at a coffee shop later that day, going on to assure a wary Carroll that he wasn't in trouble.

Carroll, who requested that his real name not be used, showed up early and waited anxiously for Swanson's arrival. Ten minutes later, he says, a casually dressed Swanson showed up, flanked by a woman whom he introduced as FBI Special Agent Maureen E. Mazzola. For the next 20 minutes, Mazzola would do most of the talking.

"She told me that I had the perfect 'look,'" recalls Carroll. "And that I had the perfect personality—they kept saying I was friendly and personable—for what they were looking for."

What they were looking for, Carroll says, was an infor-mant—someone to show up at "vegan potlucks" through-out the Twin Cities and rub shoulders with RNC protestors, schmoozing his way into their inner circles, then report-ing back to the FBI's Joint Terrorism Task Force, a partner-ship between multiple federal agencies and state and local law enforcement. The effort's primary mission, according to the Minneapolis division's website, is to "investigate terrorist acts carried out by groups or organizations which fall within the definition of terrorist groups as set forth in the current United States Attorney General Guidelines."

Carroll would be compensated for his efforts, but only if his involvement yielded an arrest. No exact dollar figure was offered.

"I'll pass," said Carroll.

For 10 more minutes, Mazzola and Swanson tried to sway him. He remained obstinate.

"Well, if you change your mind, call this number," said Mazzola, handing him her card with her cell phone number scribbled on the back.

(Mazzola, Swanson, and the FBI did not return numerous calls seeking comment.)

Carroll's story echoes a familiar theme. During the lead-up the 2004 Republican National Convention in New York City, the NYPD's Intelligence Division infiltrated and spied on protest groups across the country, as well as in Canada and Europe. The program's scope extended to explicitly non-violent groups, including street theater troupes and church organizations.

There were also two reported instances of police officers, dressed as protestors, purposefully instigating clashes. At the 2004 Republican National Convention, the NYPD orchestrated a fake arrest to incite protestors. When a blond man was "arrested," nearby protestors began shouting, "Let him go!" The helmeted police proceeded to push back against the crowd with batons and arrested at least two. In a similar instance, during an April 29, 2005, Critical Mass bike ride in New York, video footage captured a "protestor"—in reality an undercover cop—telling his captor, "I'm on the job," and being subsequently let go.

Minneapolis's own recent Critical Mass skirmish was allegedly initiated by two unidentified stragglers in hoods—one wearing a handkerchief over his or her face—who "began to make aggressive moves" near the back of the pack. During that humid August 31 evening, officers went on to arrest 19 cyclists while unleashing pepper spray into the faces of bystanders. The hooded duo was never apprehended.

In the scuffle's wake, conspiracy theories swirled that the unprecedented surveillance—squad cars from multiple agencies and a helicopter hovering overhead—was due to the presence of RNC protesters in the ride. The MPD publicly denied this. But during the trial of cyclist Gus Ganley, MPD Sgt. David Stichter testified that a task force had been created to monitor the August 31 ride and that the department knew that members of an RNC protest group would be along for the ride.

"This is all part of a larger government effort to quell political dissent," says Jordan Kushner, an attorney who represented Ganley and other Critical Mass arrestees. "The Joint Terrorism Task Force is another example of using the buzzword 'terrorism' as a basis to clamp down on people's freedoms and push forward a more authoritarian government." ➤

Police Raid Anarchist Homes in Advance of RNC
Matt Snyders

SEPTEMBER 3, 2008

Just over three months ago, we wrote of the FBI's effort to recruit moles to infiltrate and report back on peace activists throughout the Twin Cities. Upon the story's appearance in print, bemusement gave way to outraged speculation on message boards and in conversation. The idea of the federal government keeping tabs on "vegan potlucks" seemed at the time almost too absurd to be true.

But any doubts were eliminated Friday when the Ramsey County Sheriff's Department and St. Paul police—working under the direction of federal agencies, including the FBI—began raiding homes of protesters throughout the metro. Before the weekend was through, authorities would arrest six people and detain dozens more in a preemptive strike against would-be RNC rabble-rousers.

It began Friday night when officers stormed through the St. Paul headquarters of the RNC Welcoming Committee, an anarchist/anti-authoritarian group. Committee member Brian Hokanson, 21, was upstairs in the cavernous "Convergence Center" on Smith Avenue when he heard a large uproar downstairs.

"It sounded like a huge fight had broken out," he says. "Lots of yelling, lots of commotion."

In less than a minute, rifle-wielding officers rushed upstairs and herded about 25 anarchists to the center of the room. "Get down on the ground!" the cops commanded. "Nobody move!"

The anarchists complied and were handcuffed. At that point, one of the captives began singing Bob Marley's "No Woman, No Cry."

"We're 99 percent sure he [the singing captive] was the infiltrator who told the police when to show up," says Hokanson. "Because right when he started singing, the officers let him up and led him outside. That was the cue. It didn't feel like an arrest. The police didn't say anything."

With that, the authorities began separating the detainees by gender.

"They took the women one-by-one to an adjoining room and patted them down for weapons," says Hokanson. "Shortly thereafter, they started processing the men. They never patted down the men."

The activists were handcuffed for nearly an hour before being set free. No one was arrested, though officers seized numerous computers and equipment as evidence.

The Ramsey County Sheriff's Department has confirmed that it planted moles in the Welcoming Committee, as well as in other groups. In a press release, Ramsey County Sheriff Bob Fletcher stated, "The 'Welcoming Committee' is a criminal enterprise made up of 35 self-described anarchists who are intent on committing criminal acts before and during the Republican National Convention."

But authorities didn't stop with the anarchists. The next morning, the cops ransacked three more homes in south Minneapolis—one a "hippie house" inhabited by activist group Food Not Bombs—before returning to St. Paul, where agents stormed two additional homes.

Shelby Eidson and five of her colleagues with I-Witness, a New York-based citizen journalism outfit, were in town for the RNC. They stood on the porch of a two-story St. Paul duplex that afternoon awaiting a taxi. Having captured footage during the RNC in New York City—some of which led to the dismissal of charges against hundreds of arrested protesters—the crew knew what to expect. Which is why they weren't entirely surprised to see 20-odd law enforcement officers storming down Iglehart Avenue with rifles drawn.

"Two agents had already come by that day and we had heard about the other raids," said Eidson. "So we already knew we had to get the fuck out. They were obviously listening to our cell phone conversations, because they knew when we were leaving and timed their arrival just as we were going."

The six ran inside the duplex and locked the door as the police detail reached the porch. Through the thin glass front door, police explained to them that if anyone stepped outside, they'd be detained. The cops didn't have a warrant, "but one's on the way," an officer claimed.

The team staked out the perimeter of the house, each officer about 15 feet from the next. Meanwhile, Eidson and company placed frantic phone calls to Coldsnap Legal Collective, a group of attorneys providing free legal assistance to protesters. I-Witness members also sent word to various media outlets during the one-hour standoff.

When the warrant finally arrived, officers burst through the door of the adjacent duplex where some of the I-Witness members had been staying and handcuffed three people inside. Officers went on to sift through boxes, search cabinets, and peruse computer files.

"Only they didn't seem to be looking for anything," says 34-year-old Daniel Haynes, an out-of-work social studies teacher. "They weren't thorough at all. It was almost like it was just for show."

Officers led Haynes, his roommate Julian Grant, and owner Mike Whalen—all in plastic handcuffs—to the backyard, where they would sit for 45 minutes. Back inside, officers kicked open an upstairs door to the adjoining section of the duplex and rushed down the stairs, guns drawn. Six activist journalists were similarly detained and led outside while authorities sorted through their possessions.

By this time, numerous media outlets had arrived. When *Democracy Now!* host Amy Goodman attempted to climb the rusty, four-foot-tall chain-link fence in the backyard in order to question the policemen, she was met with a wave of officers. A minor fracas ensued, with several voices shouting for the officers to unhand Goodman. Perhaps wary of the many television cameras in attendance, the authorities relented.

"That's when the entire tone changed," says Eidson. "Almost right after that, they let us go and told us to go back inside. Then they took off. They didn't take any of our stuff with them."

Bruce Nestor of the National Lawyers Guild, who is representing five jailed activists, contends that the raids were politically motivated.

"We have not been allowed to see the affidavits that were filed in support of the search warrants," he says. "We're confident they'll wait until the 10 days are up, until after the RNC."

Yet local authorities maintain that the raids were justified.

"I can tell you that there was sufficient probable cause, and there would have been violence had we not executed the warrants," says Tom Walsh, the spokesman for the St. Paul Police Department. "I would suggest that that possibility has been minimized. Not eliminated, but certainly minimized."

On Monday morning, the RNC Welcoming Committee participated in a makeshift press conference in St. Paul. A diverse group of 35 activists gathered around a couch propped before dozens of television cameras. On a corner less than a mile from the Xcel Energy Center, RNC Welcoming Committee member Jesse Sparkles addressed the crowd.

"For our political beliefs and our efforts to organize healthy communities outside the spectacle of electoral politics, five activists remain locked up," she read from a prepared statement. "The people of Minneapolis, St. Paul, and the world must take back control of their communities."

Later that day, authorities raided the RNC Welcoming Committee's communication center. Nine people were arrested on charges of conspiracy to riot. ➥

"HOW I GOT THAT STORY"

Matt Snyders is a Minneapolis-based reporter and staff writer for the Twin Cities altweekly City Pages. A graduate of the University of Iowa, his work has appeared in L.A. Weekly, the Village Voice, and other publications. These stories on aggressive police tactics to infiltrate protest movements made national news; as a result,

Snyders appeared on Fox News Live, *MSNBC's* The Ed Show, *and Rachel Maddow's radio show on Air America.*

How did you find Paul Carroll, the subject of your original article, and what did you do to try to verify his story?
I discovered Carroll via a tip from an attorney source with whom I kept in regular contact. The student, "Paul Carroll," had approached my source seeking legal aid. There wasn't much he (the attorney) could do, but he passed along his contact information to me and wondered aloud if there might be a story there. It was immediately apparent that indeed there was if the story checked out.

The next day, I met with Carroll, who, after recounting what happened, produced the business card the FBI agent had left him. Scribbled on the back was the agent's name and cell phone number. That was enough to move forward.

Were you already familiar with the NYPD's spying in 2004? How did you get the information on what happened in NYC and on the Minneapolis Critical Mass ride?
I broke the story about the Critical Mass bike ride nine months earlier through pure serendipity: it unfolded just outside my apartment building. After hearing a cacophony of sirens in the streets and helicopters in the air, I ventured to find the immediate aftermath of the tussle. I interviewed a half-dozen witnesses—four of whom were cyclists who had either been maced or roughed up, two of whom were neighbors who had seen the fracas unfold. Their stories were more or less identical. The police version, meanwhile, was frankly preposterous.

Did you cover Gus Ganley's trial? How did you come to include that connection in your story?
I didn't cover Ganley's trial. A source alerted me to the pertinent testimony, which I later confirmed and included in the house raids story.

What was the reaction to your first story and how closely did you cover the protester community between its publication and the RNC?
The reaction to the story was generally positive, particularly among non-cops who were involved in the incident. This established a level of credibility with the protest community and activist attorneys who represented them. They kept me abreast of their goings-on up until the RNC.

Did you have any doubts about the descriptions of police tactics by Hokanson and Eidson? What did you do to try to verify their stories?
"Doubts" is probably too strong of a word, but you always want to verify. As I would find, their stories jived with other witnesses' accounts. Also, there were no major differences between protesters' and police's versions. They had vastly different

interpretations of what had transpired, of course, but the chain-of-events and chronology were fairly cut-and-dried.

How much of the second story did you personally witness (such as the press conferences, police standoff, and Amy Goodman arrest)?
I attended press conferences, but had to rely on witnesses, police reports, and video footage to summarize the police standoff and Goodman's arrest.

How was your relationship with the police throughout your reporting? And how is it now?
Tenuous, yet professional. It remains so.

Have you developed a sense of how widespread these kinds of police practices might be in other U.S. cities? And have you seen any significant official remorse over these tactics after passions cooled or do you think they would behave the same way during future gatherings of this magnitude?
Where other cities are concerned, all I can offer is speculation. Suffice it to say there's not much that would surprise me. Authority tends to do what it wants, especially when it's (a) state-sanctioned, and (b) armed.

No significant remorse has been voiced on behalf of law enforcement. I don't see why national and local law enforcement agencies might act any differently during similar gatherings in the future.

How has covering this story changed your political views or journalistic practices?
It hasn't. The 2008 Republican National Convention confirmed my conviction that centralized power is highly irrational and perverse, regardless of party affiliation or ideology.

John McCain's Gramm Gamble

Patricia Kilday Hart

MAY 29, 2008

In the early evening of Friday, December 15, 2000, with Christmas break only hours away, the U.S. Senate rushed to pass an essential, 11,000-page government reauthorization bill. In what one legal textbook would later call "a stunning departure from normal legislative practice," the Senate tacked on a complex, 262-page amendment at the urging of Texas Sen. Phil Gramm.

There was little debate on the floor. According to the *Congressional Record*, Gramm promised that the amendment—also known as the Commodity Futures Modernization Act—along with other landmark legislation he had authored, would usher in a new era for the U.S. financial services industry.

"The work of this Congress will be seen as a watershed where we turned away from an outmoded Depression-era approach to financial regulation and adopted a framework that will position our financial services industry to be world leaders into the new century," Gramm said.

Watershed indeed. With the U.S. economy now battered by a tsunami of mortgage foreclosures, the $30-billion Bear Stearns Companies bailout and spiking food and energy prices, many congressional leaders and Wall Street analysts are questioning the wisdom of the radical deregulation launched by Gramm's legislative package. Financial wizard Warren Buffett has labeled the risky new investment instruments Gramm unleashed "financial weapons of mass destruction." They have fed the subprime mortgage crisis like an accelerant. While his distracted peers probably finalized their Christmas gift lists, Gramm created what Wall Street analysts now refer to as the "shadow banking system," an industry that operates outside any government oversight, but, as witnessed by the Bear Stearns debacle, requiring rescue by taxpayers to avert a national economic catastrophe.

While the nation's investment bankers are paying a heavy price for their unbridled greed (in billions of dollars of write-offs), Gramm has fared quite nicely. He currently serves as a vice president at UBS AG, a colossal, Swiss-owned investment bank, the post, no doubt, a thank you for assiduously looking out for Wall Street interests during his 23 years in public office. Now, with the aid of his longtime friend Arizona Sen. John McCain, Gramm may be looking at a quantum leap in power and influence.

Gramm serves as co-chair of the McCain 2008 presidential campaign. As one of the candidate's chief economic advisers, he is mentioned as a possible secretary of the treasury in a McCain administration. Their friendship was forged in the Senate as they worked against the Clinton health care proposal, and cemented when McCain served as national chairman of Gramm's own (ill-fated) 1996 presidential bid.

During McCain's rocky road to the nomination, it was Gramm as much as anyone who helped smooth the way. Last July, when it looked as though McCain's campaign would go bankrupt, Gramm, who once called money "the mother's milk of politics," advised him to slash his costs and assisted him with fundraising. Throughout the marathon primary season, Gramm has made numerous appearances with McCain and served as an ambassador to conservative groups. This spring, when conservative commentators attacked McCain as too liberal, McCain shored up his conservative bona fides by (according to the Huffington Post) bringing Gramm to a meeting with the editorial board of the *Wall Street Journal.*

But ask Gramm about his influence with McCain and it's clear that the former senator has not lost his talent for political spin. "My position [with the campaign] is, I am the senator's friend," he aw-shuckses in a telephone interview. "It would be a mistake to call me an economic adviser." Calling himself "a private citizen," Gramm claims ignorance of McCain's appearance two days earlier on Jon Stewart's *The Daily Show.*

"I'm so out of it, I don't even know who Jon Stewart is," he says in his trademark Georgia drawl.

It's hard to imagine that anyone remotely connected to politics is unaware of Stewart, but the remark fits well with the homespun persona that Gramm has carefully crafted for public consumption. Despite his false modesty, Phil Gramm remains a powerful force in Republican politics. Here in Texas, his many protégés—most notably Gov. Rick Perry, the beneficiary of a whopping $612,000 in campaign donations from Gramm's Senate campaign reserves—give him significant reach in Lone Star public policy.

Gramm might be interested in downplaying his role with the McCain campaign because, while the alliance might help with conservatives, it's at odds with the maverick image McCain has worked so hard to project. Gramm is more closely aligned with the kind of influence-peddling represented by the Keating Five scandal, in which McCain intervened with federal regulators on behalf of a campaign contributor with a failing savings and loan. The scandal shredded McCain's reputation and convinced him of the efficacy of reform.

In Gramm, McCain has chosen for a campaign adviser a former senator who espouses free market, conservative principles, but whose actions in public office served wealthy contributors and even himself. Exhibit A: Gramm's cozy Enron Corp. connections. Not only did CEO Ken Lay chair Gramm's 1992 re-election campaign, but Gramm's wife, Wendy, earned $50,000 a year as an Enron director from 1993 to 2001 (not counting perks that included stock options). Meanwhile Gramm pushed the company's aggressive—and ultimately self-defeating—political agenda to escape government scrutiny.

That Gramm is now advising the Republican nominee for president on economic matters "shouldn't give people a lot of comfort," says University of Maryland law professor Michael Greenberger, a senior official at the Commodity Futures Trading Commission in the late 1990s. "Gramm has been a central player in two major economic crises—the credit crisis and the incredibly high price of energy. . . . He's got his fingerprints all over legislative efforts that led to this."

Nonetheless, Gramm holds fast to his ideology. "I've never seen any evidence that opening up competition among banks and insurance companies in any way contributed to this," he says with the patience of the college prof he once was. "You've got a lot of people trying to rewrite history. You've got people with an ax to grind. They always wanted more government regulation, and when you have a problem, they want the government to regulate more."

His critics say that Gramm's anti-regulatory rhetoric failed the bulk of his constituents—which included thousands of hapless Enron employees who lost their life savings—but lavishly rewarded a few wealthy pals, like Ken Lay. University of Texas economist James Galbraith says Gramm is "not against government at all. His career has been finding ways to make money for his friends. It's a predator relationship. [Government] is his food supply."

When Gramm retired from the U.S. Senate in 2002, Texas Democrats celebrated that a powerful nemesis would no longer be a force on the national scene. Wrote Molly Ivins: "Gramm both looks like a snapping turtle and has the personality of one. When he ran for president in 1996 and finished fifth in Iowa, all the profiles written of him included the line 'Even his friends don't like him.'" She concluded: "We'll sure miss that sweet style." Clearly Molly's jubilation was premature.

It's easy to understand why Democrats were so eager to say goodbye to Gramm, who began his political career when he was elected to Congress in 1978 as a Democrat—and then quickly broke ranks with his party.

Gramm often jokes that he "didn't go to Washington to be loved, and was not disappointed." In his telling, his lack of popularity stemmed from his uncompromising stand on issues. Democrats who served with him, however, felt deeply betrayed by his actions as co-author of Ronald Reagan's austere first budget.

Former House Speaker Jim Wright recalls in his memoir, *Balance of Power*, that he learned to his "chagrin and sorrow" that Reagan sought counsel from a fellow Democrat who "was the beneficiary of my help and recipient of my naïve faith. His name was Phil Gramm."

In 1981, Gramm pleaded with fellow Texan Wright to help him win a seat on the powerful House Budget Committee, a privilege he had been denied by his Democratic peers, who found him unreliable. "Phil Gramm promised me . . . that if he were favored by a Budget Committee assignment, he would make his arguments within the committee and then would close ranks and back whatever budget resolution the committee majority approved," the former speaker wrote. "That sounded fair enough." Later, Wright would be "flabbergasted" to learn that Gramm met clandestinely with Reagan budget guru David Stockman to strategize and defeat a Democratic budget plan. Reagan's "Gramm-Latta" budget would prevail.

Having led the charge for a Republican president's budget plan that, among many other things, drastically cut Social Security benefits, Gramm resigned in 1983 and forced an election for his House seat, which he won as a Republican. In a 1984 special election hastily called by then-Gov. Bill Clements, he waltzed to victory in the contest for longtime Republican John Tower's seat in the U.S. Senate.

When his new party won control of the Senate, Gramm rose to chairman of the Senate Banking Committee, where he was able to put his anti-regulation views into law. The Gramm-Leach-Bliley Act of 1999 repealed laws put in place after the Great Depression setting up protective barriers between commercial banks, investment banking firms, and insurance companies.

Consumer groups strenuously opposed the landmark legislation. "It was strongly deregulatory and . . . did not address safety and soundness," says lobbyist Ed Mierzwinski of the public interest group U.S. PIRG. But more powerful interests were pushing for the law, and they had a deadline. In 1998, Citicorp Inc. purchased Traveler's Insurance Group. Under the old law, the new company had a two-year grace period to divest either its insurance or banking functions. Instead, it went to Washington, D.C., and got the law changed—with Gramm's help.

"Some people jokingly refer to it as the Citigroup Relief Act," says University of North Carolina law professor Lisa Broome. "Normally, they would have had to spin off their insurance activities."

Another beneficiary: Gramm's future employer, UBS, which was able to absorb the brokerage house Paine Webber. (As of March 31, UBS employees and company-related PACs have given the McCain campaign $82,865, according to the Center for Responsive Politics.)

Banks had been chipping away at the barriers through Federal Reserve rules for decades. But Gramm's sweeping deregulation "stripped away restraint," says Broome.

While Gramm denies any link between the current subprime mortgage crisis and his legislative efforts, Mierzwinski, Broome, and even some Wall Street analysts trace a direct connection.

Michael Panzner, a Wall Street veteran and author of *Financial Armageddon*, says the massive deregulation encouraged "aggressive, swashbuckling, high-risk practices that might have been frowned upon in the banking industry, but which were viewed as typical, say, on Wall Street." Eventually, those practices "became the modus operandi throughout the financial services industry."

Panzner also believes that Gramm-Leach-Bliley "may have even set the stage for both the collapse and the subsequent 'rescue' of Bear Stearns by the Federal Reserve." The deregulated financial services industries were "encouraged to push the envelope in terms of risk-taking, and were not entirely dissuaded from thinking that the public purse would be available if things went horribly wrong."

Still others blame Gramm's Commodity Futures Modernization Act. Prior to its passage, they say, banks underwrote mortgages and were responsible for the risks involved. Now, through the use of credit default swaps—which in theory insure the banks against bad debts—those risks are passed along to insurance companies and other investors.

Maryland law professor Greenberger believes credit default swaps "were a key factor in encouraging lenders to feel they could make loans without knowing the risks or whether the loan would be paid back. The Commodity Futures Modernization Act freed them of federal oversight."

Before passage of the modernization act, the Commodity Futures Trading Commission was attempting to regulate the swaps market through rule-making. The modernization act, Gramm noted in his remarks on the Senate floor, provided "legal certainty" for the growing swaps market. That was necessary, Greenberger says, because at the time, "banks were doing these trades in direct violation of federal law."

Greenberger has also been critical of former Clinton Treasury Secretary Robert Rubin, who supported Gramm's banking deregulation. But Greenberger insists that it was Gramm's slick legislative move that prevented government regulators from halting the spread of the risky financial instruments.

"Without Phil Gramm adding that 262-page bill onto an 11,000 page appropriations bill in 2000, it never would have seen the light of day," Greenberger says. "It was a lame duck Congress . . . racing off to Christmas recess. It was not an orderly process."

A more notorious feature of the modernization act was the "Enron loophole," which allowed energy trading to escape federal oversight. It was Enron's electronic trading that led to the California electricity crisis of 2000 and 2001, as well as Enron's own demise.

The issue of regulating electronically traded energy futures had been a pitched battle at the Commodity Futures Trading Commission throughout the'90s. One chairman advocated so passionately for deregulating energy futures that she persuaded her fellow commissioners to agree to a rule exempting them from oversight. Who was that? Wendy Gramm, the senator's wife, who served on the commission from 1988 to 1993. Shortly after her resignation, she was welcomed onto the Enron board of directors, where she would ensconce herself on the happily deaf-blind-and-mute audit committee.

The exemption received broad criticism from an array of sources—including the President's Working Group on Futures Markets, and then-chairman of the Federal Reserve, Alan Greenspan, who believed it contributed to market volatility.

Efforts to reverse the policy became moot when Gramm's amendment on that December evening gave the exemption the force of law—at a time when his wife served on the board of the one company that would ultimately most abuse it.

The impact of the "Enron loophole" has been enormous. Since its passage, the Senate Permanent Subcommittee on Investigations has concluded that the loophole contributed to inflated energy prices for American consumers. In 2006, its report found credible expert estimates that the loophole— by encouraging speculation—accounted for $20 of the price of a barrel of oil, then at $70. In 2007, the same committee blamed the loophole for excessive speculation by hedge fund Amaranth Advisors that led to the distortion of the natural gas market.

After Enron's demise, Wendy Gramm ultimately participated in a $13-million settlement personally paid by Enron directors for insider trading, when they collectively sold some $276,000 worth of stock early in the company's decline. Consumer advocacy group Public Citizen has reported that Enron paid Wendy Gramm between $915,000 and $1.85 million from 1993 to 2001 in salary, attendance fees, and stock options.

Last September, Michigan Democratic Sen. Carl Levin introduced legislation to close the loophole, citing two congressional reports blaming it for excessive speculation that has "unfairly increased the cost of energy in the United States."

In announcing his legislation on the Senate floor, Levin noted that the Enron loophole was "inserted at the last minute, without any opportunity for debate, into commodity legislation that was attached to an omnibus appropriations bill . . . in the waning hours of the 106th Congress.

"The loophole has helped foster the explosive growth of trading on unregulated electronic energy exchanges," Levin said. "It also rendered the U.S. energy markets more vulnerable to price manipulation and excessive speculation with resulting price distortions."

Asked about Levin's legislation, Phil Gramm expresses ignorance. "I don't know what provision in the law he's talking about."

Gramm apparently has long been touchy about the subject. When Enron collapsed, law professor Greenberger remarked to an interviewer that "all that [unregulated electronic energy trading] was made permissible by Gramm." A few days later, the phone rang.

"He called me up at my home to tell me I was wrong," Greenberger says. "I was sitting in my study preparing for classes. He started arguing with me that I was wrong. I said, if you insist on believing that, then you don't know what your own legislation did. I had to terminate the call because he would have kept me on the phone forever."

Similarly, Gramm today denies any linkage between the subprime crisis and his deregulatory legislation. "I wouldn't blame [swaps] for the problem. You could make the argument that without them, things would have been worse," he says. Congress should "look at the lessons of the subprime problem and learn what we can learn—loan generators and how they are compensated, what banks ought to be required to find to lend a variable rate," he says. "I'd be open to look at those things."

Says Greenberger, "I am quite confident Phil Gramm didn't understand what his legislation did. It was written by the banks and hedge funds."

Increasingly, many Wall Street titans agree that Gramm's efforts should be reversed. In May, Richard C. Griffin, founder of the $20 billion hedge fund Citadel Investment Group, told the *New York Times* that "fixing" Wall Street would require more regulation.

"Investment banks should either choose to be regulated as banks or should arrange to conduct their affairs to not require the stopgap support of the Federal Reserve," Griffin said. He also told the *Times* he sees a need for "new government oversight of the arcane world of credit default swaps, a business with a notional value and risk of $50 trillion."

Said the *Times*: "It was the interlocking relationships between thousands of investors and banks over credit default swaps that pushed the Fed to help rescue Bear Stearns."

Gramm isn't one to engage in mea culpas, regardless of the evidence against him. Take, for example, his reaction when California was plunged into an energy crisis in 2001 by Enron traders manipulating the energy markets. Mimi Swartz recounts in her book, *Power Failure,* that Gramm exploded to the *Los Angeles Times*: "As [Californians] suffer the consequences of their own feckless policies, political leaders in California blame the power companies, deregulation, and everyone but themselves, the inevitable call is now being heard for a federal bailout. I intend to do everything in my power to require those who valued environmental extremism and interstate protectionism more than common sense and market freedom to solve their electricity crisis without short circuiting taxpayers in other states."

Greenberger predicts that the fallout from Gramm's legislation will continue to grow, with capital drying up for all kinds of borrowing, including student loans. Meanwhile, Wall Street firms have begun considering a voluntary clearinghouse system for swaps and derivatives, an acknowledgement, Greenberger says, that some sort of policing is lacking.

Ironically, one of the big losers in the subprime mortgage crisis has been UBS, Gramm's new employer, which has announced losses of $19 billion and acknowledged that number could grow.

Gramm was recently quoted in *The Washington Post* as saying he was unaware that the company had invested in subprime mortgage instruments. "That's like Claude Rains [in *Casablanca*] saying he was 'shocked, shocked' to find out gambling was occurring in his establishment," says UT's Galbraith.

Perhaps Gramm has been distracted by politics. Since last July, of course, he has been investing considerable time in another enterprise—the McCain campaign.

Crony capitalism is not the only arena in which Gramm's record might tarnish McCain's campaign. While McCain has promised to end congressional earmarks, Gramm, the legislator, once bragged, "I'm carrying so much pork, I'm beginning to get trichinosis." And there's the question of whether McCain, who wants to appeal to moderates and independents, needs political coaching from a man who once told *The Dallas Morning News*, "I know a political zealot when I see one. I am one."

Yet ideologically the two largely agree, whether it's on free trade or slashing government services. Given Gramm's free market philosophy, in a McCain administration he can be expected to continue his push for privatization of important government functions, particularly Social Security. McCain now says he would favor "maybe giving people the option" of personal retirement accounts, opting out of the Social Security system.

If a federal appointment fails to materialize for Gramm, there is always Texas. Much like the late Lt. Gov. Bob Bullock, Gramm has nurtured a "farm team" of younger Republican elected officials with whom he confers frequently.

Says Texas Secretary of State Phil Wilson, who served as state director of Gramm's Senate office, "Gramm in many ways really built the Republican Party in this state. He would actively recruit candidates to run. He would go to a fundraiser for anybody who would ask. He would do endorsements for people who were elected officials or who wanted to be elected officials, from county commissioner to state rep to state senator."

More importantly, he showed them how to raise money. "By being there to help them raise the money, that spoke in volumes about credibility, because you can't run an effective campaign without being able to do television advertising," Wilson notes. Republican U.S. Rep. Jeb Hensarling of Athens is another former Gramm staffer, as is Republican nominee for Congress Pete Olson, who is challenging Rep. Nick Lampson for Tom DeLay's old seat.

Still, Gramm's first foray into lobbying at the state level bombed: His efforts to sell so-called "dead peasants" insurance to the Teacher Retirement System of Texas went nowhere. Under the dead peasants scheme, UBS would have sold TRS annuities and life insurance policies on retired teachers and kept the proceeds when teachers died.

His company's proposal to sell the Texas Lottery is still alive. His protégé Perry (Aggies Gramm and Perry became close when both bolted the Democratic Party in the early 1980s) startled legislative leaders in 2007 when the governor proposed selling the lottery to private investors for between $14 billion and $20 billion. By investing that money, UBS argues, the state could earn hundreds of millions more in interest than the $1 billion earned annually now.

Perry first learned of the idea from Wilson, who, according to *The Dallas Morning News*, passed along Gramm's interest in the subject. There are other UBS connections as well: The investment bank employs Perry's son, Griffin, and retains former Perry spokesman Ray Sullivan as a lobbyist.

In 2007, lawmakers ignored the lottery sale idea. But Lt. Gov. David Dewhurst gave interim charges to both the State Affairs and Finance committees to study the proposal. And Texas House Appropriations Chair Warren Chisum, a Republican from Pampa, has told reporters "[proponents of the sale] are already here visiting with folks to lay out their case." Senate State Affairs Chairman Robert Duncan, the Lubbock Republican who plans to hold hearings in August, confirmed this, saying lobbyists are "circling their wagons since the issue is in play."

A huge obstacle will be making the numbers work—which, according to a recent report by campaign watchdog Texans for

Public Justice—would require a huge expansion of gambling operations.

UBS estimated that the Texas Lottery could be worth between $10 billion and $16 billion if per capita sales increased 2 percent a year; a 7 percent annual growth would make the lottery's value as high as $24 billion. But the group's report noted, "These projections assume that Texas could match the per capita sales rates of lotteries in Maryland, Georgia, and Virginia. Yet part of what drives higher sales in those states are games now prohibited in Texas. . . . The UBS proposal also suggests the Texas Lottery could boost sales by moving into interactive television and the Internet." In short, the Wall Street consensus is that maximizing the value of the Texas Lottery requires an expansion of gambling into new games and new venues, and even into cyberspace.

While convincing the legislature to expand gambling is an enormous crapshoot, if anyone is connected enough to do it, it's Gramm. No one can tout a free market ideology that happens to benefit friends and family better than he.

On January 10 Gramm introduced Perry at the annual banquet of the Texas Public Policy Foundation, a conservative think tank.

At first blush, Gramm's homage might seem to be the obligatory appearance of a dutiful husband (Gramm's wife, Wendy, serves as the foundation's board chair), or a loyal Perry friend.

Gramm's remarks at Austin's Sheraton Hotel to a friendly crowd of 500 loyal conservatives revealed just how deeply involved and powerful the former senator remains in the Perry administration and the Republican Party, both in Texas and nationwide. Pronouncing Perry the "greatest governor" of his lifetime, Gramm ticked off a list of reasons that spoke volumes about not only his subject, but himself.

Predictably, he praised Perry for no new taxes and passage of the Republican redistricting bill.

More revealing was his praise of Perry for seeking "private sector solutions" to government problems. Translation: *cha-ching.*

Perry was equally effusive about Gramm when he responded to his old friend's introduction. "Americans made a huge mistake in 1996," he declared. "I can't fathom where we would be . . . had Phil Gramm led this country for eight years."

When it comes to the economy, a McCain victory in November might make that dream come true. ➤

"HOW I GOT THAT STORY"

Patricia Kilday Hart is a 1977 graduate of the University of Texas, where she majored in journalism and served as managing editor of the Daily Texan, *the college newspaper. After a year at the* Corpus Christi Caller-Times, *Hart went to the* Dallas Times Herald, *where she spent nine years, most of it in the Austin bureau covering state politics. Since 1989, Hart has been doing freelance writing about state politics, mostly for* Texas Monthly. *She lives in Austin with her husband and has three sons.* San Francisco Bay Guardian *news editor and AAN Editorial Committee member Steve Jones conducted this interview.*

Had you covered Gramm much before starting on this story? What was your relationship like, and was he a hard interview?
I had met Phil Gramm only a few times, in public-press-conference-type situations. So, no, I did not have a relationship with him. It required a couple of phone calls to his corporate office at UBS to get him on the phone, but he was quite cordial when he did consent to the interview.

How did you get onto this story and how much of the information that you covered were you aware of before you started working on it?
I must honestly tell you that I believe this story simply connected a lot of dots already uncovered by a lot of other very good reporters. My editor at the *Texas Observer* and I first thought this story was just going to be about McCain and his relationship with Gramm and what that meant for a possible McCain presidency, given Gramm's strongly conservative outlook on economics and opposition to strong governmental regulations in the banking and finance industry.

How about the corporate connections of Gramm and his wife? Where did you dig up that information?
I already knew about Wendy Gramm's Enron connection, having closely followed the reporting on the implosion of that politically powerful corporation. A nonprofit group, Texans for Public Justice, has a helpful database on political contributions which helped me provide a context for the Gramm-Enron relationship.

What were your main sources of information on Gramm's actions in Congress, such as his late insertion of the Commodity Futures Modernization Act, and its connections to the financial meltdown?

Soon after I began researching the story, I heard Terry Gross's interview of Maryland law professor Michael Greenberger, in which he mentioned the Commodity Futures Modernization Act. I find Google "alerts" very useful when I research stories. I followed up with my own interview and found other experts to weigh in on his theory of Gramm's role in the financial meltdown, which began looking more and more solid as the spring of 2008 wore on. I looked up the vote in the Congressional Record and drew my quotes from that.

What do you think was the key to unlocking this story?

I think the greatest help to me in writing this story was my long attention to Texas politics and knowing the relationships and issues. I do think the story did a good job of putting into context how Gramm's economic theories— espoused throughout his career in Texas politics— ultimately failed on a major scale.

Your reporting seems pretty prescient given the full financial meltdown that followed. Do you think your article had an impact on the race and do you think the average voter connects deregulation to the financial collapse?

I got real lucky with timing: about a month after my piece ran, Phil Gramm told the Washington Times that the country was in a "mental recession" and that the U.S. had become "a nation of whiners." I remember being very happy the story had run.

What do you think this relationship ultimately said about John McCain's fitness to be president?

For journalists, this story is a reminder that we can learn a lot about presidential aspirants by their friends and allies. In John McCain's relationship with Gramm, we saw that McCain was too willing to abdicate an important issue—the economy!—to a friend without seriously probing his background or his ideology. Ultimately, of course, McCain's inability to "vet" members of his administration (for example, Sarah Palin) was his downfall.

ACKNOWLEDGMENTS

"Holly Collins Returns," "Local Couples Fight for Gay Rights in Wake of Proposition 8," and "Midwest Oil Mining a Crude Idea to Many" by Beth Walton, originally published in *City Pages (Twin Cities)*. Copyright © 2008 *City Pages (Twin Cities)*. Reprinted by permission of *City Pages (Twin Cities)*.

"Double Whammy," "Turn Off the Radio," and "Taming the Wild West" by Phillip Bailey, originally published in *LEO Weekly*. Copyright © 2008 *LEO Weekly*. Reprinted by permission of *LEO Weekly*.

"Stimulus, Chicago-Style" by Ben Joravsky, originally published in *Chicago Reader*. Copyright © 2009 *Chicago Reader*. Reprinted by permission of *Chicago Reader*.

"The Mayor's Press Pass" by Tom Robbins, originally published in *Village Voice*. Copyright © 2009 *Village Voice*. Reprinted by permission of *Village Voice*.

"Solo Ingles Derrotado" by Jeff Woods, originally published in *Nashville Scene*. Copyright © 2009 *Nashville Scene*. Reprinted by permission of *Nashville Scene*.

Heroin, including "Long Highland," "Junk Bonds," "Heroin Claims Another," "Editorial: Shame on Massapequa," "Save My Kid," and "Natalie's Law," by Robbie Woliver, Tim Bolger and Michael Martino Jr., originally published in *Long Island Press*. Copyright © 2008 *Long Island Press*. Reprinted by permission of *Long Island Press*.

"The Jackie Walker Story," "Local Hero," and "A Promise Kept" by Betty Bean, originally published in *Metro Pulse*. Copyright © 2007, 2008 *Metro Pulse*. Reprinted by permission of *Metro Pulse*.

"Moles Wanted," "Police Raid Anarchist Homes in Advance of RNC," and "Dozens of Journalists Arrested at RNC" by Matt Snyders, originally published in *City Pages (Twin Cities)*. Copyright © 2008 *City Pages (Twin Cities)*. Reprinted by permission of *City Pages (Twin Cities)*.

"John McCain's Gramm Gamble" by Patricia Kilday Hart, originally published in the *Texas Observer*. Copyright © 2008 the *Texas Observer*. Reprinted by permission of the *Texas Observer*.